3-16-65

## DATE DUE

| | |
|---|---|
| NOV 22 '76 | |
| DEC 1 3 1982 | |
| MAY 7 3 1996 | |
| | |
| | |
| | |
| | |
| | |
| | |
| | |
| | |
| | |
| | |
| | |
| | |
| | |
| | |
| | |

$5.00

1964-65

# JESUS, MASTER AND LORD

# JESUS
# MASTER AND LORD

*A Study in the Historical Truth*
*of the Gospels*

BY

## H. E. W. TURNER

*Sometime Fellow of Lincoln College, Oxford; Canon of Durham;*
*and Van Mildert Professor of Divinity in the University of Durham*

LONDON
A. R. MOWBRAY & Co. LIMITED

First printed in 1953
Second Edition, 1954
Fifth Impression, 1964

PRINTED IN GREAT BRITAIN BY
JOHN DICKENS AND CO LTD, NORTHAMPTON

To

## MY SON MARK

who asked why the other writers used 'his
Gospel' without his permission, in the hope
that it may one day be useful to him for
ministering

'Ye call Me, Master, and, Lord: and ye say well; for so I am. If I then, the Lord and the Master, have washed your feet, ye also ought to wash one another's feet. For I have given you an example, that ye also should do as I have done to you.'

ST. JOHN xiii. 13-15.

# PREFACE

'OF making books there is no end,' wrote an Old Testament sage, and, though he obviously cannot have had books on the Gospels in his mind, his dictum certainly applies here. It is a mark of the abiding importance of the Gospels, and of the life and work of the figure of Whom they tell us, that books from various points of view on the subject have poured from the press in a steady stream.

I have ventured to add yet another to their number chiefly because I have long felt that there is no single book which offers in convenient form to the general reader, the working clergyman, the teacher of Divinity in schools, or the theological student what I have tried to offer here—a positive crystallization of the chief results of the critical study of the Gospels.

Some readers may be inclined to distrust the critical method as a barren tool serving only to shake the faith of the reader and wielded only by those who are frozen in heart themselves. Such at least has not been the experience of some fifteen years of professional study on the part of the author. An intelligible picture of the One Who is the object of the Church's worship has gradually begun to appear as study went on, and at no time has the sense of the spiritual responsibility involved in the work of trying to become a professional theologian become dimmed.

This book makes no claim to deep originality, though it does contain a number of suggestions and some views which have not, so far as I know, been put into cold print before. I have tried in the format of the book to keep its projected public in mind, keeping references to other literature and bibliographies down to a minimum, explaining as simply as I could the few technical terms which could not be avoided, and avoiding as much as possible any use of Greek words and

5

phrases. For the same reason I have avoided almost entirely the use of footnotes which would tend to distract the attention of the kind of reader whom I have in mind without adding greatly to the value of the book. I have, however, added frequent and copious references to the New Testament in all essential points.

It is hardly likely that all readers will register complete agreement with the views expressed. Some will find the book too conservative in tone because I have not thought fit to bow the knee to all the theological Baals which it has become fashionable to venerate in recent years. Others again may find the work too critical in certain respects for their particular taste. That is perhaps inevitable. I have sought in all points to be honest and not to beg questions or to misinterpret what appears to be the evidence. I have tried to state fairly and accurately views from which I was compelled to register dissent. Above all things I have aimed at clarity.

There are signs that to-day we are on the threshold of great developments in the field of Gospel study. Many theological and critical axioms have begun to be questioned and new trails to be blazed. The work of scholars like Dr. Austin Farrer in the field of theological exegesis and of Abbot Butler in the realm of pure criticism have appeared too recently for scholars as a whole to see their work in its proper perspective. The bulk of this manuscript was already produced before their works were published. We are promised important commentaries by Drs. Dodd and Lightfoot on St. John. Dr. Vincent Taylor has just published his monumental commentary on St. Mark. Work by scholars of such eminence cannot leave the course of Gospel studies unaffected.

I cannot leave my words of introduction without a word of gratitude to my former pupils both at Lincoln College, Oxford, and in the University of Durham for whose stimulus I cannot be sufficiently grateful. If much of this book will be familiar to many of them, it owes not a little to their vigorous help in discussion as well as to the urgent need of which I was continually aware that the Master and Lord Whom we serve in common should not disappear in the clouds of theological debate and in the minutiae of critical scholarship.

My grateful thanks for help with the proofs are due to the Rev. Douglas R. Jones, Lecturer in Theology in the University of Durham.[1]

H. E. W. TURNER

THE COLLEGE
DURHAM

---

[1] To him too I owe the excellent suggestion that some readers may prefer to start at Chapter iv and to read the first three chapters last of all.

# CONTENTS

## *PART I*

## HOW DO WE KNOW OF THE LIFE OF JESUS?
## THE DOCUMENTS

## *PART II*

## CAN WE RECONSTRUCT THE MINISTRY OF JESUS
## FROM THE GOSPELS?

## *PART III*

## THE PERSON OF JESUS CHRIST

## *PART IV*

## THE TEACHING OF JESUS CHRIST

## *PART V*

## THE CONCLUSION OF THE WHOLE MATTER

## PART I

# HOW DO WE KNOW OF THE LIFE OF JESUS?
## THE DOCUMENTS

CHAPTER I

# THE SOURCES OF THE LIFE OF JESUS OUTSIDE THE GOSPELS

IT may seem strange perhaps to some readers that in seeking to introduce the subject of the Life and Teaching of Jesus Christ we must begin with a section devoted to the sources. Many will probably have never thought about them. Some will certainly feel inclined to take this section as read and to turn to other parts of the book which seem at first sight more relevant or more rewarding. Yet there are questions which have been asked in the past and which perhaps some are beginning to ask themselves now. How do we know about the life of Jesus? Have non-Christian writers of the first Christian centuries anything to tell us about Jesus and, if so, do they show any sources of information which are not available to us? Is it an advantage or a handicap that the Gospels which are the chief source of our knowledge are Christian books? Do they lack veracity or impartiality just because they are Christian books? What sort of books are the Gospels anyway? Biographies? Historical novels? Confessions of faith? Or are they perhaps something not quite like anything else in literature? Here are questions which deserve an answer before we begin our task of the reconstruction of the story of the life and teaching of Jesus.

Or put it another way. Some readers may be historians, learning the task of interpreting the past. You will find that it involves a good deal of discussion of sources which form the raw material of the history which you read in the books. That is true of Gospel history no less than any other kind of history; and just because the events of the life of Jesus happened in history, we are bound to apply and to let others apply the same kind of technique to our Christian documents which secular historians apply to their chosen periods and subjects of study. Sometimes scholars have stopped their studies just when they were in an excellent position to begin. In such cases we might say that the work of source analysis has been carried on without regard to the equal task of the historian to present as careful and accurate a picture as possible. In other cases scholars have tried to pass to the constructive side of their work without any real regard for the task of analysis which should have preceded it. In the long run a subject like our Lord Himself has a habit of taking care of itself and periods of critical analysis and historical construction have a habit of alternating with each other. There are reasons for believing that we are passing at this moment from the one to the other, from a period devoted perhaps too exclusively to analysis to one in which scholars are beginning once again to ask the kind of questions which will lead to a further effort of construction.

Another analogy will help us here. A bridge-builder will want to be sure before he starts his work that his materials are well chosen for the special purpose which he has in hand. He will analyse it carefully and make inquiries about the strains and stresses to which it will be subjected. This will ensure that the bridge will be adequate for the traffic which will pass over it. No doubt those who pass over the bridge do not reflect on the particular part of the work which went on before the piles were driven home and the stonework built. They would soon know if the work were ill or carelessly done. If Christ is the bridge by Whom humanity passes on its journey to God, the same principle applies. It is the responsibility of New Testament scholars to examine the sources much as the practical engineer needs to be sure about his materials, and a picture of Jesus which ignores this duty will be about as reliable as a bridge whose builder was too much in a hurry to examine his material before he set to work.

This book attempts both to introduce you to the constructional work behind the more positive side of its task and to present in outline something of the picture which emerges. Both parts of the treatment are presented in outline. Many greater works have been written on each part of the subject, but the time seems ripe for a presentation which will be clear and straightforward in its analysis and positive in its approach for those who are beginning to study the subject seriously for themselves or who are trying to introduce others to it, as well as for the general reader who wishes to pursue his study of the subject further.

We can divide the subject of the sources into two main divisions. The first will be the sources for the life of Jesus outside the New Testament. Here we have three sources of information—secular writers in Greek and Latin, material derived from Jewish writings, and the scanty material contained in Christian and near-Christian writings which never found a place in the Canon of the Church. The second great division and by far the most important will be the New Testament itself, chiefly the Four Gospels but partly the letters of St. Paul. It is with the former that this present chapter will be concerned.

## 1. *Secular sources*

These are more scanty than we should wish. We do not possess, for example, any account of the life of Jesus from the point of view of Pontius Pilate or any other official record of the life and ministry of Jesus. It is true that at a later date so-called *Acta Pilati*, official records of proceedings, were forged. One such was written to support the pagan reaction against Christianity just before its establishment under Constantine the Great at the beginning of the fourth century. Two reasons for the absence of any such authentic record may be noted. In the first place the official documents of the Roman Empire have rarely been preserved. If the Roman Empire had anything corresponding to the Public Record Office in this country, it has long since disappeared, and the official pronouncements which have been preserved have either come to us in inscriptions or in papyri or in literary historians who preserved short complete documents or extracts from such documents as happened to come their way or to have interested them for some particular reason. If the problem in modern history is the plethora of official sources, it is a very different question for the history of the ancient world.

The life of Jesus is therefore in no different case from many other topics in the history of the period.

But there is another and deeper reason for this absence of official evidence. Jesus was an unprivileged subject of a third-rate province of the Roman Empire. He was not a Roman citizen, and therefore had no protection from the point of view of Roman Law. The governor who caused Him to be put to death is unlikely to have made an official report about proceedings which reflected little credit on him personally. We know from the Jewish apologist and philosopher Philo that Pilate was denounced at Rome for putting to death people who had been improperly tried, together with other conduct which indicated that he was not a satisfactory governor from either the Roman or the Jewish point of view. As a result he was removed from his post in A.D. 36, a few years after the Crucifixion of our Lord. All that Pilate was concerned about was the avoidance of an open outbreak at the Passover Festival and the maintenance of law and order in Palestine. If the avoidance of an open riot told in his favour, the means which he took to do so reflected so little credit upon Roman justice that it would be hardly likely that he would have made a special report to Rome on the subject.

We are thus left in the absence of official records with the references that may be found in the writings of the secular historians. Here again it may be noticed that the three most important witnesses, Tacitus, Suetonius, and Pliny the Younger, were not concerned primarily with describing events in Palestine in the first half of the first Christian century. Tacitus is primarily concerned with weightier events in the Roman Empire than the judicial murder of an obscure provincial and only mentions Christians in connexion with the fire at Rome which took place under Nero (A.D. 64) and for which the Emperor made the Christians at Rome convenient scapegoats. He turns aside for the moment to examine the origins of the sect:

The name Christian comes from Christ who, during the principate of Tiberius, was put to death by the procurator Pontius Pilate. Checked for the moment this detestable superstition broke out again, no longer simply in Judaea where the evil took its birth, but even in the city [i.e. Rome] whither every kind of shameful frightfulness betakes itself and wins many followers.[1]

The genuineness of this passage is admitted by nearly all scholars. The last sentence is typical of the fastidious pessimism of Tacitus himself who regarded the history of the Roman Empire up to his own day as the record of a progressive degradation. It is very unlikely that he had a Christian informant. (The picture of the sect as dying down and flaring up again does not, for example, correspond to the account given in the Acts of the Apostles which represents the first Christian history of the Church.) Nor is it likely that he got his information from a Jewish source, in view of the low opinion of the Jews displayed in the fifth book of his *Histories*. Nothing suggests a source of knowledge outside the channels of information which a pagan writer sufficiently interested could have obtained without going out of his way to get it. Name, date, and governor are all correct, but there is nothing more, and Tacitus had no need for his purposes to get any further details.

The second writer of this group is Suetonius, a somewhat gossipy writer of the lives of the earlier emperors who lived like Tacitus in the first half of the second century. Tacitus died about A.D. 115; Suetonius probably was about twenty years younger and died about the middle of the century. He has two references to Christians. In his *Life of Claudius*[2] he records the expulsion of the Jews from Rome (cp. *Acts* xviii. 2) as the result of troubles instigated by a certain Christus or Chrestus (the manuscript evidence is uncertain here). It looks as if he thought of the personal presence of the ringleader at Rome itself, but he may more probably be referring merely to trouble caused in the Jewish ghetto at Rome by the arrival of Christianity to Rome. The variant reading 'Chrestus' may be a simple slip. Suetonius would not necessarily trouble to get such an insignificant detail (as he would have thought it) right, or it might be a contemptuous alteration made deliberately. 'Chrestus' means good and was often used in a rather

[1] Tacitus, *Annals*, XV, 44.　　[2] Suetonius, *Life of Claudius*, 25.

contemptuous sense (good, simple, silly fellow), and if the read-
ing is right he might have been deliberately altering Christus
(Messiah) to Chrestus (simpleton). The nickname Messiahmen
or Christians might be easily altered into 'Simpletonians.'
There is no suggestion that for his information here Suetonius
looked outside the pagan circles of his own day. His *Life of
Nero*[1] confirms the evidence of Tacitus about the use of the
Christians as scapegoats in connexion with the Fire at Rome.

The younger Pliny was more directly concerned with
Christians. When he was governor of Bithynia about
A.D. 106 he was especially concerned with the problem of
illegal *collegia* or associations. Among them he discovered the
Christians and obtained fairly full information about them
from some renegades and from deaconesses under torture.
Among the information which he transmits to the Emperor
is that they sing hymns to Christ as to God or as a god.[2] This
tells us nothing about our Lord except His Name. Pliny's
previous ignorance of Christians, although he was a barrister
at Rome with an important practice before he was sent out
to Bithynia, shows that acquaintance with Christians and, still
more, knowledge of Christ, was not particularly widespread
at this period. His sources of information are known, and we
have no need to look outside for the facts which he relates.
He is an administrator professionally interested in Christians,
not a scholar eager to discover facts about Christ Himself.

It is a strange fact that a later historian, Dio Cassius, who
lived about the middle of the third century when Christians
were an important element in the population of the Roman
Empire, never mentions either Christ or Christians, at least in
the portions of his work which have survived. If this is a fair
inference from what is left of his writings, we can only ascribe
it to a singular piece of historical blindness or to a perverse and
deliberate hostility. It looks as if we have here the case of a
reputable Roman historian who could go to the lengths of
'sending the Church to Coventry.'

There is a possible intriguing allusion to the Gospel narrative

[1] Suetonius, *Life of Nero*, 44.        [2] Pliny the Younger, Epistle X, 96.

which does not even mention the Name of our Lord.[1] A Byzantine chronicler quotes a fragment of a lost Christian writer, Julius Africanus, who refers to the darkness which accompanied the Crucifixion. He notes that a certain Thallus, in the third book of his *Histories*, accounts for this as an eclipse. The modern historian would agree with Thallus, though Julius Africanus thinks him wrong. The Thallus in question has been thought to be a freedman of Tiberius of Samaritan origin. If this identification be correct, it would represent a detail from the Passion narrative known to a contemporary and sufficiently striking for explanation of it to be attempted. Thallus would represent, if not a Jewish, at least a near-Jewish source.

## 2. *Jewish sources*

We can now pass to the Jewish evidence. Here we will take first the evidence of Josephus who took part in the Jewish War from A.D. 66 to 70, but who later became a collaborationist with the Roman government and acted as a Jewish publicist and apologist under the Flavian Emperors. His work was written in Greek, though a Slavonic edition with important variations has recently become a storm-centre of controversy.

We will begin with the two references to Jesus in the Greek edition of his work.

The first reference raises no difficulties. It occurs in the twentieth book of the *Antiquities of the Jews* where he mentions the death of James the brother of Jesus called the Christ.[2] There is nothing here that a Jewish writer could not have written. There is, however, a longer passage two books earlier which runs as follows:

Towards the same time came Jesus, a wise man, if he should be called a man at all. For he was a miracle worker and the master of men who receive the truth with joy. He attracted to himself many Jews and Greeks. He was the Christ and when, on the denunciation of our leading citizens, Pilate had him condemned to crucifixion, those who had first loved him

---

[1] Thallus, quoted in George Syncellus, edited in C. Müller, *Fragmenta historicorum graecorum*, III, pp. 517 ff.

[2] Josephus, *Antiquities of the Jews*, XX, 9.

did not cease to do so, for he appeared to them three days afterwards risen from the dead as the divine prophets had announced both this and countless other marvels about him. And the group called Christians has not yet disappeared.[1]

This remarkable passage occurs in all the manuscripts of the Greek version, although Origen, one of the most learned of the Greek Fathers, denied that Josephus believed Jesus to be the Christ. It would be hard to believe that he could have maintained this if this passage had occurred in the text of Josephus which he had studied. The difficulty is that if Josephus wrote these words he was either a Christian or as good as a Christian. Yet if Christian influence may be suspected, the whole passage does not read like an interpolation, but only as a passage strengthened in the Christian direction by a later hand. It is hard to discover what the original might have been, but the following reconstruction may be attempted for the purpose of comparison with the original:

About the same time came Jesus a wise man and a teacher who attracted to himself many of the Jews and of the Greeks. He was called the Christ and, when on the denunciation of our leading citizens, Pilate had him crucified, his disciples went on believing on him, and the group called Christians has not yet disappeared.

It is possible that a slight expansion of the faith of the early Christians in the Resurrection without, of course, implying its truth might have formed part of the original passage. Any reconstruction is, however, highly conjectural.

There remain four passages in the Slavonic edition of Josephus which are not found in the Greek version. We know that the Slavonic edition was made by order of Jaroslav between 1054 and 1100 as part of a wider scheme for the popularization of the Greek classics, and that considerable liberties were taken with the text of other authors translated by the commission. It would not therefore be surprising to find the text of Josephus handled in this kind of way. The difficulty, as will appear plainly, is to decide whether an independent tradition is here contained or, if these passages are interpolated, in whose interest it was done. It will be

[1] Josephus, *Antiquities of the Jews*, XVIII, 3.3.

noted that here, except for the inscription on the Cross, the Name of Jesus is never actually mentioned.

The first is by far the longest and most important:

Then appeared a man, if it is permitted to call him a man. His nature and his exterior were those of a man, but his appearance was superhuman and his works divine. He accomplished astonishing and powerful miracles. So I cannot call him man. On the other hand considering his community of nature (with us), I will not call him an angel either. And all that he did, by a certain invisible force, he did by word and commandment. Some said, 'It is our first legislator who is risen from the dead and who brought to light many healings and proofs of his wisdom.' Others believed that he was sent by God. He disobeyed the Law in many respects and did not observe the Sabbath according to the custom of the ancients. Yet he did nothing shameful, nor any manual work, but arranged everything solely by his word. And many of the people followed in his train and listened to his teachings, and many souls were disturbed thinking that it would be by him that the tribes would liberate themselves from the hands of the Romans. He had the custom of keeping himself outside the city on the Mount of Olives. It was here that he dispensed healings to the people. And near him there gathered together one hundred and fifty servants and among the people a great number, seeing this power and the fact that he accomplished everything that he wished by his word. They asked him to enter into the town to massacre the Roman troops and Pilate and to reign over them. But he was not anxious to do so. Later the Jewish leaders took cognisance of him; they gathered together with the chief priests and said, 'We are powerless and weak to resist the Romans seeing that the bow is bent. Let us go and tell Pilate what we have learnt and we shall be clear of trouble. If he ever learns of it through others, we should be deprived of our goods, cut in pieces ourselves and our children driven into exile.' They went and told Pilate. He sent men, killed many of the people and brought back this worker of miracles. He made an inquiry about him and learnt that he did good and not evil, that he had neither revolted nor was greedy of royal power and released him. For he had healed his wife who had died. And coming to his accustomed place, he did the accustomed works. And again as a larger number of people gathered round him he was famous for his works more than all. The doctors of the law were stricken with envy and gave thirty talents to Pilate to put him to death. He took the money and gave them permission to execute their desire themselves. They seized him and crucified him contrary to the law of their ancestors.

It is certainly hard to know what to make of this passage. It seems fairly clear that the author had in front of him the Greek text of Josephus. The attempted assessment of Jesus in the earlier part of the passage recalls the shorter passage from

the Greek text of Josephus. The healing of Pilate's wife comes
from the Apocryphal Gospels, which we shall mention later on
in this chapter. Other details look like garbled versions of
canonical Gospel material. The thirty talents recall the thirty
pieces of silver given to Judas Iscariot as the price of betrayal.
The record of opposition to the Law and working of miracles
by a word only, come from the authentic Gospel tradition.
The author clearly knows of a Jerusalem ministry and even
where Jesus stayed (on the Mount of Olives). The attempt to
make Jesus a King recalls the interesting note in St. John vi. 15.
The reference to Moses suggests the Transfiguration, and the
belief that He was sent from God the popular ideas about Jesus
mentioned before the Confession of Caesarea Philippi. The
Galilean ministry is never mentioned, though the details of
the passage are drawn indiscriminately from the Synoptic and
Johannine Gospels. There is a curious prejudice against manual
work, and an emphasis upon action by the word only which
does not fit any known source. The reference to his community of nature with us is an echo of the Christological
controversies of the fifth century. Some passages seem like a
reminiscence of the Jewish apologetic against Christianity.

It may perhaps be the attempt made by a Christian to
rewrite and enhance the Greek passage which he found in
Josephus. If this be so, it is not very intelligently done, and
the passage gives the impression of a collection of bits and
pieces derived from many different sources. The theory that
it is a Jewish interpolation does not really fit the facts, and the
scanty material about Jesus preserved in Jewish sources does
not lend any support to this hypothesis. If there is any authentic evidence about Jesus which is not contained in the other
sources at our disposal embodied in the passage, it is to be
feared that it cannot now be disentangled with any certainty.
The probability is that there is nothing of the kind there.

The second passage gives the inscription over the Cross as
'Jesus the king who never reigned, crucified by the Jews because
he announced the ruin of the city and the desolation of the
Temple.' This looks like a piece of Jewish counter-propaganda
to the authentic inscription over the Cross to which much

objection was clearly taken (*St. John* xix. 21–2). The statement that He was crucified by the Jews cannot, however, form part of such a counterblast, and is not even strictly historically true. Crucifixion was a Roman, not a Jewish, punishment, and under the Roman rule the Jewish authorities could not put any one to death themselves.

The third passage speaks of the rending of the veil of the Temple recorded in all three Synoptic Gospels (*St. Mark* xv. 38, *St. Matt.* xxvii. 51, *St. Luke* xxiii. 45):

This veil before this generation was whole because men were pious but now it is a pity to see it, for it was suddenly torn from the top to the bottom, because a good man, who because of his works was shown not to be a man at all was delivered to death through bribery. And many other frightening signs, so it is told, took place there. And after being killed and buried it was said that he could not be found in the tomb. Some in fact claimed him as risen and others, stolen by his friends. I do not know who speaks the more truly. For a man could not raise himself but by the aid of another just man unless he were an angel or some other celestial power, or else that God Himself should appear as a man and accomplish all that He wished, walk with men, fall, lie down and rise up again according to His will. Others said that He could not have been stolen (from the tomb) since about the tomb had been a guard, thirty Romans and a thousand Jews. This is what was said about the veil and the reason for its rending.

Here there is nothing that is not contained within the Gospels themselves though the numbers of the guard are obviously inserted for the sake of greater historical vividness. Once again the interpolator takes the standpoint which he conceived that Josephus might have taken. His own conclusion is obviously here in principle a Christian one.

The fourth and last passage speaks of the Jews being pushed into war by an ambiguous oracle found in the sacred books which said that at this time one of the land of Judah should reign over the universe. There are different explanations of this. Some believed that it was Herod, others this wonderworker, others again Vespasian. The basis of this passage is to be found in St. Matthew ii. 1–12, while the fulfilment of the prophecy in Vespasian is also found in Tacitus from whom it may be possibly derived.[1]

[1] Tacitus, *Histories*, V, 13.

Taken as a whole the evidence is not in support of the view that we have here a source of information supplementary to the Gospels. At some points the writer seems to have picked up the Jewish end of the controversy between Jews and Christians which he may have retailed as suitable material for the pretended author. At other times he takes the Christian estimate of Jesus and twists that into a shape which it could be imagined that Josephus might have used. At other times he uses ordinary Gospel material slightly altered, perhaps in order to disguise a Christian hand and embellished by material from the Apocryphal Gospels. It would perhaps be too much to have expected anything less confused and fumbling from any one who thought the attempt worth making at all. In fairness it should perhaps be said that a few scholars have found here a supplementary source and one even gave the data given by the Slavonic Josephus a high place in his reconstruction of the Life of Jesus.[1]

Other evidence from Jewish circles is included in certain passages in the Talmud, the collection of Rabbinical writings which was not complete until the fifth or sixth century after Christ. The form of the writings, Rabbinical opinions on matters of religious jurisprudence, would not lead us to expect the preservation of much material on any kind of Jewish history, and least of all of any data about Christ Whose religion was in bitter mutual controversy with the Jewish Faith. In general, any historical reference contained in a work of jurisprudence would be secondary to its main purpose, and the Talmud does not belie this expectation. There are, however, a few references to Jesus in the Talmud which the Jewish scholar, Klausner,[2] believed to contain authentic material not derived from the Gospels. The most important passage occurs in the *Tractate Sanhedrin* (concerned with the procedure of the Jewish court of that name). It runs as follows:

On the eve of the Passover Jesus of Nazareth was hanged. For forty days a herald went before him crying, 'He must be stoned because he has worked magic, seduced Israel, and dragged it to rebellion. Let any one who has anything to say to justify him, come forward and do so.'[3]

[1] R. Eisler, *The Messiah Jesus and John the Baptist.*     [2] J. Klausner, *Life of Jesus.*
[3] *Tractate Sanhedrin*, 43 a.

As it stands the passage is contradictory. Jesus is condemned to be stoned (the appropriate penalty under Jewish Law) and yet is actually hanged. The forty-day interval seems a rather weak Jewish reply to the Christian charge, already latent in the Gospels, of too great haste in the judicial procedure which led up to His death. There is little ground for believing that here is additional information of an historical kind.

The second is a group of passages which refer to 'Jesus ben [son of] Panthera' (or Pandara).[1] Now we know from inscriptions of a certain Sidonian archer, Tiberius Julius Abdes Pantera who belonged to an auxiliary unit formerly stationed in Palestine but transferred to the Rhine in A.D. 9. But the cycle of passages suggests rather a coarse attempt to dispose of the Virgin Birth and the story of Davidic lineage at a single blow. Ben Panthera looks like a garbled version of the Greek, phrase son of a Virgin (parthenos), and it is very unlikely, despite Klausner's defence, that we are confronted by anything more than Jewish defence against Christian claims.

## 3. Non-canonical Christian sources

We must turn finally to a brief review of the evidence for the life of Jesus from Christian sources outside the Canon of the New Testament.

First we may mention the Apocryphal Gospels. These represent literature of the Gospel type which did not succeed in finding a place within the New Testament. Some of this literature had a directly heretical motive. It formed an attempt to give Scriptural warrant or half-Scriptural warrant to theories about the Christian Faith which could not be supported from the evidence of the New Testament itself. The Baptism of Jesus was peculiarly liable to such attempts at rewriting. But there were other Apocryphal Gospels which do not seem to have had any doctrinal bias, but were directed to fill up gaps in the story. What John Oxenham called the 'Hidden Years' —the infancy and boyhood—were a favourite period for such inventions. Again, attempts were made (often with a heretical motive but sometimes without) to give greater prominence

[1] Aboda Zara, 40 d.

to the secondary characters of the Gospel tradition, particularly to little-known Apostles. Such literature has been called the 'Pleasant Sunday Afternoon' reading of the early Christian Church. The data which it contains is either directly based upon the New Testament or the fruit of pious imaginings.

One document alone, the *Gospel of Peter*, has been claimed to represent a substantially true historical narrative of the Resurrection. While the Four Gospels out of sheer reverence do not contain any account of the Resurrection itself, the Gospel of Peter seeks to remedy the defect. Material from this source has even been used by some modern scholars in their reconstructions of the sequence of events in the Easter narratives of the Gospels. It is, however, evident that such material must be used with great caution and it is almost beyond belief that an account of the action of the Resurrection should have been preserved untarnished and unwritten for over a century after the events themselves.

The second group of material from Christian or near-Christian sources are the so-called *Agrapha* (unrecorded sayings of our Lord). These are isolated sayings contained for the most part in the papyri discovered at Oxyrhynchus shortly after the opening of the present century. They need skilled and careful handling, since, although some may possibly be genuine, some must and more may have come from the heretical *Gospel of the Egyptians*. Each individual saying needs separate treatment. There is no difficulty in believing that some isolated but authentic sayings of Jesus might possibly be transmitted without being written down in a Gospel. The Beatitude 'It is more blessed to give than to receive' (*Acts* xx. 35) is such an example. And even the Fourth Gospeller with pardonable exaggeration could speak of the large number of books that could be written about the words and deeds of Jesus (*St. John* xxi. 25). This must at least mean that he is making a mere selection. The likelihood of independent and genuine material being preserved decreases in direct proportion to the time which has elapsed between the life of Jesus and the date at which the material was committed to writing.

A similar find of material was made and published just before the war. It was hailed as containing fragments of a fifth Gospel, and together with some new material contained many echoes particularly of the Fourth Gospel. The evidence is too slight to support the rash title popularly given to the fragments as belonging to a fifth Gospel. Here again there may be some original and authentic touches, but the bulk of the material is clearly edited from the Gospels as we now have them.

It is clear, then, that apart from a few possible details, we are virtually thrown back upon the New Testament evidence for the life of our Lord. At its most favourable estimate, the evidence which we have reviewed in this chapter could only convince us that there was a certain Jesus Who lived in Palestine, was a teacher and wonder-worker, and died a violent death. Secular writers for reasons which we have briefly indicated pay little attention to the life of Jesus. They mention Him when their narrative demands it, but there is no attempt to go out of their way to discover or to transmit information. The traditions preserved in Jewish writers obviously echo the war of apology and counter-apology which took place in the early Christian centuries.

Yet the evidence, however scanty, is sufficient to exclude the theory of the Christ-Myth which is at intervals reshaped with great ingenuity but little intrinsic probability. There can be few better examples of straining at gnats and swallowing camels than this theory, which necessitates the acceptance of mountains of hypothesis to explain away the historical existence of Jesus Christ.

If, however, the external sources might be considered adequate evidence for the existence of Jesus, it is clear that for anything more than the barest information about Him, we must turn to the New Testament itself.

## BIBLIOGRAPHY

M. Goguel, *Jésus* (second French edition 1950), contains by far the best treatment of these sources at present available.

The relevant passages (except for the Talmud and the Slavonic Josephus) are collected in Texts for Students No. 1, *Select passages from Josephus, Tacitus, Suetonius, and Dio Cassius illustrative of Christianity in the First Century* (S.P.C.K.).

The passages from the Slavonic Josephus are translated in H. St. J. Thackeray, *Josephus* (Loeb edition), Volume III, pp. 635 ff.

The recent evidence from Egypt may be consulted in H. G. E. White, *The Sayings of Jesus from Oxyrhynchus*, and H. I. Bell and T. C. Skeat, *Fragments of an Unknown Gospel and Other Early Christian Papyri* (British Museum).

An able short critique of one form of the Christ Myth theory is to be found in H. G. Wood, *Did Christ Really Live?* (S.C.M.).

## CHAPTER II

# THE NEW TESTAMENT DOCUMENTS

OUR last chapter will have served to convince us that for all practical purposes we are restricted to the New Testament evidence for the content of the life of Jesus, and here naturally pride of place must be given to the Four Gospels. The first three—those of Matthew, Mark, and Luke—are called the Synoptic Gospels, because they give a common point of view and outlook upon the person and work of our Lord while the Fourth Gospel, though overlapping in some respects and continuous in character with the other three, stands somewhat apart from them.

We must face two difficulties at the start. The Gospels are unique. In literature they stand by themselves. They fit into no prefabricated literary type. There is no parallel in the Old Testament, and the only example of such religious biographies in the Gentile world is the *Life of Apollonius of Tyana*, written by Philostratus in the middle of the third century, and here the circle for which it was produced suggests that the existence of the Christian Gospels had some influence upon its production. The Gospels are a blend of piety and of history, at once written for believers by believers, and narratives about an historical person recorded because they were believed not merely to be edifying but also to be true. The distinctive difference between Christianity and its rival cults, Judaism and Hellenic paganism, was focused in history in such a manner as to make the historical character of the narratives which the Gospels contain a vital part of its message. The absence of any parallel contemporary or earlier documents, however, makes it difficult for the modern scholar to frame his criteria objectively, and he is apt to ask of the Gospels a standard of detail and of accuracy which would be rare even in a modern historical work resting upon abundant evidence and written by scholars expert in probing large masses of material. Even if examined from this point of view, the Gospels stand any reasonable—and even much unreasonable—scrutiny. It is as well, however, to bear in mind that many modern critics apply to the Gospels tests which would lead to the rejection of much more modern and scientifically handled material. In such cases it is the critic and not the Gospels who is at fault if their evidence is rejected as inadequate and unreliable. Not every modern question which we put to the Gospels is sure of a full and adequate answer. It is, however, a compliment to what the Gospels do actually contain that such questions are framed and put; it is no slur upon them if the answers which would satisfy some modern scholars do not happen to be forthcoming.

The second difficulty also arises out of this tendency to set impossibly high standards of historicity and then to condemn the Gospels for not fulfilling them. It is urged that because they are Church documents, they cannot be impartial and therefore they must be condemned as unreliable. Here surely is a clear fallacy of method. Granted that the aim of the modern historian is to be impartial, it is also his aim to be an interpreter. The compilation of collections of documents or source-books is an historical instrument of great value, it is, however, only preliminary to the writing of genuine history. Fact without interpretation is as blind as interpretation without fact is empty. We cannot therefore condemn the Gospels for offering to us both. They appear neither to offer us a full-scale itemized table of the words and deeds of Jesus, without reference to their significance in the life of Jesus taken as a whole, nor a mere interpretation left in the air without factual support, and therefore at the mercy of every blast of doubt and disbelief. We may be grateful that neither of these represents the true state of the question.

It is often said in these days as if it were a truism that the Gospels are not biographies of Jesus. This is in effect merely a half-truth. If it is meant that the Gospels do not resemble the three-volume biography of Mr. Gladstone written by John Morley, the statement is true. The Gospels never pretend to be a complete chronicle of the words and works of Jesus. The Fourth Evangelist is quite conscious of the fact that the material has been selected from a wider range than has been preserved to-day. But in fact most modern biographies are compelled by the very nature of their art to be in some measure selective. The exhaustive would be quite unreadable, and what is more, it would hardly interpret its subject in the best possible manner if it did not select its material. Much of the life of all men is common ground. There is nothing distinctive in the precise number of hours which I sleep, the domestic concerns and duties which fall to my lot, the routine time-table of a teacher or a professor, the exact number of services which I take or attend in the course of a year. The good biographer selects the significant, the representative, or the typical, and makes no claim to a theoretically possible exhaustiveness. It is clear, then, that the selectivity of the Evangelists cannot be set in the balance against their historical truth. Again, a good historical treatment must necessarily, as we have seen, be an interpretation. We can indeed offer different interpretations, and perhaps judge the data either opposed to or insufficient for the interpretation proposed, but neutral history would in fact be inadequate history. Morley's *Life of Gladstone* was written by a Liberal about a Liberal. There might be room for a Tory *Life of Gladstone*, and if one were produced, it would be our duty to examine, compare, and contrast both, and then to form our assessment accordingly. We do not, however, condemn Morley's *Life* out of hand because it is written from a particular point of view. Indeed, it is possible that there were aspects of the life of Gladstone which could not reveal themselves to any other interpreter than one who was a distinguished disciple of the great Liberal leader.

If, however, the existence of selectivity and of interpretation in modern historical studies does not invalidate their claim to be historical biographies, we should be very careful not to let the modern tag 'The Gospels are not biographies' blind us to the elements of error which lie within it. Where it is true, it is little more than a truism; where it is in error, it conceals a dangerous half-truth. The Gospels are both books for believers by believers and records of a factual nature about an historical figure. Here is a tension between the subjective and objective side of the Gospels, their interpretative significance and their factual content which is a puzzle which all readers of the New Testament must face for themselves. The point is that we do not rid ourselves of the paradox by the simple expedient of ignoring one side of the problem.

Our next chapter will be concerned in greater detail with this problem of the historical assessment of the Gospels, but before we can discuss it with profit we must turn to a consideration of the process by which the Gospels have reached their present form. It would, however, clearly be wrong to embark upon this project before stating the root question which removes our next inquiry from the regions of the purely academic. The question 'How did we get our Gospels?' must inevitably have light to throw upon the fundamental issue, 'Can we trust the Gospels?'

Scholars have sought to distinguish three periods which we can usefully examine. Working backwards from the Gospels as we have them, which constitute the third and last stage, scholars have tried by inference to shed some light upon the period of written sources from which the Gospels as we now possess them were derived. Naturally, in the absence of these documents, the conclusions reached can only be regarded as in the nature of inferences; but inference, provided that it is based upon evidence, is not without logical value. It cannot be finally proved; it can only lead to conclusions which may possess varying degrees of probability dependent upon the nature of the grounds from which such inferences are made. But the Gospels as we have them are capable of being studied from another point of view and to provide some indication of the nature of the material which the Gospels now contain while it was still in the stage of oral tradition. This sounds at first sight quite incredible, and it ought always to be remembered that conclusions in this field must be regarded as very tentative. It is due, however, solely to the character of the Gospels and the nature of the record which they convey that this should be possible at all. More sophisticated historical records, such as, for example, the historical writings of a Tacitus or a Josephus, do not lend themselves to such methods.

The Gospels, as the product of a less conscious art and of less finished performance, make it possible for us almost to overhear the Church from time to time in the very process of oral transmission.

## 1. *The period of oral transmission*

Jesus Himself committed nothing to writing, and we have no evidence that any technique of shorthand reproduction was used in connexion with His teaching. Nor did the disciples belong to circles in which the practice or the technique of book-production was at all familiar. Moreover, there may have been contributory reasons why the Church did not at first turn her attention to writing down the traditions which she possessed about our Lord. Many early Christians appear to have believed that our Lord would come again to judge both the living and dead within their own lifetime. This would mean that the day of the Lord was at hand, and that the time of the Consummation was drawing near; and that therefore the task of putting their oral tradition into written form would hardly appear to be an urgent necessity.

It is, however, necessary, on the other hand, not to overpress these facts beyond due limits. Jesus the Teacher clearly cared that His teaching should be remembered, and took pains to set this teaching in a memorable form. And the disciples, if without modern aids to memory, belonged to an age in which memorization formed a far greater part of religion than it does normally in the modern West. Country folk, whatever the deficiency of their educational discipline, possess proverbially good memories.

Nor could it be concluded that because the day of the Lord was coming quickly the historicity of the Gospel tradition would become irrelevant, or interest in it seriously impaired. He Who should come was the same Jesus Who had companied with them in Galilee and suffered, died, and rose again in Jerusalem. This was a vital ingredient in the Christian conviction about the Last Things. Many, perhaps all, Jews believed in a day of the Lord which should prove a decisive fact in history, and perhaps even end the historical process altogether.

What was distinctive in the Christian belief about the Last
Things (what theologians call eschatology) is that this hope
was embodied in One Whom they already knew. It would
therefore be surprising if even the most thoroughgoing
eschatological belief should cut the painter from the historical
life and teaching of Jesus Himself.

Can we trace anything of this period of oral transmission
behind the New Testament as we now possess it? It is believed
by many scholars that we can. Dr. C. H. Dodd has attempted
with considerable success to disentangle the primitive Christian
proclamation of Christ (called by its Greek name the *Kerugma*
or the heralding) by a careful analysis of the early Christian
sermons contained in the Acts of the Apostles and some of the
more formalized passages in the letters of St. Paul.[1] The result
is extremely interesting. A summary of this Apostolic message
can be given somewhat as follows:

> The prophecies have been fulfilled and the New Age has dawned
> The long expected Messiah, born of David's line, has come
> He is Jesus of Nazareth, who, after John's Baptism
>> did mighty works by God's power
>> died for our sins
>> rose from the dead
>> was exalted at God's right hand
>> and will come again as judge
> Therefore let all who hear repent and be baptized for the forgiveness of
> their sins.[2]

A similar stereotyped pattern seems to underlie the ethical
teaching of the Apostolic Church which can be called the
*Didache* or the teaching. This has been the subject of independent study by Dr. E. G. Selwyn and Archbishop P. C. Carrington of Quebec, whose results show a high degree of unanimity
in a difficult field of study.[3]

It has been suggested that we can go further and trace not
only behind but within the Gospels evidence of oral transmission. Although recently other and more complex theories
of the arrangement and ordering of St. Mark's Gospel have

---

[1] C. H. Dodd, *The Apostolic Preaching and its developments.*
[2] This is the summary given in A. M. Hunter, *Interpreting the New Testament*, p. 35.
[3] E. G. Selwyn, *The First Epistle of St. Peter*, pp. 363–467; P. C. Carrington, *The Primitive Christian Catechism.*

been proposed which assign a higher degree of conscious construction by the author himself,[1] it has been customary in recent years to hold that the former part of St. Mark's Gospel has been constructed of sections of material which bear close to their surface the indications of this period of oral transmission. St. Mark i. 15–31 has been taken to represent a sample or typical day in the life of Jesus, as if the Christian catechist were saying to his class of converts, 'To-day I am going to tell you something of how Jesus spent His time in His earthly ministry.' There may be elements in this conjecture which are not entirely convincing, but the probabilities are greater in the chapters which immediately follow. St. Mark ii. 1–iii. 6 is a collection of controversy stories. It is inherently unlikely that controversy was canalized into a relatively short space of time at the beginning of the ministry and then died down until the last week. It is probable that here we can overhear the Christian catechist saying to his class, 'The ministry of Jesus was attended by controversies; here are a few cases in which Jesus was engaged in controversy with the religious authorities of His day.' St. Mark iv. 1–34 is a collection of parables. It is hardly likely that Jesus once delivered a discourse of parables arranged 'end on,' and then dropped so typical a form of teaching for a time; it is more likely that the material is here arranged again in catechetical form round the theme, 'Jesus was a great teacher. His use of parables was a characteristic feature; let me give you a few examples.' St. Mark iv. 35–v. 44 is composed of a series of miracles; here again the teaching motive of the Christian catechist may well be suspected. There follow two cycles of traditions composed of a feeding, a controversy, and a healing (vi. 30–vii. 37 and viii. 1–26). It is harder to see the same principle of selection at work here, but it still appears probable that we have to do with an arrangement of material which goes behind the present compilation of the Marcan Gospel.

But the principles of oral transmission have been traced not

---

[1] A. M. Farrer, *A Study in St. Mark*, offers a very different interpretation of the Second Gospel. It is as yet too recently published a work to determine how far its method and conclusions will stand the test of critical examination.

only in the compilation of the Gospel as a whole but even within the limits of individual incidents and sayings. This type of criticism has been called Form Criticism and came to the fore in this country and in Germany in the period between the wars, although some important contributions were made on the Continent before and during the First World War.

### (1) *Form Criticism applied to incidents*

Here three main groups of material have been distinguished and discussed.

(*a*) Attention may first be called to an important group of material which consists in an incident which has as its climax a saying of Jesus. Vincent Taylor, the most careful and conservative English interpreter of Form Criticism, speaks of 'Pronouncement stories.' Bultmann described them as 'Apothegms'—a term taken from Greek rhetorical literature —and notes parallels from Rabbinic and Greek literature. This description throws the accent upon the saying with which the incident closes to the possible detriment of the incident itself. The term itself means in Greek a terse, set, or pointed saying. Admittedly the saying is the climax of the story, and the details are frequently lightly sketched; but such an example as the Healing of the Sick of the Palsy does not suggest that the incident itself is secondary. Dibelius describes them as 'Paradigms' or set examples, but this again throws the incident rather than the saying into relief. Both are equally important in the Gospels. An excellent example is the question about the tribute money. Here the details of the story are not emphasized. The actors are generally described; time and place (other than Jerusalem in the Last Week) are not given in any detail; and everything leads up to the saying of Jesus, 'Render unto Caesar the things that are Caesar's and unto God the things that are God's.' There are many such stories in the Gospels, and most scholars are agreed in finding them of a high degree of historical value. It is, of course, possible that some stories in the Gospels which at present lack a saying at their conclusion, and some sayings which have no story attached, originally formed one component of a Pronouncement Story of which the distinctive character has been lost in the course of transmission.

Individual critics offer further subdivisions of this material. Albertz, for example, concentrated upon the controversy stories which he divided into two groups: discussions with friendly inquirers and debates with hostile critics. Bultmann makes a subdivision between controversial and biographical apothegms, thus calling attention to the same group of material as Albertz. The difference is rather between a scene with one single central figure and one with a number of figures so grouped that One is still central. In each case the background is a matter of purely formal scenery. Dibelius besides the Paradigms finds a number of so-called 'Chreiae,' a term derived from Greek rhetorical writing and meaning apparently much the same as Apothegms. They have a more secular ring, are characterized by greater 'joy in the telling,' but the saying still remains central. It is clear that the distinction between these two groups can be very fine-drawn and will depend in large part upon the taste of the individual critic.

It is worthy of note that the sayings with which such Pronouncement stories end do not usually bear upon the main controversies of the Apostolic Age, but reflect rather, as might be expected, the setting of the ministry of Jesus Himself.

(b) The second group is composed of stories which lack a saying at their close, and where therefore presumably the story is the all-important feature. Dibelius calls these 'Novellen' after the German name for stories told by a professional story-teller about some important figure. To explain the existence of this material, he is compelled to assume the existence of a group of professional story-tellers about Jesus, of whom no trace has been left in the literature of the Apostolic Age. They do not occur, for example, in the lists of Christian functionaries which appear from time to time in the Pauline Epistles. Bultmann and Vincent Taylor prefer to call them simply 'miracle-stories.' This description does not raise the problems of the existence of a hypothetical class of Christian agents and is a more accurate description of the type of story which belongs to this group of material. They contain

an introduction, as it were setting the stage; a description of
the cure, calling special attention to the treatment given; and
a conclusion recording the effect upon the bystanders. This
might be described as a 'choral ending' to the narrative. The
fact that there are parallels both pagan and even modern to
such stories has no real relevance. From a formal point of
view one doctor's case-book is similar in style to any other,
and Dr. Kirk was not in error in finding a remarkable un-
designed parallel in the 'Night Starvation' advertisements of
the modern newspaper. The 'choral ending' is here remarkably strongly developed! It is just worth noticing that in the
most accurate description of such material, the critic imper-
ceptibly passes from Form to Content.

(c) The third group has been found even more difficult for
the Form Critic to describe. Bultmann calls them 'Legenden.'
He insists that he merely means by this the type of story told
about a holy man; for example, in the mediaeval Chronicles
about St. Cuthbert. The modern association of the word with
a story which you believe at your own risk is too strong
to make the description an altogether happy one. In fact,
Bultmann in his analysis of this kind of material seems to pass
without any sense of difficulty from one use of the word to
the other; Form and Content are close together in the mind
of this critic. Dibelius further distinguishes between 'Legenden'
which he insists merely means stories about Jesus and 'Mythen,'
stories which introduce supernatural beings as in the Temptations, the Baptism, and the Transfiguration. It is clear that
here too is a term which covers a serious ambiguity. Myth, in
the sense of a story in which one of the characters is a supernatural being, and myth as a story in which no reliance can be
placed, are dangerously close together. Vincent Taylor calls
them all 'Stories about Jesus,' as in fact they are, and Redlich
is even more cautious and faithful to the facts in calling them
simply 'Formless stories.' Certainly a common form behind
the stories of the Temptation, the Baptism, and the Transfiguration is wholly to seek.

This brief analysis will serve to introduce the reader to the
criticism passed by Erich Fascher upon Form Criticism in

general: 'Form Criticism is a tool of limited utility.' So far, the results obtained, though not without interest, have a limited range and significance. That they are reached by purely inferential methods cannot be regarded as a valid objection against them; but it is worthy of notice how easily argument which begins on formal lines converts itself to conclusions which are reached in the main by considerations determined partly by the content or the subject-matter and partly by the personal assessment of the individual critic working upon both Form and Content.

Despite these reservations, to which we shall turn more directly in our next chapter, it remains a probable conclusion that many of the units out of which the written Gospels were constructed were at one period orally transmitted either as single units or, at a slightly later stage, as collected series of similar material.

## (2) Form Criticism applied to the sayings of Jesus

The study of the Parables of Jesus made by Adolf Jülicher before the First World War was a pioneer of the classification of the sayings of Jesus along formal lines. He distinguished the metaphor, the sample case, the typical incident, and the full-scale allegory. Such a study was valuable and unexceptionable because it confined itself to strictly formal considerations, and to a type of material sufficiently uniform and extensive to make such study profitable.

Bultmann, however, offers a much more ambitious treatment of the teaching of Jesus, extending even to the individual sayings, and attempts to assign a different historical value to the various strands in the tradition. He divides the material into five classes:

(*a*) Calls to repentance;

(*b*) Eschatological sayings, or sayings concerned with the Kingdom of God and the life of the world to come;

(*c*) Gnomic sayings, or sayings of a generalized, semi-proverbial kind;

(*d*) 'I-sayings' which embody a claim made by Jesus for Himself;

(e) Church or community rules.

Bultmann regarded the first two groups as alone fully authentic. The third stood next nearest to Jesus, but reflect rather a Hellenistic Jewish *milieu* which is unlikely to have been that of Jesus Himself. The fourth group of material is paralleled by Hellenistic non-Jewish cults and therefore is again unlikely to be historical, while the last group appeared to him to be relevant to the life of the Church, and therefore more likely to be Church creations than authentic sayings of Jesus Himself.

Now the difficulty about this classification is that it is really not Form Critical at all. This was pointed out by Easton, who noticed that from the strictly formal point of view there is no difference whatever between three sayings which Bultmann places in different classes:

'Whosoever shall be ashamed of me and of my words, of him shall the Son of Man be ashamed'—an eschatological saying.

'Whosoever exalteth himself shall be abased'—a Gnomic saying.

'Whosoever putteth away his wife and marrieth another, committeth adultery against her'—a Community Rule.

It is obvious that the classification is really made on grounds of content and, still more, that the valuation of the material in terms of its content is an historical judgement in which the general presuppositions of the critic play their full part. There is still, however, no reason to doubt the soundness of the general conclusion that sayings as well as incidents were orally transmitted before they were committed to writing.

2. *The period between the oral transmission of the material about Jesus and the compilation of our present Gospels.*

If the first period which we have noticed may have taken a short generation, the second period may well have taken not less than thirty years, with some overlap with the first stage of the progress from word-of-mouth testimony to written Gospels.

It is perhaps a rather curious fact that our earliest New

Testament writings are not the Gospels, but the Pauline Epistles; not the conscious attempts to convert the oral tradition about Jesus into a written form, but interpretations of the Christian life built upon them. The Pauline letters form part of the correspondence of a busy missionary thrown off often at a speed too fast for his own pen and that of an amanuensis to meet particular pastoral situations which had arisen in the Churches for which he had direct responsibility. The two partial exceptions are the Epistle to the Romans, a more extended defence of his theology to a Church which was of another man's building, and, possibly, the Epistle to the Ephesians which may have been a pastoral encyclical to the Churches of Asia Minor written at a much later stage of his ministry. All the Pauline letters which are considered genuine were written before the Marcan Gospel saw the light. Their purpose is not the same as that of the Gospels. What is primary in the Gospels is secondary in the Epistles, and what is primary in the Epistles is secondary in the Gospels. The Gospels are primarily documents about Jesus, though the apologetic motives of their authors have a secondary significance. On the other hand, the Epistles are chiefly concerned with the day-to-day problems of the Apostolic Church, though we shall see that they also imply the existence and the knowledge, both by the writer and the recipients, of an oral tradition about Jesus. It is not therefore a valid objection against the importance of a factual tradition about Jesus that St. Paul says relatively little about it. He is above all an interpreter, and it is no defect in an interpreter that he is not continually retracing his steps to the tradition which he is interpreting.

Those who seek to force a definite gap between St. Paul and his Lord, as was fashionable in some circles in the last century, have not taken sufficient account of the real nature and character of the Pauline letters. But the gap between Jesus and St. Paul can be narrowed still further.

i. Dr. Dodd found no difficulty in tracing the existence of the primitive Christian proclamation about our Lord, which dealt in the main with the saving facts of His life, death, and Resurrection within the Pauline letters no less than within the sermons of the Acts of the Apostles. If then the Pauline Gospel rests upon the Primitive preaching, the life of Jesus cannot have been a matter of indifference to the Apostle of the Gentiles.

ii. Special studies of the knowledge by St. Paul of the facts have from time to time been made. These range from R. J. Knowling's careful and thorough book written towards the close of the last century,[1] through Dr. Anderson Scott's more manageable summary,[2] to Dr. Hunter's recent study on Paul and his predecessors which takes account of the more recent material.[3] The general conclusion reached by these studies is not only that Paul had a fairly detailed knowledge of the life and teaching of Jesus, but also that his teaching is more deeply embedded in the general Apostolic tradition than it has sometimes been fashionable to suppose. The grandeur of St. Paul is not in the least impaired by this recognition of a general background of indebtedness both to his predecessors and his Lord.

iii. There is a further general point which is not without its force. We know that St. Paul was continually exposed to criticism from his opponents upon such matters as the conditions of the Gentile Mission. At times this reached the pitch of an accusation that he had deserted the true Gospel. It is not difficult to imagine the storm of protest which would have ensued if he had been found to be sitting loosely to the fundamental factual basis upon which the Church depended for its very existence. If this were so, we should have expected it to be plainly reflected in the documents.

iv. Paul himself shows a clear recognition of the difference in authority resting in a saying of Jesus and in an opinion which he himself expressed on his own responsibility. In 1 Corinthians vii. 10–12 he is careful to distinguish what the Lord says and what he thought himself. 1 Thessalonians v. 2–4, 'the day of the Lord cometh as a thief in the night,' summarizes teaching of Jesus in such passages as St. Matthew xxiv. 43 and St. Luke xvii. 24.

[1] R. J. Knowling, *The Witness of the Epistles*.
[2] C. Anderson Scott in *Cambridge Biblical Essays*.
[3] A. M. Hunter, *Paul and his Predecessors*.

v. But more significant still are two sections in which the purpose of his argument leads him to appeal directly to Gospel material. In 1 Corinthians xi, where he is dealing with the practical difficulties which had arisen in the conduct of the Eucharist at Corinth, he includes an account of the institution (23–6) which is remarkably close to that which forms part of the Lucan Gospel, while his theology of the Resurrection is introduced by a list of the Post-Resurrection Appearances which alludes even to some which form no part of the present Gospel tradition (1 *Cor.* xv. 5–8). This strongly suggests that he could appeal in case of need to a rich Gospel tradition.

But if we admit so much, we are still faced with the further problem why St. Paul does not in fact include more material than he does. This has in part been answered by the preliminary suggestions which we made about the nature and character of the Pauline Epistles. There is, however, a further point which we need to consider. The whole centre of St. Paul's existence as a Christian was the conversion vision on the Damascus Road. He believed that what had happened to him could happen to any one irrespective of acquaintance with the historical Jesus. His whole philosophy of the Christian life depends upon the continued availability of the Risen Christ. Yet St. Paul says enough to make it overwhelmingly probable that, in common with the rest of the primitive tradition, he regarded the Risen Master as continuous with, and derived from, the historical Jesus. The Risen Lord is still 'this same Jesus' transposed, as it were, to a different key and exalted to a different mode of existence. The Risen Christ is not another Lord but the same Master manifesting Himself in a different manner. If St. Paul's theology, then, is differently orientated from the Gospels, it rests upon precisely the same basis as they do themselves.

We can now turn to the Gospels themselves. Here it is inevitable that in certain respects we must run together our account, such as it is, of the second and third stages, the passage from oral to written sources and the transition from these sources to the Gospels. This is due to the fact that we must see what we can infer from the Gospels themselves of the probable or possible sources from which they are derived.

The starting-point of all recent source-criticism of the Gospels is the priority of Mark. This conclusion, highly probable in itself, was completely strange to the earlier tradition of Gospel study. The Fathers, almost without exception, comment on Matthew and omit any independent treatment of Mark. St. Augustine, who speaks of Mark as 'the abbreviator and as it were the lackey' of Matthew, was merely summarizing the general opinion of scholars of his day. Modern scholars, however, with rare exceptions would assert the priority of Mark.[1]

The reasons which have led scholars to reverse the verdict of antiquity on this question are as follows. There is the general ground that it is curious to find the longer account of many incidents in the shorter Gospel. Three examples are given by Streeter. The stories of the Gadarene demoniac, the Raising of Jairus' daughter, and the Feeding of the Five Thousand amount to 325, 374, and 235, words respectively in Mark, while Matthew employs 136, 135, and 157 words for the same incidents. The point is not that it is surprising to find one Gospel abbreviating another, but, first that the longer accounts appear in the shorter Gospel, and that, if Mark copied Matthew, it is surprising to find him preferring longer accounts of such incidents while omitting passages like the Sermon on the Mount and the Infancy narratives. It is hard to imagine what his principle of selection might be. It would, however, be completely in keeping for one who sought to include fresh material to prune the more vividly told narratives of his predecessor in order to save space.

That this conclusion is the more probable one is strongly supported by six pieces of evidence:

i. Mark contains a number of vivid details which Matthew omits as unnecessary to his narrative. Thus in St. Mark vi. 39–40, which forms part of the account of the Feeding of the Five Thousand, it is recorded that they sat down in ranks on

---

[1] The older view is, however, still maintained by Roman Catholic scholars; see John Chapman, *Matthew, Mark, and Luke*, and B. C. Butler, *The Originality of St. Matthew's Gospel*.

the green grass. The phrase translated 'in ranks' could be better translated 'flower-beds' referring to the gaily-coloured outer garments of the multitude. The grammatical construction is also vivid and unusual, a repetition of the noun in the nominative case. Matthew omits the touch altogether, and the adjective 'green' with the mention of grass (*St. Matt.* xiv. 19). Again, in St. Mark iv. 35–41 there is a mention of other ships on the lake, and of the pillow in the stern of the ship on which Jesus was asleep. Matthew omits both details as unessential (*St. Matt.* viii. 23–7). Again, in his brief account of the Temptation Mark adds the note that Jesus was with the wild beasts (*St. Mark* i. 13). Despite his fuller narrative of the Temptation from another source, Matthew dispenses with this detail.

ii. Where Mark has a difficult passage, Matthew tends to omit or to smooth it away. St. Mark vi. 5 records that Jesus could do no mighty work at Nazareth, thereby implying in some sense that He was conditioned by the faith of His recipients in doing miracles; Matthew contents himself with the bare statement that Jesus 'did there no mighty works,' thus avoiding a serious theological problem (*St. Matt.* xiii. 58). In the narrative of the storm at sea (*St. Mark* iv. 38) Mark records the despairing cry of the disciples, 'Master, carest Thou not that we perish?' Matthew replaces it by the words, 'Lord, save us, we perish' (*St. Matt.* viii. 25). He could not tolerate in his account any hesitation on the part of the disciples on the concern felt by Jesus for their safety.

iii. Vivid words in Mark which the later evangelist found difficult to understand are either omitted or weakened. Matthew omits the touch in St. Mark x. 21 that our Lord loved the young man. This might suggest too obviously a feeling of strong human emotion. In the story of the Anointing at Bethany, Mark uses the trade term 'pistic' or genuine for the nard; Matthew simply omits (*St. Mark* xiv. 3). The technical term 'token' given in the Marcan account of the betrayal (*St. Mark* xiv. 44) is replaced in Matthew by the more usual word 'sign' (*St. Matt.* xxvi. 48). Again, 'forecourt' (*St. Mark* xiv. 68) is replaced by 'gateway' or 'entrance'

(*St. Matt.* xxvi. 71). Other difficult words which are not always easy to interpret even to-day are simply omitted by Matthew. Examples are St. Mark i. 43, 'straitly charged' or perhaps 'looking keenly at'; xi. 4, 'in the open street'; xii. 4, 'wound in the head' ; and xiv. 41, 'He is at hand,' or perhaps 'he has received the bribe.'

iv. Latinisms or Aramaisms, that is, words of Latin or Aramaic origin either merely transliterated or rendered literally into Greek, which occur in Mark are omitted by Matthew. The following are examples. In St. Mark ii. 23, where the Greek is a literal translation of the Latin 'iter facere,' to make a journey, and v. 9 where the demoniac calls himself 'Legion' or Regiment of the Roman Army. Aramaic words simply transliterated occur in St. Mark v. 41 (Talitha cumi, Damsel arise), St. Mark vii. 34 (Ephphatha, be opened), and St. Mark xiv. 36 (Abba, Father). The difficulty is not so much that one Gospel should omit local colour which another Gospel inserts, but that the shorter Gospel should be the one to introduce such vivid touches to the exclusion of much more significant material.

v. Two details in the Marcan Gospel which suggest local interest or local knowledge are omitted by Matthew as too trivial to mention. It has often been supposed that the young man who left his cloak behind him in the Garden was St. Mark himself (*St. Mark* xiv. 51-2); that he was a figure of great significance is hardly likely. Matthew simply omits. A similar Matthaean omission occurs in the description of Simon of Cyrene, the passer-by pressed into bearing the Cross for Jesus, as 'the father of Alexander and Rufus.' They are possibly well-known members of the Church to which St. Mark was writing.

vi. It is a curious fact that Mark 'never spares the Twelve.' Matthew, on the other hand, always treats them as worthy of every respect as becoming figures of considerable prestige in the Apostolic Church. One example of a modification which is due to this change of tone between the two Gospels is to be found in the request for places of prominence in the coming Kingdom claimed by James and John, the sons of Zebedee

(*St. Mark* x. 35). Matthew, who cannot believe that the two sons of Zebedee themselves were so devoid of understanding, attributes their request to their mother (*St. Matt.* xx. 20).

Such evidence is cumulative and all points in the direction of the priority of St. Mark's Gospel.

A second conclusion to which modern criticism as a whole points is the deduction of a document other than, and additional to, Mark behind the First and Third Gospels. In the nature of the case this can only be at best a probable inference, for this presumed second source has long since disappeared. No satisfactory or even plausible reconstruction has been found possible, though some have been attempted; but this should not be regarded as in any sense a final objection, since, assuming the loss of Mark, we should find this equally difficult to reconstruct from the two Gospels concerned.

This source is normally described by the letter Q (German *Quelle* or source), and the grounds which lead scholars on the whole to assume its existence are roughly as follows. Matthew and Luke contain three classes of material. The first is material derived from Mark. This causes no problem, for, whatever view is taken of the relation between the first three Gospels, we need not go outside them for its solution. Secondly, there is material which obviously does not come from Mark but which is common to Matthew and Luke. This amounts to some two hundred verses, about half of which contains a very considerable proportion of common words (over 80 per cent).

Theoretically there are four possible explanations of this phenomenon. The common material may be explained either as evidence for Matthew's use of Luke; or of Luke's use of Matthew;[1] that both used a third source; or that both drew independently upon the same circle of oral tradition. The last view does not really explain the passages in which an almost exact correspondence in the words used occurs; and, though there are some scholars who consider that the first two possibilities are worth exploring, the great majority believe in the existence of an earlier source used in addition to Mark by both

[1] Dom John Chapman, a Roman Catholic scholar, considers that instead of Q we should speak of Luke's use of Matthew. The theory has been framed but not as yet published that it represents Matthew's use of Luke.

Matthew and Luke. To this source can be ascribed with confidence the hundred verses with very close agreements, and with great probability the other hundred verses with less striking resemblances. Some of the material which belongs to one of the two longer Synoptic Gospels may well belong to Q, but in the absence of a 'control' passage in the other Gospel we can never make it a really probable conclusion.

The source Q, so far as it is possible to construct it on broad lines, is largely concerned with the teaching of Jesus, though there is reason to believe that it contained at least a few incidents such as the Temptation of Jesus (*St. Matt.* iv. 1–11; *St. Luke* iv. 1–13), the healing of the Centurion's Servant (*St. Matt.* viii. 5–13; *St. Luke* vii. 1–10), and possibly an account of the Beelzebub controversy (*St. Matt.* xii. 25–37; *St. Luke* xi. 17–23). Burkitt believed that it contained a Passion Narrative. This is possible but it depends upon the status of the Lucan Passion Narrative and cannot be regarded as proved. Matthew, who closely follows Mark here, is no help; and we cannot in the absence of our second witness securely infer that the Lucan material derives from Q. It is equally impossible to say how much of Q has been lost. Burkitt has found few scholars to agree with him that perhaps up to a third of the source has perished. Not only can this not be proved; it is certainly improbable. It is hard to believe that the Primitive Church should have been so careless of material about the Historic Jesus as to allow a considerable amount once committed to writing to pass out of circulation. It is probable that Q was compiled at an earlier date than the Marcan Gospel, and that its centre of origin was Jerusalem or Galilee.[1]

So far we appear to be led in the direction of a Two Document Hypothesis—the belief that Mark and Q underlie the First and the Third Gospels. Can we go further than this? Streeter thought that we could, and his starting-point was an examination of how Matthew and Luke used Mark. Here a few figures are of importance. The authentic text of Mark contains 661 verses. Of these Matthew reproduces the sub-

---

[1] J. M. C. Crum, for example, entitled his reconstruction of Q, *The Original Jerusalem Gospel*. His instinct as to the place of origin may well be more probable than the actual reconstruction which he made.

stance of over 600, although in actual vocabulary Matthew only contains 51 per cent of the Marcan words, owing to his frequent habit of abbreviating and paraphrasing Mark's material. Thanks to this treatment of Mark, he is able to add as much material again from other sources. It is clear, however, that the shape of Matthew is of an edition of Mark newly enlarged and in great part rewritten. The statistics for Luke, however, bear a different character. Luke uses only about 65 per cent of Marcan material as against 90 per cent in Matthew, but his percentage of Marcan words is slightly higher than that of Matthew. This implies a more faithful reproduction of considerably less material. These figures leave open the possibility that Matthew and Luke used Mark in different ways. If Matthew treats Mark as the backbone of his work, Luke seems on the whole to prefer non-Marcan material to Marcan in the course of his Gospel. Streeter proceeds to try out the further hypothesis that Luke possessed a non-Marcan framework into which he proceeded finally to fit his Marcan material, as occasion served.

The starting-point for this theory is the fact which appears at the outset that there seems to be something rather queer about the third chapter of Luke in relation to the first two. The Gospel starts unexceptionably with a rather formal prologue and the Infancy Narratives occur naturally enough at the beginning of the book. Chapter Three begins with a rather formal and careful date such as might be the beginning of a book, while the genealogy of Jesus, Who has, of course, been mentioned several times in the course of the first two chapters, occurs in the middle of the third chapter at the first mention of His Name in the chapter itself. This procedure is so surprising, especially in view of the straightforward way in which Matthew opens his Gospel with the genealogy, that it has been suggested that at one time the Gospel of Luke was current without the first two chapters. The Infancy Narratives would then form a kind of appendix inserted at the beginning, possibly taken from material made available to Luke by the Blessed Virgin herself.

If this be a probable hypothesis, we can examine the rest

of the Gospel with new eyes. Scholars have frequently noticed two long sections (*St. Luke* vi. 20–viii. 3 and ix. 51–xviii. 14) which bear little or no trace of Marcan influence. Some of the material can be derived from Q in view of Matthaean parallels, while the rest is either peculiar to Luke himself (called L by Streeter) or possibly in some cases derived from Q but lacking the Matthaean control which would afford an indication of this. On the assumption that both Matthew and Luke made use of Mark in precisely the same way, they used to be called the lesser and greater 'non-Marcan interpolation' respectively. Streeter, however, suggests that they ought to be regarded as part of the foundation document, and that Luke used Mark not as his primary but as his secondary source. This is confirmed by the fact that, at least in the Passion Narrative, the Marcan touches are put in exactly the Marcan order, which in the light of this theory suggests, though it does not prove, that Luke is enriching a non-Marcan Passion Narrative with material derived from Mark's account. Streeter gave the name 'Proto-Luke' to this original non-Marcan nucleus of Luke, and Vincent Taylor published a connected narrative of this under the title of 'The Original Draft of Luke's Gospel.'

This theory has many attractive features, but it has not succeeded in convincing all scholars. It was accepted and used by T. W. Manson in his work *The Teaching of Jesus*. Vincent Taylor is also a weighty champion in his book *Behind the Third Gospel*, as are American scholars like B. S. Easton and A. M. Perry. Some detailed tests, for example, of Lucan vocabulary and style must be applied if the theory is to be taken further. It has met with a certain amount of rejection. J. M. Creed, for example, in his commentary on St. Luke explains all the phenomena which Streeter held to point to an independent Passion Narrative as editorial glosses and expansions of a fundamentally Marcan tradition. Dr. A. M. Farrer in his recent study of St. Mark's Gospel roundly asserts that the theory is incapable of reasonable defence. This judgement at least appears much too sweeping even if we cannot claim the same probability for it as we can for the inferred existence of Q.

The theory has, however, important consequences. It is perhaps an insoluble problem whether, supposing it to have existed, the document was more than a stage in the writer's notes; we have no warrant that the Gospel was in circulation in its draft form. It would suggest important corollaries about the meaning and purpose of St. Luke. Some writers like Dr. R. H. Lightfoot (and probably also Dr. Farrer) would regard St. Luke as a great interpreter, a creative artist of great force and originality. This theory, on the other hand, would rather suggest that his aim was to gather up the fragments of the tradition that nothing be lost. This might agree well with the Prologue to the Gospel. If it could be proved, the theory would point to the material in the so-called first draft as an early source, perhaps as early as St. Mark's Gospel, and would lead to a considerable enrichment of early material in our disentanglement of the various strands of the Gospel tradition. One objection has been raised to the whole theory which is not, however, well-founded. If we read Vincent Taylor's reconstruction of the document in question, we are impressed by its unlikeness to Mark. While Mark has a good and clear form which many regard as true in general sequence and order to the pattern of the historical ministry, Proto-Luke appears positively formless. This is confirmed by the difficulty which even many good scholars have in remembering where exactly in the Lucan Gospel any particular piece of material comes. But perhaps, as Vincent Taylor suggests, the real problem is not the formlessness of Proto-Luke but the formfulness of Mark.

Streeter completed his expansion of the Two-Document theory to a Four-Document hypothesis by an examination of the material special to Matthew which he believed to represent a written source called for convenience M. Here fewer scholars have been convinced; though it is easy to see why, after an examination of other probable written sources, Streeter was led to make the assumption that this too was written. But the material special to Matthew does not appear to me to have sufficient homogeneity to make a written source really probable. There are, it is true, the Sermon on the Mount and the Denunciation of the Pharisees, some of which plainly derive from Q. There are a few incidents of which the most formal are to be found in the Infancy Narratives and the cycle of Post-Resurrection appearances. Apart from this there are three Petrine supplements, some details in the Baptism, and the Passion Narrative. There are a few Parables and a number of sayings. While Dr. A. M. Hunter, in his recent review of New Testament studies, finds a written source at least for the sayings probable, I must confess myself less confident. There is little to suggest a written source rather than editorial modification and oral tradition.

We can now pass to the Fourth Gospel. Here the difficulty has long been felt that it is markedly different from the Synoptists. Indeed, as we have seen, that title was given to the first three Gospels to mark the fact that they present a common picture of our Lord in contrast to that of the Fourth Gospeller. Two theories have been framed to account for its difference in character: the first may be called 'the supplementary theory,' the second 'the interpretative hypothesis.'

According to the former the Gospel represents a deliberate attempt to supplement the facts of our Lord's Ministry as given in the Synoptic Gospels. The writer, finding that less than justice was done to the Jerusalem Ministry and possessing himself important additional sources of information, set himself the task to fill in this gap. The difference in the type of teaching contained in the Gospel is explained as a deeper note struck for the more theologically perceptive audience at Jerusalem.

Now there seems little doubt that the Fourth Evangelist does frequently offer a factual tradition which differs from that of the Synoptists and which may in certain respects even be preferable. T. W. Manson has recently noted a significant change in critical studies in favour of this theory: 'It is no longer possible to say "If the Fourth Gospel contradicts the Synoptists, so much the worse for the Fourth Gospel." '[1] If

[1] *Bulletin of the John Rylands Library, Manchester,* May, 1947.

this be taken as a piece of customary British critical conservatism, attention may be directed to the way in which M. Goguel, himself certainly no conservative, finds himself prepared to discover historical traditions within the Fourth Gospel.

It is probable at the outset, even from the Synoptists, that Jesus did fulfil a ministry at Jerusalem. In the Q passage (*St. Matt.* xxiii. 37; *St. Luke* xiii. 34), 'O Jerusalem, Jerusalem, thou that killest the prophets, and stonest those who are sent unto thee, how often would I have gathered thy children together and ye would not,' the first half might suggest merely an unfulfilled intention, but the latter half suggests strongly an actual ministry. It was suggested in support of this hypothesis, though with rather less probability, that the Raising of Lazarus is just the kind of incident necessary to explain the Triumphal Entry which is otherwise left hanging in the air. It is normally held that there is a discrepancy between the date of the Last Supper in the Synoptists and St. John, and many scholars are prepared to find the correct date in the Fourth Gospel. It is also urged that the evidence afforded by the Fourth Gospel that the earliest disciples were attached to John the Baptist before they embarked upon discipleship of Jesus may well help to explain the otherwise sudden call which we find in the Marcan Gospel. This is merely a selection of points, not all equally convincing, urged in support of this theory. There is little reason to dispute its main contention that there are many factual supplements contained within the Fourth Gospel; there are, however, other facts which might well make us doubt whether this is the only or perhaps even the principal reason for the writing of the Fourth Gospel.

It is to these facts that the second theory of an interpretation of the Jesus of history makes its chief appeal. First, we can notice the probable controversial bent of many passages in the Gospel. The strong anti-Jewish bias of much of the Gospel calls for no comment. It seems, however, rather different from the denunciations of the Pharisees contained in the Synoptic tradition. 'The Jews' appear rather as an external body rather than, humanly speaking, kith and kin to our Lord.

It is possible, too, that part of the purpose of the Gospel was to correct the picture of John the Baptist given in the Synoptists. We read in the nineteenth chapter of Acts of a body of John the Baptist's disciples existing as a circle or Church at Ephesus. The Fourth Gospel contains some material very relevant to meet such a situation. It is curious for a modern Christian to find in the middle of the exalted theology of the Prologue the statement that John the Baptist was 'not that light.' He is inclined to murmur, 'Whoever supposed that he was?' The controversial motive might be reasonably suspected here. In the Fourth Gospel the Baptist points to Jesus personally and directly, not to the Christ officially and subsequently to Jesus identified with the Christ. This could be fitted easily into such a theory. Some scholars have found traces of a controversial purpose in the silence about Simon of Cyrene in this Gospel and the insistence that Jesus carried His own Cross (*St. John* xix. 17). There are traces in Gnosticism of some who believed that Simon of Cyrene was crucified instead of the Christ, Who was not capable, on Gnostic theories, of suffering. Gnosticism as a whole, like Simon Peter at Caesarea Philippi, said to the Christ, 'That be far from Thee, O Lord.' It must, however, be pointed out that this interpretation, though possible and in some ways attractive, is not at all compelling. Both facts are obviously true, and the Evangelist may simply by his selection between them be emphasizing the essential humanity of the Master. That this was another motive of the Gospel is proved by the poignant verse that 'Jesus wept' at the death of Lazarus (xi. 35), and perhaps also the statement that water and blood flowed from the wounded side of our Lord on the Cross (*St. John* xix. 34). Although the figure of Jesus in the Fourth Gospel is full of glory, it is clear that the writer also takes pains to safeguard the essential humanity of the Master.

But the interpretative elements within the Fourth Gospel seem to go much deeper than a few relatively superficial controversial touches. One important principle may be suggested here: it is the tendency of the writer to see the end of the process in its beginning. It might be called 'the principle

of teleological interpretation,' and examples to which it applies
can be seen throughout the Gospel. John the Baptist acclaims
our Lord as the Lamb of God that taketh away the sin of the
world (*St. John* i. 29). It is unlikely, as a point of historical
fact, that he saw in Jesus all that He was afterwards to show
Himself to be. That is, however, what Jesus actually was, the
great saving fact which underlies His Life and Ministry. Then
why not say so at once? argues the Evangelist and thus puts
his readers in possession of an important clue at the very
beginning of his Gospel. The same explanation probably
applies to the transposition of the Cleansing of the Temple
from the last week to the beginning of the Ministry. It does
not appear very likely (though some scholars have been found
to support each view) either that there were two cleansings of
the Temple or that the Johannine order is historically preferable. The Synoptic account makes the Cleansing of the
Temple the action which proved the decisive break with
Judaism and was recognized as such. But the Fourth Evangelist may have argued that Temple Judaism was in principle
superseded from the very moment at which the Public
Ministry of Jesus opened, and have taken this opportunity of
showing it. The two discourses on Gospel Sacraments (*St. John*
iii and vi) are perhaps placed early in the Gospel so as to put
the reader in immediate possession of two clues to the understanding of Jesus as early as possible. But most characteristic
of all is the treatment of the Passion of our Lord. It is, in fact,
the climax of the interpretation of the Passion found in the
Four Gospels. For Mark the Passion marks a crescendo of
gloom until the Resurrection (known by its effects) bursts
upon our astonished eyes. The 'happy ending,' though prepared for in an earlier part of the Gospel, is kept carefully
in the background. Luke, however, stands beside us all
through the Passion story reminding us that we are assisting
not at a stark tragedy but at the Martyrdom of the Suffering
Servant of God Who is sure of His vindication. John carries
the interpretation a stage further and shows us not that the
Passion is the prelude to the Glorification, but that it is in fact
the Glorification itself. 'Until Jesus should be glorified' is a

characteristic way of alluding to the Passion in the earlier part of the Gospel. This fact may well have determined him to omit the incident of the Transfiguration which would on other grounds have appealed greatly to him.

It is not suggested that this is a skeleton key to open all the secrets of the Fourth Gospel, but rather that it represents one clue towards its better understanding.

It is clear then that neither the factual supplement theory nor the interpretative hypothesis is adequate by itself to account for the rich and manifold contents of this Gospel. Fact and interpretation are subtly blended. It is difficult to take the Gospel and to enter in the margin the comments, 'This is fact,' 'This is interpretation' with any conviction of producing an objective analysis. One suggestion may, however, be hazarded for further thought. It has sometimes appeared to me that the structure of the Fourth Gospel rather resembles the bony structure of the middle part of the human body with a 'vertebra' of fact issuing in a 'rib' of interpretation, to be succeeded by another vertebra and yet another rib. If, however, this suggestion is made, it must be remembered that here we have not a mechanical but an organic process.

It remains to try to assign dates and places for the origin of the various Gospels and to mention the most probable conjectures with regard to authorship. Nothing appears to forbid the opinion that the Second Gospel was written by St. Mark himself at Rome about A.D. 65, as tradition suggests. There is also much to be said for the belief, which has of recent years largely under Form Critical influence become unfashionable, that it contains a degree of Petrine reminiscence. We shall need to discuss this matter further in the next chapter. It is difficult to assign definite dates for the other Synoptic Gospels. Much is bound to depend upon the amount of time necessary for the Marcan Gospel to become known and the subsequent compilation of the two Gospels in question. If we allow between ten and twenty years, that would perhaps be sufficient. The Third Gospel may perhaps be a trifle the earlier. Its place of origin must be a Church with a predominantly Gentile approach. Nothing forbids Lucan authorship. Tradition assigns Achaea as its place of origin but critical confirmation is inevitably lacking. It is not now regarded as probable that St. Matthew was the author of the Gospel which bears his name, although the tradition derived from Papias may be interpreted as opening the way to the ascription of the authorship of Q to the Apostle. It is believed on the grounds of its outlook to be slightly later than Luke. Streeter thought that its place of origin was Antioch, but the more probable conjecture is that of Bacon that it was some place further to the east.

The question of the authorship and place of origin of the Fourth Gospel still remain in doubt. Opinion is rather hardening against direct authorship by the son of Zebedee in favour of authorship by another John, of whom there are some traces in early tradition. It is still disputed whether the author was acquainted with the Synoptic Gospels as we at present possess them; there is a balance of opinion in favour of the view that the author knew Mark and Luke; no evidence to suggest that he knew and used Matthew. The rehandling of the Synoptic tradition tells heavily in favour of the Gospel as representing at second-hand the interpretation of John, son of Zebedee. It would be difficult to believe that a Gospel which presented so different a picture from that given by the Apostolic writings could have gained universal currency without the aid of some such assumption. The place of origin is traditionally given as Asia Minor, and there is much in the content of the Gospel to confirm this. Mr. J. N. Sanders, however, has made out an interesting case for Egypt as its place of origin. The use made by the Egyptian Gnostics of this Gospel and the early papyrus fragments found there, dated by experts between A.D. 90 and 125, are weighty arguments in support of this theory. Its date is a matter of conjecture, but critical opinion has swung back to the belief that it was probably written during the last decade of the first Christian century.

To sum up, the Christian sources for the life of Jesus consist virtually in the Four Gospels written from faith to faith, by believers for believers, related to each other and to the oral tradition upon which they rest in a rather complex way. All blend fact and interpretation in different ways. The difference may perhaps be put as follows: whereas in the Synoptic Gospels fact appears to control interpretation, in the Fourth Gospel interpretation seems to take control of fact. The difference is, however, one rather of degree than of kind, and such generalizations can at best only represent partial truths. The Gospels do, however, present a vivid and fundamentally reliable witness to the One Who was not only the object of the Church's worship, but also the Master Who lived, taught, suffered, and died in Jerusalem and rose again to be the Living Companion of Christians from that day until the end of time.

## BIBLIOGRAPHY

For any close study of the Synoptic Gospels a Synopsis either in English or Greek with the parallels arranged side by side is indispensable. The best Greek Synopsis is Huck-Lietzmann-Cross, *A Synopsis of the First Three Gospels*.

A general survey of modern critical opinion given with admirable clarity is to be found in A. M. Hunter, *Interpreting the New Testament 1900–1950*.

### 1. FORM CRITICISM

E. B. Redlich, *Form Criticism*,
B. S. Easton, *The Gospel before the Gospels*,
Vincent Taylor, *The Formation of the Gospel Tradition*,
are the best introductions in English.

A fuller treatment from one point of view is given by M. Dibelius, *From Tradition to Gospel*.

### 2. SOURCE CRITICISM

B. H. Streeter, *The Four Gospels*, is the basic work here.

Vincent Taylor, *Behind the Third Gospel*, is an excellent detailed treatment of the Proto-Luke Theory.

G. D. Kilpatrick, *The Origin of the Gospel according to St. Matthew*, is a masterpiece of minute and careful criticism.

B. W. Bacon, *Studies in St. Matthew*, from a different point of view, will repay careful attention.

### 3. THE FOURTH GOSPEL

Standard commentaries are J. H. Bernard (International Critical Commentary), E. C. Hoskyns, and F. N. Davey, *The Fourth Gospel* (difficult but rewarding).

Articles of importance on the Fourth Gospel are to be found in *Cambridge Biblical Essays* (A. E. Brooke and W. R. Inge) and by Baron von Hügel in *Encyclopaedia Britannica* (eleventh edition).

W. Temple, *Readings in St. John's Gospel*, is much more than a devotional commentary.

## 4. THE SYNOPTIC GOSPELS

Reference may here be made to:

F. W. Green, *St. Matthew* (Clarendon Bible).

A. E. J. Rawlinson, *St. Mark* (Westminster Commentaries).

J. M. Creed, *St. Luke*.

## PART II

# CAN WE RECONSTRUCT THE MINISTRY OF JESUS FROM THE GOSPELS?

## Chapter III

## HISTORY AND THE GOSPELS

THE questions which this chapter will be concerned to answer are once more real problems, even if few readers may have asked them for themselves. Why is there not one single standard or, to use the language of reviewers, definitive life of Jesus in existence? Why are there so many which seem to reflect different points of view? Why for the last few years has there been so little apparent interest in this branch of study? And why are so many good and careful scholars whom we would otherwise gladly follow anxious to tell us that the Gospels are not biographies?

Up to the beginning of the present century these would not have been urgent questions. Many Lives of Jesus kept on appearing, each hoping to be greeted as the biography for which Christians were looking. It was never doubted that a scholar, provided that he was good enough and clever enough, would some day produce such a biography, starting from exactly the right assumptions and dealing satisfactorily with all the available material. With the peculiar patience of the tribe of scholars the failure of such a work to appear was regarded as a mere accident.

Looking back upon these efforts in the light of our present knowledge we can notice four important features.

i. They were based upon a faulty treatment of the sources. This is a feature for which it is impossible to blame them, but it is nevertheless true. That there were differences in the approach of the Four Gospels had long been known. Tatian in the second century produced a Harmony of the Gospels which for some centuries became the official Gospel text in the Syrian Branch of the Church. St. Augustine sought to harmonize the Four Gospels in a treatise on the subject. No one, however, suspected that the interrelation of the Gospels was as complicated and difficult a matter as we have come to realize to-day. Although from the point of view of the biographer of Jesus this is the least important factor in the situation, the determination of a proper text of the Gospels had hardly begun. This work was the product of the careful and minute study of manuscripts and texts which was a marked feature of classical and New Testament scholarship in the nineteenth century, and many of the most important discoveries were the product of the last hundred and fifty years. It is by no means certain that further treasures will not come to light as the resources of Eastern monasteries become more generally available to scholars. The work of source-criticism, perhaps carried as far as it can be taken, for the present at least, was the work of the first half of the present century, while the tool of Form Criticism was only forged during the last thirty years and its results have only been assimilated slowly. These developments of recent years give the appearance of false confidence to the older Lives of Jesus owing to the fact that the necessary structural engineering had not (and indeed could not) be attempted at an earlier date.

ii. From the days of the Enlightenment (the close of the eighteenth century onwards) many scholars had worked on a basically false assumption. It was believed that behind the Christ of the Church's worship was a nuclear historical Jesus Who could be reached by stripping off the accretions with which the Church had overlaid Him. The nineteenth-century scholar said in effect to the Church, 'You have taken away my Lord and I know not where you have laid Him.' By the time the scholars had finished their task, the Church could be heard (and with greater reason) to make the same complaint. Originally, in the most optimistic part of the period, it was believed that all that was needed was to remove a few 'ecclesiastical' embellishments to explain away a few obviously 'impossible' miracles, and the Historical Jesus would stand revealed in all His impressive simplicity, a fully human, magnificently rational figure. But the difficulty was that the process of pruning the tradition did not turn out to be so simple as had at first been thought, and that the fundamental

masonry of the Gospels showed an unfortunate tendency to
come away as well. The Christ and His Church were shown
to be far more integrally related than appeared at first sight,
and the latest scholar to attempt this task, Rudolf Bultmann,
in an essay called *The Demythologising of Jesus*, does not appear
to have been any more successful. The *reductio ad absurdum* of
this whole procedure was reached in the article on Jesus Christ
in the *Encyclopaedia Biblica* written by the Swiss scholar P. W.
Schmiedel, whose search for 'pillar passages,' that is, passages
which could not be unhistorical, resulted in the disentanglement of nine sayings, most of which were notoriously difficult
texts and which did not amount either to a rich or a coherent
picture of the Master. It is only fair to Schmiedel to say that
these were not the only passages which he accepted as genuine;
they were only the passages which could not in his opinion be
regarded as anything else. The result, however, casts doubt
upon the correctness of the principle which he accepted.

iii. The attempts which were produced were not without
their significance. If they threw relatively little light upon the
Person of our Lord, they were most significant for the character
and interests of the would-be biographer. No man can write
a Life of Jesus on whatever principles without laying bare the
very structure of his own soul. Renan produced a Life which
approximated Jesus to a gentle, meditative Breton peasant;
Harnack revealed Jesus as the ideal Liberal Protestant; Conrad
Noel presented One Who would have been the natural leader
of any extreme Left-Wing political party; Schweitzer presented an eschatologist possessed by a spirit of heaven-assailing
aggressiveness, a veritable storm-trooper of the Kingdom of
God. Archbishop William Temple made a wise remark about
the nineteenth-century pictures of Jesus: 'Why anybody should
have bothered to crucify the Christ of Liberal Protestantism is
an unsolved mystery.'

iv. The authors were never averse to supplying 'missing
links' in the narrative, and in particular psychological missing
links. While it is possible that no Life of Jesus can dispense
with this procedure, it is well to remember with Dr. Mascall
that we cannot know by introspection what it meant to be the

Incarnate Son of God, and to be rather chary of speaking of
the development of the inner consciousness of the Master. I
would not personally regard this as an objection in principle
to any possible Life of Jesus; it is certainly true that in actual
fact this procedure was applied without reserve and with
considerable abandon by many earlier scholars.

It is given to few books to open a new epoch. Yet it is
hardly an exaggeration to regard Albert Schweitzer's *Quest of
the Historical Jesus* as fulfilling such a role with regard to the
writing of the Life of Jesus. It simply blew the whole effort
of producing a Liberal Life of Jesus sky-high. The bulk of the
work is in the form of a series of extended and critical reviews
of Lives of Jesus 'from Reimarus to Wrede' of which the only
work to receive even a modicum of praise was the latter's book
on the Messianic Secret. The constructive part of the work is
confined to the last two chapters. Here Schweitzer has one
important thing to say: the eschatological teaching of Jesus
(the teaching of Jesus about the Last things and their future
and even impending approach) was a part of the Gospels
which most of his predecessors had been content to ignore;
wherever the clue to the right understanding of Jesus lay, it
could not be here. With Schweitzer the stone which the builders
rejected has become the head of the corner. He leads us rather
to infer from his sharp way of putting things that here is a
Sketch of the life of Jesus to end all sketches. In the ferment
of his new discovery he adopts a somewhat magisterial 'Either-
Or' approach to the subject. When we examine the positive
side of his work, we are, however, disappointed to find that
he has not himself avoided any of the dangers which he was
quick to point out in others. If they are selective, so is he. He
builds much on the eschatological passages, many of them
drawn from the material special to St. Matthew, which they
ignore; but he himself passes somewhat lightly over the
Lucan interpretation of Jesus. Whether Schweitzer was here
right or wrong, here is certainly selection carried to a fine
pitch. He accuses others of offering psychological reconstructions to tide over difficult places in their task. Yet his descrip-

tion of the Passion: 'The wheel of fate would not turn, the expected *Parousia* (decisive coming of God in history) tarried. Jesus flung Himself upon that wheel and is left there hanging still,' although a vivid metaphor, is liable to the same accusation. It does not impose itself from the documents, and is rather read into them than out from them.

Again, Schweitzer adopted a somewhat high-handed attitude to his material when it would not 'turn at his call.' He transposes, for example, the Confession at Caesarea Philippi and the Transfiguration in the interests of his theory. It is true that before Form Criticism made its appearance he insisted that the only material which could be regarded as trustworthy was the sayings and incidents, and that the connexions between them were not so much unguaranteed as nonexistent. It can, however, hardly be a strength to any reconstruction which has to switch its material about without explanation. In a later chapter we shall have to examine in greater detail the interpretations of 'Son of Man' and 'Kingdom of God' in the Gospels, given by Schweitzer. It is important, however, to offer so much criticism now in order to show that he offers merely another Life of Jesus and not a radically new methodology. His own solution is exposed to precisely the same criticisms in principle which he makes of the efforts of others. That is inevitable because all of them are inherent in the historian's task and precisely in so far as he claims to be writing history they are true of him as well. He cannot escape them merely by shouting louder than any one else.

The effect of Schweitzer's work was immediate and considerable. Here was a book of real power, clear-cut in concept and forceful in tone. It had wide scope and profound learning. Its portrait of Jesus as an eschatological storm-trooper was arresting and vividly depicted. It took the theological world by surprise, almost by storm. It killed stone dead a movement which was already beginning to die of slow inanition. It is not therefore surprising that it had an immediate psychological effect on the world of scholarship.

But it also laid bare a real problem—eschatology—and

forced scholars to take into account a whole new field of inquiry which had previously been shelved. New documents which came from the Apocalyptic world of Judaism—that queer remodelling of the open prophetic message in symbol and vision of which the Book of Daniel in the Old and the Revelation of St. John the Divine in the New Testament are the most familiar examples—had come to light in languages other than Hebrew and Greek and needed the close examination which they received by R. H. Charles and others, while the place of eschatology in the Gospels was reviewed by many, most notably by E. von Dobschutz in *The Eschatological Question in the Gospels*.

Further problems, as we have seen, were soon to arise. The work of Source Criticism has been treated in an earlier chapter. It meant that the material had to be sorted, sifted, and labelled afresh. It was important now to ask what strand of the written tradition contained the material which the historian wished to use. He had to weigh the relative historical value of what was considered to be early and what could be regarded as late. The inference from early to historical reliable, and from late to historically unreliable, if made, needed to be justified and, as we have seen, even after Streeter's masterly study, inferences from the Gospels to their sources have varying degrees of probability. Perhaps the best attempt to use them in the interests of historical reconstruction was that of T. W. Manson in his book *The Teaching of Jesus*, a work suggestive alike in method and result.

But Source Criticism did not answer every historical question; above all it left the problem of the shadow generation between the saving facts and the first written record. That is not to condemn it as either critically or historically valueless but only to point out its necessary limitations. It was to fill in this gap that Form Criticism arose. Erich Fascher, its principal German critic, calls it 'the child of disappointment.' This disappointment is a threefold one. First, it was disappointment with failure to provide a convincing biography of Jesus; secondly, with the inferential and in some respects uncertain results of Source Criticism; and thirdly, with the gap already mentioned which in the nature of the case Source Criticism could do relatively little to bridge. It could carry us back some years behind Mark but not to the events themselves. Since Form Criticism supplements and does not supersede Source Criticism, the amount of preliminary sorting of the material has been at least doubled for we must now ask not only the possible written source of a passage but whether it belongs to a particular form which Form Critics regard as reliable, and as the Form Critics themselves are far from unanimous, this is by far the more complicated proceeding of the two. More discouraging still, from the point of the writer of the Life of Jesus is the widespread assumption among Form Critics that any vestige of reliability left by Schweitzer to the so-called historical framework of the Gospels has been removed. What Schweitzer left as a mere hint, Form Criticism exalted to the status certainly of a principle, almost to that of a dogma which must not be questioned.

Thus in the last fifty years we have seen the death of one scepticism succeeded by the birth of another. The century opened with the scepticism born of the exhaustion of the Liberal hypothesis; it was replaced by a scepticism at first sight more dangerous born of the critical study of the material by different detailed methods.

In fact, however, the Gospels know how to take care of themselves. It can hardly be believed that the minute and careful work that has been put into the study of the sources will not produce in the end positive results, despite the initial stage of bewilderment and scepticism to which these methods have sometimes led. And already there are signs that a new positive approach is being built up on far firmer foundations and a far deeper basis than the relatively superficial studies with which the century opened. The return to a more positive and constructive approach was heralded in England by the publication of studies of particular aspects of the life and ministry of Jesus, such as Dr. Newton Flew's *Jesus and His Church*, Dr. Vincent Taylor's *Jesus and His Sacrifice*, and Dr. William Manson's difficult work *Jesus the Messiah*. All three are fully abreast of source-critical and form-critical studies and set themselves to approach particular aspects in a constructive way. The results are not only conservative in conclusions but illuminating in approach. It is difficult to see how they could have been written without the detailed work that had gone before them. They stand with regard to Form Criticism much as T. W. Manson's work to Source Criticism as a kind of firstfruits of constructive scholarship.

An even more interesting symptom of the return of a concern for historicity is Maurice Goguel's patient *Life of Jesus*. The remarkable part of the work is the space devoted to critical prolegomena, which occupy more than half the book. Many readers are disappointed in the constructive side of the work, and perhaps not without reason, but it must be remembered that the production of any Life of Jesus on this scale at the period at which it was first produced, and from a scholar with the critical proclivities of M. Goguel, was little short of a portent.

Finally, to remind us that the production of Lives of Jesus was merely postponed, we have Principal Duncan's *Jesus, Son of Man* and Dr. Hunter's *Work and Words of Jesus*. The former does not claim to set out all its rough working in detail, but it did set out to show to a post-war theological generation that an effort to present a picture of its Lord and Master was not impossible. The latter is slight, but careful, sympathetic, and scholarly; never claiming to be a Life of Jesus, but certainly the kind of sketch or outline which might precede some greater and more systematic construction.

The way is now clear to restate the question and to get more closely to grips with its difficulties. As I see it we are faced with two unavoidable tensions in our study of the Gospels. There is first what may be called the tension between the objective and the subjective, between what we find in the Gospels themselves and what inevitably appears of ourselves in our interpretations of them. This is due to the fact that history is concerned not less with interpretation than with fact. We have seen this to be true of various modern Lives of Jesus which might almost have convinced the reader that in delineating the portrait of Jesus some writers have merely succeeded in delineating themselves. Is then the life of Jesus merely a well at the bottom of which we simply see ourselves? Surely not, though it must certainly be admitted that the subjective element of the scholar himself is inescapable even here. And this applies not only to sacred history but also to secular. During the early part of the last century two histories of Greece were written, one by Mitford and the other by Grote. They were both histories of Greece, but their difference was that Mitford's was Tory history and Grote's Whig history. Both emphasized different points of importance and advance in writing that kind of history can only come by assimilating and transcending both. Such methods of writing the history of Greece have no doubt gone out of fashion, partly owing to the necessity of assimilation of abundant new material from inscriptions and partly by the breaking up of the field into smaller studies from a specialist point of view; but the difficulty with these nineteenth-century products is not that they offered interpretations but that these interpretations were too narrowly based and that of necessity there was much spade-work to be done on sources and documents before such an enterprise could be attempted afresh. The parallel to the position with regard to the Gospels is surely fairly complete. A period in which the accent was put upon the subjective aspect of the interpretation of the writer has been succeeded by a fresh assessment of the material, and that again by the publication of detailed studies in some way preliminary to wider unities.

But there is another tension in the Gospels themselves. For the modern scholar in his capacity of Mr. Interpreter is confronted with the fact that some one has been doing this task before him. For the Gospels are, as we have noticed earlier in this work, both historical documents about Jesus and Church documents. This should be a truism in view of the fact that they belong to the Church's Canon of Scripture, and the older works have sections upon the characteristic interests and concerns of the various writers. The existence of this aspect of the Gospels was therefore known even before the rise of Form Criticism, but it was reserved to Form Criticism to exalt it into a primary principle and to press forward with this method of interpreting the Gospels. We can get closer to this aspect of the problem of the relation of history and interpretation in the Gospels by considering first what Form Criticism makes of this approach and next by setting over against it by way of comparison and criticism the case for historicity as some of us see it.

Form Criticism made this attempt upon two lines: first, by an attempt to answer certain questions which appeared to it urgently pressing and which have real significance for all students of the New Testament; and secondly, by way of critical attack upon the opposite hypothesis. Positively it asked the question, 'What motives, apart from the belief that it was recording true history, led the Church to select and to preserve the material which we find in the Gospels?' To answer this question different scholars took different clues which they believed would lead them most nearly to the truth. Thus, for example, Bultmann hazarded the conjecture that one motive for the preservation of Gospel material was the existence of debates within the Palestinian community. This conjecture is perhaps unfortunate for two reasons: first, that the only example of such a debate which we know—the Council of Jerusalem in Acts xv—makes no mention of Gospel material; and secondly, in a more general way, it has been noted that the interests and concerns of the Gospels and of the Apostolic Church were by no means identical.

Dibelius offers two clues for the preservation of material. The first is obviously important, the Christian sermon, particularly mission preaching to Gentiles. Here Dibelius is the good Lutheran and Erich Fascher says not inaptly that 'for Dibelius—in the beginning was—the Sermon.' The early Christian preaching, if Acts is any test, contained a good proportion of solid historical teaching besides ethical and spiritual appeal. It is on the grounds that they make good sermon material that Dibelius assigns so high a value to Pronouncement Stories, and there may well be much truth in his contention that the detailed Passion Narrative constitutes a preaching or proclamation of the Cross. But there is much material that cannot be so guaranteed for Dibelius, and so he is compelled to assume the existence of a class of story-tellers about Jesus to account for the second class of material—the 'Stories about Jesus.' Here it is harder to follow him, since the lists, admittedly probably not exhaustive—of Christian functionaries given in the Pauline letters give no hint of such a body. It is by no means true that his original preference for the Sermon could not be extended to cover this class of material. Canon Alan Richardson, for example, in his study of the Miracle Stories of the Gospels, has shown that they contain within themselves much of the Gospel. There might be some reason for extending the concept of preaching, or possibly that of teaching, to cover much material not directly concerned with Mission Preaching at least at first, and yet useful for converts to know, which has in any case been preserved within the Gospels. Should we call this the subject-matter of preaching or of teaching? It is hard to say. Yet it obviously must on Form-Critical grounds have been preserved for some reason. Again, the early Church was a controverting society as well as a preaching society, and here the controversy stories studied by Albertz find their appropriate niche. If controversy dogged the steps of the Master, the servant should not be surprised if it confronted him too. The influence of cult must equally not be forgotten, and this was the clue pursued by Bertram and Loisy though the latter took it as a corrupting rather than as a preserving element. Those who maintain this point of view see the developed Passion Narrative as a kind of Palm Sunday Gospel in which to-day the Passion Narrative is read as a whole. Archbishop Carrington has recently published a study of St. Mark from the point of view of the early Christian calendar.[1]

Now clearly such questions are right and reasonable in themselves and the world of scholarship has learnt about the New Testament as a whole and the Gospels in particular from those who set themselves to pursue each individual clue. It may, however, be noted that each is necessarily partial, and reflects in a high degree the ecclesiastical susceptibilities of the writer concerned. It is possible to argue, for example, that the

[1] *The Primitive Christian Calendar*, Part I.

concerns of teaching and of cultus have been much neglected in German theological circles.

The real difficulty comes, however, when it is implied either that these are the only questions that can be asked with good hope of an answer or that we can claim a better or more complete answer to these questions than we can secure in asking of the Gospels historical questions about Jesus. Two points can be made here:

i. The Form Critic speaks of the 'Setting in Life' (*Sitz im Leben*) of the material in the life of the Primitive Church. This is a proper subject for inquiry, though some might well regard it as a secondary one. But we can also speak of a setting of the material in the life of Jesus Himself; and it by no means follows that, because the first question is proper, the second is an improper object of inquiry. May we not rightly speak of a double setting in life for the material without implying that either one or the other is an impossible question?

ii. It is difficult, in fact, to believe that we can secure a firmer historical answer to this type of question than we can to the other. It is true that the Gospels are Church books. That is an obvious fact, but their primary *raison d'être* is not to be books about the Primitive Church but to embody the historical record about Jesus Himself. Or rather they are only Church books by being books about Jesus. Granted that we may not be able to answer from them all the questions that we should like to raise about the Master, our knowledge of the Apostolic Church from the same source is no more likely to be complete. This does not mean that we are condemned to scepticism on both counts; that I should be far from wishing to maintain. It appears to me, however, that we are in precisely the same position with regard to the Church in the Gospels as we are with regard to the Life of Jesus in the other documents of the Apostolic Age. What is primary to the one is secondary in the other. What is direct in the one is inferential in the other. The Gospels as evidence for the Life of Jesus are balanced by the Acts of the Apostles for the life of the Apostolic Church. Both appear to be broadly reliable for their own chosen objects of study, though both are selective and interpretative. The evidence of St. Paul is partly direct and partly inferential for both the Life of Jesus and the life of the Apostolic Church.

The position with regard to the completeness of the evidence is in fact exactly the same in both cases. It may easily be admitted that we do not possess an exhaustive account of the life of Jesus from any source. But we are in exactly the same position with regard to the life of the Primitive Church. The clues suggested by Form Critics for the preservation of Gospel material possess, as we have seen, their varying value. They are neither exhaustive nor in many cases mutually exclusive. It would be hard to deny either of the two clues for the preservation of the Passion Narrative in so complete a form in the interest of the other. We cannot therefore assert that the state of the evidence is such as to give any decisive priority to the questions which seek to assign the Gospel material to the life of the Primitive Church over those which seek to set the material in its place in the life of Jesus. This may seem obvious to the reader, but T. W. Manson had good grounds for his protest that 'it is not the higher criticism but the higher credulity that boggles at a verse in Mark and swallows without a qualm pages of pure conjecture about the primitive Christians' psychology and its workings in the pre-literary tradition.'[1]

iii. Form Criticism tends to split up the material in the Gospels into single incidents or small sections, and to suggest that while the material was given, the connexions were constructed. We have already seen that this is only an extension into a principle of a hint already given by Schweitzer in pre-Form Critical days. Clearly if the Form Critics are right here, the effort to construct a Life of Jesus is wounded grievously, even if not fatally. It was argued that matters of time and place had little interest for the earliest Christians, and that for the sequence of events they were content to rely upon constructions which reflect rather the interests of the early Church than an understanding of the historical continuity of the Life of Jesus. The Christian evangelist was content to pass somewhat lightly over the earlier part of the Ministry of the Lord,

[1] *Expository Times*, May, 1942.

and to focus his attention upon the Passion; for him, as for some later Church theologians, Christ was 'sent to die' (*mori missus*). Before the Passion, therefore, the Church was content to leave the continuities of the stories of Jesus to community creations, based upon the deep instinctive theology of the Church herself.

This is admittedly a serious attack made upon the fortress of historicity; but, before marshalling the arguments which can legitimately be ranged against it, we may well regroup our forces by seeing what in fact the Marcan Gospel taken as a whole has to teach us.

We have already agreed that the Form Critic is probably right in his contention that much in the earlier part of the Gospel is arranged by topic rather than in strict historical order. There is no difficulty in this. Any biography will for large tracts of its subject's life adopt such a procedure by selecting out of a mass of possible material what is most representative of its hero or most of interest to its readers. We can thus explain the 'Sample Day,' the controversy stories, the Miracle stories, the Parables. It is harder perhaps to explain the duplicate cycles of traditions in St. Mark vi. 30–vii. 37 and vii. 1–26. He would be a conservative scholar indeed who was prepared to maintain the exact temporal sequence either of these sections or of the material contained within them. Those who are doubtful about accepting this position should ask themselves whether they seriously believe that controversies, healings, or parables were so largely canalized as the record suggests. Here, however, the character of the narrative changes. A northern journey takes place, the Confession at Caesarea Philippi and the Transfiguration follow each other, and the teaching of the disciples takes on (as T. W. Manson has shown us) a radically new character. Jesus sets His face to go up to Jerusalem; miracles almost entirely cease; the shadow of the Cross begins to fall over the record, and before long we are in Jerusalem assisting at the closely-knit and dramatically fast-moving scenes of the Passion. The second half of the Marcan Gospel appears to the attentive reader to be much more closely knit than the first.

With this brief reminder of the state of affairs in Mark we can pass directly to a consideration of the claims to historicity which can be made for the Gospels. They appear to be remarkably strong:

i. It may be·urged first that the real differentiation between the Church and its rivals lay in questions of history. The headings of its apologetic against Judaism can be extracted from Luke—that the Messiah was Jesus and that the Messiah must suffer. The differentiating feature of Christianity was not that it believed in a coming Messiah (that doctrine was held by many Jews) but that the Messiah was Jesus. Here was a straight matter of history; for the way in which Jesus had so recently lived and died did not fit any of the patterns of Messiahship which were current among the Jews. The scandal lay not in the expectation of a coming Messiah, but in the actual Messiah whom Christians believed to have come. If Jesus had been a different person living in a different way and undergoing different experiences, the scandal might never have arisen, or, if it had arisen, might have assumed very different proportions. Further, the second ground for dispute between Christian and Jew—that the Messiah must suffer—in addition to a keenly felt problem of Old Testament interpretation, once again forced the Church back on the history of the Messiah Who had come and suffered before entering into His Glory.

Nor was the matter different with regard to paganism. The idea of a redemption derived from a certain pattern of mystical experience was quite commonly held in the pagan world. St. Paul recognizes that the pagan world had 'Gods many and Lords many' (he might also have added 'Saviours many'). Each tolerated and received tolerance from his rivals or colleagues in the task of mystical redemption. On the whole it might be said that if Christianity had been willing to cut the painter from the Historical Jesus and to stress without reference to historicity an experience of the Risen Lord, few pagans would have been greatly concerned. But the Pauline attitude to these 'Lords many' would appear to any pagan regrettably uncooperative. Not simply in addition to them, but against

them, stood 'ONE LORD JESUS CHRIST.' This challenge involved
the assertion, monstrous to a pagan, that the spiritual experiences which a Christian shared were in some way bound up
with a human figure who underwent a certain set of factual
experiences, a particular figure living in a given time and place
and finally undergoing a peculiarly shameful death at the hands
of the Roman provincial administration in Judea. This Great
Divide of historicity which separated paganism and Judaism
alike from the Christian Church in the Apostolic Age was
precisely identical with that which a century or so later was to
mark off Christianity from any form of Gnosticism. If the
claim to historicity had been waived or abated, the difficulties
confronting the Church in its missionary situation would have
largely disappeared; but it is no mere debating point to add
that the Church itself would long since have disappeared
together with its difficulties and its distinctive message of
comfort and help to the world.

This conclusion is confirmed by the solid fact to which we
have already appealed, that the earliest Christian preaching, as
disentangled by Dr. Dodd, is to a surprising extent a factual
proclamation.

We have already examined and set aside the most weighty
objection to this point: the character and content of the
distinctive Pauline Gospel. Perhaps we should have gone on
in our preceding paragraph to note that the distinctive feature
of the Christian message was not merely that salvation
depended upon a particular historical character (that is wholly
true), but also upon the belief that this historical character was
Risen, Ascended, Glorified, and universally available to His
people. The two are clearly continuous, and the one fact does
not detract in the least from the importance of the other. If
the distinctive interpretation of St. Paul stressed the one factor,
it does not imply that he lacked concern and interest in the
other. Nor is it really probable that a Church which was quite
capable of attempting to cry halt to some Pauline practical
innovations would really have permitted any interpretation of
the Gospel which did violence to its distinctive character.

   ii. A feature of some importance which has been discounted

by many Form Critics is the existence of eyewitnesses. Yet it is clear from the account given in the early chapters of Acts of the choice of Matthias in the place of the traitor Judas, that this was one of the primary qualifications for the Apostolate. 'Of the men therefore which have companied with us all the time that the Lord Jesus went in and went out among us, beginning from the baptism of John, unto the day that He was received up from us, must one become a witness with us of His Resurrection' (*Acts* i. 21-2). The Prologue to the Lucan Gospel speaks expressly of 'eye-witnesses and ministers of the word' (*St. Luke* i. 2). Moreover, there is a tradition that St. Mark's Gospel depends closely upon the witness of St. Peter. R. O. P. Taylor, indeed, interprets the crucial passage from Papias as implying that St. Mark was the teacher to whom St. Peter handed over his converts for further factual instruction. It might even be claimed that when, in the Pastoral Epistles, it is said 'Bring Mark with thee: for he is useful to me for ministering' (2 *Tim.* iv. 11), it is for some such purpose as this that the writer is thinking.

Form Critics (not wholly surprisingly on their premises) are inclined to be critical of the relationship of St. Peter to the Second Gospel. It is argued that the tone of the Gospel is too impersonal and objective for this tradition to be favourably regarded. This might, however, mean little more than that Peter was that kind of man himself. And there are phenomena within that Gospel for which it is difficult to account in any other way. The unfavourable attitude to the Twelve is quite remarkable for a writer who was not himself of their number, and who lived at a time when the Apostles were important key-figures within the Church. The struggles of St. Paul with the problem of his own apostolate proved quite clearly not only that the Twelve guarded their own privileges and status, but also that they held such a position in the Church as to make his own claim to equality a vital one to establish. We can legitimately ask on whose authority St. Mark makes the disparaging reference that he does to a group who were regarded as the pillars of the Christian Church. Again, the Confession at Caesarea Philippi with its rapid changes of pulse and beat can hardly have come from any other source than St. Peter himself. Nor can the story of the Denial which, natural enough as a personal reminiscence, gives rise to the most elaborate and unconvincing conjectures from the more radical critics. Finally, the vivid touch in St. Mark xvi. 7, 'Go, tell His disciples and Peter,' behind which (especially if reinforced by a vision to St. Peter now lost to us) lies a whole history of personal renewal, and which had as its motive the fear that Peter having denied should also despair, seems to point irresistibly to the same conclusion. C. H. Turner even held that the bare third person plural of much of the Gospel could easily be turned into 'We passages' by slight grammatical alterations. This argument might extend considerably the area of Petrine reminiscence, though it is not altogether convincing in view of the fact that it rests upon a grammatical inference. Possibilities must not be converted into certainties on such slender grounds as these.

Vincent Taylor wisely presses this stress on eyewitnesses as a very vulnerable point in the armour of Form Criticism: 'If the Form Critics are right, the disciples must have been translated to heaven immediately after the Resurrection.' 'The one hundred and twenty at Pentecost did not go into permanent retreat; for at least a generation they moved among the young Palestinian communities, and through preaching and fellowship their recollections were at the disposal of those who sought information.' Negatively, too, there was always the risk that the Christian preacher would unexpectedly be confronted by a member of his audience who could say, 'I was there myself and it did not happen at all as you describe.'

iii. Certainly the evidence tells heavily in favour of the view that Jesus meant His teaching to be remembered, and to this end cast it in a readily memorable form. We shall have occasion to study this in greater detail when we turn to consider Jesus as the Teacher. Moreover, if one saying of His is rightly reported, much depended upon exact recollection of what He had said. St. Mark viii. 38 (followed closely by St. Luke ix. 26) runs, 'Whosoever shall be ashamed of Me and of My words in this adulterous and sinful generation, of him

shall the Son of Man also be ashamed.' This does not guarantee
either complete or exhaustive memory; it is a pertinent reminder to the Form Critics that not only personal eye-witness
but also accurate memory are factors with which their theories
have to come to terms.

iv. As against the Form Critical assumption that the early
Christians were uninterested in matters of time and place, there
are points of importance to urge. Here Dr. Lightfoot in his
important book, *Locality and Doctrine in the Gospels*, accepts
their premises. He points out, for example, that, although St.
Paul has a rich list of post-Resurrection Appearances, he never
troubles to record where they took place. He therefore
develops the hypothesis that the geographical indications with
regard to the Resurrection narratives should be studied from
a different point of view, the doctrinal. His Pauline starting-
point is, however, most precarious. St. Paul is not intending
to tell us all that he knows (if that had been so, we should have
been more completely informed than we are about the events
which followed the Resurrection), but only what is sufficient
for his purpose. This purpose was not biographical, but
controversial. If, as others have told us, Jerusalem is in these
appearances the place of evidence, whereas Galilee is the place
of commission, this is, as we shall see, precisely what we should
expect as we work towards a harmonization of these traditions.
But the lack of interest in geographical detail in the Gospels
has been much overdrawn. Granted the impossibility of what
might possibly be called a 'Bradshaw' knowledge of the Life
of Jesus, details about time and place are not wanting. The
broad outlines are secure enough; Nazareth the home town,
Capernaum the headquarters, and the Lake and the surround-
ing country with occasional excursions across it to Decapolis
fall naturally into place. A saying from Q (*St. Matt.* xi. 21;
*St. Luke* x. 13) speaks of mighty works done in Bethsaida and
Chorazin sufficient to convert sceptical Tyre and Sidon, all
trace of which have perished from the records. A ministry at
Jerusalem traced in the Fourth Gospel is hinted at in another
Q passage (*St. Matt.* xxiii. 37; *St. Luke* xiii. 34) where repeated
failure is more likely than unfulfilled intention. It is certainly

not easy to plot Samaritan and Peraean journeys with the data available, but it is not the existence of such movements which is difficult. A further Q passage (*St. Matt.* viii. 20; *St. Luke* ix. 58) depicts Jesus and His disciples as a wandering band: 'The foxes have holes, and the birds of the air have nests; but the Son of Man hath not where to lay His head.'

The most difficult problem for those who believe strongly in the factual character of the notes of time and place in the Gospels is to be found in the Northern Journey recorded in the Marcan Gospel. If we plot the movements recorded in St. Mark vii. 31, 'Tyre through Sidon to Galilee through Decapolis,' they can hardly represent a direct route from one place to another. Sidon is north of Tyre and therefore further away from Galilee, and Decapolis is on the further side of the Sea of Galilee. Burkitt, however, suggests that to read the journey in this way is to misconceive its purpose. It is not really a journey from one place to another; it is rather a journey without fixed point avoiding a given area, the domain of Herod Antipas, ruler of Galilee. The death of John the Baptist for boldly rebuking vice in the highest quarters is recorded in St. Mark vi. 14–29, and Jesus had certainly been connected with John the Baptist at an earlier period; what if He were still so associated in the public mind? In St. Mark viii. 15 the disciples are told to beware of the leaven of Herod as well as of the Pharisees. In the question asked of Jesus at a later stage about divorce (*St. Mark* x. 1–12) Burkitt found in the reading of an important manuscript (D) in verse 12 a direct allusion to the position of Herodias. This piece of evidence is, however, disputable and is not essential to the case. More significant is the passage in St. Luke xiii. 31–3, where certain Pharisees (perhaps friendly) came to Jesus to tell Him that 'Herod [Antipas] would fain kill Thee!' Our Lord answers, 'Go and tell that fox. Behold, I cast out devils to-day and to-morrow and the third day I am perfected. Howbeit I must go on My way to-day and to-morrow and the day following; for it cannot be that a prophet perish out of Jerusalem.' From this evidence Burkitt constructed the attractive theory that the Northern Journey was taken by Jesus and His disciples to avoid the long arm of Herod's secret police. It might be objected that this places Jesus in a most unfavourable light, and contrasts sharply with His decision to set His face to go to Jerusalem. The difference may well be found in the Lucan passage already quoted. In Johannine language it would be described that Jesus did not believe that His hour had yet come. There was still much to do with His disciples before He could press forward to the decisive challenge which issued in His death. The real difference between the two situations is the Confession at Caesarea Philippi which might be called the necessary preliminary to the final thrust into the heart of Judaism itself. It is therefore possible that at the point at which criticism was most strongly directed to the Evangelists' interest in chronology a reasonable defence can nevertheless be made. It may well be granted to Dr. Lightfoot that the several Evangelists have their own interpretation of the topographical details of the Gospel tradition to set before us; that does not imply that the whole tradition, because capable of being interpreted in different ways, is factually unreliable.

v. Form Criticism is inclined to scout the historical value of the connecting links between the various sections of traditional material. If this could be proved, fundamental doubts would be cast upon the possibility of constructing anything more than a series of unconnected vignettes of the Life of Jesus. Here a valuable starting point for discussion is afforded by an article by Dr. Dodd[1] in which he calls attention to the strange fact that some of the most disputed connecting links in the Marcan Gospel can be concentrated into a single narrative section which would be quite unexceptionable by strict Form Critical standards. The argument does not depend for its force on the actual existence of such a section. It is rather a valid debating point that the Form Critic could not in fact have disputed the material if it had been placed together in a single section, and that therefore there can be no insuperable difficulty about the same data when scattered and dispersed abroad.

If, however, the historical basis of the details of time and place and the general framework of the Gospels be rejected,

---

[1] *Expository Times*, Vol. XLIII, 396–400.

then one of two theories must be accepted. Either they must (with perhaps much more) be assigned to the Primitive Community in general or they must be ascribed to the work of particular Evangelists.

Those who find the origin of material in the Primitive Church may adopt either a wider or a narrower hypothesis. On the wider front, more than the mere connecting links is ascribed to the community. But in this particular form the theory is exposed to two grave objections. If the Primitive community created much of the material connected with its Lord, who then created the community? The greater the role assigned to the Church, the more urgent does this question become. Moreover, if such an assumption is accepted, the Church appears to have done its work uncommonly badly. The main problems concerned with the teaching of the Gospels are not those which directly interested the Primitive Church, and the burning questions of the Primitive Church find no real place in the Gospel narrative. The Spirit and His gifts, the circumcision issue, the admission of the Gentiles, the nature and life of the Christian community itself are questions on which the Gospels are wholly silent or offer at best indirect testimony. Great Gospel terms like 'Son of Man' and 'Kingdom of God' are not the dominant themes of the Apostolic Church, while the concepts of Justification by Faith and Union with Christ ('in Christ'), which are central to the Pauline understanding of the Christian Life, have little or no place within the Gospels themselves.

But the theory has a less extended form which sees the material as on the whole received by the community, but the connecting links or the outline of the Ministry as a community creation. German scholarship has coined a special term for this instinctive rudimentary theology of the Christian community, *Gemeinde Theologie* or 'Community Theology,' and it is to this that the Marcan outline, for instance, is often ascribed. On this point the judgement of F. C. Burkitt is well worth quoting: 'The outline does not read to me like *Gemeinde Theologie*; nothing but a strong element of personal reminiscence could have produced it.' It is difficult to believe that the

Church merely retained an accurate memory of the incidents and sayings as isolated units and then strung them together completely upon a thread of its own making. If it is impossible to believe that facts without interpretations were ever current, it is equally hard to imagine events and sayings recalled and their connexions simply constructed. No doubt a topical arrangement was adopted for some material in which the element of connexion was not specially significant. That has been already fully admitted, and some explanation attempted as to why it should be so in the very nature of biography as such. It does not follow that we must in consequence regard every connexion as necessarily suspect for this reason. No doubt the information here is not as complete or as invariable as we should wish; it does not follow that it is non-existent.

One example may well be given here. Dr. T. W. Manson in his work, *The Teaching of Jesus*, calls attention to the Great Divide in the teaching of Jesus which is constituted by the Confession at Caesarea Philippi. The section which immediately follows it in the Marcan Gospel claims to represent a deliberate attempt on the part of Jesus to carry His disciples deeper into the implications of the Confession of Messiahship. It was not the acknowledgement of Him as MESSIAH as such that answered all questions and raised no problems. It was rather the acknowledgement of HIM·as Messiah which was to involve a complete revaluation of what Messiahship meant. The whole section is splendidly expounded in Dr. Lightfoot's *History and Interpretation in the Gospels*, but it is expounded there primarily from the point of view of interpretation, as part of the pattern as St. Mark presents it. Dr. Lightfoot does not raise the further question in that work whether it also represents historical fact. Seen in its context the particular chapter clearly must not be taken to imply that Dr. Lightfoot does not believe it to be historical fact; despite the mention of history in its title, his book is really concerned with interpretative elements within the Gospels. But the further conclusion that it represents substantially the historical facts appears irresistible. If it be argued that this would divert attention from our Lord and be merely a chapter in the unrecorded biographies of the disciples, the answer is clear enough. The disciples recognized Jesus as a Teacher. Part of the truth about any great teacher lies in his teaching method as well as in the content of the teaching which he gives. It would not be surprising if the section were recorded as part of the evidence about Jesus the Teacher. It is not written to the greater glory of the disciples, for there is no glory that they possess of themselves; it is recorded to show the steps by which Jesus led them out of their blindness and insensitiveness to spiritual truth, into the clear knowledge of Him and of the Father through Him.

Others, however, would prefer to see the Evangelists themselves as responsible for the connexion between the material which they had received. This is inherently a better theory than the attempt to make the community as such responsible for this task. Communities preserve and maintain; they do not create. And apart from St. Paul who, for reasons given above, is not available for this purpose, the Primitive Church contained on his own testimony 'not many wise, not many mighty' (1 Cor. i. 26). In comparison with many other Churches the Church at Corinth appears richly endowed. The Evangelists as individuals seem much more likely to be cast for this role. It is rather to this hypothesis that Dr. Lightfoot has lent the weight of his scholarship. If the individual idiosyncracies of the various Evangelists had been sketched and recognized before his time, no single scholar has done more to make us aware of the essential greatness of those who gave us the Gospels. Their role was not simply mechanical transmission of their material. If a different point of view is stated here, the difference between it and the much more weighty conclusions of Dr. Lightfoot is rather one of degree than of kind. Dr. Lightfoot speaks of the *Doctrine* of St. Mark's Gospel. But is 'doctrine' the right word? It suggests something too formal and stereotyped for the presentation which the Evangelist gives us. Certainly neither St. Paul nor, if the point be pressed, the other Evangelists, saw it anything so fixed. In his recent book, Dr. Lightfoot speaks rather of *The Gospel Message of St. Mark*. There is certainly selection (it

could not well be otherwise). There is also interpretation; but
the question must be taken rather further than that. For what
really matters is whether an interpretation is elicited from the
facts or imported into them. Does St. Mark read into the
material what is not there, or does he spell out what is in fact
there waiting to be elicited? Such an interpretation is the
raw material for a theology rather than a doctrine already
composed.

It all depends what impression the Evangelists make upon
the reader. St. John, no doubt, is the great creative artist who,
though narrating facts unrecorded by the other three Gos-
pellers, is more concerned to offer an interpretative picture of
Christ. But what of the others? St. Matthew combines nearly
the whole Marcan Gospel with other material which, as we
have suggested, comes from another source. Much, though
not all, of his special material looks rather like preoccupation
with his own interests. St. Matthew makes clear the essentially
Jewish background of the Life and Teaching of Jesus, but he
also reflects a great interest in the life of the Christian community as well. Debate has raged chiefly round St. Mark and
St. Luke. Are they great creative artists or primarily Ministers
of the Word, recording, and no doubt interpreting in recording, the oral or written traditions that came down to them?
Dr. Lightfoot regards St. Mark as possessing a real doctrine
of the Person and Work of Christ. That is certainly true, but
reasons can be given for the belief that he also stands in his
interpretation very near to the facts themselves. He is interested in developments. He sees things from the disciples' point
of view. He makes us follow the ministry step by step as
though we were the original disciples themselves. There is a
general air of breathlessness about his Passion Narrative. We
know that a storm is about to break, but we cannot tell when
or how or what the outcome will be. The 'crowning mercy'
of the Resurrection, if we have followed his narrative with
due care and attention, breaks upon us as suddenly and as
mysteriously as it does upon the first disciples. It is hard to
believe that we are not in the presence of historic fact in this
process set so vividly before us. Dr. Hunter well notes: 'The

earliest witnesses to Jesus of Nazareth were no followers of cunningly devised fables. They were men who were set to bear witness to the truth.' It is difficult to subscribe at the moment to the theory of Dr. Farrer, who sees in St. Mark the writer of a Gospel with an elaborate and conscious 'plot.' This is in part a matter of taste; Dr. Farrer sees Mark in one way, I in another. On the whole the character of the book does not suggest a complicated figure with great literary ingenuity. There is certainly simplicity and vividness. He tells a story well and to the point, but does his mind really move in such a complicated way? I hardly think that future ages will believe that it did.

St. Luke is rather more difficult to handle. There are facts which suggest the faithful recorder of traditions. His faithful use of Mark, down to the very vocabulary in the sections where he is indebted to him, the stress upon exact historiography in the Prologue to the Gospel, suggest one who gathers up the fragments that remain that nothing be lost. The long sections not dependent upon Mark, which appear to be based upon factual traditions which would otherwise have perished, all point in the same direction. And yet in many ways his interpretation of Jesus stands halfway between those of Mark and the Fourth Evangelist. He reminds us throughout the Passion Narrative that Jesus is really the martyred Servant of God and that the things concerning Him have an end. He can bring himself to use the title Lord for the period before the Resurrection in a manner foreign to Marcan idiom. Already the backlash of the Church's understanding of the Master, derived from His Post-Incarnate existence, begins to make itself felt. But it still remains true even here that fact controls interpretation, and if the interpretation of Jesus is clear enough, there is still considerable evidence in support of the view that his Gospel retains much of fact that is not contained in the other recorded Gospels. A reassessment of St. Luke in the light of recent discussion is urgently needed. If he may not be so much of a fact-grubber as Streeter makes him appear, there is little doubt that despite his interpretations of Jesus, fresh facts emerge through his Gospel and support the interpretation which he gives. Modern work on the Acts of the Apostles (his second volume) confirms this opinion. It has taken two directions, the one confirming his substantial accuracy on matters of fact, the other expounding the principles of selection which underlie his use of his material. Neither Gospel nor Acts is photographic history, but neither is simply inspired meditation.

So far we have been concerned to set out general principles, to analyse the reasons for scepticism on matters of history which have been most widely accepted and to give the reasons why these grounds do not appear completely convincing. It remains to give a single example in greater detail of the two opposite interpretations of the Gospel evidence. We shall select the theory of the Messianic Secret which has been widely used to discredit the historicity of the Marcan Outline. This was first expounded by Wrede at the beginning of the present century. It received 'honourable mention' from Schweitzer, and is sympathetically regarded both by Dr. Lightfoot and Dibelius.

The theory calls attention to the frequent injunctions to secrecy addressed both to demons and men in the Second Gospel. This suggested to Wrede that the work is rather a book of secret appearances, a revelation made to a few, but concealed from the many, of the Messiahship of Jesus. The injunctions to secrecy occur as follows: to demoniacs i. 21–7, 34, iii. 11–12; to human beings after a cure i. 40–5, v. 43, vii. 36, viii. 26. Dr. Lightfoot summarizes these instances as follows: 'It is as if St. Mark said, "Here was a manifestation of His Messiahship; but it passed unrecognized and it was the will of the Messiah that it should so pass." ' If the latter part of the Gospel does not contain any such injunctions, it is because demoniacs disappear from the scene, acts of power virtually cease and, since the teaching is directed to the disciples alone, conditions of secrecy are guaranteed. The same theory is said to underlie the use of Parables. What appear to us vivid pictorial means of revealing truth to the many are regarded as attempts to conceal the truth from all but a few. Great weight is attached to the difficult passage on the significance of

Parables in St. Mark iv. 11–12: 'Unto you it is given to know the mystery of the Kingdom of God, but to them that are without all things are done in Parables: that seeing they may see, and not perceive; and hearing they may hear, and not understand; lest haply they should turn again, and it should be forgiven them.' Even the Confession at Caesarea Philippi is interpreted not as the Revelation of the Messiahship of Jesus, but rather as the prohibition of revealing it to any one else.

Such a theory looks at first formidable and strongly supported, but two questions naturally arise, Is the theory of the Messianic Secret the most natural interpretation of the facts? and, Is this or whatever theory better explains them more likely to be true history or Church interpretation or comment made by the Evangelists?

On the former question the following considerations are of importance:

i. If the theme of the Marcan Gospel is the concealment of the Messiahship from the disciples during the earthly life of the Master, what in fact decided them to accept the Messiahship of Jesus? In the form in which the theory was phrased by Wrede, the answer given was the Resurrection. But while the Resurrection was a most powerful vindication of whatever theory they themselves held, it could not by itself suggest one. So far as we know, no pattern of Messianic expectation held by the Jews involved or even allowed for a Resurrection.

ii. It is argued in Form Critical circles that the injunctions to secrecy can be easily detached from the sections to which they are conjoined. This is held to establish that they are interpretative additions to the narrative. But the fact that they can be detached, in most cases easily, merely because they are the last item in the story, does not by itself prove that they ought to be detached.

iii. Granted that there are cases, particularly where demoniacs are concerned, in which the cure is placed in a Messianic setting, the majority of cases give no hint of Messiahship in the context. It is possible, of course, that the total background of acts of healings is deemed to be Messianic. It is, however, surprising if the theory were true that in so many cases it is left simply to be inferred.

iv. The section on the significance of parables is pressed much too hard by Wrede. It is admittedly difficult, but it may in fact mean little more than 'Spiritual truth must be worked for if it is to be attained. Those who attend to it receive it in fuller measure; those who do not, find it progressively slipping further from their grasp.' The Semitic mind is notoriously prone to telescope effect and intention. This is due in part to its concern for primary causes (God) at the expense of secondary causes (created agencies), which contrasts sharply with the modern tendency to reverse the procedure. T. W. Manson considered that behind the Greek word for 'in order that' lies an Aramaic particle which might convey either purpose or simply a weaker causal connexion. It may not be wise to lay too much stress on supposed Aramaic originals, but enough has been said to show that the interpretation given is neither the only nor even the most probable interpretation of the passage.

v. Wrede called attention to the prominence of demon-possession and the revelation of our Lord put into their mouth in the Gospels. Modern scholarship is apt to ignore or to gloze over the frequent mention of this puzzling phenomenon in the New Testament and even in later times. An impeccably learned, but rather impish-minded professor of theology once suggested that many people went to Church in the early centuries in order to get out of the way of the demons! The relation between demon possession and certain acute forms of mental disorder is not as yet fully determined. The Evangelists certainly believed in demon-possession; it is probable that Jesus did so too. While this may possibly be the only real element of interpretation in the story, it is not altogether certain that they were wrong in so thinking.

If, then, the case in favour of the theory of the Messianic Secret does not appear nearly so overwhelming as it appears at first sight, we are bound to ask what alternative theory might be framed to meet the difficulties to which Wrede called attention. It is possible that what he regarded as a Messianic

Secret ought rather to be described as a Messianic cross-purpose between Jesus and His contemporaries. There is sufficient evidence that in many Jewish circles at the time of our Lord it was the political idea of Messiahship which was dominant. The 'Son of David' Messiahship in the seventeenth of the Psalms of Solomon would suggest as much. The Temptation narrative, derived from the early source Q and recorded in both Matthew and Luke, indicates that Jesus rejected this conception as a wrong tack. If this were so, it would plainly be unwise to claim Messiahship either directly or prematurely for fear that many people would interpret the mission of Jesus in terms of the pattern of Messiahship existing in their own minds. Such a cross purpose would naturally lead to a relative indirectness of Messianic claim. Such a suggestion meets all the facts to which Wrede called attention without becoming exposed to the exaggerations of the evidence which his theory involved. If it is objected that this is an interpretation which involves certain elements of reconstruction, it can be replied with some truth that the same is equally true of the Messianic Secret. This is a theory not strictly given in the Marcan Gospel, but elicited from it and constructed to meet certain difficulties in the narrative, and that, for the reasons given above, does not commend itself with compelling force.

There remains the question whether either theory is more likely to be definitive history or constructed interpretation. For myself I cannot see the difficulty in assuming that it is the former rather than the latter. That there was a Messianic cross-purpose is suggested by the documents and confirmed by data outside the Gospels. That Jesus adopted an indirect approach to the question of His Messiahship is again plainly stated in the Gospel tradition. That the two are associated is indeed an inference, but it is an inference which lies close to the surface. There is no need to invoke either community theology or evangelistic invention to account for it.

This defence of the fundamental historicity of the Gospel tradition does not indeed carry us all the way. It is not offered as the explanation of all the difficulties or as the supplement to all possible gaps. There are many questions which we should like to ask about the Life of Jesus to which in the present state of the evidence either no certain answer or no answer at all can be given. It is, however, offered to challenge the mood of historical pessimism which has come of late years over historical criticism and to prepare the way for the suggested outline reconstruction which it will be our task to attempt in the next chapter.

## BIBLIOGRAPHY

Reference should be made to the works on Form Criticism already mentioned. See also R. H. Lightfoot, *History and Interpretation in the Gospels, Locality and Doctrine in the Gospels, The Gospel Message of St. Mark.*

Discussions on the first principles of the problem are contained in
E. F. Scott, *The Validity of the Gospel Record.*
C. H. Dodd, *History and the Gospels.*
B. S. Easton, *The Gospel before the Gospels.*

Studies of a detailed nature covering particular aspects of the Life and Teaching of Jesus include
Vincent Taylor, *Jesus and His Sacrifice.*
R. Newton Flew, *Jesus and His Church.*
William Manson, *Jesus the Messiah.*
T. W. Manson, *The Teaching of Jesus.*
A. Richardson, *The Miracle Stories of the Gospels.*

Essays towards biography are manifold; mention may, however, be made of
W. Sanday, *Outlines of the Life of Christ.*
F. C. Burkitt, *Jesus Christ; A Historical Outline.*
C. Gore, *Jesus of Nazareth.*
G. S. Duncan, *Jesus, Son of Man.*
A. M. Hunter, *The Work and Words of Jesus.*
M. Goguel, *Jésus.*

## CHAPTER IV

## THE LIFE OF CHRIST—AN HISTORICAL SKETCH

IT is our purpose in this chapter to offer an outline sketch of the life of our Lord without attempting to examine in any detail the critical problems which may be involved, or to fit into place all the Gospel data. Such a sketch is bound to be selective, but it need not for that reason be condemned as misleading. It should be treated rather as a necessary biographical background for the more detailed discussion of particular topics in later chapters. Footnote reference will be made to the principal later treatments on particular heads. The Resurrection is reserved for more extended discussion in a later chapter.

The story will be presented as an historical narrative, as if its subject were merely a human being. While it is not in the least the object of this book to present Jesus as such, we are here trying to align ourselves with the disciples, who clearly, at the outset at least, regarded Jesus as being such. We are trying to let the narrative speak to us as it unfolds itself before us. Yet at the same time it should be read in the light of the reasonable faith of the Christian Church that when we look at the sayings and deeds of Jesus, we can say, 'God the Son of God died, suffered, and taught this for us men and for our salvation.' Where interpretative links even of a psychological kind appear to be necessary, we shall not hesitate to insert them, though it must be borne in mind that they must be regarded as tentative and as far as possible contained within, or suggested by, the narrative itself.

It is the faith of the Church that Jesus was born of a pure Virgin without the normal human intercourse between man and woman which precedes a human birth. This miracle is called the Virginal Conception or, less accurately but more commonly, the Virgin Birth. It is not to be confused with the

Immaculate Conception which some Christians regard as its corollary.

The historical evidence for this Virginal Conception is contained almost exclusively in the Infancy Narratives of the First and Third Gospels. Whatever explanation we may give of this fact, the rest of the New Testament appears to all intents and purposes to be silent on the subject. No early Christian preacher within the New Testament bases an appeal to believe in Jesus on the Virginal Conception. It seems to be generally agreed that we stand nearer to the facts in St. Luke's Gospel than in St. Matthew's account. The Lucan Infancy Narrative is very primitive in tone, and reflects the point of view and the experiences of the Mother herself. Both accounts agree in treating the event with the utmost reverence and reserve. No attempt to heighten the miracle can be found. Perhaps the best explanation of all these facts taken together is that Mary hid these matters within her heart and disclosed them late in her life to St. Luke, the 'dear doctor' of St. Paul. We know from the 'We passages' of the Acts that he was with St. Paul in Palestine (*Acts* xxi. 8).

Although the family home was at Nazareth, both accounts agree that Jesus was born at Bethlehem. Joseph, His foster-father, was of the Davidic lineage and fulfilled the trade of a carpenter. Joseph disappears relatively early in the Gospel narrative. We hear of four 'brethren' and of 'sisters,' though it is not quite clear how we should express their relationship humanly to our Lord. We may be able to glean a few details of the home at Nazareth from the setting of the parables, a humble, busy home, where every penny counted.

Of the boyhood and young manhood of Jesus we are told virtually nothing in the Gospels, probably because there was nothing of special interest to record. John Oxenham calls these years the 'hidden years,' and we are probably to envisage them as spent in the normal education, religious and otherwise, of a Jewish boy and in the usual duties of an artisan family. At the age of twelve a Jewish boy became a 'Son of the Law,' taking upon himself the adult duties of the Jewish Faith much as in some churches his Christian brother is confirmed at a similar age. It was at this age (though we are not told that it was on such an occasion) that Jesus went up with Joseph and Mary to Jerusalem at the Feast of the Passover. No special reason for this visit is assigned, since the Passover was one of the Pilgrimage Feasts of the Jews when the Holy City was thronged with pilgrims from all parts of the world. It would be natural for those who lived nearest to Jerusalem to make the journey with the greatest frequency. On this occasion Jesus spent His time hearing the learned men of His religion and asking them questions. Absorbed in this employment, He got separated from the rest of the company, and His family circle, thinking, no doubt, that He was with other members of the pilgrim party, started on their journey back to Galilee without Him. Discovering His absence, at the end of the first day's journey, they returned to Jerusalem and found Jesus in the Temple, still absorbed in the quest for knowledge. In answer to His Mother's expostulations, Jesus replied, 'Wist ye not that I must be in My Father's house?' (or 'about My Father's business' or 'among My Father's people.' The exact shade of meaning of the Greek is not wholly clear, but the general sense is plain enough.) Here the curtain of His own inner consciousness is lifted for a moment. This unique sense of Divine Sonship was to determine His whole attitude to His family circle in the years to come.

The curtain falls back again until about His thirtieth year, when a remarkable phenomenon occurred within the religious life of Judaism. For many centuries the voice of prophecy had been silent, but now in the person of John the Baptist the old authentic accents of a prophet were being heard once more. It was a simple message of daily duty and inner repentance or change of heart. An Amos might not have disowned the message of John the Baptist, while in dress, manner of life, food, and even the place where his ministry was being fulfilled, he closely followed Elijah. But his message was not merely prophetic. It was eschatological or even apocalyptic, pointing to One Who should come. Although the word 'Messiah' is not expressly used, we should probably not be wrong in identifying the Coming One with the Messiah. As Elijah ran before Ahab to Jezreel (1 *Kings* xviii. 46), and as the prophet Malachi looks forward to the coming of Elijah before the great and terrible day of the Lord (*Mal.* iv. 5–6), so John the Baptist came to 'turn the heart of the fathers to the children, and the heart of the children to their fathers,' acting as the forerunner to One Whom he knew not. John appears to have gathered disciples about him, and certainly used water baptism as the means of expression and instrument of his mission of repentance. How closely this mission is connected with the coming of Jesus is indicated by the opening words of St. Mark's Gospel: 'The beginning of the Gospel of Jesus Christ—John came baptizing.' The Baptist started what would to-day be called a religious revival, and many of all classes and types came out to hear his message, to be baptized, and to receive the ethical and spiritual advice appropriate to their condition.

While he was baptizing at the fords of Jordan, John received —in circumstances which suggest that they were alone at the time—the One Who was alike his cousin and his Lord. There is every reason to believe that the two branches of the family had not been in any close association with each other during the past years. The Temple priest and his wife, who were the parents of John the Baptist, might not have met at all frequently the artisan household at Nazareth. Matthew shows that the first question which frames itself in the mind of a modern reader—what was Jesus doing receiving a baptism for repentance, if He were, as Christians have always believed Him to be, positively sinless?—was already before the minds of the early Church. The answer which the First Gospel gives is in substance the one which we should give to-day, that Jesus willed to make Himself one as fully as possible with those whom He came to seek and to save. 'For so it becometh us to fulfil all righteousness.' As He came out of the water the Holy Spirit in the form of a Dove rested upon Him, and a voice from heaven said: 'This is My Beloved Son in Whom I am well-pleased.' The exact status of this experience from a factual point of view is difficult to assess, but the meaning of the words is clear enough. The coronation of the Messiah and the ordination of the Servant of God are here combined. The words are taken in part from the second Psalm regarded as Messianic and from the Servant Songs of the great prophet of the Exile whom we call Second Isaiah. Behind both these concepts stands the unique consciousness of His Sonship of God to which reference has already been made. Jesus henceforth knew Himself to be Messiah, and John dared to hope, despite certain later hesitations, that here was the One to Whom his ministry had pointed all the time.

Jewish expectation about the Messiah, though widely held, never assumed any uniform character. There was no agreement about the identity or even the character of the expected Messiah. Many believed that He would be a great political figure Whose purpose would be to make Israel once again a strong and independent nation. Others saw in Him a supernatural figure Who should come with power and great glory from Heaven. Others again held a belief in a Messiah without any clearly formulated expectation either of what He was to be or what functions might devolve upon Him.[1]

The Temptations of Jesus are closely associated with this question of Messianic Vocation. There is little difficulty in believing that Jesus was really tempted. It is only the spiritually mature who can really feel the force and significance of moral evil. These Temptations belong to Jesus considered as the Christ and not merely to Jesus as a mere human being. No doubt He had His full share of ordinary human temptations; the author of the Epistle to the Hebrews, for example, describes Him as 'tempted in all points like as we are, yet without sin.' Nor are these three Temptations the only occasions upon which even what might be called special Messianic Temptations beset Him. Luke adds the significant detail (iv. 13) that the 'Devil departed from Him for a season.' The stinging rebuke to Simon Peter which Matthew records at the Confession at Caesarea Philippi, 'Get thee behind Me, Satan' (*St. Matt.* xvi. 23), points in the same direction. It is clear, too, that the Agony in the Garden has a similar implication. Graphically told as the Temptations are both in Matthew and Luke, we need not necessarily assume an externally visible struggle, but rather an

[1] See Chapter vii.

inner wrestling with wrong ways of fulfilling His Messianic Call.

(a) Was Jesus to become an economic Messiah? In His personal hunger during the fast which accompanied His struggles, He may have imagined that the smooth wind-swept stones resembled the flat cakes of bread which form the ordinary 'cottage loaf' of the district even to-day. He knew that He could rely on God's power for God's purposes. Why should He not turn these stones into bread here and now? But the Temptation, if it may have begun here, must be seen against a wider context. There were many hungry people in the Palestine of His day. Economic realities have always had an absorbing concern. Could He not do much good as a bread-giving Messiah? But would this have been the greatest good? While not denying the necessity of material goods, Jesus saw them consistently as a by-product and secondary. 'Seek ye first the Kingdom of God, and all these things shall be added unto you.' Man is not simply an economic animal though he clearly cannot live unless his economic needs are supplied. And the answer to the Temptation came from a passage in Deuteronomy: 'Man shall not live by bread alone, but by every word that proceedeth out of the mouth of God.'

(b) Was He to be a sign-giving Messiah? Once again the assumption is that Jesus possesses God's power for God's purposes. The difficulty of securing recognition from the religious leaders of Judaism must have been a subject of deep reflection to Him even before the Public Ministry opened. The claim to be Messiah was neither a light nor an easily verifiable claim. The background of Messianic expectation was an open and flexible one, and yet in popular expectation opinion had crystallized in the direction of a politically-conceived Messiahship. In any case the attitude of religious authorities appears in general to be weighted—not always wrongly—in the direction of conservatism. There was, however, an expectation that the Messiah should come from Heaven. Could not Jesus show His divine origin in what would be for Him a kind of acted Parable? If He mounted one of the high pinnacles of the Temple and threw Himself

down from thence into the Temple Courts in full view of the
religious authorities and of the ordinary worshippers without
harm to Himself, He might at one blow represent His Divine
authority and silence any possible opposition for the future.
There was a Divine promise in Psalm xci which might almost
seem to cover such a case. But the answer came also from the
Book of Deuteronomy, 'Thou shalt not tempt the Lord Thy
God.' Such an act would be an abuse of God's power for His
own purposes, in order to make His own work easier. The
rejection of this Temptation meant that even if Jesus in fact
worked many miracles, He could not think Himself as a mere
wonder-worker or the miracles as ends in themselves.

(c) Was He to become a political Messiah? Many, and
perhaps the bulk of those who held a clearly-formed Messianic
expectation, thought of the Messiah as One Who should
establish Israel firmly in a position of political domination such
as she had hardly enjoyed previously except at certain fugitive
moments. There were certainly disciples of Jesus who even at
a late stage in the Ministry seem to have thought much along
these lines—James and John (*St. Mark* x. 35–7; *St. Matt.* xx.
20–8), probably Peter (*St. Matt.* xvi. 22), and possibly also
Judas Iscariot. The prospect of Jesus as a juster and wiser
Caesar, reigning not from Rome but from Jerusalem, opened
up a glittering, and not wholly contemptible, prospect. But
was this enough? Would it not be fighting God's battles with
the Devil's weapons? or at least making the good the enemy
of the best? Jesus rejects this Temptation with yet a third
quotation from Deuteronomy, 'Thou shalt worship the Lord
thy God, and Him only shalt thou serve.' At times the
Christian Church has been busy reversing this judgement of
its Master, but it has never been able to prove Him wrong.
A kingdom which is not of this world can never become a
kingdom within this world without a fundamental loss of
spiritual power.

What then was left? Simply to be a spiritual Messiah Who
should fight God's battles with God's weapons, through the
way of lowly service and of utmost sacrifice. Whether or not
Jesus foresaw the Cross at this precise moment, it became

inevitable at this point; for such a pattern of Messianic conduct leaves itself no weapon except suffering against the blindness and incredulity of man.[1]

After these Temptations Jesus came back from the wilderness not only as the designated Messiah of God, but also as One Who knew sufficiently how this pattern of Messianic conduct was best to be fulfilled. He returned to Galilee, not to the carpenter's shop, but to begin His public Ministry.

If we follow the order of St. John's Gospel, which frequently offers supplementary information to that given by the other three, we shall think of a preliminary period, perhaps only a short one, in which Jesus worked almost side by side and certainly simultaneously with John the Baptist (*St. John* i. 35, iv. 1–2). It strongly suggests that some at least of the disciples of Jesus had been attached to John the Baptist, and softens somewhat the suddenness of their calls by Jesus as recorded in the other Gospels. Mark certainly dates the opening of the Galilean Ministry—which is virtually all that concerns him—after the arrest of John the Baptist.

The Ministry of Jesus falls roughly into three periods. The first (*St. Mark* i. 14–vii. 31) is marked by expansion, first to the call of the Twelve and then to the public Ministry in Galilee as a whole. The two latter are characterized by contraction. The second phase, running from St. Mark vii. 31 to x. 52, involves a withdrawal from the crowds of Galilee and is devoted in large measure to a closer training of the Twelve culminating in a journey to Jerusalem; while the third and last phase (*St. Mark* xi. 1–xv. 47) covers the events of Holy Week and Good Friday in which the circle is narrowed still further through the failure of the disciples and ends in the crucifixion of Jesus, lonely upon His Cross and silent in His grave.

It is with the first that we are now concerned. There is little doubt that much of the material has been arranged by St. Mark according to topics without any special regard to the interests of chronology, and we have given reasons in a previous chapter why we need not be unduly alarmed by this fact.[2]  Neverthe-

---

[1] Chapter vii.          [2] Chapter iii.

less, the main outlines of the Ministry can even here be observed.

Jesus begins by calling His disciples. James and John, the sons of Zebedee, Simon, and Andrew were fisher-folk who had been acquainted with John the Baptist before they received their call to follow Jesus. To them was soon added Levi or Matthew, a customs' officer, and therefore not only a man of some education but also a collaborationist with Roman rule. As the number of followers grew, Jesus made a selection of Twelve. Simon He nicknamed Peter for no very obvious reason. He does not appear particularly the Rock-man, his behaviour in the Gospels being characterized rather by impetuosity. It might be a playful reference to his personal lack of stability or it might be a prophecy of what in the service of the Master he was afterwards to become. James and John were called Boanerges or Sons of Thunder probably as youthful hotheads. It will be remembered that they wished to call down fire upon a Samaritan village which refused to receive Jesus (*St. Luke* ix. 54). Philip and Andrew have Greek names meaning 'lover of horses' and 'brave' respectively, a reminder of the mixed culture of Galilee at that period. Bartholomew, perhaps identical with Nathanael in the Fourth Gospel, has a name which, though Aramaic in form, has probably a Greek component and means 'son of Ptolemy.' Matthew is followed by Thomas surnamed 'Twin,' a second James, another disciple whose name is not securely known, a second Simon called the Canaanean or Zealot (alternative descriptions for a political extremist, perhaps a liberationist), and finally Judas from Kerioth, the only non-Galilean of the company, 'who also was the traitor.'

The list of names does not suggest a particularly impressive body of people, nor is our expectation belied if we follow their career through the Gospels. They were, however, chosen neither simply for their own sake, nor because there were no others from whom to choose; but because Twelve was the number of the Twelve tribes of Israel and thus they formed (if the expression may be allowed) the nucleus or even the 'right markers' of the New Israel. St. Mark tells us that they were called for two purposes, 'that they might be with Him, and that He might send them forth.' They are to be first disciples and then Apostles. If the individual calls of some of them are recorded in the Gospels, this might be called their corporate commission or perhaps their ordination. One further fact is recorded about them in this part of the Gospel. They were 'apostelled' or sent forth on a preaching tour of the Kingdom of God and given the power to cast out devils and to heal disease. Here they are to act as the deputies of their Master. Those who received them received Him, those who rejected them rejected Him. They were sent forth two by two, travelling light, and relying on the hospitality which they received as they went. It is sometimes thought that the Galilean Mission was a failure. Jesus, however, seems to have greeted the return of the Seventy with almost ecstatic enthusiasm: 'I saw Satan fall like lightning from Heaven' (*St. Luke* x. 17 ff.).

Jesus sought to reach the multitude in three main ways. In the earliest days of His Ministry He seems, at least on some occasions, to have enjoyed the 'Freedom of the Synagogue.' Mark records one such instance at Capernaum (*St. Mark* i. 21–8), while Luke records that His inaugural sermon at Nazareth (*St. Luke* iv. 16–30) also took place in the Synagogue. This fact, surprising as it is, betokens at least a favourable impression made upon the synagogue authorities initially. It is on any showing surprising to find some one without any theological qualifications enjoying this privilege. But, as the result of controversies to which we shall shortly turn, this first advantage is soon denied Him, and it was rather by the lake or in the hills that much of His work for the future was to be done. It was by the lakeside, for example, that He entered into Simon's boat and taught from there (*St. Luke* v. 1–11), and a parallel incident is recorded in St. Mark iii. 9. The Twelve were called by Him on a mountainside (*St. Mark* iii. 13), and it is with a mountain that the famous Sermon is connected by St. Matthew (v. 1).

The effect of His teaching upon the common people was remarkable. Already in St. Mark i. 22 it is recorded that they were astonished at His teaching 'for He taught them with authority and not as the scribes.' There was a ring of first-hand authority about His teaching which contrasted sharply with the appeal to the authority of others which characterized scribal teaching. People marvelled at His wisdom (*St. Mark* vi. 2), while St. Luke tells us that the words of Jesus were characterized by authority and attractiveness or grace (*St. Luke* iv. 22 and 32). It appears probable that the form in which His teaching was put contributed largely to the latter.[1] That this mission to the multitude had no little superficial success is proved by the crowds of 5,000 and 4,000 whose feeding and teaching formed, as it were, the climax of this period. When it is realized that the direct teaching of the crowd by Jesus was followed by the Mission of the Twelve, and possibly even by the Mission of the Seventy which Luke alone records, it will be seen that quite a considerable amount of the population of Galilee may well have been reached at least superficially during this phase of the Ministry. How long it lasted it is difficult to envisage, but it is probable that it covered at least a year. The note of time indicated in St. Mark vi. 39, 'they sat down upon the green grass,' is a valuable indication in view of the short duration of the lovely Galilean springtide.

The message of Jesus, given both in word and deed, had a single theme: it concerned the coming of the Kingdom of God. It is true that St. Matthew iii. 2 mentions 'The Kingdom of God is at hand' in a summary of the teaching of John the Baptist. If this is more than a mere anticipation of the message of Jesus, it must here be used in a sense other than it bears in the teaching of the Master Himself. For John, the Kingdom of God, if coming, had not as yet come; it could only be described as imminent; for Jesus the Kingdom, if not as yet all that it was afterwards to become, was already in a real sense present, and present in and with Himself.[2]

The coming of the Kingdom is expressed in two main ways:

i. In mighty works. These are not merely accidental or irrelevant to the essential work of Jesus the Teacher. They represented outgoings in power of the Love which is central to the Kingdom of God. If they were indeed acts of rescue

[1] Chapter v.     [2] Chapter ix.

to people in need, they were also manifestations of the presence of the Kingdom of God, particularly in the victory over the forces of evil. This is certainly true of the exorcisms of Jesus. 'If I by the finger [or 'by the Spirit'] of God cast out demons, then is the Kingdom of God come among you' (*St. Matt.* xii. 28; *St. Luke* xi. 20). While it is clear that Jesus (particularly in the light of the second Temptation) never built much upon these so far as individual faith of other people went, they were nevertheless evidence, for those who had eyes to see, that the Kingdom of God was already in some sense in their midst. If He never appeals to them as a mere wonder-worker would naturally do as evidence for what He was, it would be equally untrue to the facts to regard them as without significance for His deepest purposes.[1]

ii. In teaching. Here again we find a certain indirectness of approach, and for a very similar reason. If to have set too much store or to have focused too much attention upon the miracles might have been to suggest that here was a wonder-working Messiah, and thus to have evoked faith on the wrong grounds or for the wrong reasons, to have given His teaching in too direct a form would have been to reduce the element of free personal response which Jesus regarded as of such supreme significance. It is not that Jesus despised the multitude and therefore wrapped His teaching up in forms which would be unintelligible or unacceptable to them. If that had been the case we should neither have expected that He would have spent so much time among them nor that His welcome among them would have been so warm and so widespread. Ordinary simple people have a shrewd enough judgement about those who really care for their needs. But two reasons, one general and one special, can be assigned for this indirectness which showed itself in the use of parables as His principal instrument of teaching for the ordinary man. In the first place, the truth about God is not something which can be handed over without a living response from its recipients. Some forms of truth—even perhaps theology—can be crammed; but the knowledge of God is not of this order. Parables bring the

[1] Chapter vi.

truth about God within reach of ordinary people with a point and a relevance which is quite unmistakable; nevertheless, they demand considerable thought for their deeper understanding. The rubric, 'Go and work it out for yourselves,' could without difficulty be inserted at the end of each parable; indeed, this is an almost perfect paraphrase for the saying of Jesus, 'He that hath ears to hear, let him hear.' This motive for the use of parables as demanding co-operation of the hearer with the speaker is borne out, though set somewhat sharply, in the difficult Marcan saying on the use of Parables (*St. Mark* iv. 10–12). But there is also a special reason for this indirectness when teaching about our Lord's own Person is in question. To claim to be Messiah directly and without explanation would be to invite one of two possible misconstructions. It might leave matters too wide open, allowing those whose contact with Jesus was neither very deep nor very close the possibility of being satisfied with a designation to which no very precise connotation might be attached by them. Or, alternatively, in the light of the general expectation of a political Messiah, a more direct emphasis upon the idea of Messiahship might lead to a premature assumption that they knew all about it, with the temptation not to stretch their minds any further than the belief that they had previously held demanded. The fact that Jesus, Messiah though He was, came to fulfil a pattern of Messianism quite different from any which was expected at the time indicates how vital such a relative indirectness of Messianic claim was to the fulfilment of our Lord's true mission.[1] This situation sheds light upon two features which are at first sight rather puzzling. The first is that, although the healing of demoniacs is expressly mentioned as an evident sign of the coming of the Kingdom, and demoniacs were believed to possess supernatural knowledge not shared by more ordinary mortals, Jesus nevertheless silences their reluctant acknowledgements of what He was and refuses to use them as evidence for others of His Person and Glory. The second is the equally surprising fact that Jesus apparently does not recruit His inner circle of the Twelve from

[1] Chapter iii.

the ranks of those who had received in acts of healing the marks of the Kingdom in their own person. Neither the Kingdom of God nor the Master Who brought it can in the long run be received except for their own sakes.

We are able to catch glimpses of the opposition which attended the earlier period of our Lord's Ministry. We have no means of knowing how far this was sponsored by the Jerusalemite authorities or how far it arose solely within Galilee itself. It is probable that the former was the case, for there was apparently a more open and less rigid atmosphere about Galilean Judaism than prevailed in the closer proximity to the leaders of religion in Jerusalem. Controversies arose with regard to the Sabbath Law concerned not only with trivial acts like plucking and rubbing the ears of corn in fields already white to harvest which the Pharisees regarded strictly as a form of reaping and therefore included under the general prohibition of work, but also with the healing of the man with the withered hand, which, although in itself a laudable act, would not appear to a strict Sabbatarian Jew sufficiently urgent to preserve life to be performed on the Sabbath Day. These issues already revealed the fact that the new teacher was hardly a stickler for the letter of the Sabbath Law, whatever view His opponents might take themselves. Hand in hand with this went a far more serious matter: the claim to forgive sins, which ran clean contrary to the fundamental Jewish dogma that none could forgive sins but God alone. Despite the unheard or unheeded warnings that the days might come in which the disciples of Jesus should fast, they stood in the Galilean springtide of the Ministry sharply apart from the practice alike of official Judaism and of the disciples of John in this matter. A legal religion would naturally on its own premises look askance at a group which Jesus describes as a happy bridal party (sons of the bridechamber), and therefore refused to obey its provisions on the matter. Jesus even criticized the law of ritual purity in the interests of a deeper purity of heart and conscience. He paid not the slightest attention to the kind of discipline which put groups of people like tax-gatherers and harlots outside the pale, and showed no

reluctance to be in their company. He could even carry the
war into the enemy's camp and offer—whether at this period
or at a later date—the most scathing denunciation of the
precisionists of the Law.

But there was more even than that. Religious opposition
might well have been expected. Political opposition was yet
to follow. The execution of John the Baptist, who had boldly
rebuked vice and was therefore suffering patiently for the
truth's sake, may have reminded the authorities that Jesus had
once been associated with the Baptist. The Herodians make
a sinister appearance with the Pharisees (*St. Mark* iii. 6).
Although we have no further record of the Herodians, we
can tell fairly plainly what they were. They seem to represent
the court party of Herod. The disciples are bidden not only
to beware of the leaven of the Pharisees but also of Herod
(*St. Mark* viii. 15). If the leaven of the Pharisees is further
defined as hypocrisy, no further indication is given of the
meaning of the leaven of Herod. It probably means the evil
influence of Herod. Each, no doubt, refers to a party bitterly
hostile to Jesus. St. Luke xiii. 31 actually records a warning
given by some (apparently) friendly Pharisees to Jesus that
Herod was seeking to kill Him. This was answered by the
defiant reply: 'Go tell that fox, Behold, I cast out devils and
perform cures to-day and to-morrow, and the third day I am
perfected.' Jesus would fulfil the Divine Mission and His
death (is Luke's 'perfected' the equivalent of John's 'glorified'?)
would not be either at that time or at Herod's hands.

The second main phase of the Ministry of Jesus is covered
by a Northern Journey which it is as hard to explain as it is
to plot intelligibly on the map. There is a mention of the
'borders of Tyre and Sidon' where Jesus healed the daughter
of the Syrophenician woman (*St. Mark* vii. 24–30), a return
journey through Sidon to the Sea of Galilee through the midst
of the borders of Decapolis (*St. Mark* vii. 31). There is a
mention of Bethsaida in St. Mark viii. 22–6, and a journey to
the villages of Caesarea Philippi where the Confession of the
Messiahship of Jesus by Simon Peter took place. A week later
there took place the Transfiguration on the mountain-top

probably to be identified with Mount Hermon. From that time forward in the Marcan Gospel Jesus set His face to go up to Jerusalem. The southern end of His journey carried Him across the Jordan through Peraea to Jericho (*St. Mark* x. 1) and thence up to Jerusalem. Not unnaturally the other Evangelists find this journey difficult. Matthew, indeed, mentions Caesarea Philippi and the Mount of Transfiguration and links on again at the southern end of the journey on the other side of the Jordan. Luke (ix. 10) notes a withdrawal to Bethsaida, the Confession and the Transfiguration, and then follows with a long section (ix. 51–xviii. 14) in the form of a journey to Jerusalem. Since this mentions both Samaria and Jericho, which were situated on two possible but mutually exclusive routes from Galilee to Jerusalem, it is clear that one single journey cannot be in question, but a conflation of material associated with different journeying in Palestine. The Q saying that 'the foxes have holes and the birds of the air have nests, but the Son of Man hath not where to lay His head' (*St. Matt.* viii. 20; *St. Luke* ix. 58) provides the necessary authority in the earliest and best strains of material for the view that Jesus and His disciples might well have made many journeys up and down Palestine. The picture given in the Fourth Gospel of frequent visits to the capital on pilgrimage feasts would be in close accord with this.

Three explanations of this Northern Journey with which the difficult travel section opens are popular. The first suggests that Jesus made a withdrawal from Galilee on realizing that the 'broadcast' mission to the crowds was never likely to produce the result which He most desired. It was attended by great enthusiasm (St. John vi. 15, for example, even goes so far as to suggest that they wanted to make Him a King); it resulted, however, in a limited committal which contrasted sharply with the thoroughgoing and costing demands which Jesus made upon His would-be disciples. Others regard it as simply an extended 'retreat' in which Jesus breaks off contact with the crowds in order to concentrate further upon the Training of the Twelve. Finally, F. C. Burkitt with great ingenuity pieced together the evidence in the Gospels which suggested that the

Northern Journey was virtually a flight from the long arm of
the police of Herod Antipas. His hour was not yet come and
it would be unwise in view of the failure of His disciples to
face as yet the full implications of His Messiahship to force a
final issue with the entrenched authorities of the Judaism of
His day. We know too of His conviction that a prophet could
not perish outside Jerusalem.

It may be said at once that these three motives may not be
incompatible. Quite apart from the opposition of Herod
Antipas, the other two motives were not negligible. For all
their widespread, though superficial response, the Galilean
crowds gave no reason to believe that a mass movement in the
direction which Jesus wished to take was possible. The recent
attempt to make Him a King showed how far the crowds
were from the truth. Nor clearly were the disciples themselves ready. It is no doubt possible that they had some
inkling that Jesus was the Messiah; it is clear that they had not
as yet made any definite confession of Him as such, and the
sequel was to show that, even after such a Confession, they
were far from realizing the implications of that Messiahship as
Jesus understood it for Himself. Many Christians have an
instinctive dislike of the theory of a voluntary flight. It contrasts so sharply with the heroic courage displayed by our Lord
in His journey to Jerusalem and in the events of Holy Week
and the Passion itself. It becomes more explicable in the light
of the two previous points. The Fourth Gospel makes much
of the expression 'my hour' (in the mouth of Jesus) and 'his
hour' (on the lips of the Evangelist). If the actual expression
is lacking in the Synoptic Gospels, the idea is clearly present.
The reply to Herod quoted above from St. Luke's Gospel
conveys the same idea of a planned destiny with Jesus in
control, while the prophecies of the Passion contained in
St. Mark contain the significant term 'must.' Here is a statement of Divine Destiny rather than of human inevitability.
Jesus is to suffer not as the plaything of blind forces or the
victim of human machinations, but as the chief actor in a
pattern of Divine action. Perhaps it is against this background
of steps to be taken and of a destiny to be fulfilled that the

Northern Journey must be viewed, not as a flight for personal reasons but rather as a withdrawal for the fulfilment of steps which still needed to be taken if the final bid for the soul of the nation could be reasonably undertaken.

It was on this Northern Journey in the villages of Caesarea Philippi that Jesus asked the disciples Who they thought Him to be. This must be taken closely into connexion with the striking fact that the earlier part of the Gospel is concerned rather with teaching about the Kingdom of God than with questions concerning His own Person. True, this question had not passed without comment. Demoniacs had made announcements which Jesus had promptly silenced. John the Baptist had thought along similar lines, though in the close confinement of prison his faith had for the moment wavered. Perhaps the minds of the disciples could hardly help asking the same question. The attempt to make Jesus King could hardly fail to suggest or to confirm Messianic ideas in their minds. On the other hand, there is a considerable difference between half-formed ideas passing through their minds and convictions maturing to decisions. Thus we may not be wrong in seeing the Confession at Caesarea Philippi as marking a new stage in the disciples' understanding of Jesus; not perhaps as marking the dawning of a Messianic idea in their minds, but rather as bringing to the fore ideas which had not received open acknowledgement before. It is important to realize that this was no mere accurate reproduction of an idea put into their minds by Jesus shortly before, but a genuine inference or even a revelation occurring within their own minds. Jesus first asks them what were the popular conceptions of His Person and Work current among the general public. He then asks the disciples what they themselves thought. Peter as their spokesman answers that He is the Messiah, the Anointed One of God. The passage which Matthew inserts here seems almost necessitated by the context in Mark. Jesus offers a personal Beatitude of Peter, 'Blessed art thou, Simon Bar Jona: for flesh and blood hath not revealed it unto thee, but My Father in heaven.' The acceptance of Jesus as Messiah was not apparently here regarded as the intelligent repetition of a lesson previously learnt by heart, or as a skilful inference from the facts themselves, but rather as a direct revelation of God Himself. For Peter this Confession appears almost a final goal, at least as the appropriate halting-place of his striving to understand; for Jesus it was merely a starting-point. Once He was confessed by the disciples as the Messiah, and confessed without, as it were, putting the word into their mouths, He could begin to explain to them what sort of a Messiah He was. 'And He began to teach them that the Son of Man must suffer many things and be rejected of the elders and of the chief priests and the scribes, and after three days rise again.' This is the first of the three predictions of the Passion which ring out like a warning-bell in the middle section of St. Mark's Gospel. The background is the Suffering Servant of God from Isaiah liii, here for the first time, so far as we can tell, brought into such a close organic connexion with the Messianic pattern of action.

The warning note did not go unheeded. Peter, who had a moment before received such a commendation of his confession of our Lord, is scandalized, and his protest shows how little the disciples had as yet understood anything of the full stature of the teaching of Jesus. Peter is still thinking along the lines of the old pattern of Messiahship which would regard a Suffering Messiah as a thing unthinkable. If there was to be suffering, it should be suffering not of Messiah but of Messiah's enemies. Matthew records his words of remonstrance to Jesus, 'God be gracious to Thee [a mild expletive 'Mercy me']. This shall never happen to Thee.' Jesus, however, rebukes him, 'Get thee behind Me, Satan, for your thoughts are the thoughts of man and not of God.' The vigorous denunciation with the epithet 'Satan' suggests that Peter's words unwittingly carried Jesus back to the Temptations in the wilderness. If their rejection then carried with them (whether Jesus consciously realized it or not) a Cross, that Cross was becoming plain enough now. Here was one of His own disciples, even the one who had just made his Confession of Jesus a moment before, playing the role of the Tempter bidding Him accept an easier and less exacting role.

Here is certainly, as T. W. Manson has shown, a real

turning-point in the Ministry. Jesus had already begun to focus His attention upon the Twelve. Clearly this attention must be redoubled and redirected. Healings almost entirely cease. Public teachings are no longer heard. Teaching about the Kingdom of God in general is replaced by teaching about the Son of Man and the nature of His mission. If beforehand Jesus had insisted upon absolute obedience to His call, the forsaking of all lesser ties in His service, now He links that discipleship far more plainly with cross-bearing. In the light of these aspects of His teaching, Jesus and His disciples have been aptly compared to a party of condemned men bearing their own crosses to the place of execution. No happy bridal party here! The disciples must deny themselves as Jesus puts out of His own mind all thoughts but those of the Suffering Son of Man. That the Son of Man must suffer is the dominant note of the central section of the Marcan Gospel.

A week later, as Mark tells us, there occurred the Transfiguration probably on the snow-capped Mount Hermon. It is difficult to conjecture what the exact status of the Transfiguration may be, how inner experience is linked exactly with outward event, but its significance is clear enough. If the Baptism can be regarded as the seal of God on the call of His Son to Messiahship, the Transfiguration is a similar seal upon the Mission of Jesus as Suffering Messiah. Elijah and Moses are present not as welcoming Jesus into 'the goodly fellowship of the prophets' but as the witnesses to our Lord of the old order of the Law and the Prophets. St. Luke adds that they were discussing the 'exodus' which He was about to accomplish at Jerusalem. It is just possible that this may merely mean 'death.' (The Revised Version translates it 'decease' just to show that it is a slightly unusual word.) It is, however, far more probable that it means 'deliverance' and points like the Last Supper not obscurely to a greater deliverance which He was to accomplish through His Death and Resurrection. The Voice from the cloud again resembles the Utterance at the Baptism. It is a combination of the Messiah and the Servant with a similar background of unique Filial Consciousness. 'This is My beloved Son; hear Him.' The vision faded and the privileged three saw no man any more save Jesus only, and returned down the mountainside to find at its foot a scene of human need, and failure on the part of the rest of the disciples to meet this need.

The narrative now takes on a different turn. It is cast in the form of a hurried transit through Galilee (*St. Mark* ix. 30). The disciples are now the principal objects of their Master's attention. Their disputes about precedence are rebuked by taking a little child and setting him in their midst. The request for positions of honour in the coming Kingdom made by James and John is countered by a reminder that His Kingdom must be judged in terms of sufferings rather than of privileges. The conditions of discipleship itself appear to be the constant theme of His Teaching, and the company now turns south. Mark gives a vivid picture alike of the purposiveness of Jesus and the bewilderment of the Twelve: 'And they were in the way going up to Jerusalem; and Jesus was going before them; and they were amazed; and as they followed, they were afraid' (*St. Mark* x. 32). Jesus was going up to Jerusalem not so much to die but upon a journey which could only end in death. His aim was a final bid for the soul of the nation which could scarcely have any other end. St. Mark leaves us with the impression that this was His first visit to the capital; there are good reasons for believing that St. John is right in suggesting previous visits to Jerusalem before this time. It would be hard otherwise to account for some of the details of the Passion Narrative, even as St. Mark sets them before us. This is no single 'take it or leave it' venture, but the natural climax of a whole pattern of ministering which includes, but is not exhausted by, the Galilean Ministry.

The third and final phase of the Ministry opens with the Entry into Jerusalem. As they draw near to the city Jesus makes preparations for a solemn entry into the city. Not only was He Himself clear about the purpose and character of His coming, He makes sure by an action which had the character of a prophetic action or a sermon in deed that others should have the opportunity of judging as well. He takes as His model here a prophecy in Zechariah ix. 9 where the prophet envisages a King Who comes not on the war-horse or charger, but upon the humble ass, the customary beast of daily usage in the Palestine of His day. (It is perhaps necessary to point out that only one beast is really in question both in the action of Jesus and in the original prophecy of Zechariah. The impression that two beasts were provided merely comes from a misunderstanding by Matthew of a customary idiom of Hebrew poetry by which a single fact is stated twice over in slightly different language for the sake of emphasis and variety.[1]) If any special reason for this Triumphal Entry were deemed necessary, it might well be found in the narrative of the Raising of Lazarus which the Fourth Gospel records in this place. In any case, however, Jesus did not lack sympathizers not only in Galilee but also in Jerusalem. The former would by this time be beginning to converge upon the city in large numbers in readiness for the celebration of the Feast of the Passover in a few days' time. But the Messianic cross-purpose which has already been mentioned makes itself felt even here. He comes a lowly King; they greet Him with cries more appropriate to a conquering hero. Nobody appeared to notice a figure which to Jesus was of the essence of the scene—the ass itself.

On the very next day (apparently) there took place the cleansing of the Temple. The Fourth Gospel puts this earlier on in the record, perhaps in accordance with its general principle of antedating incidents which appear to have great significance in the understanding of Jesus. It is generally agreed that the incident fits better as St. Mark gives it. It is not merely a prophetic manifesto in action such as Amos (for example) might have performed at Bethel. It was a direct assertion of Messianic and even more of Filial authority against a desecration of the Father's House. The traffic against which Jesus protested seems to have been of two kinds. There was first the sale of sacrificial victims in the Temple Courts already guaranteed to be ceremonially clean in accordance with the provisions of the Priestly Law. It is easy to romanticize the character of sacrificial worship as we find it in the Old

[1] See the forms of Hebrew poetry discussed in Chapter v.

Testament. The sale as well as the slaughter of victims has its repellent side to modern taste. It is sometimes forgotten that the corollary of such worship was that the Temple in some at least of its aspects presented the combined character of Smithfield Market and a public *abattoir*. It is, however, against the sale of such victims in the Temple Courts rather than the other feature of sacrificial worship which Jesus is chiefly protesting here. The second scandal was the changing of the secular currency into Temple coinage, no doubt with its attendant profits to the money-changers.

That the authorities were alive to the challenge presented by the entry of Jesus into Jerusalem and His subsequent conduct is proved by the questions asked of Him. The problem of the Tribute Money was a living issue asked as a test-question. It was one which must have genuinely exercised the minds of many Jews at the time. The attitude which Jesus would take up with regard to it involved His whole approach to the question of political Messiahship and its implications. To accept the principle of tribute as a duty would be to disavow automatically any political aspirations. To repudiate it would be to assent, even if only by implication, to the breach between the Jews and their Roman overlords which many felt it to be their duty to widen to breaking-point. Jesus first asks for a denarius to be produced, stamped as it was with the Emperor's head. This is not a mere debating point or an attempt to play for time. It was a sharp reminder that here was a question which could not be regarded as purely external to the questioners themselves. The reply of Jesus, 'Render unto Caesar the things that are Caesar's and unto God the things which are God's,' threw back the question for further consideration by the questioners themselves. What, in fact, are the things that belong to Caesar? In effect, the very recognition of a sphere of operations which belonged to Caesar implied the legitimacy of the imposition of tribute and the necessity of paying it.

The question about authority was again a natural one which Jesus had envisaged as long ago as the Temptations. But the very nature of the type of Messiahship which Jesus knew

Himself to be called to fulfil precluded the possibility of producing any external evidence for its authority. Jesus asked a counter-question about the authority of John the Baptist and by this technique reduced His adversaries to silence.

A more theological question follows in which the question was rather of the order of a logical puzzle than of a living issue. The doctrine of the future life was a relatively latecomer on the scene of Jewish theology. It was accepted by the Pharisees, but rejected by the more conservatively-minded Sadducees, partly on the ground that it was not contained within the Law of Moses. It is evident that for the purposes of misrepresentation the Sadducees used a puzzle which depended for its plausibility upon the conception of the future as qualitatively the same as life here and now. On such premises the hypothetical case of the woman with the seven husbands successively on earth, who would presumably meet them simultaneously in heaven, presented insuperable difficulties. Jesus met this problem by rejecting entirely at the outset the premises upon which it was based. Life in eternity is not at all of the same order as life as it is lived here and now. Here we live as creatures of flesh and blood, there we are 'as the angels of heaven.' Jesus then proceeds to find an argument for the future life from the very Law of Moses which carried greatest weight with the Sadducees themselves.

A further question appears in comparison an innocuous request for information. It was, however, a famous question in Rabbinic circles. The question about the first commandment might in fact cover two such questions. It might first involve the problem (which is involved in any highly complicated legal religion like Judaism) as to which commandments were light and which were heavy (that is, more and less binding). It might also cover the less practical but also important question what was the basic premise from which all else in the Law might be derived. This would clearly have importance as indicating the place at which a particular teacher laid the greatest stress. There is little reason to doubt that this was a perfectly serious question. And Jesus answers it by an appeal to two passages from the Law of Moses, one

from His favourite Deuteronomy. Here the collection of
controversy stories ends with a wholly unparalleled example.
Normally it is Jesus Who receives the questions, here He takes
the initiative in asking one. It appears at first sight merely to
concern a dry point of scholastic exegesis; in reality it is a
shrewd counter-attack upon the assumptions which underlay
the popular conceptions of Davidic Messiahship. Behind the
scribal (and popular) assertion that the Messiah was to be the
Son of David lay the mysterious figure of David's Lord.

The Last Week continues. The Passover draws nearer and
the authorities decide to strike. We are told that they wished
to avoid the Feast Day itself, and if this was to be the case, time
was beginning to press. At this juncture they received an offer
of betrayal from Judas Iscariot. The motive which led him to
betray his Master has long been a matter for conjecture. We
can safely reject the theory that he wished to do Jesus an
indirect service by putting Him into a position in which He
would have to make a bid for political Messiahship. It is
equally difficult to believe that it was a matter of greed.
Thirty pieces of silver is hardly a miser's paradise and in the
background of Old Testament symbolism (*Zech.* xi. 12; *Exod.*
xxi. 32) it represents the price of a slave. It is more probable
that the disappointment which attended the realization that
Jesus was not going to make a bid for political power led to
his action. What he actually betrayed was probably the place
and time at which Jesus could be most conveniently arrested
than anything more profound like the fact that Jesus was or
believed Himself to be the Messiah. An authority which could
not have guessed as much from the events of the last few days
was hardly an authority worthy of the name.

In the meantime, Jesus was not without plans. It is clear
that He set great store on celebrating this particular Passover
with His disciples. Although many excellent authorities
believed that He lived to do so, the view is here taken that He
did not.[1] He does, in fact, the next best thing which, as events
were to prove, was a far better thing. Accommodation for
the Passover had been reserved for Jesus and His disciples and

---

[1] Chapter x.

prepared in fitting manner for the Passover Observance. The night before the Passover was actually celebrated Jesus resorted thither with His disciples, and in the course of a hunger-satisfying meal He did something new with bread and wine. He took, blessed, and brake the bread, saying, 'This is My Body,' and distributed a cup which He had also blessed with the words, 'This is My Blood.' Here was a rite which replaced the Jewish Passover for Jesus and His disciples on this occasion, and was to do so equally for later disciples as well. If it looked back to the great acts of Divine Deliverance wrought in ages past, it also looked forward to a greater deliverance wrought by Jesus Himself on the Cross. The Passover was related to the great national deliverance from Egypt; there is some evidence (and much stronger presumption) that it was also related to the prospective Messianic Deliverance on which many people set their hopes. Jesus saw it as closely connected with the deliverance for all mankind which He, the Martyred Servant of God, should bring to pass. The Last Discourse which the Fourth Gospel puts in this part of its narrative might well represent the kind of conversation which took place at and immediately after the meal.

Supper ended, Jesus and His own left the Old City and began their return journey to their lodging at Bethany over the rise of the Mount of Olives. At the Garden of Gethsemane, as the ascent from the valley began, Jesus turned aside for prayer. The Gospels frequently record occasions on which Jesus is said to have prayed; here was indeed grave matter for prayer. Betrayal, He knew, was imminent; He was also aware through whom this act of treachery would take place. The result of betrayal could only have one end; and the Temptation to evade this must have been wellnigh overwhelming, recalling at perhaps a more intense level those which He had met in the wilderness at the beginning of His Ministry. The writer of the Epistle to the Hebrews is surely not in error in seeing in the Agony in the Garden an incident of deep significance in the Life and Ministry of our Lord. Clear in mind and steadfast in purpose, Jesus began to lead His disciples up the hill when the traitor arrived attended by a body of Temple police and high-priestly servants. He greeted our Lord with the kiss of fellowship which was the prearranged sign of betrayal, and perhaps to the surprise of His captors, Jesus allowed Himself to be taken prisoner without even a show of resistance.

Once Jesus was in their hands, the authorities were determined to make the most of this unexpected opportunity. If we are right in thinking that the Feast of the Passover began on the next day, the time-factor was beginning to press them hard. Probably after a preliminary examination at the house of Annas, the father-in-law of Caiaphas and himself once High Priest before his deposition by the Roman authority, Jesus was led to a meeting of the Sanhedrin. This was hastily summoned and appears to have contained certain illegalities. This question turns upon the contents of the Jewish *Tractate Sanhedrin*, which may either represent an idealized picture of the procedure of this court or an essentially historical account of the actual functioning of the court at the time of our Lord. It is not improbable that the latter view is nearer the truth. If this be admitted, then the trial before the High Priest Caiaphas was illegal in three main ways: first, the trial was held by night; secondly, the admission that false testimony was produced should have been sufficient to quash further proceedings. (Here the evidence is not confined to the *Tractate Sanhedrin* alone; the point is corroborated by the story of Susannah and the Elders contained in the Apocrypha.) The third trace of illegality lies in the direct adjuration of the prisoner by the judge himself. Surprisingly enough in Jewish Law the prisoner was not permitted to bear witness in his own cause. (This is again confirmed by St. John v. 31–2.) Thus at the bar of history it is Caiaphas rather than Jesus who is on his trial here.

The status of the trial is not without its difficulty. It is overwhelmingly probable (and the Trial before Pilate is sufficient to suggest as much) that at this period the Jews did not possess the right to pass or to execute sentences involving capital punishment. Certainly, as matters stood, nothing short of the death of Jesus would satisfy the authorities now. From the point of view of the Jewish authorities the trial before Caiaphas was the decisive proceeding; from the Roman point of view it could have at best the character of 'Grand Jury proceedings,' a preliminary trial to see whether a further action at law would lie. The object of the Jewish trial appears to have been to establish a conviction for blasphemy. This was approached along two lines. At first an attempt was made on the basis of a saying of Jesus (something like an authentic saying is in question here) to show that He had spoken against the Temple. (This has special significance since other evidence makes it probable that the Roman authorities tended to accept such a charge, if substantiated, almost automatically as a ground for the imposition of the death penalty. This can be explained not by any special Roman sensitiveness with regard to the Temple but by a shrewd and realistic assumption that nothing could wound Jewish susceptibilities more and therefore provide matter for a grave breach of the peace than sacrilegious conduct.) When the evidence for this broke down, the High Priest changed his tactics and adjured the prisoner on oath to say whether He was the Messiah or not. St. Mark records an emphatic 'Yes,' although Matthew makes Jesus shift the onus for the statement on to the shoulders of the High Priest himself. Now it is obvious that to claim to be Messiah was not in itself a blasphemous statement. If this were true, it would immediately condemn to frustration any expectation that a Messiah should ever appear and be recognized as such. The real difficulty lay in the kind of Figure that Jesus presented, claiming or being acclaimed as Messiah. Jesus was in fact condemned not for claiming to be the Messiah but for being the wrong kind of Messiah. Here is obviously a situation heavily charged with irony. Jesus is condemned for being what He actually was; and secondly, if He had been the wrong kind of Messiah, almost certainly His judges would have been among those who would have acclaimed the very Messiah Whom they put to death.

On the conclusion of these Jewish proceedings, it was necessary to secure Roman approval. Here the Jewish authorities were lucky in their governor. Pontius Pilate was not the best representative of Roman Administration. He had been governor since A.D. 26, and some few years later, in A.D. 36, he was recalled in disgrace and banished. His long tenure of the Procuratorship was due to the rather cynical policy of Tiberius who prolonged governorships not only to avoid the necessity of making fresh appointments but also to ensure that a province should not be subjected to the tender mercies of too many governors all anxious to make their piles at the provincials' expense. The policy of Pilate towards the Jews vacillated between outbursts of violent repression and ill-considered acts of appeasement. Already two adverse reports had preceded him to Rome, and the third complaint to Rome was destined to prove fatal to his tenure of office. Before him the charge was altered from blasphemy against the Temple to one of high treason against Rome. This change may appear surprising, but it is in the circumstances perfectly natural. If Pilate had been concerned with a well-attested case of blasphemy against the Temple amounting to sacrilege, he would not have been interested in a charge which amounted to being the wrong kind of Messiah. But a charge of high treason, based upon the political implications of Messiahship (implications which it is clear that Jesus rejected), was one which Pilate would have to take with the utmost seriousness, especially in view of the need to show himself 'Caesar's friend.' Here again the irony of the situation leaps to the eye. Had Jesus been a Messiah of the type which the charge presupposes, not only would His accusers never have framed the charge, it is possible that they would themselves have followed Him against the very governor before whose tribunal they were to press for His condemnation.

There is nothing inherently impossible in the dispatch of the prisoner to Herod Antipas. The fact that Jesus was a Galilean seemed to open up this way of escape for Pilate. No doubt Herod ('that fox,' as Jesus had called him) was flattered by the attention paid to him by the Roman governor; he was quite unwilling to act as substitute for Pilate in this particularly unpleasant situation, and returned Jesus to Pilate for trial. The Roman governor next tried to discharge Jesus by taking advantage of the custom of giving a special release to a single prisoner at the Passover. (We have no other evidence for this practice but there is little reason to doubt its historicity; it is just the rather fatuous concession that a weak and unpopular governor like Pilate might very well make.) The contrast between the two prisoners could not well be more profound. The Fourth Evangelist sums up clearly the force of the message of Jesus in the words which he records: 'My Kingdom is not of this world.' Barabbas, 'a notable prisoner,' appears in the pages of the Gospels as an 'activist,' possibly even of a Messianic, certainly of a political, kind. The *claqueurs* of the High Priest, however, thwarted Pilate's plan, and Jesus, untried and guiltless as He was of the charge of *maiestas*, replaces Barabbas, guilty, tried, condemned, and awaiting execution on the same charge. Next, Pilate tries an appeal to pity. He orders Jesus to be scourged, a terrible punishment under which prisoners often died. The Synoptic Gospels show that the punishment was deemed to be part of the sentence of crucifixion and there is much evidence outside the New Testament to show that it was usually so regarded. St. John, however, treats it as a lesser punishment designed to satisfy the Jews. If this were the case, the appeal to pity failed, and Pilate found himself compelled to utter the sentence of crucifixion.

This was a punishment which no Roman citizen could be called upon to undergo. Criminals so sentenced had as part of their punishment to carry the heavy cross-bar to the place of execution; but Jesus, weak from the scourging, stumbled under the Cross, and a brawny passer-by, Simon of Cyrene, was pressed into service. St. Mark shows that at least his two sons afterwards became disciples of Jesus, cross-bearers in another sense. With Jesus were also crucified two malefactors, perhaps men of a similar type to Barabbas. A cross normally had attached to it a notice giving the reason for the condemnation of its victim as an awful warning to others who might meditate committing the same offence. That placed over the Cross of Jesus ran: 'Jesus of Nazareth, the King of the Jews.' St. John tells us that it was written in the three official languages of Palestine, Latin, Greek, and Hebrew or Aramaic. It was meant to be a last slap in the face for the Jews—a weak gesture of contempt and defiance on the part of the impotent Pilate.

Of the words from the Cross St. Mark records one only—the opening words of Psalm xxii, 'My God, My God, why hast Thou forsaken Me?' (Mark records them in Aramaic; Matthew approximates them to the original Hebrew.) The choice of the words is significant. Psalm xxii is the Psalm of a Righteous Sufferer, and though it begins in accents of despair, it ends in a note of confidence. It belongs to a circle of literature akin to, and probably influenced by, the Suffering Servant song. It is, I think, just possible that Jesus was quoting the whole Psalm to Himself with the 'happy ending' in His mind. But this is a rather superficial explanation and it is far more probable that it is in a deep and mysterious sense a cry of dereliction, not so much of mere human despair as of separation from God arising from the burden of the sin of the world which Jesus was carrying, and which shut off, difficult to conceive as this may be, the Son of God Incarnate, from His Father's presence. Crucifixion was always a degrading, often a lingering, death which lasted for several days. For Jesus, however, weakened as He was by the scourging and the continual strain of the preceding days, it lasted but six hours. Significantly the Fourth Gospeller records that He died about the time that the Passover Lambs were slain in the Temple Courts, a mightier victim fulfilling a better sacrifice. St. Paul probably has the same thought, 'Christ our Passover is sacrificed for us.'

Among other words from the Cross recorded by St. John is a final cry of triumph, 'It is finished.' That cry might have been echoed in different senses by other groups round the Cross. 'It is finished,' might have said the disciples. 'We had trusted that it had been He that should have redeemed Israel. We are masterless men once more and we know not what to do next.' 'It is finished,' might have said the Jews. 'Now our ecclesiastical influence will be secure. He will never trouble us again. How differently it might have turned out if Jesus had known how to mobilize the popular support that was with Him almost to the last. As it was, it had its awkward moments and we were, of course, lucky in our procurator. But it's over now and we can rest secure.' 'It is finished,' might have said Pilate with his troubled conscience. 'Well, that's over, thank goodness. A nasty corner turned. Of course, Jesus was innocent, but even a miscarriage of justice is better than a riot at Passover time.' Man's last word had been said at the Cross but, as so often happens in human history, man's last word is but the prelude to God's first word. Men were crying failure, but God's word was 'triumph.' At the Resurrection at the close of the earthly life of His Son, just as at the Virginal Conception at its beginning, the Father said, 'This is My Beloved Son, in Whom I am well pleased.' The centurion at the Cross, whom St. Mark sets out as the typical confessor of the Gentile world, in his words, 'Truly this man was the Son of God,' had spoken wiser than he knew.

## BIBLIOGRAPHY

Lives of Jesus are almost without number and vary alike in scope and in presuppositions. Perhaps the three best are:

G. S. Duncan, *Jesus, Son of Man*.
A. M. Hunter, *The Work and Words of Jesus*.
C. Gore, *Jesus of Nazareth*.

## PART III

# THE PERSON OF JESUS CHRIST

## CHAPTER V

## JESUS THE TEACHER AND PROPHET

WE can now pass to examine what the Gospels tell us of the Person of Jesus, and will begin with an examination of the evidence for Him as Teacher and Prophet.

It is significant evidence of the essential historical reliability of the Gospels that they afford such clear evidence that during His lifetime both within and outside of the Apostolic company Jesus was regarded as a teacher and a prophet. This is where the disciples began, although it is certainly not where the disciples finished, in their assessment of the Person of their Lord. The evidence for this is interesting, and is spread remarkably evenly over all four Gospels.

The actual Hebrew word *Rabbi* transliterated into Greek occurs thrice in Mark, twice in Matthew, and three times in John. Its absence in Luke should occasion no surprise in view of the Gentile destination of the Third Gospel. The natural translation into Greek (*Didaskalos*) occurs twelve times in Mark, ten in Matthew, eight in Luke, and six in John. In addition, Luke uses a Greek equivalent distinctive of him six times. There are thus some numerical differences between the Gospels, but they are not specially significant and do nothing to shake our confidence in the conclusion to which they point. The use of the title is confined neither to the disciples nor to those outside their company. The Gospel usage is all the more distinctive because Jesus lacked any official authorization from the Rabbinic schools; it appears to have been a courtesy title which both friends and others simply find it natural to use.

Superficially there were many similarities between Jesus and the accredited religious teachers of His day. Like Jesus, they gathered disciples about them who attended them and learnt what they were concerned to teach. Again, Jesus, like other more officially accredited teachers, was at least once given

what is called 'the freedom of the synagogue' or an opportunity to give his teaching during a regular synagogue service.
Indeed, the account given by St. Luke in iv. 16–30 of the
sermon at Nazareth is extremely valuable and early evidence
for synagogue procedure.  Rabbis, no less than John the Baptist and Jesus, gave their disciples model prayers for private
use.

But the evidence of the Gospels carry us further than this.
As we read them attentively the Gospels indicate that in many
respects the teaching of Jesus had a close connexion with
religious matters widely discussed in Rabbinic circles.  What
might be called the universes of thought and discourse of
Jesus and the Rabbis to some extent overlap.  In a later chapter
we shall see how relevant the question upon divorce was to a
matter widely canvassed between the two rival Rabbinical
schools of Hillel and Shammai.  Here Jesus probably took a
distinctive line, though St. Matthew's Gospel suggests that He
agreed whole-heartedly with the teaching of Shammai.  Again
the controversies about the Sabbath bring Jesus both into
connexion and conflict with Rabbinic legalism.  'Remember
the Sabbath Day to keep it holy' was a provision of the Jewish
Law so sacred that one writing outside the Old Testament
Canon represented the angels in heaven as strict Sabbatarians.
The duty of keeping the Sabbath holy involved abstinence
from any form of work.  But what constituted work?  Here
the Rabbis were concerned by a series of further definitions to
leave the ordinary Israelite in no doubt where his duty lay.
Among other prohibited occupations were threshing and
reaping.  But how far was this to be carried?  On one occasion
Jesus and His disciples were passing through a cornfield on the
Sabbath Day and plucked the ears of corn and rubbed them
with their hands to remove the husk.  The Sabbath was a good
day for feasting, but a prohibited day for harvesting.  Did the
disciples stand convicted of a breach of the Sabbath Law of
work?  His critics pointed to what seemed to them a glaring
breach of one of the pillar institutions of Judaism.  Jesus
condoned a technical breach of the law in favour of human

need: 'The Sabbath was made for man, and not man for the Sabbath' (*St. Mark* ii. 23–8).

The next section in Mark (iii. 1–6) raises the problem of the Sabbath Law in another form. No one doubted that there were actions of such importance that even the exact fulfilment of the Sabbath Law could be waived in their favour. No legalistic religion can dispense with the principle 'if the hour demanded it.' A rebellious teacher of the law could, for example, be put to death on the Sabbath Day on the principle that one Sabbath might be broken so that others should be kept. Actions which would lead to the saving of the life both of man and beast could reasonably be performed, whatever breach of Sabbath Observance was involved. When, however, Jesus healed a man with a withered hand on the Sabbath Day, the legal precisionists among the bystanders were led to protest. Here was a condition which could reasonably wait for healing until the Sabbath was over. But Jesus maintained that an action directed to giving greater life was as justified as an action necessary to prevent death. It was their positive end and not their negative necessity which characterized actions which could be performed on the Sabbath Day.

A final example of even greater interest can be given in the question about the greatest commandment. Here two problems are involved, each of great importance for a legalistic religion like Rabbinic Judaism. The first is the distinction between 'light' and 'heavy precepts.' All religious duties imposed within legal Judaism were clearly not of the same importance. Some, described as 'heavy,' must stand whatever the circumstances; others were 'light' and could be safely postponed if they came into conflict with some heavier precept. This is the issue correctly stated in St. Matthew xxiii. 23 and implied in the corresponding passage in St. Luke xi. 42 (obviously based upon Q). 'Ye tithe mint, anise, and cummin [condiments] and neglect the "heavier" matters of the Law, judgement, mercy, and faith.' But equally, in a highly complex legal religion, if the wood were not to be lost sight of in the multitude of the trees, it was necessary to offer in addition to this some hierarchy of principles, for the guidance of the plain man. It is not surprising that at the very time at which the Canon Law of the Church of England is being revised, many of the laity are demanding a short and simple summary of the duties of their religion. This is the attitude of the proselyte who came to the Rabbi Hillel demanding to be taught the whole Law while he was standing on one leg! He is not the last to make such a request of his spiritual pastors and masters. Hillel did, in fact, do more than many Rabbis would have done in the face of such a request: he gave him what was in effect a negative form of the Golden Rule, but added the proviso, 'The rest is commentary; go and study.' Jesus gives two root principles in answer to a similar request: 'Thou shalt love the Lord thy God with all thy heart, soul, mind, and strength and thy neighbour as thyself' (*St. Mark* xii. 28–34). Matthew sets his conclusion in exactly the right Rabbinical form: 'On these two commandments hang all the Law and the prophets' (*St. Matt.* xxii. 40). Later Rabbinical Judaism was much exercised over this question. In the third century, for example, Rabbi Simlai is recorded (in *T.B. Makkoth* 23b) to have made the following attempt. According to him Moses gave 365 positive precepts (one for every day of the year) and 248 negative ones (one for every bone in the human body). David established them as eleven (*Ps.* xv); Isaiah reduced them to six (*Isa.* xxxiii. 15); Micah to three (*Micah* vi. 8); Isaiah again to two (*Isa.* lxi. 1); and Amos finally to one (*Amos* v. 4). Rabbi Nahman ben Isaac, however, found his unitary principle in Habakkuk ii. 4. Thus Jesus at least in answer to this question accepts the legitimacy of such a treatment of the Law and finds its Lowest Common Measure in two sovereign principles (*Deut.* vi. 5 and *Lev.* xix. 18). Rabbi Aqiba, some fifty years later than Jesus, treated the passage from Leviticus as his sovereign principle (*Sifre* on *Lev.* xix. 18) while the Golden Rule at least in a negative form occurs both in the Book of Tobit (iv. 15) and in the anecdote of Rabbi Hillel noted above.

But the similarities between Jesus and the Rabbis do not even end here. The following parallel to the Lord's Prayer can be constructed from the Rabbinic and Liturgical literature of Judaism: 'Our Father, Who art in Heaven, Hallowed be Thy exalted Name in the world which Thou didst create according to Thy Will. May Thy Kingdom and Thy Lordship come speedily and be acknowledged by all the world that Thy Name may be praised in all Eternity. May Thy Will be done in Heaven and also on earth do Thou give tranquillity of spirit to those who fear Thee, yet in all things do what seemeth good to Thee. Let us enjoy the bread daily apportioned to us. Forgive, O Father, for we have sinned. Forgive also all who have done us wrong, even as we forgive all. And lead us not into temptation but keep us far from all evil, for Thine is the greatness and the power and the dominion and the glory and the majesty over all in heaven and on earth. Thine is the Kingdom and Thou art Lord of all beings for ever.' The detailed parallels are remarkably close, and prove that here again Jesus and the Rabbis stand relatively near together. It must, however, be remembered that while the Lord's Prayer actually existed as a prayer used by Christians from the earliest times, this parallel is constructed by scholars using material which is never actually found together in this form and which comes from different periods in the development of Jewish thought.

We are accustomed to think of the method of teaching by parables as characteristic of Jesus. Here again we find Rabbinic parallels. Here, for example, is a parallel to the Parable of the Wedding Feast: 'Rabbi Jochanan ben Zakkai uttered this parable. It is like a King who invited his servants to a feast, but he did not fix any time. The wise ones among them arrayed themselves and sat at the entrance of the King's palace. They said, "Something is still wanting in the King's palace [that is, we shall not have long to wait]." But the foolish ones among them went on with their ordinary work saying, "Was there ever a feast without long waiting?" Suddenly the King called his servants. The wise ones went in fitly dressed as they were, but the foolish ones entered his presence all dirty as they were. Then the King did rejoice over the wise ones, but he was wrath with the foolish ones; and he said, "Let those who arrayed themselves fitly for the feast recline and eat and drink, but those who did not array themselves, let them remain standing and watch the others." ' A second parable offers both comparison and contrast to the Parable of the Labourers in the Vineyard; it is recorded in *Debarim Rabba* 6: 'A King hired some labourers and sent them into his garden. At evening he inquired of the work of each of them. He summoned one, "Under what kind of a tree didst thou labour?" "Under this." "It is a pepper plant. The wage is a gold piece." He summoned another, "Under what tree didst thou labour?" "Under this." "It is a white-flowered tree [an almond]. The wage is 200 zuzim." They said, "Thou shouldst have informed us which tree would earn the greatest reward, that we might work under it." The King said, "Had I informed you, how would my whole garden have been worked?" '

Finally, there are parallels to individual sayings, though these may well be popular proverbs used alike by Jesus and the Rabbis. The first example is found in *T.B. Becharoth* 8b: 'Salt, if it has lost its savour, wherewith shall it be salted?' Clearly this is a popular proverb. The second is more interesting. A saying of R. Tarphon (perhaps the Trypho who was the Jewish opponent of Justin Martyr in the second century) is recorded in *Arachin* 16b: 'Rabbi Tarphon doubted whether any one in his generation could bear reproof. If a man said to his neighbour, "Take away the splinter from your eye," the other would reply, "Remove the beam from your eye." ' Either we have here another popular proverb or possibly a case in which an opponent of Christians well versed in the Christian literature has adapted for his own purposes an authentic saying of Jesus!

At first sight the evidence looks very impressive and might almost suggest that Jesus was little more than another Rabbi with a more liberal attitude towards the Law and an independent line towards the controversies of the Jewish schools. In fact the situation is very different from this.

i. In the first place the dating of the Rabbinic material is a notoriously difficult problem. It is far from clear how much of the vast amount of Rabbinic material can be traced back to the first Christian century. It is a fact that the century of the New Testament is the most difficult of all to interpret from the point of view of the religion of Judaism. The Old Testament is completed, the Apocryphal writings largely though not completely composed, and the real flowering of the Rabbinic movement which culminated in the Mishna and the Talmud.not fully under way. Some of the material must go back to this period, some, though later in date, may still be representative of first-century Judaism; but fixed points are few and far between. It cannot therefore be assumed that where there are parallels, the Rabbinic material is the earlier. Some of the material may be popular and traditional and antedate both; much can be explained by the common heritage of Jewish life and thought which underlies both Jesus and the Rabbis.

ii. But there is a second reason which makes it difficult to assess the real value of Rabbinic parallels even when attested and discovered. The point is well put by the late Dr. C. G. Montefiore who as a Liberal Jew can hardly be accused of any controversial Christian bias. He declared that no one was fit to be trusted to handle this problem until he had read the Talmud through four times carefully. And if at that stage his learning was sufficient he might well fail for want of another gift—a flair for picking out what was distinctive of the Rabbinic Literature and for setting aside what was not. Here again is a genuine further difficulty. It is said that Adolf Jülicher, when his attention was called to some Rabbinic parallels, replied: 'It is a pity that they said so much else.' Herein lies part of the difficulty of any comparison. The Gospels are a lean, spare tradition which appears to have suffered remarkably little from accretion. The Rabbinic literature, however, rather resembles a garden which has become overgrown for lack of pruning. The Parables of Jesus are, for example, like gold refined in the furnace. They are vivid and pointed. Rabbinic Parables are multitudinous, but many are trivial and insignificant. There is a wise statement of Bousset that when it came to Parables, 'the Rabbis stammered, but Jesus spoke.' We can, however, gladly acknowledge without any detriment to our Lord the excellence of many of the Parables attributed to Rabbi Jochanan ben Zakkai.

iii. The differences, however, strike even deeper. Even where Jesus and the Rabbis handle the same problems, there is with Jesus a straightforward directness which can see unfailingly to the heart of a problem. Jesus could, if necessary, cut through layers of tradition in order to reach its heart. Where tradition overlaid and overcomplicated a problem, our Lord would bring it back to first principles and see it in the light of God's common sense. This is the case with the problem of divorce, which He sets squarely in the light of the primary vocation of marriage itself. It is true also of refusal to become impaled on the horns of the dilemma about the Tribute Money, or to get involved in a *reductio ad absurdum* in the Sadducees' question about the nature of the Resurrection. There is on this count some truth in the claim of Montefiore that we should be unwise to compare Jesus and the Rabbis too closely because, while each have distinctive excellence, they are really doing different things and spring from different roots. The legalism of religious teachers who thought their task undone so long as a single duty was left unclarified, differed profoundly from the teaching of Jesus, Who always insisted upon moving the previous question and checking developments against the first principles on which they claimed to be based and the ideals which they were framed to support.

iv. The Gospels themselves call attention to the very feature in the teaching of Jesus which, for all His similarity to them, distinguishes Him from them: 'He taught them as one having authority [or possibly as one possessed of kingly power], and not as the scribes.' At least in its later and classical period Rabbinism was an affair of the schools, and therefore lacked just this note of first-hand authority. It preferred to amass and to lean upon opinions. It possessed little of the spirit of 'Ye have heard that it was said by them of old time, but I say unto you.'

The concept of Jesus as the Teacher is not restricted to an assessment, however incomplete and fragmentary, of the Rabbinic parallels. Whatever be the merits of the Rabbinic literature (and they are solid and manifold), no one could accuse them of containing to any superlative degree either the form or the spirit of poetry. It is, however, becoming increasingly clear that C. F. Burney was right in calling attention to the poetry of our Lord. Jesus, good teacher as He was, provided that His teaching should be remembered by making it exceptionally memorable. If the Rabbis used epigram and aphorism, and, in certain periods, parable and similitude as well, Jesus added to both a poetic form comparable to that of the older sages and prophets.

The rediscovery of the principles of Hebrew poetry goes back to the work of Bishop Lowth at the end of the eighteenth century. While both Hebrew and English poetry make much of accent and stress, Hebrew poetry differs from English in making much of sense-parallelism and little of rhyme. If we are to make any study of the poetical form of the teaching of Jesus, we shall need to note the main principles upon which the Hebrew poetical tradition was based. Four kinds of sense parallelism can be traced:

(a) *Synonymous parallelism*, in which the second half of the verse adds nothing to the sense but, as it were, marks time! It could virtually without loss of sense be reduced to one-half of the verse only. The best example is Psalm cxiv where the closest possible parallelism exists through the whole Psalm.

When Israel came out of Egypt; and the House of Jacob from a strange
    people
Judah was his sanctuary; and Israel his dominion.
The sea saw it and fled; Jordan was driven back.
The mountains skipped like rams; and the little hills like young sheep.
What aileth thee, thou sea, that thou fleddest; thou Jordan that thou wast
    driven back?
Ye mountains that ye skipped like rams; ye little hills like young sheep?
Tremble thou earth at the presence of the Lord; at the presence of the God
    of Jacob;
Which turned the rock into a standing water; the flint into a fountain of
    waters.

The parallels can even extend within the various parts of the verse as well as between the complete verses themselves. An example is to be found in Psalm xix. 1-2:

The heavens      declare      the glory      of God.
and the firmament      sheweth      His handiwork.

Day unto day        uttereth   speech
and night to night  sheweth    knowledge.

There are obvious parallels in the oracles of the prophets.
Examples which might be given include Amos v. 21–4;
Isaiah xl. 29–31 and lv. 6–7.

(*b*) *Antithetic parallelism*, where the principle of parallelism
between the first and second half of the verse is still observed
but the form which it takes is not a straightforward repetition
but a repetition by means of the denial of the opposite. Obvious
examples are found in the Book of Psalms i. 6:

For Jahweh knoweth the way of the righteous
But the way of the ungodly shall perish;

and x. 16:

Jahweh is King for ever and ever.
The heathen are perished out of the land.

It is, however, especially characteristic of the Wisdom Literature, where it suits admirably the black and white coloured
ethics which it contains. Thus, for example, Proverbs x. 1:

A wise son maketh a glad father
but a foolish son is the heaviness of his mother.

(*c*) *Synthetic or constructive parallelism*. Here a genuine
advance in the sense can be marked in the second half of the
verse; though there is always a link in the sense, the second
half is continuous rather than identical with the first half.
Many examples might be chosen but perhaps the best is
Psalm xl. 1–3:

I waited patiently for the Lord,
and He inclined unto me and heard my calling.
He brought me up out of the horrible pit, out of the miry clay,
and set my feet upon a crag; He steadied my steps.
And He put a new song in my mouth,
even praise to our God.
Many shall see it and fear
and shall trust in Jahveh.

(*d*) The fourth type of parallelism is called *step or stair
parallelism*, because the idea contained in the verse is worked
up into a crescendo or climax in the final part of the verse.
It is a somewhat rare form of poetry in the Old Testament,

but is specially characteristic of the Song of Deborah. The examples that follow are taken from the English version:

He asked water and she gave him milk;
               she gave him butter in a lordly dish.
She put her hand to the nail,
and her right hand to the workmen's hammer.

At her feet, he bowed, he fell, he lay:
At her feet he bowed, he fell:
             Where he bowed, there he fell—dead!

To Sisera a spoil of divers colours,
       a spoil of divers colours of needlework,
            of divers colours of needlework on both sides!

The extent of poetry in the Old Testament should be noted before we pass to a consideration of the poetry of Jesus. That the Ode of the Heroic Age of Israel, the Song of Deborah, is written in poetry is clear. That the Psalms are also written in poetry also goes without saying. It is not always so clearly understood that much of the Wisdom Literature is written in a poetical form, though it is mostly set out in this form in the Revised Version. The English reader may not be as familiar as he should with the fact that the prophetical oracles are also in many (though not in all) cases in verse. This is due partly to the fact that the Authorized Version which most people still use was translated before Dr. Lowth's great discovery and partly to the textual difficulties which beset any translator of many of the prophets.

Dr. Burney's book *The Poetry of Our Lord* shows that we can use these principles of Hebrew poetry and apply them to the form of the teaching of Jesus even in the present Greek form of the Gospels. It is, in fact, a genuine piece of Form Criticism and suggests strongly that we are here confronted by a Teacher Who, by the very form in which He gave His teaching, ensured that it should be remembered.

(*a*) *Synonymous parallelism.* The most striking use of this form of parallelism extending over a complete passage occurs in St. Mark x. 38 ff.:

Can ye drink    of the cup of    which I drink?
Or be baptized  with the baptism  wherewith I am baptized?

> The cup of which I drink     shall ye drink;
> and with the baptism wherewith I am baptized shall ye be baptized:
> but to sit on My right hand and on My left is not Mine to give:
> but for those for whom it is prepared     of My Father.
> The princes of the nations exercise lordship over them;
> and the great ones exercise authority over them.
> But it shall not be so among you; but
> he that would be great among you, let him be your minister:
> and he that would be first among you, let him be your servant.

Individual sayings with two or three clauses have the same characteristics. St. Mark iv. 30, cp. St. Luke xiii. 18:

> How shall we liken the Kingdom of God?
> Or in what parable shall we set it forth?

St. Matthew vii. 7–8, cp. St. Luke xi. 9–10:

> Ask, and it shall be given you;
> Seek, and ye shall find;
> Knock, and it shall be opened to you.
>     For
> every asker receiveth;
> and the seeker findeth;
> and to the knocker it shall be opened.

St. Matthew x. 24–5, cp. St. Luke vi. 40:

> The disciple is not above his master,
> nor the servant above his lord.
> Enough for the disciple that he be as his master,
> and the servant as his Lord.

St. Matthew vii. 6:

> Give not that which is holy to the dogs,
> neither cast your pearls before swine,
> lest they trample them under their feet,
> and turn again and rend you.

Examples of this form of parallelism occur in the Fourth Gospel no less than the other three.

(b) *Antithetic parallelism* is equally frequent. Here we have clear evidence for the influence of the Wisdom Literature upon the teaching of Jesus. Examples may be given as follows:
St. Matthew vii. 17:

> Every good tree bringeth forth good fruit;
> but a corrupt tree bringeth forth evil fruit.

St. John iii. 6:

> That which is born of the flesh is flesh;
> and that which is born of the Spirit is spirit.

St. Matthew vi. 14–15:

> If ye forgive men their trespasses,
> Your heavenly Father also shall forgive you.
> But if ye forgive not men their trespasses,
> Neither shall your Father forgive your trespasses.

St. John iii. 18:

> He that believeth on Him is not condemned:
> He that believeth not is already condemned.

Especially simple and effective is an antithesis formed by the inversion of clauses (the figure known to Greek grammarians as *Chiasmus*):

St. Matthew x. 39:

> He that findeth his life shall lose it;
> and he that loseth his life for My sake shall find it.

St. Matthew xx. 16:

> So the last shall be first,
> and the first last.

St. Matthew xxiii. 12:

> Whosoever exalteth himself shall be humbled;
> and whosoever humbleth himself shall be exalted.

St. Mark ii. 27:

> The Sabbath was made for man,
> and not man for the Sabbath.

One bye-form of this type of parallelism, the *a fortiori* argument, is especially characteristic of Jesus:

St. Matthew vii. 11, cp. St. Luke xi. 13:

If ye, being evil, know how to give good gifts to your children,
How much more shall your heavenly Father give good things to those who ask Him?

St. Matthew x. 25b:

If they have called the Master of the House Beelzebub
How much more those of the household?

St. Luke xxiii. 31:

If they do these things in a green tree,
What shall be done in the dry?

St. John iii. 12:

If I told you of earthly things and ye believed not,
How shall ye believe if I tell you of heavenly things?

St. John v. 47:

If ye believe not his writings,
How shall ye believe My words?

(c) Of the third form of parallelism (*synthetic parallelism*) a single consecutive example will suffice. It is taken from St. Matthew xxiii. 5–10:

> They make broad their phylacteries,
> and enlarge their fringes,
> and love the chief seats at the feasts,
> and the salutations in the market places,
> and to be called of men 'Rabbi.'
> But be ye not called Rabbi:
> For one is your teacher,
> and all ye are brethren.
> And call no man your father upon earth:
> for One is your Father, the heavenly.
> Neither be ye called masters:
> for One is your Master, even Christ.

(d) It is perhaps rather surprising to find that Jesus makes *step or stair parallelism* a distinctive feature of His poetic form. It differs in one important respect from the primitive type to which attention has been called in the Song of Deborah, for the step-like units are not mere fragments repeated for the sake of greater emphasis, but units of sense. Thus, for example, St. Mark ix. 37:

He that receiveth this child in My Name, receiveth Me:
> and he that receiveth Me, receiveth Him that sent Me.

St. Matthew x. 40:

He that receiveth you receiveth Me,
> and he that receiveth Me receiveth Him that sent Me.

St. Luke x. 16:

He that heareth you heareth Me;
and he that rejecteth you rejecteth Me;
                    and he that rejecteth Me rejecteth Him that sent Me.

The three examples just quoted have a strong family likeness
and may indeed be three variants of a single saying.

Other examples less striking but more varied are as follows:
St. Matthew vi. 34:

Therefore be not anxious for the morrow:
                    for the morrow shall be anxious for itself.

St. Matthew v. 17:

Think not that I am come to destroy the Law and the Prophets:
          I am come not to destroy, but to fulfil.

This evidence, spaced throughout the Four Gospels, and
from all the sources made probable by Source Criticism,
suggest strongly that we stand close to the words of our Lord
in the Gospel tradition. It is much less probable that, while
Jesus did not use verse, the Evangelists one and all happened
to have a bent that way. We cannot press the argument to
the extent of believing in a virtual shorthand reproduction of
the whole teaching of Jesus, but it is strong enough to suggest
that accurate memorization not only was intended, but in
many cases actually took place. It would be a very risky
procedure to suggest emendations on purely metrical grounds.

It is now regarded as probable that Jesus did not in fact speak
in Greek but taught in Aramaic. Objective evidence for this
is found in the Aramaic phrases scattered throughout the
Marcan Gospel. It would be most improbable that in a Gospel
addressed to Gentiles they should be introduced without direct
warrant, though it is easy to imagine that they were so deeply
embedded in the tradition that St. Mark, perhaps with Petrine
reminiscence behind him, felt impelled to leave them in his
Gospel and to offer a translation in each case.

But can we infer the Aramaic original behind the Greek
Gospels, and would it in any respect modify our conclusions
on this subject if we could? Much pioneer work in this field
was done by scholars like Wellhausen and Dalman, and they

have been succeeded by the more ambitious attempts of C. F. Burney, who stoutly maintained that the whole of the Fourth Gospel had an Aramaic original, and C. C. Torrey, who not only inclined to the view that an Aramaic original lay behind the early chapters of the Acts of the Apostles but offered a retranslation of the Gospels based upon what he imagined to be their original Aramaic form. At this stage the inquiry lacked any objective scaffolding, and while the impression left by the controversy upon an outsider is that the belief that Jesus used Aramaic in much of His teaching seems established, it was doubtful whether to any appreciable extent the actual words used could be inferred. Recently, however, the patient work of Matthew Black, *An Aramaic Approach to the Gospels and Acts*, studies the subject in a far more objective manner from the standpoint of Aramaic grammar, and it appears possible that a fresh start can now be made in this branch of study with better hope of agreed results. In view of the thoroughly objective approach which Black adopts, his conclusion reads most impressively:

The impression which the sayings of Jesus make in Aramaic is of carefully prepared and studied deliverances; we have to do with prophetic utterances of the style and grandeur of Isaiah, cast in a medium which can express in appropriate and modulated sound the underlying beauty of the sentiment or the passion out of which the thought arose, soft and gentle in the kindly sayings, as in the promises to the heavy-laden, inexorable and hard in the sayings about offences, strongly guttural or mockingly sibilant where hypocrites and the rest of mankind are contrasted with the Christian disciples.

From the pens of some scholars this might appear to be the rather monotonous grinding of a particularly favourite axe; the careful linguistic and grammatical work upon which this conclusion rests lifts it into a wholly different category.

If, however, we are confronted with an additional reason why we can believe ourselves close to the actual words of Jesus the Teacher, there are corollaries sometimes drawn from it which can only be accepted with great reserve. Some have maintained that besides the forms of parallelism which would remain unaffected by the translation from one tongue to the other, and besides the adaptation of sound to sense suggested by Dr. Black, at least an elementary use of rhyme can be observed. The most probable example is to be found in a Q passage[1] in which the agreement between Matthew and Luke is extraordinarily high. The following Aramaic original has been suggested.

Hōlēlnā l'kōn w'lā raqqedtōn
Ailēlnā l'kōn w'lā aspedtōn

This illustration, remarkable as it is, does not prove that Jesus used rhyme, as the saying is obviously a proverb and therefore does not of necessity carry with it into rhyming form the teaching in which it is set.

Attempts to use a possible Aramaic original as a basis for the emendation of the Greek text is possible, but necessarily a risky procedure. Dr. Torrey, indeed, offers many such emendations in his retranslation of the Gospels, but they are not all such as will commend themselves as necessary to the attentive though Aramaic-less reader. He seems to omit the one which appears to be the most probable. In St. Matthew vii. 6 the connexion between 'Holy' and 'pearl' is far from obvious. In Aramaic, however, the word for 'holy' and that for 'ear-ring' possess a common root. The link is, no doubt, that ear-rings had in primitive times a possible magical use.

The emendation of 'holy' to 'ear-ring' to which only the Aramaic could give a clue completes the verbal parallelism and is probable. On the other hand, the emendation which Torrey admits into his translation of St. Matthew v. 48, 'Be ye therefore catholic [that is, all-inclusive] as your father in heaven is catholic' appears much more forced than the perfectly reasonable received text 'be ye therefore perfect as your Father in heaven is perfect.' Few will feel that the improvement in the sense here is so striking as to justify any alteration of the current reading.

From Jesus the Teacher Who was also a poet to Jesus the Prophet would be to a first-century Jew an easy, even perhaps almost an imperceptible, transition. Not only the Wisdom writers, the great ethical teachers of Judaism, but also the prophets at a much earlier stage used the vehicle of verse.

[1] St. Matthew xi. 17; St. Luke vii. 32.

Indeed, it might well be doubted whether the Hebrews ever thought of the poet as a separate person. Poetry was a vehicle, not a vocation. Sage and prophet used a poetic vehicle, and the consideration of the poetical form of His teaching really places Jesus in one, if not both, of these two categories.

That His contemporaries regarded Jesus as a prophet is clearly stated in the records. St. Mark vi. 15 with its Lucan parallel records that 'Some say Elijah, others a prophet like one of the prophets.' There is a very similar passage in St. Mark viii. 28 and parallels (the confession by St. Peter at Caesarea Philippi), where Mark repeats his earlier formula and Luke stands close to him. Matthew, however, interestingly enough, adds Jeremiah. The crowd who acclaim the Triumphal Entry in St. Matthew xxi. 11 greet Jesus as the prophet from Nazareth, while the disciples on the road to Emmaus (*St. Luke* xxiv. 18) with striking irony describe Him to His Risen Self as 'Jesus of Nazareth a prophet mighty in word and deed before God and all the people.' This corresponds closely with the Christology of the early chapters of Acts, and illustrates the feeling for history and doctrinal reserve which is so striking a feature of the Gospels even when the adoption of later insights into the Person of our Lord might appear most tempting. The Fourth Gospel here agrees with the other three in its description of Jesus as a prophet. There is even one passage recorded in all four Gospels in which Jesus appears to accept the title and apply it to Himself (*St. Mark* vi. 4; *St. Matt.* xiii. 57; *St. Luke* iv. 24; *St. John* iv. 44). It is, however, quite clear that 'A prophet is not without honour save in his own country' is a proverbial saying, perhaps roughly comparable to the 'Charity begins at home' of our proverbial literature and 'the knee is closer than the shin' of classical times.

Some scholars are prepared to go further and find in the Gospels an attempt to portray Jesus in incident and detail in terms borrowed from the old prophets. One particular form of this theory portrays Jesus as the new Elijah. There are at first sight obvious parallels. Both fast forty days and raise the dead. Both are concerned with feeding miracles and call disciples. While Elijah is translated to heaven in the chariot of fire, Jesus ascends to the Father's throne. There are, however, significant differences as well. There are no parallels in our Lord's life to several of the vital episodes in the life of Elijah—the trial of strength on the Carmel spur, the incident of Naboth and Ahab, the rain-making, or the vision on Mount Horeb culminating in the revelation given through the 'still, small voice.' And if the most significant incidents in the life of Elijah have no parallel in the life of our Lord, it is even more clear that the most crucial incidents in the life of Jesus have no foreshadowing in the cycle of incidents about Elijah which have been preserved to us.

Even where parallels have been noted, the differences are even more significant than the similarities. The story of the widow's cruse at Zarephath does not in fact offer any very close parallel to the Feeding Miracles of our Lord. Loisy finds a closer parallel to these in 2 Kings iv. 38–44, associated with Elisha, and even here the analogy extends only to the general sequence of events—the multiplication of loaves, the objection of the servant, the repetition of the order, and its ultimate fulfilment. If the call of Elisha is sudden, like that of the first disciples of Jesus, it should not be forgotten that, while Elijah raises no sort of objection to the natural request of Elisha to be allowed to go and visit his father, Jesus replies to the would-be disciples, 'Let the dead bury their dead.' It is, of course, possible, perhaps even probable, that the would-be disciple of our Lord was asking for a longer postponement of actual following than Elisha, but the difference can plainly be noted. The Forty Days of both fasts is plainly enough a round figure for a good long time. Montefiore suggested that traces might be found in the Gospels of a tendency to make Jesus outdo the miracles of Elijah and Elisha, but this is to misinterpret seriously the miracles of Jesus. There is no tendency to overpress the external machinery of miracle-working in the Gospels and the strong note of reserve which characterizes the miracle-working of Jesus tells against this suggestion. There is good reason for the caution of the otherwise radical scholar, Loisy, who finds the influence of the Elijah traditions in a few details only. Nor can it be forgotten that, despite Schweitzer's protest to the

contrary, the real parallel to Elijah in the Gospels is not Jesus
but John the Baptist. In dress, diet, place of ministry, and
message the Baptist closely follows his Old Testament precursor. Both appear on the scene as it were from nowhere.
Both 'boldly rebuke vice and patiently suffer for the truth's
sake.' Malachi iii. 1 proves that Jewish expectation held that
Elijah should return before the day of the Lord. If Elijah
appears with Moses on the Mount of Transfiguration, it is not
to welcome Jesus into the goodly fellowship of the prophets
but as the representative of prophecy under the Old Order
paying its tribute to the Fulfilment of Prophecy in the New
Age.

Elijah is not, however, the only Old Testament prophet
brought into close connexion with our Lord in the days of
His Ministry. Jesus Himself, for example, used the sign of the
prophet Jonah as a type of His own Resurrection.

Parallels of more far-reaching importance can be found with
Jeremiah and with the Servant Songs contained in Isaiah xl–lv.
We have already noticed that Matthew in an exceedingly
interesting passage speaks of one form of popular expectation
about our Lord as concerned with the prophet Jeremiah. If
we have direct information that in some quarters Elijah was
expected to return as the herald of the New Age, we have not
the slightest hint that anything corresponding would be connected with Jeremiah.[1] There is, however, an exceedingly
interesting hint in 2 Maccabees xv. 14, where Judas Maccabeus
receives a sword from a supernatural visitor described as 'the
lover of the brethren who prayeth much for the people and
the holy city, Jeremiah the prophet of God.' That Jeremiah
should be regarded as the prophet of prayer need cause no
surprise; that he should carry with him the sword with which
Judas was to smite down the enemies of the Lord's people
must appear slightly ironical in view of the not-unfounded
accusation of pacifism made against him during his lifetime.
Two important features in the Book of Jeremiah appear to
have influenced the mind of our Lord. The first and most
direct is the New Covenant passage of Jeremiah xxxi, of which
there are obvious echoes in the Last Supper, and the 'Lamb led

[1] My attention has, however, been called to 2 (4) Esdras ii. 18.

to the slaughter' of Jeremiah xi. 19, which is taken from one of the so-called 'Confessions of Jeremiah,' autobiographical and devotional passages which reflect even more directly than the rest of the book the inner experience of Jeremiah in his prophetic vocation.

In fact, however, it is likely that the second passage in Jeremiah may have influenced Jesus not directly but through the Servant Songs scattered throughout the chapters usually assigned to Second Isaiah. Jeremiah xii. 3 is indeed directly caught up in the last and longest of these songs which speaks of the Servant as one who should suffer (*Isa.* liii. 7). It is beyond dispute that the Evangelists saw in Jesus the Suffering Servant of the Unknown Prophet. This is amply proved by the frequent references to the Servant Songs which they insert as it were in the margin of the narrative. The question, however, has been raised by F. C. Burkitt whether this Servant Christology really goes back to Jesus Himself. Burkitt saw in it the very earliest Christology outside the Gospels. It occurs chiefly in the early chapters of Acts, in the hymn to the humiliated Christ (*Phil.* ii. 5–11), behind which many scholars incline to find an Aramaic original and therefore a pre-Pauline origin, and some passages in the First Epistle of St. Peter. But the Primitive Church was, Paul apart, not so fruitful in profound and original ideas as to invent one of great and rich significance and then to allow it so quickly to recede into the background. And it is more likely that the marginalia of the Evangelists are drawing out the significance of what was for Jesus already there rather than importing into the facts a significance which they did not possess. There is one important clue which tells much in favour of the view that Jesus saw Himself foreshadowed in the Suffering Servant. St. Mark x. 45 contains the famous phrase, 'to give His life a ransom for many.' This has sometimes been regarded as an interpolation from Pauline theology, but it can hardly be regarded as distinctive of Pauline thinking and it has a more natural source in Isaiah liii. 10. If this is its true setting, there is nothing to forbid the view that it derives directly from our Lord Himself.

But the significance of Jesus as a prophet is not exhausted

by the discovery of parallels of varying degrees of closeness with prophets of the Old Testament. There is much in His own office and ministry to suggest not a copy or even a fulfilment of Old Testament figures, but a prophet acting as a prophet would in the new circumstances of His own Ministry.

i. The Old Testament prophet is what is known as a spiritual or charismatic man. These terms need a word of explanation. When to-day we speak of any one as 'deeply spiritual' we mean that he lives close to God in such a manner that any one who associates with him can see the effects for himself. In fact, we see what is called 'spirituality' through the eyes of 1 Corinthians xiii. But in the Old Testament and in certain parts of the New Testament a wholly different expectation is associated with the idea of spirituality. The spiritual person was expected to show his closeness to God by the possession of powers which were denied to the ordinary man. His spiritual experience was to be shown in forms of ecstasy and vision. He could read the inner secrets of the heart in a manner which is regarded as a spiritual gift in 1 Corinthians xii. 10. The working of miracles by Old Testament prophets, though not necessarily regarded as a vital part of such a concept, was at least in agreement with such a mission.

The significance of this concept of spirituality and its value in interpreting the life and ministry of our Lord was first emphasized by Rudolf Otto, who spoke of Jesus as 'the charismatic man,' a term derived from the Greek word used by St. Paul to express particular gifts or endowments of the Holy Spirit. It has also recently been studied with characteristic care and thoroughness by Mr. C. K. Barrett in his book *The Holy Spirit and the Gospel Tradition*. In fact, however, there are limitations to the use of this concept in relation to Jesus. The Pauline refusal to overvalue directly 'spiritual' experiences and his emphasis upon Love as the Master gift of the Spirit is a lesson which he learnt from the historic Ministry of his Lord. A few such unusual experiences are, however, mentioned in the Gospels with as little emphasis laid upon them as St. Paul does upon the vision experience in which, as 'the man in Christ,' he was caught up to the third heaven. Jesus sees a vision of Satan falling from Heaven (*St. Luke* x. 18). Immediately afterwards we are told that He rejoiced in Spirit (*St. Luke* x. 21). He passes unharmed through a crowd of assailants (*St. Luke* iv. 30). It might indeed be objected that these examples all come from an Evangelist whose interest in the Holy Spirit and His operations in the Church is clearly marked in the Acts of the Apostles. This interest, however, is more likely to explain the selection of such material from the tradition than to suggest its invention. He Who promises that the disciples should receive the endowment of the Holy Spirit can hardly have lacked such endowment Himself. All the Gospels indicate that Jesus had special insight into the thoughts and lives of people. The Johannine statement that 'He knew what was in man' (*St. John* ii. 25) is thoroughly faithful to the whole Gospel tradition. Perhaps part of the horror which His critics felt at His association with tax-gatherers and sinners was due to the conviction that He ought to have known by some spiritual instinct what sort of people they were (*St. Luke* vii. 39). The whole gift is parallel to the spiritual gift whereby St. Peter could read the hidden motives of an Ananias and a Sapphira in Acts. Some have sought to explain the meaning of the miracles along these lines, but the Gospel records link them more closely with Messiahship than with prophethood. Though the actual form which might be taken in individual prophets might vary, it was clearly expected that a prophet should in some manner display what might be called the 'control' of the Spirit. If such a test were applied, Jesus would certainly not be found wanting.

ii. An important element in the task of a prophet was prediction. Scholarship has varied much in the significance which it attached to the predictive elements in prophecy. It was a key argument for the truth of the Christian Revelation in the early centuries, and carried as much weight for Gentile pagans as it did for Jews. The writings of the second-century Apologists afford clear evidence of this. Nineteenth-century scholarship emphasized rather the predicative than the predictive element in prophecy. The prophet was a forthteller rather than a foreteller. There are signs, however, that a fuller recognition of the importance of foretelling in prophecy is beginning cautiously to be made. It is clear from the Gospels that Jesus neither ignored nor overestimated prediction. He disclaims, for example, all knowledge of the date of the Parousia (*St. Mark* xiii. 32). The attempt to assign times and seasons is not indeed specially characteristic; He did not come to tell us what was going to happen, but to bring to pass what was actually occurring. Yet it is becoming increasingly recognized that He did foretell the Fall of Jerusalem. Such a factual prediction is deeply embedded in the eschatological discourses. While the last generation of scholarship regarded the prophecies of His own death as prophecies inserted after the event, the careful and detailed work of Dr. Vincent Taylor in his book *Jesus and His Sacrifice* has made it probable that some at least are genuine predictions which go back to Jesus Himself. The Shadow of the Cross is cast over much of the Ministry, and the event itself did not take Jesus by surprise. It is surely only an over-scrupulous scholarship which can regard all such predictions as attempts to read back into the tradition predictions which had no historical right to be there. There are mysterious foreshowings of His Resurrection such as the sign of the prophet Jonah and the saying about the Temple of His Body which hardly bear the stamp of later invention upon them. A prophecy composed after the event would have been much more direct and self-explanatory. One of the incidents in the mockery before the Crucifixion speaks of the soldiers as covering His head and bidding Him to 'prophesy' who smote Him. The sting may lie either in the demand to prophesy to order or to use such a gift on such trivial occasions.

iii. There is much in the content of His teaching which recalls the teaching of the older prophets in contrast with the special concerns of the more recent legalism. If an historical generalization may be permitted, by the time of our Lord prophecy as understood and received from the eighth century to the Post-Exilic period had virtually disappeared. Certain passages from the later parts of the Old Testament and the Apocrypha indeed suggest that prophecy was not only dead but officially buried. Elijah had given place to Moses, and the later legalism had become, at least for official Judaism, the main line of historical development. In many respects, however, the teaching of Jesus recalls strongly the interests and tone of the older prophecy. His attitude to sacrifice and the Law, for example, had much in common with that of the eighth-century prophets. A concern with the national destiny as distinct from the more ecclesiastical aspects of Jewish life was also characteristic of the older prophecy. Yet we must not exaggerate the indebtedness of Jesus to the older prophets. A strong case might be made out for Jesus as the heir of the Wisdom tradition on the basis of His Gnomic or proverbial sayings; His connexion with the Apocalyptic is equally strongly marked; while the Sermon on the Mount in its present form suggests that Jesus may from time to time have envisaged Himself as a new Moses giving a better Torah. If Jesus echoes the older prophetic tradition, it is not because He set Himself to fulfil this to the exclusion of other parts of the Jewish tradition. He is the Amen to the promises of God, as St. Paul envisages Him; the One in Whom all religious traditions meet, are fulfilled, and are carried further by being associated in Himself.

iv. Even more characteristic of the teaching of Jesus is the use of prophetic symbols. Here a word of explanation is essential. Modern research on the prophets has called attention to the significance of what the Hebrews called an ôth. This is an act or an experience which at once symbolizes what it represents and is actually believed to bring it to pass. When, for example, Ezekiel drew upon a tile a rough picture of a besieged city, he meant not only to illustrate vividly what he believed would happen to Jerusalem, but actually to bring it to pass. The same belief underlies the symbolic names like Maher-shalal-hashbaz (Speeds Booty, Hastens Spoil) and Shear-jashub (a Remnant shall return) given to his children by the prophet Isaiah. Such a procedure seems indeed strange to the modern mind and it is very probable that at the most primitive level its background is to be found in the practices of sympathetic magic which occur in the Old Testament as late as the lifetime of Elisha. But at the period of the writing prophets with whom we are here concerned, the theological background was rather different. It is closely related to the theology of the Word of Jahveh, which was thought of as self-fulfilling and self-authenticating. This is virtually said in a passage from the Book of Isaiah (lv. 11): 'My Word shall not return unto me void, but it shall accomplish that which I shall please, and prosper in the thing whereto I send it.' The ôth or prophetic symbol is simply a Word of Jahveh given through an action rather than through an utterance of the prophet, with the same divine origin and the same theological explanation. It is this conception which probably throws light upon the story of the Cursing of the Barren Fig-Tree. It is not impossible that this is a parable interpreted by the tradition as a miracle. The relation between a spoken and an acted Word of the Lord to which we have called attention would make the transition here somewhat easier. It is Israel, the barren fig-tree, which is envisaged here, and its blight is the direct result of its rejection of the One Who came in the Name of Israel's Lord. It was without spiritual fruit, and its pretended religion was 'nothing but leaves.' But most significant of all from this point of view is the Last Supper, where symbol and instrument pass into each other. Here are both the Old Order and the New, and Jesus the Prophet, performing an ôth of rich significance and mighty range, is shown as more than a prophet, One Who, as a later Christian thinker was to put it, 'gives Himself with His own hand.'

## BIBLIOGRAPHY

A. JESUS AND RABBINIC LITERATURE
  Israel Abrahams, *Studies in Pharisaism and the Gospels* (two series).
  C. G. Montefiore, *The Synoptic Gospels* and *Rabbinic Literature and Gospel Teachings*.

B. THE FORMAL CHARACTERISTICS OF THE TEACHING OF JESUS
  C. F. Burney, *The Poetry of Our Lord*.
  T. W. Manson, *The Teaching of Jesus*.

C. The Aramaic Original of the Teaching of Jesus

C. F. Burney, *The Aramaic Origin of the Fourth Gospel.*

C. C. Torrey, *Our Translated Gospels* and *The Four Gospels: a New Translation.*

Dalman, *Jesus-Jeshua.*

Matthew Black, *An Aramaic Approach to the Gospels and Acts.*

D. Jesus the Prophet

C. K. Barrett, *The Holy Spirit and the Gospel Tradition.*

C. H. Dodd, 'Jesus as Teacher and Prophet' in *Mysterium Christi.*

R. Otto, *The Kingdom of God and the Son of Man.*

W. A. Curtis, *Jesus Christ the Teacher.*

## Chapter VI

## JESUS THE WONDERWORKER

IN most circles to-day the reception accorded to this aspect of the life and ministry of Jesus contrasts sharply with the welcome given to Jesus the Teacher and the Prophet. There can be few who take the trouble to study the Gospels with care and attention who are not attracted by the Teaching of the Master; there are, however, many even within Christendom who have a real feeling of uneasiness when they turn to the miracles of our Lord. This uneasiness extends not merely to the debatable question whether miracles happen, but also to the equally important problem of what we are to think of them even if they actually occurred. Yet the stark fact remains that of the very limited repertoire of sayings and actions recorded of Jesus a surprisingly high proportion are concerned with the miraculous.

The thought of the modern world about miracles in general and those of Jesus in particular has passed through three main phases. The first of blind, uncritical, universal acceptance has for most people long since passed. It was succeeded historically by a period dominated by the older Rationalism in which it was almost a dogma that miracles had never happened and could never happen. During this period any explanation, however incomplete and however improbable, could be accepted as an alternative. The difficulty with this type of criticism is that it failed to distinguish between explaining and explaining away. If these explanations were correct, it would be hard to explain how the stories ever came to be recorded in the first place, and recorded as miraculous in the second. Trivial explanations have a habit of coming home to roost to the disadvantage of those who propound them.

The second phase belongs to the New Enlightenment or the Modernist movement at the beginning of the present century. Typical of this movement are two short books by Mr. J. M.

Thompson entitled *The Miracles of the New Testament* and *Through Facts to Faith*, the latter being the St. Margaret's Lectures for 1912. They created no small stir at the time, but represent ably and sympathetically a fresh approach to the question of the miraculous. Mr. Thompson drew a very clear distinction between the assumptions and the procedure of the Older Enlightenment and the premises with which he was working. He would have nothing to do with the older explaining away of the miracles, but he was equally firm that miracles did not occur. Either miracles did not occur, or they were non-miraculous in character. If the older Rationalism rejected the supernatural in favour of the natural, the more recent move-ment rejected the miraculous in favour of the supernatural. In fact, as Mr. C. S. Lewis points out, for this movement the natural and the supernatural were different names for the same set of realities as seen from different points of view. Nature and Supernature are the same orders of being, obey the same laws, but while Nature is Reality scientifically treated, Supernature is this same reality religiously regarded. This is what Mr. Lewis means when he speaks of the under-lying philosophy of this school of thought as Monist. I am reminded of a long poem of which I have forgotten all but the refrain at the end of each verse: 'Some call it Evolution, but others call it God.' Since, then, the miraculous as classically understood was inconsistent with the natural as they inter-preted it, this school of thought was bound either to reject miracles in their entirety or else to offer an interpretation of them consistent with the premises about the natural which they accepted. It might even be maintained that in principle Mr. J. M. Thompson rejected miracle for what he conceived to be a religious no less than a philosophical or scientific reason.

The second feature of the work of this school was to develop what might be called the historical argument against miracle. Mr. Thompson noticed the marked shrinkage in the area of the miraculous during the last few centuries. In earlier times it mattered little whether an event was called natural or super-natural, but the disentanglement of many so-called laws of

nature gave rise to at least a well-grounded confidence that
within certain areas facts were likely to happen in one way
and not in another way. Such an establishment of confidence
(not always well-grounded) led to a grave suspicion of any
events which could not be fitted into this mould. Belief in
ecclesiastical miracles was the first to be widely challenged,
and certainly many such miracles appear to require a singularly
robust faith for their acceptance. The Old Testament miracles
were the next to be tried and found wanting, while Mr.
Thompson claimed that the final stage was reached during
this present century when critical examination might turn
upon the miracles even of the Gospels. Use was made of the
recent developments of Source Criticism to determine 'the
relative density' of the miraculous in the various sources. Mr.
Thompson called attention to a steady crescendo in the
records of the miraculous between Q and the Fourth Gospel.
The factual side of his analysis has never been successfully
challenged, though from time to time he tends to press
doubtful cases into too close conformity to his views. The
spate of literature evoked by these two books was much more
largely concerned with the religious and philosophical presuppositions behind his work than with the historical side of
his argument.

The most recent phase of the study of the miracles of
Jesus is represented by Canon Alan Richardson's work *The
Miracle Stories of the Gospels*. Here the discussion has passed
on to other grounds, and rests on quite different premises.
The great question which Mr. Thompson asked was whether
in fact miracles had happened historically. The very title of
his St. Margaret's Lectures, *Through Facts to Faith*, is indicative
of this. Canon Richardson, however, doubts whether this is
precisely the right question, or, if it is, whether it can be
answered satisfactorily. For him the question about miracles
is not a simple factual question, 'Did they happen or not?' It
is a Christological question only capable of being answered as
part of a total taking of sides with regard to our Lord. Thus
the factual question really resolves itself into a Christological
question, 'Is Jesus Christ the sort of Person of Whom miracu-

lous action can sensibly be predicated?' Mr. Thompson invites us to examine the evidence as it were from outside, and in the light of this to determine our attitude to Christ, Canon Richardson insists that we must look at the total Person of Christ first, and in the light of this determine our own approach to the miraculous. A further important line of demarcation between the two points of view concerns what Canon Richardson calls the 'Bible view of Miracles.' To Mr. Thompson this must take second place to what it is reasonable to expect a modern man to accept about the miraculous; to Canon Richardson it is the Biblical view of miracle which is the norm, and modern man must first of all determine this and then make his decision about it. After all, whose are the miracles, the Bible's or ours? Mr. Thompson, however, jettisons the Bible view of miracle as obsolescent and irrelevant. Canon Richardson as a representative of the new Biblicism urges us to start where the Bible starts, even if it means finding a new perspective and acclimatizing ourselves to what are for us strange presuppositions.

In this matter I do not find it altogether easy to align myself fully with either Mr. Thompson or Canon Richardson. With Mr. Thompson I find the question of historicity of the greatest importance; if the miracles did not in fact happen, it is obviously irrelevant from what point of view they are regarded. On the other hand, I can cordially agree with Canon Richardson that the Biblical attitude to Miracle has much more importance than Mr. Thompson assigned to it, and that in such a question it is of the first importance to examine not only the Biblical evidence but also the presuppositions with which we ourselves approach it.

In this chapter we must ask four questions with regard to miracles and attempt some answer to them:

1. What is the Biblical background to the Gospel miracles?
2. How did the Evangelists approach the miracles of Jesus?
3. How did our Lord treat His miracles?
4. What is the best approach towards the miracles which a twentieth-century Christian can take up?

It is clear at the outset that the distinction between the second and third questions cannot be drawn with absolute precision. Our discussion of the sources in an earlier chapter will have indicated that the Gospels are not merely biographies of Jesus; they are written from faith to faith. We can, with John Wick Bowman in a recently published book, examine the 'Intention' of Jesus. But we can also with Dr. Lightfoot in a less recently published work speak of 'the interpretative elements within the Gospels.' But the fact that our answer to the one question inevitably tends to pass over to the second question does not mean that we can only ask the second question intelligently, or that our answer to the second question is more likely to be right than our answer to the first. While there are obviously areas within the selfhood of our Lord which we cannot really penetrate, it does not follow that all that the Evangelists have to tell us on this head must be discounted as interpretation. The Gospels are concerned after all with the self-revelation of Jesus to His disciples, and we must be on our guard against assuming that every interpretation which they offer of Him is imported by them into the record rather than contained within the historical facts.

## 1. *The Biblical Background to Miracles*

Here we can readily follow the able exposition of Canon Richardson. The Hebrew and Christian Biblical tradition in theology started from the concept of God as Power. By contrast with Greek thought, which interpreted the fullness of Being which characterizes God as virtual immobility, the Biblical pattern of thought about God is as the living and true God Who displays His Almighty Power most chiefly in creative act and revealing Word. If, for the Hebrew, God is dynamic within the historical process, the Greek conception of Godhead was static, sometimes conceived of as within, but more often as outside and above, that process. That God should intervene in natural events was for the Hebrew an axiom; to the Greek it would cause a certain theological scandal, not, as for many modern thinkers, because the natural order was sacrosanct, but because it was difficult to discover any valid reason why God should so demean Himself. At a level of thought more primitive than the full development of either Hebrew and Greek thinking it made little difference whether an act was called natural or miraculous. Hebrew thinking was, of course, more developed than this, but the notion of a selective intervention of God in human history was one which no Biblical writer would find in the least difficult. Such historical selectivity is in fact part of the message which the Bible is concerned to give. The God Who initiates the whole process of creation, and Who sustains it by His continuous activity of creation, can also intervene within it without the slightest taint of theological scandal. The point is not that the Hebrews lacked completely the sense of the orderly process of nature. The latter part of the Book of Job, and in a less coherent and attractive fashion the Book of Wisdom in the Apocrypha, is sufficient evidence to the contrary. The point is rather that they based their belief in the uniformity of nature upon theological rather than upon strictly scientific grounds, as we should expect from a people which made no contribution to physical science comparable to the development of their understanding of the ways of God. It is significant confirmation of this point of view that their contribution to the philosophy (or, to put it more exactly, the theology) of history was much earlier and more distinctive than the achievement even of the rudiments of a philosophy or theology of nature.

This concept of God as Power is fundamental to the understanding of Biblical theology. One of the favourite reverential substitutes for the direct use of the Name of God was 'The Power' (*St. Mark* xiv. 62). St. Paul almost equates God and His power in a famous passage in Romans i. 20. It is through creation that we have the evidence for His invisible power and divinity. All power flows from God, and all things are possible to Him (*St. Mark* x. 27). The miraculous powers of Jesus are therefore set clearly by the Gospels against the background of the Divine Power (*dunamis*) which works within Jesus and flows from Him (*St. Mark* vi. 15; v. 30). It is the same power which raised Jesus from the dead (1 *Cor.* vi. 14;

2 *Cor.* xiii. 4). Linked with this in the Gospels are words like authority (*exousia*), Spirit (*pneuma*), and Kingdom (*basileia*). The proof of the teaching of Jesus is to be seen in the authority by which He casts out demons (*St. Mark* i. 27). It is by the finger or the Spirit of God that He casts out demons (*St. Matt.* xii. 28; *St. Luke* xi. 20—a Q passage). The Kingdom of God which the Ministry of Jesus ushered in comes with power (*St. Mark* ix. 1). As with the Master, so with the servants of Jesus in the Apostolic Age, there are spiritual gifts, mighty and manifest tokens of the presence of that power of God present within them through the Spirit.

Part of this whole complex of Biblical ideas is the conception of Jesus as the spiritual or charismatic man to which reference was made in the last chapter. It is in the miracles that this aspect of His life and mission is most clearly displayed. To ignore it would be to be unfaithful to an aspect of Jesus which was full of significance to the Biblical writers within the framework of their thought about God. Yet if we are to be true to their pattern of thinking we can safely dismiss at once two opposite points of view. The Gospels give no warrant either for an exaggeration of the importance of miracles in such a manner as to make Jesus simply a wonderworker Whose miracles bear no close relation to the rest of the evidence, or for the minimizing of their importance so as to make Jesus a Teacher and Prophet Whose alleged miracles can be safely left out of account by the Christian theologian in his estimate of the Person and work of his Lord. The efforts of Mr. J. M. Thompson to convince us that the shining mystery of Jesus is improved rather than impaired by the elimination of the miraculous must be regarded as one of the less successful parts of his modernist apologetic.

## 2. *The Attitude of the Gospels to the Miracles of Jesus*

If we examine the Gospels as they stand, without entering into any kind of critical question whatever, we are at once impressed with the high proportion of miraculous material which can be found in them. We should normally infer from this that such material was deeply embedded into the texture of the Gospel tradition, and that considerable, though not necessarily overriding, importance was attached to it by the Gospel writers. But the method of inquiry called Form Criticism with its belief that the material was at one time floating in the form of separate incidents in the Oral Tradition, is (at least in some quarters) inclined to see in the Miracle Stories a relatively secondary and late stage in the Oral Tradition about Jesus. The grounds upon which this judgement rests appear rather arbitrary and subjective. The danger of breaking up the Gospel material in such a manner is that less than justice is done to the picture of Jesus as a whole; it is therefore easy for this method of criticism to take the miracles out of their context and to treat them as evidence that Jesus was in some circles regarded merely or primarily as a wonder-worker. But it can readily be seen that there is a great difference between a picture of Jesus which among other traits regarded Him as a worker of miracles and one which focuses its attention exclusively upon this. There is a grave danger that Form Criticism at least by implication should pass from the former conclusion to the latter. The study of the Miracle Stories of the Gospels in isolation led to two conclusions. In support of the theory that Jesus was in some circles thought of as a wonderworker *par excellence*, appeal was made to the parallel stories about miracles which are found in non-Christian sources both Jewish and Gentile. A number of notable parallels have been collected by writers like Bultmann, Weinrich, and Fiebig, to whom Canon Richardson refers in his study of the Gospel Miracles. The Temple of Asclepius at Cos, for example, gathered round it the reputation of being a veritable pagan Lourdes. But the argument from parallels proves little. Any story of a cure is bound to parallel other stories of similar medical happenings. One doctor's case-book must read monotonously like another's. A story which consists basically in a description of the disease or disability, treatment, and cure, together with an expression of wonder or gratitude on the part of bystanders and patient, naturally appears remarkably similar to any other story of the same type. And the force of the argument from parallels is considerably weakened by the fact that Jesus uses it Himself. There is, of course, no reason to believe that Jesus or His disciples were familiar with the cures claimed by the Temple of Asclepius.

The position is entirely different with regard to exorcisms. In the Q passage concerned with the Beelzebub controversy in which His critics argued that it was through Beelzebub, the prince of the demons, that Jesus wrought His cures, He replies: 'If I through Beelzebub cast out demons, by whom do your sons cast them out? Therefore shall they be your judges' (*St. Matt.* xii. 27; *St. Luke* xi. 19). And the disciples who were scandalized by the action of the strange exorcist and expected our Lord to forbid him to 'practise,' found that Jesus refused to silence him (*St. Mark* ix. 38-40; *St. Luke* ix. 49-50). Neither incident is consistent with the picture of Jesus as a mere wonderworker. If that were so, we should expect to find traces of a professional jealousy of which there is not the slightest indication.

A further example may well illustrate the danger of building too much upon parallels to the exclusion of the rest of the picture of Jesus which the Gospels present. The healing of a blind man by the use of spittle is recorded of the Emperor Vespasian by Tacitus (*Histories*, IV, 81), which has striking similarities both in method and disease to some of the cures recorded in the Gospels. Yet Vespasian, deified at death as he was, has not to-day millions who worship him in spirit and truth. The difference lies in the 'overplus' which we find in the figure of Jesus in the Gospels and in the Church. If Jesus shares His miracles with others, He is perfectly well aware that He is doing so, and the attempt to isolate the picture of Jesus as a wonderworker, legitimate as it may be for the purpose of detailed study, if treated as it is at times by Form Criticism in isolation, can put the Gospel portrait of Jesus seriously out of perspective.

But there is another argument used by Form Criticism which is equally open to question. Dibelius, for example, whose study of the Gospels considered from the point of view of sermon material has many elements of real value, is inclined to regard the miracle stories as a secondary part of the tradition in comparison with the so-called Pronouncement Stories. Even adopting his standard of historicitiy it might be sufficient to point out that some at least of the Pronouncement Stories have the story of a miracle deeply embedded in their structure. But we can with perfect safety go further with Canon Richardson, who reminds us that there is scarcely a miracle story in the Gospels which lacks a sound devotional or homiletic point. They contain within themselves much of the Gospel. The message of the forgiveness of sins is closely associated with the healing of the paralytic. The casting out of demons must be set against the context of the widespread belief that demonic forces affected the lives of ordinary people. Victory over the demons and the release of their victims would be no contemptible part of the mighty victory of the Incarnate Lord. Control over nature underlies the miracles of feeding and the stilling of the storm. Certain cures raise, as we have seen, the question of Sabbath Observance, a religious, if not also a moral issue of the highest importance. The picture of Jesus is like the seamless robe of the Fourth Gospel; we isolate one aspect of Jesus at our risk and divide His Person and work too rigidly into compartments at our peril. There is much substance in Canon Richardson's point that the miracles of Jesus are only one element in the total Christ. Our attitude to them must be determined not primarily by a comparison with other wonderworkers outside the range of the Christian religion but by the whole Christ as He appears to us in the Gospels themselves. The difference between Jesus and other pagan and Jewish parallels is that He goes on where they stop. In Him the miracles are seen not as the whole of the relevant evidence which enables us to speak of Him as a wonderworker, but as part of the evidence which points to Him as something else.

If, then, there are dangerous exaggerations of the truth about the miracles of Jesus in some of the prevalent methods of Form-Critical study, we can begin to get a better perspective when we turn to the Gospels themselves.

The place given to miracles in St. Mark's Gospel determines in a large measure the attitude taken to them in the two other

Synoptic Gospels. The stories are told in Mark with great freshness, dignity, and reserve. This extends no less to the Nature Miracles than to the Healing Miracles. Whatever a modern Christian's distinction between them, it is quite clear that St. Mark regarded them as not essentially different from each other and told them in much the same way. Details which suggest eye-witness are indeed particularly rich in these miracles. He records the Feeding both of the Four and of the Five Thousand. The latter sat down on the 'green grass,' a valuable indication of the time of year in view of the brief, though lovely, Galilean springtide. In their coloured dress, the companies in which they sat down looked like flower-beds. When the storm on the lake arose, Jesus was asleep on a cushion in the stern. The actual Aramaic words addressed to the daughter of Jairus are preserved in the tradition. Later Evangelists, like Matthew, who wanted to cut down the amount of material taken from Mark, found no difficulty in compressing the material.

Features in the Marcan account which help to set the miracles in their proper light and contrast sharply with the idea that Jesus was merely or primarily a wonderworker may be noted as follows:

i. In many of the stories emphasis is laid upon the faith of the recipient. 'If thou canst believe, all things are possible to him that believeth,' said our Lord to the father of the epileptic child whom the disciples had failed to cure. They are met by the response of faith, 'Lord, I believe, help Thou mine unbelief' (St. Mark ix. 23–4). Jairus is told, 'Only believe,' even when the report of his daughter's death reaches him (St. Mark v. 36). The faith of those who uncovered the roof in order to let down the sick of the palsy to Jesus is clearly brought out. Here is an example of what might be called vicarious faith (St. Mark ii. 5). Negatively, Mark notices that at Nazareth Jesus 'could do no mighty works because of their unbelief' (St. Mark vi. 5). Canon Richardson is inclined to interpret 'faith' in such passages as the type of faith in Christ possessed by the Apostolic Church as illustrated, for example, by St. Paul. It is possible, though by no means necessary, that the

Evangelists thought of it in such a way. I am not personally convinced that St. Mark, for example, means us to understand as much as this. In the context of the actual ministry of our Lord it appears likely that something much more rudimentary than this is meant, and that the faith which Jesus evoked has more in common with the faith implied in faith-healing than Canon Richardson is disposed to admit. The one, no doubt, was to lead to the other; the lesser would, as men understood Jesus better, be merged into the greater. It does not seem very likely that either a mature understanding of Jesus or a fully conscious act of faith in Him was present so early in His Ministry.

ii. The story of the woman with the issue of blood affords just a glimpse of what the healing miracles cost our Lord. As a result of His (quite unconscious) contact with the woman who desired to be healed, He perceived that virtue or power had gone out of Him (*St. Mark* v. 30).

iii. In some of the stories the means of healing are placed on record. While some of the healings took place purely as the result of a word—the sick of the palsy (*St. Mark* ii. 1–12), the man with the withered hand (*St. Mark* iii. 1–6), the Gadarene demoniac (*St. Mark* v. 1–20), the daughter of the Syro-phenician woman (*St. Mark* vii. 24–30), the epileptic boy (*St. Mark* ix. 22–7), blind Bartimaeus (*St. Mark* x. 46–52), the use of touch seems to have been characteristic of Jesus. Examples may be found in the healing of Simon's wife's mother (*St. Mark* i. 29–31), the leper (*St. Mark* i. 40–5), Jairus' daughter (*St. Mark* v. 21–43). Touch and the use of spittle together are mentioned on two occasions—the healing of the deaf mute (*St. Mark* vii. 31–7) and the blind man at Bethsaida (*St. Mark* viii. 22–6). Canon Richardson again invites us to see them as symbolic actions and gestures rather along the lines of the prophetic *ôth* mentioned in the previous chapter. It appears more likely that they represent traces of the actual means whereby the miracle was performed. It is worth noticing that the cure of the blind man at Bethsaida was a gradual cure (*St. Mark* viii. 22–6).

iv. Injunctions to secrecy are added in a number of cases,

while other miracles were performed under conditions which were sufficient to ensure secrecy. We have examined the significance attached to these by Wrede and others in an earlier chapter.[1] All that is needed here is a reminder that the mention of these limitations hardly tallies with the picture of Jesus as a mere wonderworker. It would be odd indeed to find someone whose sole stock-in-trade was miracle charging those whom he cured to keep the matter secret.

v. The lack of understanding and faith of the disciples is never concealed. In the boat, while the storm on the sea raged, they cry, 'Carest Thou not that we perish?' Their failure to cure the epileptic boy in the absence of their Master is clearly emphasized.

vi. Mark notices the human emotions of the Master when confronted with demon-possession and disease, though, of course, on other occasions as well. The look which He cast at the leper when enjoining him to secrecy is recorded in Mark alone (*St. Mark* i. 43) and contrasts somewhat curiously with the mention of the compassion which He felt towards him before the cure was performed (*St. Mark* i. 41). His stern charge to a demoniac, 'Shut up and come out of him,' is recorded in St. Mark i. 25.

In the other two Synoptic Gospels two quite opposite tendencies make themselves felt. In the first place, there is especially in Matthew much abbreviation of the Marcan record of miracles. The actual number of words used is considerably reduced. Vivid details no longer occur. Any expression of emotion by our Lord is omitted. Some parallels look like mere summaries of a miracle told fully and freshly by his source. In two cases he even combines two stories into one. Two blind men are healed (*St. Matt.* ix. 27–31; cp. *St. Mark* viii. 22–6, x. 46–52), two demoniacs cured (*St. Matt.* viii. 28–32; cp. *St. Mark* i. 21–8, v. 1–20).

Some of these omissions are no doubt designed to heighten the miraculous character of the incident. Patients become perfectly whole. The absence of cures at Nazareth is simply stated as a fact without assigning as its reasons the unbelief of its inhabitants. Demons no longer rend their victims in a final

[1] Chapter iii.

ecstasy of destruction. On the other hand, many new miracles find their place in the other Synoptic Gospels. Some of them have quite a Marcan ring about them and raise no difficulty. A few of them, however, appear to be rather secondary in character, and to heighten the tone of the miracle and even at times to make it appear rather trivial. It is instructive, for example, to compare the raising of Jairus' daughter in Mark (v. 21–43) with that of the widow's son at Nain in Luke (vii. 11–17) and of Lazarus in John (xi. 1–46). Two possible examples of rather trivial miracles occur in the Petrine supplements in St. Matthew: the walking on the water (xiv. 28–31) and the catching of the fish which contained within its mouth the coin necessary for the payment of the Temple tax (xvii. 24–7). Such instances are, however, far from typical of the tradition as a whole.

The difference between the Synoptic Gospels and the Fourth Gospel lies rather in the significance attached to miracles than in their character. The following quotation from Dr. Lightfoot from his book *History and Interpretation in the Gospels* may be taken as a fair representation of the approach of Mark. It is rather as if he said, 'Here was a manifestation of Messiahship; but it was a mystery and passed unrecognized; and it was the will of the Messiah that it should so pass.' The miracles are indeed signs but only signs to those who have eyes to see. St. John might perhaps have commented upon the statement of Dr. Lightfoot mentioned above, 'But if they were manifestations of Messiahship, then why not say so plainly?' For him the end of the process is always seen in its beginning. Just as the Passion is described as the Glorification, so the miracles are without any attempt at concealment described as 'signs,' and in the Fourth Gospel they are public enough in all conscience. The Fourth Gospeller recognizes the possibility of belief in Jesus 'for the very works' sake' (*St. John* xiv. 11), but in the light of the refusal of Jesus to give any sign to the Jews, it is hard to believe that the Synoptists would have recognized even the possibility of such a faith. If the Marcan Gospel is full of injunctions to secrecy, however they are interpreted, they clearly would have no place in the Fourth Gospel and do not occur. The possibility of an evidential argument from miracle is plainly set out: 'If I had not done among them the works which no other man did, they had not had sin, but now they have no cloak for their sin' (*St. John* xv. 24). Yet in this Gospel no less than in the previous three, miracle and teaching are closely related. The Johannine miracles formed the bases for discourses usually closely connected with their subject-matter and leading up to a total picture of Jesus which, if it includes them, certainly goes beyond them. If the Synoptists do not attach discourses to miracles, they are certainly not blind to their importance as teaching and, as we shall see in later chapters, take their own way of pointing out aspects of the Person and work of Jesus which carry us beyond that of the mere miracle-worker. It is plain that the Fourth Gospeller, while clearly starting from the Synoptic tradition of the miraculous, carries its assessment very much further than the Synoptists do.

### 3. *The Attitude of Jesus to His Own Miracles*

We have hitherto examined first the Biblical background to miracles and passed on to notice some of the aspects of the treatment of the miracles of Jesus in the Four Gospels. We must now attempt with due caution and reserve to discover, if we can, what was the intention of Jesus Himself in the miracles which He wrought.

Here there appear to be two strands in the tradition, which we must set out as it were in parallel before considering how far they can be harmonized into a single whole.

There is first the evidence that He did not overvalue the miraculous. Primary evidence for this is afforded by the Temptations. The most common view to-day is to regard the Temptations as the Temptations of Jesus as the Christ rather than of Jesus as a private person. They are certainly all concerned with different ways of fulfilling His role as the Messiah of God. Certainly one and probably two are concerned with the role of the miraculous in relation to that vocation. The first temptation urges Jesus to turn stones into bread and is answered by an appeal to Scripture, 'Man shall not live by bread alone.' While there is no trace in the narrative that any one is to be fed apart from Jesus Himself, hungry after His long fast, the principle is clear enough. A miraculous bread-giving Messiah would certainly be fulfilling a real need (there were many hungry people in the Palestine of His day). He would in fact be meeting the needs of men at too low a level. It is easy for secondary aims to be a positive hindrance to the satisfaction of the real needs of mankind. But the further temptation to cast Himself down unhurt from a pinnacle of the Temple has a more direct bearing on the place of the miraculous in the Ministry of Jesus the Messiah. Such an action would have a far greater significance than is commonly supposed. It might appear as a direct fulfilment of the expectation of the Apocalyptic books that the Son of Man should come on the clouds of heaven. It would in any case do much to overawe and to silence any possible official opposition. It would take place in the Temple Courts, the very nerve centre of official Judaism. It would silence in a single act anxious and awkward questions about the authority of Jesus, questions which apparently had already been aroused even about the lesser ministry of John the Baptist (*St. Mark* xi. 27–33). After such a miracle similar questionings could hardly have arisen at all. But Jesus puts such a suggestion from Him with the words, 'Thou shalt not tempt the Lord thy God.' A miracle-working Messiah of this type would simply be abusing the Divine Power at His command to serve others, for His own ends. This prelude to the Ministry should prepare us to find that here is One Who, if He worked miracles, certainly did not over-value them. But there is further evidence. Mark records that Jesus refused to work a sign to convince the Jews (*St. Mark* viii. 12 and parallels). A commentary on this might be found in the closing words of the Parable of Dives and Lazarus: 'If they believe not Moses and the prophets, neither will they believe if one rose from the dead' (*St. Luke* xvi. 31). It also appears to be probable that this is the real bearing of the many injunctions to secrecy so carefully studied by Dr. Lightfoot in *History and Interpretation in the Gospels*. A further pointer in the same direction may be found in the fact that the more the story of the Ministry hastens to its climax in the Passion and the Resurrection, the less part is played by miracles in the narrative. The refusal to call down legions of angels recorded by St. Matthew (xxvi. 53) is true to the whole character of the Passion Narrative.

This is, however, not the only strand in the evidence. Mr. J. M. Thompson called attention to the fact that the Q did not exactly abound in miracles. No doubt we do not possess Q in its entirety, and, if the passages which may reasonably be assigned to it are mainly concerned with the teaching of Jesus, and if incidents as a whole are the exception rather than the rule, a sufficient explanation might well be found for this fact. Yet even here in the teaching, the existence of miracle and even in some cases an elementary form of the argument from miracle can be found. Thus, for example, when the disciples of John the Baptist in his lonely prison come to Jesus on behalf of their master, they are bidden to return and tell John what they have seen and heard. The answer is made up of certain passages taken from the Book of Isaiah: 'Blind see, lame walk, lepers are cleansed, and poor are evangelized' (St. Matt. xi. 4–5; St. Luke vii. 20–2). It will be noticed that direct evidential appeal is made to the miraculous by our earliest written source. Again, Bethsaida and Chorazin are denounced for their persistent unbelief in spite of many miracles (now lost to the tradition) which would have convinced even Tyre and Sidon (St. Matt. xi. 21; St. Luke x. 13). St. Mark, for all his insistence upon secrecy, can treat successful exorcisms as indications of the authority (exousia) which underlay the new teaching (St. Mark i. 27), while Luke in the inaugural sermon at Nazareth mentions expressly, also in language derived from the Book of Isaiah, recovery of sight to the blind (St. Luke iv. 16–30). The ascriptions of praise and wonder at the ending of some of the miracle stories indicate that their significance did not pass altogether unnoticed.

Thus the suggestion that the miracles were at least on some occasions treated as signs or evidences for the Divine power which Jesus possessed is implied even within the Synoptic Gospels, though it is only brought out with full force by the

Fourth Evangelist. Indeed, with the background of the prophetic and, still more, as we shall see, the Messianic vocation of Jesus, it would be surprising if this were not so. Part at least of the answer seems to lie in the concept of the prophetic ôth already discussed. There is a common hinterland between parable and miracle. Indeed, it is possible that in one instance (the cursing of the fig tree) the borderline between them may have been crossed in the tradition. Parables are illustrations of religious truth for those who have eyes to see; it would not be surprising if miracles have a similar force. It is instructive to compare the lack of understanding displayed by the disciples with regard to the parables (*St. Mark* iv. 10–12) with the similar lack of understanding displayed with respect to the feeding of the five thousand recorded in the same Gospel (*St. Mark* vi. 52; for they did not understand about the loaves for their hearts were hardened). As Canon Richardson points out, the miracles of Jesus possess not only power but meaning. That is, after all, the meaning of the Q passage, 'Blessed are the eyes which see the things which ye see, for many prophets and righteous men have desired to see the things which ye see and did not see them, and to hear what ye hear and did not hear them' (*St. Matt.* xiii. 16–17; *St. Luke* x. 23–4). To see, of course, means not only to visualize but also to understand.

Such appear to be the main facts. How are they to be interpreted from the point of view of those who believe that we can at least to some extent discover for ourselves what was the intention of the Master Himself? Are we to regard the miracles as some Form Critics and others do, as a readily detachable and perhaps historically secondary part of the tradition which display to us Jesus as a wonderworker in manner detached from and perhaps inconsistent with the other conceptions of His Person and work? Or are we to adopt the standpoint of the Fourth Gospeller that the miracles were signs, and were meant to be perceived and accepted as such? Or is some position much nearer to that of the Synoptists, tenable and true?

As against the first interpretation we might argue that, while the miracles are part of the tradition about Jesus, and have therefore an unmistakable right to be studied seriously as part of the content of that tradition, they form only one of the many elements within it. Just as the Old Testament conception of God is not only as Power but also as Character, so Jesus is not merely the wonderworker but possesses many other and deeper aspects without which we may well grievously misunderstand the miracles of the Gospels. If the mighty acts of God in the Old Testament were cherished and valued by the Hebrew people, it was not for their own sake but as evidences of His character, His covenant faithfulness, and His lovingkindness, that they were interpreted. So with Jesus in the Gospels. The miracles are interpreted in the light of their hinterland in His Person. Jesus is, as we shall see, not simply the wonderworker, but the Messiah, and even more, the Son of God. It is in the light of this background that the miracles are seen by the Evangelists. They point beyond themselves as acts of power not only to the love and care for the sick and the sinful which they display, but ultimately to the deeper significance of the Person Who performs them. The disciples were not converted to Jesus the wonderworker, but to the total figure of the Incarnate Lord Who did in fact during His earthly life perform many miracles as the outgoing of His love and compassion to the sons of men.

But we may equally go astray in adopting too easily the second possibility. No doubt, as St. John says, the miracles ultimately amount to signs, indications of the Christ Who had come. If, however, we adopt too simply the interpretation of the process in the light of its final meaning, we shall perhaps do less than justice to other equally important factors in our assessment of the Master. We learn significant lessons about Him by observing so far as we can how the disciples learnt to recognize Him in the days of His flesh. Jesus, Who rejected as a Temptation the attractive suggestion that He might legitimately base belief in Himself on the miraculous alone, was thereby committed to a far harder and more costly way of winning men to Himself. The qualification 'for those who have eyes to see' must therefore be added to the description of miracles as signs.

Thus it might be expected that the significance of miracles should depend at least in part on what might be called the public of Jesus. To the Jews who wanted external tokens which might save them the costly spiritual adventure of following Christ and discovering in the light of this discipleship Who He was and what He might demand of them He refused to give a sign. To the sufferers themselves, whether they understood fully or followed consciously or not, here was 'the power of the Lord present to heal,' a true outgoing of the Divine Compassion in the face of the world's need. To John the Baptist, prevented in his prison from any more active following of the Master, they might serve for confirmation of faith and encouragement of spirit. The disciples might indeed find in them part of the evidence for the coming Kingdom. They were never permitted to make them even temporary resting-places of the Spirit. A true understanding of the Master must ever be made in the realm of the spirit and can never be achieved without considerable interior cost to the disciple himself. The early Christians were not in error in seeing the mighty works as part of their Christian Apologetic; they were not in error in adding to it arguments from the fulfilment of prophecy and the spiritual life of the Church itself. It is not miracles taken by themselves but miracles in their Biblical setting and significance, and the abiding spiritual miracle of the rebirth and renewal of Christians, that pointed the second-century convert to Christ. There is much in the place given to miracles here that is true of the intention of Jesus Himself.

### 4. The Attitude of Modern Man to the Miracles of Jesus

It is not proposed in this section to discuss in detail two sharply contrasted standpoints. There is first the older uncritical Biblicism which found no greater difficulty in the mastery of Jesus over nature than in His Lordship of the moral order of the world, and no greater difficulty in the raising of the physical dead than in His awakening of the dead conscience of mankind. Such an attitude is wholly right in demanding that we should view the Person of our Lord as a whole and that at some stage in our inquiry we are involved in what Canon Richardson calls 'a total taking of sides,' a transition from Facts to Faith. The older Biblicism starts from the right place, and contains many of the ingredients necessary for the right treatment of the problem; it does not really succeed in getting to grips with the problems which naturally tend to arise in an age dominated, often unconsciously, by scientific method. Nor again are we directly concerned with the older Rationalism. We shall have occasion shortly to challenge its conception of Natural Law; but even more disputable are its cheap and easy explainings away of the miracles of Jesus. The Evangelists do not appear in their records as either fools or knaves, and the many elements in the Gospels which display a deep instinctive feeling for historicity make such a treatment of miracles increasingly unlikely. Mr. J. M. Thompson with all his radical propensities is rightly contemptuous of this approach to the problem. We shall adopt the starting-point here that there are many readers of goodwill to the Christian Faith who find some difficulty with the miracles of Jesus but who are prepared to think hard about them and to reject superficial explanations or easy acceptance as equally unfounded.

To return to Mr. J. M. Thompson's dilemma. He argued, as we have seen, that either miracles did not occur or that they were not miraculous at all. His alternatives have appeared to the modern Christian much too sharply set. It all depends, of course, what you mean by a miracle. Even at the time of the controversy which Mr. Thompson's books aroused, the great and liberal-minded William Sanday regarded much of the dispute as a mere dispute about words.

It will be well to approach our problem by examining afresh what is meant by miracle. Here we can get real help in approaching the problem by examining what St. Augustine had to say about miracle in *The City of God* and other works. His treatment has quite a modern ring, and is quite independent of the fact that his own scientific views are no longer held. (His astronomy, for example, was Ptolemaic rather than Copernican, and his physics pre-Newtonian as well as, of course, pre-Einsteinian.) He starts by an examination of the idea of nature, and it does not really matter that the detailed ideas which he included under this head are very different from our own. Here he draws a distinction between acts which are 'beyond nature' (*praeter naturam*) or even 'against what is known of nature' (*contra quod est notum naturae*) and acts which are 'against nature' (*contra naturam*). The miracles of our Lord are of the first type and not of the second. What after all do we mean by 'nature'? Do we mean by it 'all that is known at any given time about the natural order' or do we mean to imply that we are fully informed about the unchanging laws of nature? Surely, if we are wise, we mean the former. No doubt there is a fixed body of laws of nature and, if we are Christians, we are bound to believe that this system is known to God and depends upon Him. We cannot, for example, believe that the changeover from Newtonian to Einsteinian physics took God (if we may put it in this way) by surprise. What we know about nature may be part of what God knows about it, but we cannot assume that we are perfectly informed about it.

These considerations have a bearing upon the status of what is called Natural Law. It is sometimes forgotten that the use of this concept is virtually a metaphor drawn from juris-prudence. The laws of England, for example, are not made to be broken and they react in punishment against those who do in fact break them. Granted that they are man-made and therefore alterable, they declare, for so long as they are in force, 'So much the worse for the exception.' But is this the case with Natural Law? Can we speak in this realm of

Laws which never shall be broken
For their guidance He has made?

No doubt we can if we look at them with the completeness of the Divine Knowledge. Such laws may be laid up in heavenly places, but this can hardly be true of the knowledge which we possess of them at any given time. If the scientist speaks of Natural Law, he means rather the sum total of the generalizations which in the present state of his knowledge he

is able to make about the world as he knows it. It is an inference from the regularity of phenomena to the explanation
which he is able to frame. No doubt there is a very high
degree of probability attaching to many of his results. We
can go to bed reasonably assured that the sun will rise to-
morrow. Our surprise if it did not would have to be phrased
in rather different terms from those which our grandfathers
would have used. They might have said, 'Here is a clear
breach of an unswerving law of nature.' We might rather say,
'Here is a case which is not covered by our previous generalization.' We should probably be equally surprised, but we should
tackle such a hypothetical exception in quite a different way.
On the older way of expressing our knowledge, the exception
must not be allowed to exist. If an exception were reported,
so much the worse for the exception; the law must stand and
the exception be bundled off into outer darkness as un-
ceremoniously as possible. The more recent attitude to the
law of nature argues differently. If there is a well-attested
exception, so much the worse for the rule. A modern scientist
is in most cases very conscious of the provisional nature of his
results. Phrases like 'so far as we know' or 'in the present state
of our knowledge' will occur frequently in his works. A
working scientist is all too conscious of the fast-moving world
of research to think otherwise. Despite the very high degree
of probability attaching to many of his generalizations, the
genuine scientist would find little to quarrel with in the
Augustinian qualification of nature by 'what is known of
nature.'

The difficulty is that the older Rationalism worked with a
harder and more cocksure idea of Natural Law, which is as
strange to the contemporary scientist as it would have been to
St. Augustine and for some centuries after his day. In the field
of physics, for example, the Newtonian system appeared so
complete and adequate an explanation of the basic facts of
nature that it was almost believed (perhaps unconsciously) to
have the status of unchanging law. The quite unexpected
revolution in the world of physics which led to the substitution

of Einstein for Newton as the master discerner of the order of nature has been a rude shock for the older rationalism.

Now not only has this discussion a most important bearing in general upon the question of miracle; it is possible to carry the inquiry into a particular field—the recent researches in medical science. It is true in general that modern science cannot (if it is true to its own best insights into what it is actually doing) be quite as ruthlessly sceptical about exceptions to the generalizations with which it works. It so happens that some of these recent advances have a direct bearing upon the miracles of the Gospels. In the days of the older rationalistic Enlightenment, the healing miracles of Jesus were no less 'irrational' than those which involved control over the natural world. Modern medical research has steadily become more familiar with a background of scientifically attested phenomena which cast much light upon the healing miracles of Jesus. The more recent advances in the field of psychological medicine are set out with great reserve and impressive caution by Mr. E. R. Micklem in his book *Miracles and the New Psychology*, and the developments in medical science which have taken place since his day have only served to strengthen and extend his conclusions. It has been established, for example, that paralysis, partial or complete, can have psychological as well as physiological causes. Certain types of skin disease are patient of psychological treatment. Blindness, though often organic in character, is sometimes functional in origin. It is perhaps doubtful how demon-possession would be phrased by a modern psychological practitioner; it is at least possible that many of them would include it under the heading of advanced cases of morbid psychology. The relation in such cases between what arises from within the depths of our own selfhood and what enters it from without is admittedly obscure. In general, what William Temple called 'the Cartesian *faux pas*,' the rigid dualism between mind and body, has been to a large extent transcended in more recent study. All this suggests not only that for medical science the scope of what might be called 'what is known of nature' has largely increased, but also that the particular advances that have been

made have a direct bearing upon the healing miracles of
Jesus.

We must beware of pressing this conclusion too far or of
accepting it for the wrong reasons. It is not claimed that Jesus
the wonderworker was simply a practitioner of psychological
medicine many centuries before His time. It is merely to point
out that this field of Gospel study is not left so much in the
air as was previously thought and that the old idea that the
healings of Jesus were 'against' rather than 'beyond nature'
must frankly be abandoned. Nor must we accept its conclusions for the wrong reasons. It would be too facile to say
that we accept the healing miracles because they had modern
parallels. That would be to convert a subjective ground for
faith into an objective principle, and virtually to surrender in
so doing to the fundamental error of the older rationalism—
the acceptance only of what is easy and congenial to ourselves
in the present state of our knowledge. We can, however,
reasonably state at this stage the conclusion that such recent
advances as we have noted in medical science form a background against which the healing miracles of Jesus can be most
appropriately understood and satisfactorily set.

We are still without any corresponding indications of a
possible area in which to look for the understanding of the
nature miracles of our Lord. In principle, however, the treatment given by St. Augustine of miracle in general is no less
applicable. They represent rather mighty acts which are
'beyond nature' or, if we will, 'against what is known of
nature' than necessarily against 'nature' itself.

On these miracles two opposite tendencies can be detected
even in the world of Christian scholarship. Some may be
inclined to 'sell out' at this point, and to adopt the least unlikely
'explanation' of the miracle in question. Some scholars
approximate raisings from the dead as resuscitations from
medical conditions too hastily diagnosed as final physical
death. Attention has sometimes been called to the actual
words of Jesus in the raising of Jairus' daughter, 'The maiden
is not dead but sleepeth'; though this saying of Jesus is better
set against the general Biblical description of death as sleep.

The account of the raising of Lazarus in the Fourth Gospel is expressly framed so as to exclude this hypothesis altogether. It is suggested that the Feeding of the Thousands may possibly represent sacramental meals earlier than, and in anticipation of, the Last Supper. In favour of this conclusion might be urged the fact that St. John attached his Eucharistic Discourse to his account of the Feeding of the Five Thousand and perhaps also that the two disciples who recognized our Lord in the breaking of bread at Emmaus and who were not at the Last Supper, may have noted something characteristic about the Master on one such occasion. The frequent squalls on the Sea of Galilee which die down as suddenly as they arise serve as a possible background to the Stilling of the Storm. But those who adopt this method of approach need to be warned against too close an approximation to the methods of the old Rationalism.

It seems on all accounts better to leave these miracles in a kind of theological 'suspense account,' admitting that we have not at present (though we might at any moment discover) the most natural means of understanding these miracles better. Here the Christological clue given us by Canon Richardson may be held to apply. Is Jesus the sort of person to Whom such a mastery over nature can reasonably be ascribed? Do we really know and can we dare to assign particular limits to the control which He might exercise in areas admittedly beyond what we know of nature?

The really difficult miracles are not these in which the problem of the absence of the necessary context of thought is all that really confronts us. They are those which appear inconsistent with the character of Jesus. It would be wrong to treat the miracles solely as demonstrations of power; they are also indications of character. Former ages may perhaps have sought too much to 'prove' the character from the power; this theological generation is right in subordinating the power to the character. We need not seek to establish the character by apologizing for the power. I have heard it said, for example, that we 'bear with' the miracles for the love that they display. Those who have followed the section on the Biblical background to miracle will see that the power that belongs to God stands in no need of an apology. But the ordinary man is not wrong in his instinctive suspicion of miracles which are not, as we might say, 'in character' with Jesus.

It may be well before summing up the conclusions which we have reached in this chapter to examine briefly the two miracles 'out of character' which occur in the Marcan Gospel and which therefore are deeply embedded in the tradition. The first is the story of the Gadarene demoniac in which the demons are permitted to enter into a herd of swine which rush madly down a steep place into the sea and are drowned. The older criticism described this as factually speaking a mere coincidence. The behaviour of the demoniac startled a herd of swine which happened to rush down the steep place into the lake beneath. It is better to start with the presuppositions of the time. It was universally believed (and not in Christian circles alone) that demonic forces actually existed. They were believed to occupy or to seek to occupy human or other material dwelling-places. The little parable of the man out of whom the demon was cast, whose last state was worse than the first, is very relevant here (*St. Matt.* xii. 43–5; *St. Luke* xi. 24–6—a Q passage). The swine were unclean animals to a Jew, a fitter abode for demons than a human being. Humanitarian considerations for animals are not the point here. Despite his tender passages about the birds of the air, Jesus appears to share the contemporary estimate of both swine and dogs. The latter comes out in the story of the Syrophenician woman (*St. Mark* vii. 24–30; *St. Matt.* xv. 21–8) which Luke omits perhaps because he sees that the point is hardly complimentary to his Gentile readers! In this case, if it was not kindness to swine, it was certainly kindness to human beings and perhaps even in the last resort to the demons themselves. The incident emphasizes the completeness of the cure. That particular legion of demons would never trouble humanity again. If this kind of approach is sound, it at least suggests that this miracle is not so completely out of character as has sometimes been thought.

The second incident is that of the Cursing of the Fig Tree,

which has been mentioned more than once already. The difficulty is that we should hardly expect botanically to find both fruit and leaves upon a fig tree at the same time. This is not quite without parallel, for I have myself seen a photograph taken in Jerusalem about Passover time of a fig tree which contained both. But such a botanical oddity cannot be regarded as the real point of the story. It is rather a parable of the Jewish nation with its promising exterior and disappointing response to Jesus. The Old Testament is full of comparisons between the nation and a growing plant, and the real point of the story really lies here. It is a solemn prophetic ôth—an anticipation of judgement rather than the somewhat peevish act of a disappointed wonderworker. Whether, in fact, it is a miracle performed with symbolic intention or a parable in speech converted by misunderstanding into a miracle must remain an open question. It is its parabolic meaning that rescues it from the petty and the meaningless.

To sum up, then, the Gospels present to us a picture of Jesus as the dynamic, charismatic man, Who revealed Himself not merely as a Teacher and Prophet of singular range and power but also as a worker of miracles, Whose mighty acts were themselves the indication of the coming of the Kingdom of God. It is clear that the Evangelists cherish this part of the tradition about Jesus, otherwise they would not have preserved so much material of this kind. We cannot therefore ourselves rest content with any attempt to reduce the miracles to a secondary or even a meaningless part of the tradition. They contain within themselves much, though not all, of the Gospel. We have seen that the miracles of Jesus must neither be ignored nor overvalued. They were indeed part of the pattern of ministering which Jesus set before Him, one of the ways in which the Divine Love through Him went out to needy souls. Yet He never allowed even His disciples to rest in an admiring contemplation of the mighty acts which He wrought. They were rather pointers to a significance in Jesus which went beyond them. Seen out of focus or as ends in themselves, they would become rather a hindrance to real belief in than a gateway to a deeper understanding of Jesus. It was certainly the power of the Lord present to heal which they display, but the presence of the Lord is not confined to such acts of power. The miracles formed part of a whole Messianic pattern of action and belief to which we shall next turn our attention. While they were indeed signs to such as could see, it was never intended by Jesus that they should be convenient ways of levering open the eyes of the otherwise blind or an obvious gateway to belief for those who wished an easy passage into Christian discipleship. For—then as now—discipleship of the Master demands the response of the whole man to all that he can see the Master to be.

## BIBLIOGRAPHY

J. M. Thompson, *Miracles in the New Testament* and *Through Facts to Faith.*

Among the literature evoked by Mr. Thompson's books may be quoted:
H. Scott Holland, *Miracles: Papers and Sermons contributed to the Guardian.*
A. C. Headlam, *The Miracles of the New Testament.*

More recent studies include:
Alan Richardson, *The Miracle Stories of the Gospels.*
E. R. Micklem, *Miracles and the New Psychology.*
C. S. Lewis, *Miracles.*

See also C. K. Barrett, *The Holy Spirit and the Gospel Tradition.*

## CHAPTER VII

## JESUS THE MESSIAH

IN his recent notable book *The Intention of Jesus*, John Wick Bowman makes a distinction between the lower and the higher Christology of the Gospels. Under the former head he groups together the designations of Jesus which we have so far studied as Teacher and Prophet and Healer, while reserving the descriptions of Jesus as Messiah and Son of God for examination under the latter head. That a division in our subject-matter may be drawn at this point need not be doubted, but the break can be made rather too absolute. No more than the disciples can we, as it were, 'rule off' certain aspects of the Person of our Lord as though we had finished with them, and then turn to examine the overplus to which the categories so far used do not apply. It is not in this way that a Christology either ancient or modern can be constructed. The Person of Jesus does not come apart in our hands into the two halves of humanity and divinity, one of which we have to set on one side when we begin to examine the other. His Personality is a seamless whole, and wherever we start in our approach to the whole Christ, we shall find ourselves unable to stop before we bring into account all the other aspects of His Being.

Two examples may be given. We have already seen in the previous chapter that the miracles of Jesus do not stand un-related to other aspects of His Person or work. We had continually to be looking backward at Jesus the Prophet for the true significance of many of them, and we found in the records more than a hint that Jesus also connected them with His Messianic Mission. We had, as it were, to pass the divide between the higher and the lower Christologies.

Again, if we glance at His teaching we shall find ourselves led well beyond the mere conception of Jesus as Great Teacher: It was a new teaching, 'not as the scribes.' Its authority (or should we rather speak of its *authorization*?) was given in the 'signs which followed.' But an examination of its content will lead us into a deeper concept of the Person of Christ. Without anticipating our treatment of this point in a subsequent chapter we can put it briefly with the aid of terms derived from the Fourth Gospel. 'Thou hast the words of Eternal Life,' says St. Peter (*St. John* vi. 68) in a passage which recalls his confession in the Synoptic Gospels. But the question at once arises: 'If Jesus teaches with such direct authority and such simple profundity about the things of God, Who then is HE?' and we are led on, no less than the first disciples were, towards the conclusion that the One Who had the words of eternal life was none other than that Life itself made man 'for us men and for our salvation.' Here again, the distinction between the lower and the higher Christology must not be made too absolute if it is to remain true to the situation in the Gospels.

The real significance of this distinction is, however, in principle a different one. It is a valid division of the categories which we must use in order to understand Jesus aright into a group which lie within our experience and a further set in which we have to pass beyond that immediate experience either into a realm of which we have no direct experience or into a region in which we are dealing with ideal figures which had never before existed although there was a widespread expectation that such figures might exist or would come.

In this chapter we shall try to deal with the second group of expectations concerned with the Jewish Messianic Hope while reserving the first group for later consideration when we examine the evidence which leads to the belief that Jesus was the Son of God.

That Jesus was the Messiah or Christ of Jewish expectation has become so much part of the Christian estimate of Him that the title 'Christ' has become virtually the second half of a proper name—Jesus Christ—and there are signs of this even before the New Testament was completed. Yet this is precisely the title which caused so much scandal in the earliest Christian times. That Jesus was the Christ was one of the most controversial statements that a primitive Christian could make. The previous aspects of Jesus which we have examined

were all at least readily assimilable to the ordinary man. He
could form a clear picture of a teacher and even, within certain
limits, of the work of a prophet or a wonderworker; but the
description of Jesus as Messiah brought his conception of Him
in touch with a whole ferment of religious ideas which lay far
beyond the range of expectation which could be applied
unhesitatingly to an ordinary man. Strangely enough this
early situation is in some ways closely parallel to the situation
of the ordinary unthinking man of to-day. He believes that
he can form a clear picture of a teacher, a prophet (or should
it be a sage or a philosopher?); he can grasp to some extent the
concept of a wonderworker. But he finds the idea of Messiahship—cluttered up as it appears to be with ancient Hebrew
ideas and images—difficult and remote. To argue thus would
be to show a defective sense of history. It is an even graver
misunderstanding of the conditions of an Incarnation. If God
is to come significantly to man, He must come in a Here and a
Now which in the passage of time must appear to be a Then
and a There. If the fact of an historical Incarnation is to have
any real significance at all for us, it must be accepted as a 'dated'
event which requires for its fullest understanding a particular
setting in history into which we must enter if we are to
understand it aright.

It is with this dated background which we are specially
concerned in this chapter. The term 'Messiah' in Hebrew, like
its Greek equivalent 'Christ,' means 'Anointed.' In the Old
Testament it is used generally of kings and priests, even on
one occasion of Cyrus, King of Persia, who was not a wor-
shipper of Jahveh at all (*Isa.* xlv. 1). When we turn to the
Gospels we find that Jesus does not make as much or as willing
use of it as might be expected. It is used freely of the expectations and doubts of others, friends and enemies alike. Jesus
Himself uses it when discussing, in the passage concerned with
the relation of David's Son and David's Lord (*St. Mark* xii. 35;
*St. Luke* xx. 41), the general state of Messianic expectancy.
Herod makes the general inquiry where the Messiah should
be born (*St. Matt.* ii. 4). False claimants to Messiahship will
say, 'I am Christ' (*St. Mark* xiii. 21; *St. Matt.* xxiv. 23). The

High Priest charges Jesus on oath to say whether He·be the
Messiah or no (*St. Mark* xiv. 61; *St. Matt.* xxvi. 63; *St. Luke*
xxii. 67). The false witnesses at the trial in the Lucan account
accuse Jesus of making this claim for Himself (*St. Luke* xxiii. 2,
without parallel in the other Synoptists). Mockers in the
Passion Narrative freely use this title about our Lord (*St. Mark*
xv. 32; *St. Matt.* xxvi. 68; *St. Luke* xxiii. 35 and 39). The
Messiahship of Jesus is confessed by St. Peter at Caesarea
Philippi (*St. Mark* viii. 29; *St. Matt.* xvi. 16 and 20; *St. Luke* ix.
20). There appears to be only one instance in which it is used
by Jesus Himself about Himself, 'Because ye belong to Christ
or the Messiah' (*St. Mark* ix. 41), where there are no parallels
in either of the other two Synoptic Gospels.

A similar situation is reflected in the Fourth Gospel. The
general expectation of a Messiah is reflected in the seventh
chapter, 'Do the rulers know that this is really the Messiah?
When the Messiah comes, will He do more miracles than this?
Will the Messiah come from Galilee?' (vii. 26–7, 29, 31, and
41). It is customarily used by others to express their belief in
Him. The first disciples say, 'We have found the Messiah' (i. 41).
The Samaritan woman tells her neighbours, 'Come see a man
Who told me all things that ever I did; can this be the Messiah?'
(iv. 29). Finally, Martha of Bethany confesses, 'I have believed
and know that Thou art the Messiah, the Son of God' (xi. 27).
The whole Gospel has as its motive, 'That ye may believe
that Jesus is the Messiah and that believing ye might have
life in His Name.' Here again, as in the Synoptic Gospels,
we do not find Jesus using the title of His own initiative.

In the light of these facts it has even been doubted whether
our Lord claimed to be Messiah at all. This would, however,
be an unwarranted deduction from the evidence. Jesus never
seems to negative directly any of the confessions of Messiahship
made about Him. More important is His answer to the High
Priest's solemn adjuration. Here, in Mark at least, He answers
in a phrase significant of the most impressive utterances of the
Old Testament, 'I am.' It is only in the other Synoptists that
any degree of ambiguity is imported into His reply. Both
Matthew xxvi. 64, and Luke xxii. 70, throw the statement

of the High Priest back to him. We should also have to discard the one positive use of the word by our Lord in Mark which has been quoted above. The facts can surely be better explained by the theory that there was a widespread Messianic expectation of a kind which Jesus Himself did not share and which made Him unwilling to treat the confession of Himself as Messiah as the real climax of belief in Him. The assumption that there was a Messianic cross-purpose between Jesus and His contemporaries makes good sense of all the evidence. It explains why Jesus accepts the title when applied to Him by others; why He refused to use it at all freely of Himself; and why He prefers to use other self-designations. This hypothesis will receive impressive confirmation from the facts as this chapter proceeds.

Messiahship was a term associated with the eschatology of the Jewish people, the distinctive way in which the Hebrews expressed their belief in the Victory of God in human history. For them it might well be said that the meaning of History was expressed in End-History. What was of faith to a Hebrew was the belief that 'the Lord God Omnipotent reigneth.' Any statement as to the means taken by God to express or to establish His Reign upon earth lay solely on the level of permitted theological thinking. Often a Hebrew writer would express his fundamental faith without hazarding any conjecture as to how this reign of God might be fulfilled. In at least one instance, the curious document known as the *Assumption of Moses*, it is inferred that God would be His own Messiah. Sometimes the Messianic agent of the Rule of God was conceived as the Faithful Remnant or nucleus of the nation— the 'Stock' of Isaiah ben Amoz or the Servant (to adopt a common interpretation of the Servant Songs incorporated into the middle part of the Book of Isaiah), or the saints of the Most High of the Book of Daniel. But in other cases the Messiah was conceived as a single individual figure to whom different titles might be assigned and different descriptions given. Thus in Jewish circles, even where it was believed that God would intervene through a Messiah, there was no uniform picture of what the Messiah would resemble when He came.

We must now pass briefly in review some of the ways in which the Messiah conceived as an individual was regarded on the basis of the documents which have come down to us:

i. The Messiah might first be regarded as an earthly ruler through Whom the Reign of God would be made manifest upon earth. The form in which such a figure was described naturally reflected the fortunes upon earth of the Hebrews themselves. During the pre-exilic period the southern kingdom remained unswervingly faithful to the House of David. It is therefore not surprising that in the prophecies ascribed to Isaiah ben Amoz the Messiah should be described as a prince of the Davidic line greater and more righteous than any actual ruler of that line. This is as natural to a south-country Jew as it would be strange and improbable in a document emanating from the north. Barring an obscure reference to Zerubbabel as the Branch, this form of the Messianic Hope remained in abeyance until the revival of Jewish nationality in the Maccabaean period. Here the actual leadership lay not with any member of the line of David but in the Levitical Family of the Hasmonaeans. It is therefore hardly surprising that in a few documents like Psalm cx, the book of *Jubilees*, and part of the *Testament of the Twelve Patriarchs*, mention should be made of a Messiah Who was a Son of Levi. This expression of the hope, however, quickly faded, as the House of Hashmon sank into lower depths of worldliness and cruelty. The result was a revival of the hopes centred in the house of David as found, for example, in the seventeenth of the *Psalms of Solomon*. It might be overpressing the evidence to speak of a Zealot Messiah, but it would not be surprising if the Zealots found material which encouraged their belief that 'direct action' was part of the plan approved by God for the establishment of His reign upon earth.

ii. There was, however, a second tendency to think of the Messiah as a supernatural or supramundane figure. A comparison between the doctrine of the Remnant in Isaiah ben Amoz and the figure of the saints of the Most High as the Son of Man in Daniel might indicate how this could take place. The curious idiom which is so marked a feature of the Apocalyptic Literature in which in a simple kind of code each order of being is, as it were, 'down-graded' shows that when the saints of the Most High, the faithful remnant, are described as the Son of Man, it is their supernatural calling and origin that is in question. For the author of the Book of Daniel angels are described as men and men as beasts. It would not therefore be surprising if the human figure of the Messiah, already regarded as an ideal figure, should become in the same type of literature a supernatural figure. It is believed that this process has actually occurred and is part of the background of the term 'Son of Man' in the Gospels.

There are, however, other usages of the term Son of Man outside the Apocalyptic Literature to which we must first turn our attention. There are two passages in the Psalms (viii. 4, cxliv. 3) where the parallelism proves that 'son of man' merely means 'man.' Here evidently is no title. And though it is just possible that it is used in Psalm lxxx. 17 as a title, a similar interpretation is probably to be preferred. The term is used in the Book of Ezekiel as a favourite form of address to the prophet by angels. On this basis some scholars have suggested that there might be a prophetic conception of the title 'Son of Man' to which our Lord might have been indebted. This is a possible interpretation of the evidence, but if we reflect upon the difficulty of seeing how the angel could otherwise address a human being without using his name the whole time we shall see how flimsy the evidence for this theory really is.

The term is also used in 1 *Enoch*, a work rediscovered only about a century ago which never formed part either of the Old Testament or of the Apocrypha and is known to scholars as a Pseudepigraph. Its date and place of origin are unknown, but it is likely to be later than the Book of Daniel. Scholars are divided on the questions whether the book is a unity and whether the title 'Son of Man' is to be thought of as canalized in a section of the work or meant to be understood throughout the book. Charles regarded it as confined to the so-called *Similitudes of Enoch* (chapters xxxvii–lxxi), though Otto with the help of a disputed reading believed that this was one of the key ideas of the book as a whole. It is also uncertain whether the title here is used in the same way as in Daniel, that is, as a group concept, or whether it describes a single, supernatural heavenly being. Charles and Otto agree in the latter interpretation; T. W. Manson thinks that it describes as in Daniel the saints of the Most High. With some hesitation I accept the judgement of Charles on both disputed points. To complete the picture it may be said that 4 *Esdras*, a work unlikely to be as early as the time of our Lord, uses the title 'Son of Man' to denote a pre-existent heavenly being rather like a demi-god.

Even if we accept the interpretation of 1 *Enoch* given above, it is still disputed whether our Lord did in fact know the work. Here again scholars are divided. Of an older generation H. L. Goudge, and among contemporaries J. Y. Campbell, G. S. Duncan, and John Wick Bowman have considered it highly dubious. As soon believe that Jesus was influenced by *Old Moore's Almanack*! It is quite clear that to a modern scholar the work seems flat, stale, and unprofitable. There can be few regrets that it found no place in the Canon. But it is not certain that it would have appeared such to Jewish eyes and its undervaluing in this connexion goes hand in hand with the modern depreciation of the Apocalyptic literature as a whole. On the other hand, Charles quotes a long list of parallels with the New Testament which at least means that we cannot exclude the possibility that it was known and even valued by our Lord Himself. It is argued that it is strange in this case why Jesus quotes not 1 *Enoch* but Daniel at His trial as authority for the statement that He was the supernatural Son of Man. To my mind a sufficient answer can be found in the fact that Daniel was Canonical Scripture to a Jew but that 1 *Enoch* was not. To have done otherwise would have been to become involved in a debate with the High Priest on the side-issue of what constituted Canonical Scriptures, or in Jewish parlance which Scriptures 'defiled the hand.' Those who are most doubtful of the influence of 1 *Enoch* are so on the ground that they prefer to trace the influence of prophetic concepts on the mind of our Lord. But surely it is not necessary to deny the one in order to establish the other. No one doubts that many of the key-ideas which Jesus used to express His unique Person and

Mission were prophetic in character, and we can hold this without reducing Jesus merely to the status of one of the prophets. But it may still be equally true that He was influenced by Apocalyptic ideas and expectations without making Him an Apocalyptist like other Apocalyptists. It is probable from the first two chapters of St. Luke that the circle into which He came was strongly influenced by Apocalyptic ideas. The combination of deep personal piety and fierce Apocalyptic expectation is not confined to certain circles in first-century Judaism; it has its parallels in some of the more determined Evangelical types of Christendom to-day. The problem to which modern scholars draw our attention of the relation between the prophetic and the Apocalyptic in the teaching of Jesus is surely rather one of balance and proportion than of two mutually exclusive sources.

It must again be emphasized before turning to the content of our Lord's approach to His Messianic Vocation that there is no single uniform conception of the Messiah current within Judaism and that, although we can with fair probability disentangle these three streams of thought, the corporate Messiah, the individual political Messiah, and the individual supernatural Messiah, we cannot be confident of the number, character, and influence of the respective circles within Judaism within which they were held. It is being increasingly realized to-day that within the unbroken front of Judaism there were many different types of thought which were current, ranging from the rigid legalism of the Jerusalem-controlled hierarchy through the pietistic Apocalyptic groups to the politically-centred Judaism of the Zealot groups.

But the Gospels are themselves evidence not only for the life and teaching of Jesus and of His Church, but also for the beliefs and practices of first-century Judaism, all the more important because they throw light upon an otherwise scantily documented period of Jewish history. Read in this sense they bear impressive testimony to a kind of Messianic ferment, keenly felt, though obscurely thought, which acted as a kind of background to the Mission of Jesus. They suggest that one ingredient at least of this popular conception of

Messiahship could be described as political in tendency, whereas in the minds of others prophetic and apocalyptic ideas were uppermost. Our study of the way in which Jesus handled the various terms and ideas with which He approaches His Messianic Vocation will therefore throw light not merely upon His own outlook upon His Person and Mission, but also upon the background of contemporary expectation against which it is set.

## 1. The Son of David

The title 'Son of David' is used by others of our Lord in the Synoptic Gospels. All three Synoptic Gospels describe its use by blind Bartimaeus in his cry for help to Jesus (*St. Mark* x. 46–52; *St. Matt.* xx. 29–34; *St. Luke* xviii. 35–43). This is the sole use of the title in Luke, whose readers might find it too Jewish for their liking. Matthew, however, is less sparing. Three examples of the almost liturgical cry, 'Have mercy upon me [or us], Thou Son of David,' occur in this Gospel. In St. Matthew xii. 23 the multitudes, amazed at the miracles of Jesus, ask, 'Is not this the Son of David?' The crowds at the Triumphal Entry and the children who accompany Him into the Temple (xxi. 9 and 15) all cry, 'Hosanna to the Son of David.' None of these passages forbid, and the last two suggest that the title had a popular Messianic, perhaps even a political, tinge in the minds of those who used it.

There are two passages in which Jesus appears to refer to a Son of David. The first is the Q passage (*St. Matt.* xii. 42; *St. Luke* xi. 31) in which He claims that something greater than Solomon is here. It has sometimes been thought significant that the 'greater thing' is put in the neuter and not in the masculine, and that therefore it is the Kingdom of God rather than His own Person that is in question. It is, however, at least equally possible that Jesus was referring to Himself, but preferred to use the vaguer neuter because the connotations of the Son of David Messiahship made it inadvisable to draw the connexion too close.

The second passage occurs in St. Mark xii. 35–7. This is a rather curious controversy about Davidic Sonship in which, rather surprisingly, the question is asked by Jesus Himself (an unusual usage for St. Mark's Gospel). The question itself, 'How say the scribes that the Messiah is the Son of David?' represents a perfectly straightforward description of the bare bones of Davidic Messiahship. Against this Jesus quotes the opening words of Psalm cx, 'The Lord said unto my Lord.' Jesus evidently regards this psalm as Messianic and uses the description of the Messiah as David's Lord to cast doubt upon the adequacy of the description of Him as Son of David. The whole section recalls the closely-reasoned verbal arguments of the Rabbinic schools. Some scholars describe the section as amounting to a denial of Davidic Sonship, but it is rather better to describe it as an assertion of Davidic Lordship. Jesus is here probably not denying Sonship of David but rather its adequacy as a description of His Messianic Mission. He is rather questioning an assumption in the minds of His hearers than asserting a negative with respect to Himself. In other words, both these passages represent an attempt to break down a fixation in the popular mind about the Messiahship as a preparation for the introduction of other concepts and fresh meanings. If Messiahship for many ordinary Jews was virtually identical with Davidic Messiahship, and this was for many again synonymous with political Messiahship, much light would be thrown not only on our Lord's attitude to this title in particular, but on His whole outlook upon Messiahship in general.

Was our Lord in actual fact of Davidic lineage? That this was the primitive tradition is clearly evidenced by Acts ii. 30 and Romans i. 3. It is also alluded to in later documents like 2 Timothy ii. 8 and Revelation v. 5 and xxii. 16. The same assumption underlies the Infancy stories in Matthew and Luke, which are probably quite independent of the references just given. But here an obvious and long-standing difficulty arises. Both documents state the belief in the Virginal Conception, that our Lord was born without the action of a human father, and yet each traces His Davidic lineage through Joseph, who, in the nature of the case, the document concerned did not believe to have been His physical father. The answer

may well lie in the greater importance attached to betrothal
in the ancient world. In the East a child born after betrothal
would be automatically credited to the betrothed pair unless
the future husband took the proper steps to disclaim paternity.
This, no doubt, suggests a rather legalistic conception of
paternity, but it may nevertheless be the correct explanation.
The only other possible explanation is one adopted by some
of the early Fathers that Mary herself was of Davidic descent.
This may well be true, but it is not what the Infancy stories
tell us. However we interpret it, belief in Davidic descent is
deeply embedded in all stages of the tradition.

## 2. *The Son of Man*

We have carried our discussion of this title through the
instances in the Psalms and the prophets to Daniel and 1 *Enoch*
and are now quite in a position to begin our examination of
the title in the Gospels.

During the earlier part of the present century critical doubts
were expressed by Lietzmann whether in the Aramaic this could
represent a possible title. These have been sufficiently answered
by scholars like Wellhausen and Dalman. But whether it
means 'Son of Man' or simply 'Man,' it suits well the love of
vague allusive titles so typical of Apocalyptic. Phrases like the
Coming One, the Elect One, full of mystery as they were,
occur freely in this literature. What difficulty was there about
a similar title 'The Man'?

That the title was used by Jesus Himself can scarcely be
doubted. Not only does it occur freely and is used characteristically in the Gospels, it is not at all prominent in the Apostolic
Church. Acts vii. 56, with a scarcely veiled reference to the
Lucan Passion Narrative, speaks of the Son of Man as standing
on the Right Hand of God. The term also occurs twice in the
Book of Revelation (i. 13 and xiv. 14), where it has even been
argued that it comes direct from Daniel and other Apocalyptic
writings without any necessary indebtedness to the Gospels.
Two other passages in which the word is not used may
nevertheless contain allusions to it (*Acts* ii. 22, 'a man approved
of God,' and 1 *Cor.* xv. 47, 'The second man is the Lord from

Heaven'). This virtual silence on the use of the title in the Apostolic Age has its own puzzles with which we are not concerned here. It makes it quite impossible to believe that the title used in the Gospels is not authentic to Jesus.

The title is used, then, solely by Jesus in the Gospels, and is always therefore used in the third person. The question has been raised whether Jesus used it of Himself or in allusion to some one else. There is no question that the Evangelists use it of Him. This is proved by the instances in which 'Son of Man' in one Gospel is replaced by 'I' or 'Me' in another. Three instances may be given. The first is the familiar passage St. Mark x. 45, 'The Son of Man is come not to be ministered unto but to minister and to give His life a ransom for many,' where St. Luke xxii. 27 renders the first part, 'I am among you as one that serveth.' An opposite example occurs in the introduction to the Confession at Caesarea Philippi, where Mark and Luke read 'Me' and Matthew inserts with some awkwardness the familiar title (*St. Mark* viii. 27, 'Whom do men say that I am?' *St. Matt.* xvi. 13, 'Whom do men say that the Son of Man is?'). The other passage is not quite so direct. St. Matthew xix. 28 records the saying, 'When the Son of Man sits on the throne of His Glory,' while St. Luke xxii. 30 renders the saying, 'That you may eat and drink at My Table in My Kingdom and sit on thrones judging the Twelve Tribes of Israel.'

But what of Jesus Himself? Two sayings can at first sight be used as evidence that Jesus was thinking of some one other than Himself. The first is found in St. Mark xiv. 62, where Jesus says, in answer to the High Priest's adjuration, 'I am, and ye shall see the Son of Man sitting on the right hand of the Power'; while the second occurs in St. Mark viii. 38 (cp. *St. Luke* ix. 26), 'Whosoever shall be ashamed of Me and of My words, of him shall the Son of Man be ashamed.' No doubt it is fair to assume that those who heard would be left in some doubt upon the point, but it is probable that in each case it is not two persons but two aspects of one person which are referred to. In the second case, for example, the difference might well lie between Jesus in His present lowly obscurity and Jesus as He will appear in His final vindication. The same contrast might well serve to explain the first passage. This interpretation, probably correct as it is in these two admittedly difficult passages, is strongly confirmed by a number of other passages, in which the allusion is so clear as virtually to leave no room for doubt. Thus, for example, the contrast between John the Baptist drawn in a well-known Q passage (*St. Matt.* xi. 19; *St. Luke* vii. 34: 'The Son of Man came eating and drinking') leaves no room for doubt that here the Son of Man represents Jesus Himself. A similar passage from the same source, 'The Son of Man hath not where to lay His head' (*St. Matt.* viii. 20; *St. Luke* ix. 58), is an obvious description of the career of Jesus as an itinerant evangelist. Again, St. Mark x. 45 (*St. Matt.* xx. 28), 'The Son of Man came not to be ministered unto but to minister and to give His life a ransom for many,' can hardly refer to any one except Jesus Himself.

The use of a rather enigmatic title in the third person might well leave open the possibility of filling it with his own content as nothing else could.

There are three groups of passages in which the title occurs:

i. There are two passages in which the use of the title stands rather by itself. As T. W. Manson points out, there are isolated instances of the title in the first part of the Gospel. St. Mark ii. 10 (with parallels in both of the other Synoptic Gospels) records the saying, 'That ye may know that the Son of Man hath power to forgive sins'; while St. Mark ii. 28 (again with exact parallels in the other Gospels) preserves the *logion*, 'The Son of Man is Lord also of the Sabbath.' Both occur in controversy stories. It has also been suggested, though in my judgement without sufficient reason, that with them should be taken a Q passage (*St. Matt.* xii. 32; *St. Luke* xii. 10) which contrasts blasphemy against the Son of Man with blasphemy against the Holy Spirit.

It is sometimes urged that in these three passages 'Son of Man' does not in fact refer to Jesus at all, but more generally to man or mankind as a whole. Now it may well be admitted that this meaning is exegetically just possible in each passage. The first might mean that man hath power to forgive sins;

the second that man is Lord of the Sabbath; and the third
might contrast blasphemy in the sense of evil speech against
man with similar evil speech directed against God Himself (the
more customary meaning of the word to-day). But in none
of the three cases is this interpretation (even if formally
possible) really to be preferred. Take first the claim to be able
to forgive sins. This must be seen in the light of the firm
belief of Judaism that God alone could forgive sins. The
astonishment of the bystanders correctly expresses the attitude
of the Jewish Church to forgiveness of sin. Judaism never
knew the pattern of a mediatorial priesthood. It is more likely
that Jesus is referring to Himself as commissioned to forgive
sins by God Himself than that He should in the saying in
question throw open the power of mediating Divine Forgiveness to the whole human race. It may be as well to meet a
possible objection here by stating that the belief in such
a mediatorial priesthood held by many Christians to-day
depends closely upon the continuation of the priesthood of
Christ rather than upon an indiscriminate opening of the
power of the forgiveness of sin to humanity as a whole. A
similar interpretation of the second saying may be preferred.
The obligation of Sabbath Observance was one of the prime
duties of Judaism; in some quarters it was even suggested that
angels were strict Sabbatarians. Despite the existence of a
Rabbinical saying 'Unto you is the Sabbath given over and
you are not given over to the Sabbath,' it remains more likely
that Jesus was thinking of Himself, and not of mankind in
general, as Lord of the Sabbath. This conclusion, though not
so overwhelmingly more probable as in the first instance, still
has the balance of probability in its support. The best interpretation of the Q passage is rather a distinction between Jesus
personally (Son of Man) and His Divine Message and Mission
(Holy Spirit). The nearest parallel is St. Mark viii. 38 where
the same contrast is expressed between shame now felt at
Jesus personally in the days of His humiliation and the shame
which will be felt in His Presence when He comes as the Son
of Man. The contrast has nothing to do with the general
contrast between God and man, but between blasphemy

against Jesus personally and Jesus in relation to His Divine Mission and Message.

ii. The second group of passages concern His *Parousia*. They present Jesus as coming in glory to judge both the living and the dead. These passages appear to be rather formal and stylized in tone. They lack the spontaneity and freshness which will be found in the third group to which attention will be called. They appear to be directly derived from Apocalyptic writers like Daniel and 1 *Enoch*. It is impossible by any stretch of critical imagination to excise them from the tradition with any degree of plausibility, but the manner of their presentation suggests perhaps that what was really distinctive in the teaching of Jesus on His Son of Manhood lies rather elsewhere. There is, however, a significant difference even here between Jesus and His probable sources. What was for them the only Coming of the Son of Man was for Him His Second Coming. It is enough at this stage of our inquiry to note that the term Son of Man is securely used of His Exaltation.

iii. The third group of passages are, however, the most distinctive and original in His teaching. These refer not to the Exaltation but to the Humiliation of the Son of Man, to His present condition and not to His Future Glory. Here the connexion is not with Daniel or with 1 *Enoch* but with the prophetic figure of the Suffering Servant of Isaiah liii. Here Jesus combines the prophetic and the apocalyptic in a manner which is all His own and which indicates that for Him the accent falls strongly upon the prophetic tradition. It may well be true, as William Manson in his great book *Jesus the Messiah* has made probable that some touches derived from the Servant Songs can already be detected in some passage in 1 *Enoch*, but these fugitive echoes do not extend to the Suffering Servant passage which Jesus makes basic to His understanding of what is involved in being the Son of Man. In 1 *Enoch* they emphasize merely the 'magpie' character of much apocalyptic literature: in the thought of Jesus the fusion is conscious, deliberate, planned, and fundamental. This will appear more clearly when we come to examine the influence of the Suffering Servant and similar passages upon the thought of Jesus. Here the

combination is noted as relevant to recent disputes about the
relationship of apocalyptic and prophetic elements in His
Teaching. It does not appear from this group of passages that
we have to choose between prophetic and apocalyptic influence
in the thought of our Lord. Both may be present, but the
blending is deeply and subtly made so as to give virtual
predominance to the prophetic strain.

So far, then, the basic facts; we can now turn to consider
the meaning of the term 'Son of Man' in the teaching of Jesus.

i. It has first been suggested, both by Schweitzer and by
Otto, that for Jesus the title 'Son of Man' meant Messiah-
designate. On this view Jesus would only later be displayed as
the Messiah. In the interim period when He was present, as
Otto put it, before His Power, He could only be described as
'Son of Man.' But it is difficult to maintain this view. It
might be feasible if the title were only applied to the days of
His Humiliation, but it is also used just as freely to express
Him in His Exaltation. This does not serve to confirm this
theory. No doubt it is true that Jesus is not in the days of His
flesh all that He will afterwards be shown to be. What the
Fathers called the doctrine of the Two Advents corresponds
to two phases in the self-manifestation of the Master. But it
is clear from the existence both of the Humiliation and of the
Exaltation passages that the term itself cannot be interpreted
exclusively in terms of one group alone. Nor again does the
general cryptic, allusive, and flexible character of the term
really support the restriction of it to such narrow limits as this
theory suggests.

ii. In sharpest contrast to this very particularized meaning
assigned to the title is an interpretation which seems to empty
it of any precise meaning whatever. In view of the fact that
the title could grammatically mean little more than 'this man,'
it was even suggested that the title meant nothing more than
'I,' or in more popular parlance 'one,' a vague and allusive way
of indicating the speaker. This would virtually evacuate the
term of any real content and convert it into a mere form of
words. This is not in itself a final objection, and we should
have to accept it if the evidence pointed that way. This theory

certainly grasps the point that it is a self-designation of our
Lord. It appears, however, to ignore the background of the
term which we have already examined, and which can hardly
go for nothing. But there are still more positive objections.
It would render nonsensical some well-attested sayings. It is
hard, for example, to rescue from a mere tautology (a mere
repetition of the same thought) St. Mark viii. 38, 'Whosoever
shall be ashamed of Me and of My words, of him shall the
Son of Man be ashamed.' As we have seen, the passage does
not imply that Jesus is here dissociating the Son of Man from
Himself, but that the two halves cannot simply be repeating
each other without any significant variation between them.
If the distinction is rather between Jesus personally and Jesus,
as it were, formally, functionally, and officially, the right
degree of distinction is preserved. Though not quite impossible, the theory which we are now discussing makes it
difficult to interpret St. Mark xiv. 62 (the answer to the High
Priest) satisfactorily.

iii. The Fathers took the term to refer to the Human Nature
of our Lord, while reserving the title 'Son of God' for His
Divine Nature. This again would appear to be very difficult
to maintain, and for a good reason. The Fathers lived and
wrote after the period in which the original clue to the term
'Son of Man' had long since been lost. The virtual cessation
in its use which occurred in the Apostolic Age proved fatal to
its correct interpretation. No doubt if the term had been used
solely of the Humiliated Christ, the theory would have
deserved more careful examination; but, taken on balance, a
case might be made out for the view that it was just as suitable
for the expression of the Divine Nature. While the Two
Natures' doctrine, in the interests of which the term was largely
used in Patristic times, may well be a legitimate and even a
necessary part of the theological explanation of the Person of
Christ, the Gospels themselves do not in fact use it and prefer
to see the whole Christ no doubt with two aspects but presented as a single whole. In view of the use of the term 'Son
of Man' in connexion with the Exaltation passages and the
weakening in the content of the term 'Son of God' in some of

the few passages in which this precise term occurs, there is hardly the clear-cut distinction between them which we should expect if this were the true solution of the problem.

iv. It has been suggested that the term must be taken to imply that Jesus was the Representative Man—the Second Adam of Pauline theology. Here is a solution more akin to the Spirit of Jesus. One can without difficulty imagine that He might have held it, and it would have the merit of reducing the gap between the title as it is found in the Gospels and the theology of the Apostolic Age. It would also help to weave the two passages from the second chapter of St. Mark more readily into the texture of Son of Man thinking. Yet even here there are difficulties to be faced. The first is a point of detail which may appear differently to different minds. If Son of Man is virtually identical with the Second Adam it is difficult to see why St. Paul should be completely silent about the term. If it is argued that it might not be readily intelligible to Gentile converts, it is possible to urge that Second Adam might not be very much more so, at least not so much more so as to lead to the abandonment of a term so deeply embedded in the Gospel tradition. After all, Messiah was equally difficult and this was retained, although we have already admitted that there exists the tendency, even within the literature of the Apostolic Age, to treat it as the second half of a proper name. Again, the term 'slave' had, as we shall see, different connotations for a Greek than for a Hebrew, yet St. Paul never scruples even in writing to Gentile Churches to describe himself as the slave of Jesus Christ. This suggests that a meaning much more strange than this must have been associated with the term 'Son of Man' if its complete absence in Pauline thought is to be explained. We may not perhaps regard this argument as completely decisive; its significance must not, however, be underestimated. Further, while the suggested meaning would make good sense of the first group of passages, and might with a struggle be made to cover the 'Humiliation' passages, it is almost impossible to assign any significance to the term on this theory in the Exaltation passages.

v. T. W. Manson made the interesting suggestion in his
*Teaching of Jesus* that the Son of Man in the Gospels is a
corporate term including Jesus and His disciples under a single
head. This has the merit of seeing the term against its background. It is universally agreed that the term had a corporate
significance in Daniel, and it is possible, though not, in my
judgement, really probable, that the same usage is to be found
in 1 *Enoch*. The use of an individual designation for a group
of people is not strange to Hebrew thinking. It is found, for
example, in the concept of corporate personality which
appears to underlie the Servant passages of Second Isaiah. The
'I' of the Book of Psalms, for example, might be either a
single individual or the whole group of faithful Israelites. That
Jesus did not lack this sense of the unity between the individual
and the group which appears so foreign at first sight to modern
Western thinking will be argued in a subsequent chapter on
the Church in the teaching of Jesus. That He taught His
disciples that 'as is the Master so shall the servant be' is plain
to every reader of the Gospels. The question is not, however,
whether such a concept was possible for Jesus, but whether it
is in fact really probable that Jesus did in fact understand the
term 'Son of Man' in this sense. Here there is grave room for
doubt. The difficulty is that there exist a group of 'disciple'
sayings in addition to 'Son of Man' sayings. These would
appear to be redundant if the concept 'Son of Man' really
included both Jesus and His own. If Manson's theory is
correct, all has already been said, and the reduplication, if
possibly safe, would be curious and awkward. But there is a
further argument against this theory. There is one passage
(*St. Matt*. xix. 28) which becomes quite impossible on this
view. It runs: 'When the Son of Man shall sit on the throne
of His glory, then shall ye also sit on twelve thrones judging
the twelve tribes of Israel.' Admittedly this is unsupported
Matthew, but whatever its source it would be frankly impossible on Manson's theory. No passage in the Gospels, so
far as I can see, really demands this interpretation, nor could
any passage really be better interpreted by adopting it. The

ideas which it embodies are certainly present in the Gospels, but they are differently expressed.

vi. We are therefore forced back upon the view that the title 'Son of Man' is a vague allusive title meaning primarily 'the Man' with an apocalyptic background used partly in the traditional manner of a Coming in glory of a supernatural kind and partly in a manner special to Jesus with the help of material extraneous to the apocalyptic but with an older prophetic origin of the lowly Servant and Saviour Whom He knew Himself to be. It interprets the claim to be Messiah both in terms of the supernatural heavenly being of the apocalyptic tradition and of the Suffering Servant of prophecy. It holds together two contrasted but necessary aspects of the Messiahship of Jesus: His Humiliation and His Exaltation. Its use may well be associated with the Messianic cross-purpose which we have seen reason to believe to have existed between Jesus and His contemporaries, and the relative indirectness of Messianic claim which it appears to have necessitated. Perhaps we may make bold to say that no term could have been better suited from its background and from the use which Jesus made of it to tell us so much of what He conceived Himself to be with so little of the dangerously false associations which belonged to other terms which embodied the hope of the Jewish people of intervention of God through a Messianic figure. If, as we believe, it was part of the intention of Jesus to take old terms and to fill them with a new and characteristic content, such a procedure would have been in complete harmony with what we can still to-day discover of His mind.

## 3. *The Suffering Servant*

We can now turn to the last leading idea which formed part of the background of the thought of Jesus upon His own Messiahship.

The figure of the Servant of the Lord forms the subject of four Songs included in the writings of Second Isaiah, the great unknown prophet of the Hebrew Exile. They are to be found in Isaiah xlii. 1–4, xlix. 1–6, l. 4–9, and lii. 13–liii. 12. These passages are most probably to be interpreted in the light of the concept of corporate personality to which reference has already been made. The background is the rather flexible concept of the relation between the individual and the community which made it possible for the thought of many Hebrew writers to pass from the individual to the group and the group to the individual without any feeling of strain. Perhaps the most probable interpretation of the Songs is that the prophet begins by reflecting upon the fortunes of his people, then passes to think of the people as the righteous remnant or spiritual nucleus among them, and finally envisages such a mission and destiny for this righteous remnant as to pass wholly beyond what was possible for a body of people, and reach a description of the Servant which could only find fulfilment in an individual and in a unique Individual at that. It is perhaps easier for us to trace a development in the writer's thought than it was for the writer himself. That is partly because our thought is not so much coloured by the concept of corporate personality and partly because we stand on the other side of the fact of Christ, and can see not only what it was possible for the Jewish people to achieve, but also what God has actually done in Christ.

These passages had a deep influence upon certain passages in the Old Testament. There are passages in the last ten chapters of the Book of Isaiah which modern scholars regard as a collection of oracles belonging to the period of the Return from Exile. Similar passages occur in two psalms (xxii and lxix) and in a picture of the Lowly King in an oracle in Zechariah ix. 9. These passages might almost be called the 'Fellow Travellers' of the Servant Songs.

Here clearly is a concept of singular beauty, range, and power. It is, however, a striking fact that the idea of the Servant of the Lord never appears to have overflowed into, still less dominated, the concept of the Messiah. Attention has been called by William Manson in his book *Jesus the Messiah* to a number of fugitive echoes to the Servant Songs in the passages in 1 *Enoch* which refer to the Son of Man. The parallels are clear enough, but they do not appear to control the thought of the writer and are easily explained by the general tendency in apocalyptic writers to use phrases and ideas culled from any part of the previous literature of the Jewish people. It is particularly important for our purpose to notice the complete absence of any allusion to the *Suffering Servant* in these passages.

It has been suggested that the only place where a real integration of the concepts of the Servant and the Messiah took place occurs in certain Aramaic Targums (or running commentaries) on the Book of Isaiah written by a certain Jonathan ben Onkelos. It is an open question whether these were already in existence in our Lord's day or not. The evidence has been reviewed in detail by William Manson, who shows that even here, while the Exaltation passages of Isaiah liii are ascribed to the Messiah, any trace of humiliation is referred either to Israel or to the nations of the Gentiles. It therefore remains true that the Gospels are the first documents consciously to link the pattern of Messiahship with the Servant of the Lord Who suffers and is glorified.

But does this identification go back to Jesus Himself or is it part of the work of interpretation introduced by the Evangelists themselves? Even if it were the latter, it would still leave open the possibility that it was nevertheless true interpretation. F. C. Burkitt believed that we are here face to face with the earliest Christology of the Primitive Church, which goes back almost, but not quite, to the time of Jesus Himself. It is clear enough that we find the idea of the Suffering Servant applied to Jesus in the earliest chapters of Acts. The term *pais*, which might mean either Servant or Son, occurs twice in Acts iv. 27 and 30.[1] If the common belief is right that the famous passage in Philippians ii. 5–12 which speaks of our Lord both as the Second Adam and the Suffering Servant has as its basis an Aramaic hymn which is pre-Pauline in origin, we should find here additional evidence for the early character of Servant Christology. The evidence of St. Luke, both in the Gospel and Acts, leaves us in no doubt that the belief that the Messiah should suffer was one of the most bitterly contested parts of the Christian Faith, and that appeal was made to the

[1] Even more striking evidence is found in Acts viii. 28-35 (the story of the meeting of Philip with the Ethiopian Eunuch).

Old Testament Scriptures in support of this conviction
(*St. Luke* xxiv. 26 and 46; *Acts* xxvi. 23). Although these
Scriptures are never fully quoted, we should not be wrong
in assuming that the Servant Songs must have been among
them. Burkitt found it significant for his theory that references to the Servant Songs in the Gospels are usually found
in the form of marginal references added by the Evangelists
(*St. Matt.* viii. 17; *Isa.* liii. 4; *St. Matt.* xii. 17; *Isa.* xlii. 1–4;
*St. Luke* xxii. 37; *Isa.* liii. 12). He accounted for the early
disappearance of this Christology even within the New Testament by the difficulty which would be found in translating
into terms which would be significant for Gentile readers.
The idea of slavery among the Greeks was one of a position
which lacked dignity. The slave was the one who did the
chores, and the Greek contempt for manual work and manual
workers was well known. In Semitic circles the term used in
a religious context did not convey quite the same significance.
Even outside Hebrew circles kings could proclaim themselves
the slaves of their God, and throughout his ministry of letter-
writing Paul like a good Semite was proud to call himself the
slave of Jesus Christ.

There appear, however, to be excellent reasons why we
should reject this theory. Granted that the difficulty of the
disappearance of the Suffering Servant Christology is a real
one, on any theory, the Primitive Church was not so rich in
creative thought as to reject a theory of such range and
significance if she had invented it herself. Creative thinkers,
St. Paul apart, were not a characteristic feature of the Primitive
Christian Community.

The very marginalia in the Gospels to which Burkitt
appealed are capable of an opposite interpretation. They are
not so much glosses imported into the records by the Evangelists but footnotes drawing out and making explicit what
was already involved in the actions and sufferings of our Lord.
Nor is influence of the Suffering Servant Songs as restricted as
this in the Gospels. It is clearly evidenced, for example, in the
saying in St. Mark x. 45: 'The Son of Man came not to be
ministered unto but to minister and to give His life a ransom

for many.' Burkitt and others find in the word 'ransom' a reading back of Pauline theology into the Gospels; but whatever might be said of the broader word 'redemption,' the narrower term 'ransom' is not at all characteristic of Pauline thought. Further, the voice from Heaven at both Baptism and Transfiguration combines echoes of Psalm ii. 7 with material derived from Isaiah xlii. 1–3. Clearly here in the basic motif of the Ministry of Jesus the idea of the Servant is clearly present. The voice, as it has been said, combines the Coronation of the Messiah with the Ordination of the Servant. But the evidence goes even deeper than this; behind what the Evangelists say, even behind what Jesus says, to what He actually was. It is impossible to mistake the influence of the Servant Passages in the silences and the indirectness of claim which Jesus imposed upon Himself. Of the Servant it is written that 'He shall not cry nor lift up His voice.' Of Jesus Himself and of His attitude to Messianic cross-purpose and Messianic popular acclaim this is deeply and vitally true. It is not suggested that this 'Elected Silence' was undertaken as a conscious fulfilment of a particular Old Testament; it is the natural reaction of One Who knew Himself to be the Servant of Old Testament expectation to the situation in which He found Himself. It is therefore preferable to regard the Servant and the Suffering Servant Christology as going back to the Intention of Jesus Himself rather than to the supposed creative originality of the Primitive Church.

The position is even clearer with regard to what we may venture to call the Fellow Travellers of the Servant Songs.

(a) The Trito-Isaianic parallels to the Servant Songs play an important role in the Gospels. One example only may suffice. The Lucan story of the Inauguration Sermon at Nazareth starts from an extensive conflation of Isaiah lxi. 1–2 and lviii. 6. Those who hesitate to regard the passage as authentic because it occurs simply in St. Luke should consider first whether it is likely that a writer for Gentiles would invent material and place it in a synagogue, and even more carefully the treatment by Israel Abrahams of the passage as one of the few first-hand accounts which we possess of synagogue proce-

dure in the time of our Lord. A quotation of similar material
from Trito-Isaiah (lxi. 1) is found in the answer to John the
Baptist in prison recorded in Q (*St. Matt.* xi. 2–6; *St. Luke* vii.
18–23).

(*b*) It would be hard to overestimate the influence on the
Gospels of Zechariah ix. 9, the prophecy of the King Who
came in lowly guise and not in the character of a conqueror.
Here is the real significance of the Triumphal Entry. Some of
the points of detail about the demonstration may be obscure;
it is not doubtful that our Lord's whole reaction to what might
easily have become a demonstration in support of a political
Messiah echoes this particular passage.

(*c*) Psalm xxii (the cry of a righteous sufferer) has a direct
influence on the Passion Narrative. The opening verse, 'My
God, My God, why hast Thou forsaken Me?' was quoted,
whether in Hebrew or in Aramaic, by Jesus on the Cross
(*St. Mark* xv. 34). Not only does its preservation in the
original Semitic languages proclaim its genuineness; on general
critical grounds even the radical Schmiedel saw in it one of the
nine 'pillar sayings' in the Gospels. It may possibly represent
a *cri de coeur* of Jesus as the burden of the world's sin which
He was carrying walled Him off from God, for the time of
His Passion. It has been suggested (although in the nature of
the case this cannot be proved) that Jesus was using the whole
psalm with its conclusion of triumphant confidence as material
for meditation on the Cross. In the light of our understanding
of the Passion we may well read the psalm as a whole, although
we have no historical warrant that Jesus actually quoted more
than the opening words. Other details in the Passion Narrative
are drawn from the same psalm (*St. Matt.* xxvii. 43, the cry
of the mockers, *Ps.* xxii. 8; *St. Mark* xv. 29, *Ps.* xxii. 7; *St.
Mark* xv. 24, casting lots for His garments, *Ps.* xxii. 18).

(*d*) Psalm lxix is a similar psalm which has left its trace on
the Gospel records. Not only are there echoes in the Johannine
account of the cleansing of the Temple (*St. John* ii. 17, cp. *Ps.*
lxix. 9, 'the zeal of thine house hath eaten me up'), but also the
offer of crude wine or vinegar to drink on the Cross (*St. Mark*
xv. 36) is compared to verse 21 of the same psalm: 'They gave

me gall to eat, and when I was thirsty they gave me vinegar to drink.'

It is clear, then, that a distinctive place in the Messianic pattern of Jesus must be assigned to the Servant passages and those which in the process of time were allied to them or dependent upon them. This association has such distinctive features that it is hard to deny that it belongs to the mind and intention of Jesus Himself.

In conclusion, three points appear to emerge from our study of the titles concerned in the Messianic Vocation of Jesus.

i. Our Lord does not appear to emphasize His own Messiahship unduly. It is not characterized (to borrow a vivid phrase from the Form Critics) by 'joy in the telling.' The evidence which led Wrede to speak of a Messianic Secret is clear enough, although the explanation which he gave of it does not appear to be particularly probable. The acclamation of our Lord as Messiah, though made at times during the Ministry, is never put into the mouth of any one by Jesus Himself. This is wholly intelligible if the inference of a Messianic cross-purpose between Jesus and His contemporaries is accepted. If, as the evidence both within and outside the Gospels renders probable, people were looking for Messiahship of the wrong kind and in the wrong way, and if the pattern of political action was associated with it in the minds of many, the reserve with respect to His Messiahship is at once made explicable. Nothing could have been more fatal to His own conception of Messiahship than a direct claim to Messiahship on His part misinterpreted by His hearers as an incitement to political disaffection. Considerations of common prudence no less than the silences and reserves suggested by the Servant concept would have been sufficient to occasion this.

ii. A fine point is made by William Manson. There are disadvantages attaching to the attempt to pass the complex associations of the term Messiah as it occurred to the mind of Jesus through a critical spectrum. A comparison of His Messianic expectation with its sources and bases in previous Jewish expectation might suggest to a careless reader that we were really attempting to measure Jesus by His sources. This would be the wrong procedure, and would in consequence be liable to give the wrong answer. For we do not in fact measure Jesus by His sources, but rather His sources by Jesus. It is not a question whether He measures up to them, but in what sense they cast light upon Him. For as William Manson rightly reminds us, Jesus Himself is part of the evidence about His own Messiahship. He is the greater which includes and transcends the less of the expectations of His predecessors. He outdistances the clues which led men to an understanding of His Person. Jesus is the Messiah Who came, all the Messiah there is, all the Messiah there is going to be; it is therefore right that we should measure the sources of the idea by Him and not Him by them. If St. Paul could rightly call Jesus the Amen of the promises of God, God's 'Yes' to the expectations of His people, this is not to forget that the answer which came was better than the promises which were given.

iii. But the meaning of the Person of Christ must in fact be carried further than His Messiahship into realms which have to do with what Christians call His Divine Sonship. Where Jewish expectations and their fulfilment stopped, the Person of Jesus went on; and it is precisely, as we shall see, this overplus of meaning which made Messiahship for Him not as for the Jews an unbelievable hope to be awaited and for any potential holder of the office a privilege to be enjoyed. For Jesus it appears to be rather a duty to be fulfilled and a burden to be borne in the light of a prior status and a greater endowment which was His already. It is to this that we must next turn.

## BIBLIOGRAPHY

William Manson, *Jesus the Messiah*.

A. E. J. Rawlinson, *The New Testament Doctrine of the Christ*.

John Wick Bowman, *The Intention of Jesus*.

F. D. V. Narborough in Rawlinson, *Essays on the Trinity and the Incarnation*.

Foakes Jackson and Kirsopp Lake, *Beginnings of Christianity*, Volume I, Part 3, Chapter iv.

G. S. Duncan, *Jesus, Son of Man*.

## Chapter VIII

## JESUS THE SON OF THE FATHER

OUR last chapter suggested that however far-reaching the concept of the Messiahship of Jesus might be when studied in the light of its Jewish sources and background, there still remained aspects of the life of Jesus which lay beyond it, and gave it, when associated with Himself, an altogether richer and deeper significance. It will be our task in this chapter to offer some examination of the evidence in the Gospels which enables us to probe deeper into the hinterland of Being that exists in our Lord.

First, and most obvious, is the title 'Son of God' as it occurs in the Gospels. To us this title appears quite conclusively to point to the full faith in Jesus as the Son of God such as is expressly contained in the Nicene Creed. We read it in the light of the full metaphysical Sonship of God which Christians have classically and rightly found in Him. If, however, we look at the use of the title 'Son of God' in the Old Testament and the Apocrypha, we shall find that it could be used in a much weaker and less distinctive sense. It could be used of Israel (*Hos.* xi. 1 and *Exod.* iv. 22 f.) or even of individuals like David and Solomon (*Ps.* lxxxix. 26 and 2 *Sam.* vii. 14). It is used perhaps honorifically of the Messiah in Psalm ii. 7 and perhaps also in Psalm lxxx. 17. In Jewish circles not wholly impervious to Greek influence it could be used in the diluted sense of a righteous man (cf. *Ecclus.* iv. 10 and *Wisd.* ii. 18). This would agree well with the tendency in some forms of Greek thought to weaken the distinction between God and man.

Yet if it is important not to claim too much for this particular term in the light of its somewhat mixed past, it is equally important not to claim too little. If the term were used of Israel in the Old Testament, its use with regard to our Lord in

213

the New Testament may well agree with the use both of the
titles 'Son of Man' and 'The Servant' in pointing to Jesus not
only as the true Israelite but as Himself the essential Israel. If
in at least one passage the Messiah is so described, we might
perhaps compare it to the conferment of a high degree of
nobility upon the Governor-General of some great dominion.
We shall see reason to believe that if, according to Psalm ii. 7,
the Messiah was Messiah first and Son afterwards, for Jesus the
order of priorities was reversed; we can speak of Him as Son
rather than Messiah, and Son before He was Messiah.

When we pass from the sources of the title 'Son of God'
to its use in the Gospels, we are at once struck by the fact that
it is not very freely used. Yet St. Mark appears to appeal to
it at all the crucial points of his narrative, and treats it as a
theme to which he frequently recurs. Many manuscripts in-
corporate the title in the 'banner headline' at the beginning of
his Gospel. It is twice found on the lips of demoniacs (iii. 11
and v. 7) as a kind of confession on the part of the unseen
world of spiritual forces. (It is clear that the Evangelists
believed the demoniacs to possess supernatural knowledge, and
this belief may constitute one reason for the imposition of a
discipline of secrecy upon those whom they were believed to
possess.) In St. Mark xiv. 61 it occurs upon the lips of the High
Priest probably as a synonym for the Messiah, but perhaps by
a kind of Marcan irony representing the testimony of the
Jewish world to our Lord. Jesus is also acclaimed as the Son of
God by the centurion at the Cross in St. Mark xv. 39 (which
again may represent in the mind of the Evangelist the opening
act of the Confession of the Gentile world). If, however, we
ask what the warrant officer in charge of the execution really
meant by it, we shall probably feel content with the weaker
meaning which the sources suggest that the title might often
have possessed in Gentile circles. It is possible that if the Gospel
were complete that we would possess an acclamation of Jesus
as Son of God by the disciples. As the Gospel stands, they are
unrepresented in this paean of praise. Even St. Peter at
Caesarea Philippi does not get as far as acclaiming Jesus as the
Son of God.

In the other Synoptic Gospels other instances of the title are found. The Temptation stories derived from Q put the term in the mouth of the devil on two occasions, 'If Thou be the Son of God.' The devil, like the demons in Mark, is believed to have a direct knowledge denied to men. There is a curious echo of this identical phrase in St. Luke xxiii. 39, where the two thieves crucified with our Lord unwittingly reopen the devil's Temptation to work a miracle in His own interest! 'If Thou be the Son of God, save Thyself and us.' In this Gospel again the words, 'the Son of the Living God,' are added to the Confession of St. Peter at Caesarea Philippi. It is possible that here, as in the Adjuration before the High Priest, the term is taken as synonymous with Messiahship. Luke adds the promise to the Blessed Virgin at the Annunciation (*St. Luke* i. 35): 'That holy thing that shall be born of thee shall be called the Son of God.' In the examination before Caiaphas, Luke adds: 'They all said, Art Thou the Son of God? and He said to them, Ye say that I am.' The title occurs eight times in all in the Fourth Gospel.

These data suggest what is at first sight a paradoxical conclusion that whereas the title 'Son of Man' occurs frequently in the Gospels and always on the lips of Jesus Himself the title 'Son of God' is never apparently recorded as being used by Jesus Himself and is far from frequent. The suggestion may be offered that its disuse by Jesus was due to the fact that it said less than He would have meant by it, and not more than He wished to convey.

It will appear, then, that our treatment of the title 'Son of God' has shown perhaps too great a reluctance to build much upon it in our search for a Gospel Christology. The situation is wholly different when we turn to the evidence for what has been called the Filial Consciousness of our Lord. By this we mean a deep, underlying sense that in the depths of His Being Jesus is essentially, even metaphysically, one with God. It will not be expected that such passages should lie upon the surface. Even in purely human relationships it is true that the greater a man the less he finds it necessary to call attention to his own greatness. It is only little men (or men who are afraid that they are not as big as they consider themselves to be) who find it necessary to parade their inmost souls or to make claims for themselves. Similarly, we should not be inclined to accept at its face value a monotonously reiterated claim that Jesus is the Divine Son. Such passages, however, in which it occur are significant and characteristic.

First of these significant passages are the two acclamations from Heaven at the Baptism and the Transfiguration. Here the Voice from Heaven in each case combines words from Psalm ii. 7 with a passage taken from the Servant Songs of Second Isaiah: 'This is My Beloved Son in Whom I am well pleased'; and at the Transfiguration: 'This is My Beloved Son; hear ye Him.' Here the Coronation of the Messiah and the Ordination of the Servant are combined. It will be argued shortly that both find their basis and as it were their 'subsoil' in the consciousness of a Unique Sonship of God. The third passage to be taken with this comes from St. Mark xii. 1 ff., the Parable of the Wicked Husbandmen, which possesses parallels in both the other Gospels. Its authenticity has been doubted by some, but has been defended with great skill by F. C. Burkitt. Here the absent householder after the rejection and murder of his servants in the past finally sends his beloved son, saying: 'They will reverence my son.' But the wicked husbandmen plot together saying: 'This is the heir; come, let us kill him and the inheritance shall be ours.' Its application to the whole economy of God's dealings with His people in the Old Testament and in Jesus makes any expository comment needless.

An important clue for our purpose is given by the term 'beloved' (*agapetos*) which is found in all three passages. This has been the subject of an important lexicographical and exegetical study by C. H. Turner.[1] He argues from both classical and Biblical Greek that what we normally translate 'beloved' should rather be rendered 'unique.' In my opinion he has proved this most important point. From classical Greek we can quote two decisive instances. Both come from Aristotle. The first occurs in the *Eudemian Ethics* (III, 6, 3; 1233 b),

[1] *Journal of Theological Studies*, Vol. XVII, pp. 113 ff.

where he is arguing in favour of his usual ethical doctrine that the mean between two extremes of conduct is probably correct. Here he takes as an example of stingy conduct and therefore the opposite pole to extravagance the hypothetical case of a rich man who prepared a wedding feast for an only son (*agapetos*) on the same scale as a banquet given for a Temperance Society. He could not plead poverty, neither could he plead that he had more sons to provide for, since the son concerned was an *agapetos* or unique son. The second example, taken from the *Rhetoric*, is equally clear. In the middle of a long disquisition upon goods (I, 7, 41; 1365 b 16), Aristotle in the light of the *lex talionis* or limitation of revenge points out that the loss of an eye is not the same punishment for a man who has normal two-ocular vision as for the man who has an *agapetos* eye. This clearly does not mean either his favourite or his beloved eye, but his unique eye, the only one that he has got! Without pausing to examine the evidence of the lexicographers, we turn finally to the evidence of the Greek version of the Old Testament. Here the same rule persists. Half the instances which occur can be rendered 'unique.' The adjective is used in connexion with the sacrifices of Isaac and Jephthah's daughter. It is therefore most probable that the adjective in the Marcan Gospel has exactly the same meaning.

But these, though in many ways the most striking, are far from the only passages which support this conclusion. There is, for example, an important Q passage (*St. Matt.* xi. 27; *St. Luke* x. 22): 'No man knoweth the Son save the Father, nor the Father save the Son, and him to whom the Son willeth to reveal Him.' Most people, if asked to assign this passage to its source on the spur of the moment, would without hesitation place it in the Fourth Gospel, and it is for this reason that Wellhausen described it as the 'Johannine Thunderbolt.' It affords a salutary warning against making too absolute a break between the Fourth Gospel and the Synoptists in the matter of teaching. Efforts have been made to weaken the force of the passage by pointing out that there is a textual uncertainty about some manuscripts, but for this there is a perfectly intelligible explanation in the lack of smoothness with which the passage runs when compared with parallel passages in the Fourth Gospel. We should expect it, for example, to begin, 'No man knoweth the Father save the Son.' The momentary pause which some of us have to make before we can quote the passage exactly from memory is evidence for the type of motive that led some scribes to try to reconstruct slightly the character of the passage. Its importance as early and valuable evidence for the 'Son-Father' complex of ideas need not be further emphasized.

A final passage may be quoted from St. Mark xiii. 32 with its parallel in St. Matthew xxiv. 36. It concerns the ignorance of our Lord of the day and hour of the *Parousia* or the Second Coming. It runs as follows: 'Of that day and hour knoweth no man, not even the Son, but the Father.' This formed one of Schmiedel's famous 'pillar passages' on the very reasonable ground that no one would have dared to invent a statement of the ignorance of our Lord. But if we accept the first part of the verse as authentic, we can hardly reject the second half with its clear use of the Son-Father terminology. Here again, then, is another well-attested instance of the term 'Son' used absolutely.

If, then, we put together all the passages which we have so far discussed, the way is prepared for the conjecture that the teaching of the Fourth Gospel, although it clearly uses this terminology with far greater frequency than the Synoptic Gospels, cannot be accused of a new invention, although it may well be following its usual procedure of developing and carrying further Synoptic usage.

We can confirm our conclusion that the Synoptic Gospels provide evidence for a deep underlying Filial Consciousness of our Lord by a further consideration of the use of the term 'Father' to describe God as used in the Gospels. Here, as in respect of the use of the title 'Son of God,' we have no reason to believe that Jesus invented the terms which He used; but we can equally note a significant development in His application of the term. The description of God as Father in a very primitive sense has its roots deep in the religious history of mankind. Some early polytheists who believed in the existence of a multitude of gods could use it of their particular deity in the sense of an almost physical paternity. This usage is even evidenced in the Old Testament itself. Thus, in Numbers xxi. 29, Moabites are described as the sons and daughters of their god, Moloch. In Jeremiah ii. 27 an idolater addresses a stock (his wooden idol): 'Thou art my father'; while in Malachi ii. 11 a heathen woman is called 'the daughter of a strange god.' The Hebrews, however, show a considerable advance from this crude conception of physical paternity. For them the real ground of their relationship to Jahveh was the Covenant Sacrifice of Horeb or Sinai. Their sonship of God was rather one of Adoption than of Procreation. This lies at the back of the most direct passage in the Old Testament (Hos. xi. 1): 'When Israel was a child, then I loved him, and brought my son out of Egypt.' Israel is rather the adoptive than the natural son of Jahveh.

A further difference between the Hebrew and non-Hebrew usage of the word strikes us at a rather later period of religious development. The idea of Fatherhood as applied to God might cover two distinct though related conceptions, that of fatherly origin and paternal rule. It is no accident that in early Christian thought both creation and providence are covered by the single idea of the Fatherhood of God. The Greek tradition stressed the idea of Fatherhood as Creation, the Hebrew and Christian tradition rather the idea of Fatherhood as Providence. To underline this point it will be necessary to appeal to evidence which comes from the Christian era, but its late date does not make it untrue to the point which we wish to make here. Greek secular thinking can be traced in the quotation which occurs from the philosophical poet, Aratus, in St. Paul's speech at Athens: 'For we also are His offspring.' Here is the Divine Fatherhood expressed in terms of creation. The second-century Christian Apologists who seek to express the Christian Faith in terms which their Greek public could understand also define the term 'Fatherhood' in similar terms. When the Greeks wished to express the idea of Providence they used a separate word (pronoia), and it is perhaps significant that it is a relatively late coinage and never secured in Greek thinking the central position occupied by the Creation and its problems.  The genuine Hebrew and Christian traditions, while not ignoring the doctrine of creation, gave a correspondingly larger place to the Divine Providence.  It is no accident that St. Paul devotes more and more intense thought to the question of the Providence of God than to His Creative action. The latter, no doubt, is taken for granted, but the agonized wrestling displayed in Romans ix–xi over the problem of the apparent rejection of Israel shows how deeply the concept of Paternity as Providence had entered into the mind of this Hebrew of the Hebrews.

If, then, there are two meanings attached to the Fatherhood of God conceived as a term with a rich doctrinal content, a third usage, more connected with devotion than with doctrine, is found in later Jewish literature.  Here Father becomes a term of personal piety.  Thus the prayer of Ben Sira (*Ecclus*. xxiii. 1) opens with the words: 'O Lord, Father and Master of my life'; while in Wisdom ii. 13 the ideal just man is depicted as calling God his Father.  As we have previously noticed, the phrase, 'Our Father, which art in Heaven,' is not without its parallel in Jewish liturgical documents.  In the use of the word 'Father' to express a devotional attitude to God, Jesus and Judaism do not stand noticeably far apart.

Yet, when we turn to the Gospels, we are once again given a sharp reminder against the danger of reducing Jesus to His sources.  It is clear that Jesus did not invent the term.  He certainly does not appear to use it with the frequency assumed by those who regard a general doctrine of the Divine Fatherhood as the principal commonplace of His teaching.  It is, for instance, far less frequent than the term 'The Kingdom of God.'  It is primarily used in teaching given to the disciples, and seldom occurs in teaching addressed to a wider public. This careful distinction preserved in the sources suggests a reserve about the use of the term which prepares us to look for something distinctive about His use of it.  Only if it is carried further by Jesus and used to express a deeper insight than that possessed by contemporary Judaism can these facts be satisfactorily interpreted.

A statistical table of the use of the term 'Father' in the Gospels will best serve to introduce a somewhat closer study of the records.

| | Mark | Q | Matthew | Luke | John |
|---|---|---|---|---|---|
| My Father | – | 2 | 18 | 4 | 24 |
| The Father | 1 | 2 | 2 | 6 | 77 |
| Your Father | – | 2 | 18 | 3 | 1 |
| Father | 1 | 3 | 6 | 3 | 5 |
| | 2 | 9 | 44 | 16 | 107 |

This table is taken from Foakes Jackson and Kirsopp Lake, *Beginnings of Christianity*, Volume I, p. 402, footnote 1. The figures given in T. W. Manson, *The Teaching of Jesus*, differ in some respects.

On this table the following observations may be made:

i. *Father*. It seems certain that the address used by Jesus in His prayers was the plain vocative 'Father,' or even a repeated vocative 'Father, Father.' The latter form is strongly supported by two important passages: Romans viii. 15 ('the Spirit of Sonship whereby we cry Abba Father') and St. Mark xiv. 36 (the Garden of Gethsemane). The retention of the original Aramaic word in both passages strongly suggests that we are very near the heart of the tradition. It appears to me probable that both Apostle and Evangelist, confronted with a double vocative (*Abba, Abba*) in the tradition, used the second *Abba* as an opportunity for translating the word for the benefit of their recipients. Further examples of this use of the vocative in the practice of Jesus are to be found in St. Matthew xi. 25–7, St. Luke x. 21 (Q: the cry of thanksgiving), and two prayers from the Cross (*St. Luke* xxiii. 34 and 46). The usage of the Fourth Gospel is identical. If these examples are relatively few in number, it is clearly significant that we have no recorded prayer of Jesus which lacks this form of address.

ii. *The Father*. We have in fact discussed the Synoptic usages of this form in our discussion of the Unique Sonship of Jesus.

The high incidence of the use in the Fourth Gospel may be noticed.

iii. *Thy Father*. This occurs solely in four passages in Matthew, all contained within the Sermon on the Mount but nowhere else, not even in the Fourth Gospel.

iv. *Your Father*. This variant of the term occurs once in Mark (xi. 25: 'that your Father also which is in heaven may forgive your trespasses'). It is found freely in the Sermon on the Mount, and in the related passages in Luke. This suggests that whereas Q read, 'Your Father,' the material special to Matthew read, 'Thy Father.' It is only found once in the Fourth Gospel.

v. *My Father*. This occurs freely in Matthew, four times only in Luke, never in Mark. It is found as often in the Fourth Gospel as in the other Gospels put together.

vi. *Our Father*. This form of the title occurs once only, in the Matthaean version of the Lord's Prayer (*St. Matt.* vi. 9). It introduces a prayer given for use by the disciples: 'And when ye pray, say Our Father.'

In summary we may conclude that, while the term 'Father' was not a new coinage on the part of our Lord, the use made of it by Him is individual and distinctive. It appears in the evidence which we have just set out that Jesus drew a clear distinction between the sense in which God is Father to Him personally and to the disciples corporately. Jesus always dissociates them from Himself in this matter. The outlook of the rest of the New Testament, that whereas Jesus is Son of God by nature, His disciples enjoy this status through Him by Adoption and Grace, seems to be clearly reflected in the use of the title 'Father' in the Gospels. Here the Fourth Gospel does not introduce new distinctions; it merely accentuates distinctions which were already there in the Synoptic tradition.

The way is now clear for a brief exposition of the view that what is really basic in the teaching and ministry of Jesus is this Consciousness of Unique Sonship of God and that all previous concepts flow from this and are, as it were, derived from it.

We can start from an incident in the Boyhood, only recorded for us by St. Luke (ii. 41–52), which has a bearing on the

question.  At the age of twelve, the normal time when a Jewish
boy became a 'son of the law,' Jesus visited the Temple Courts
with Joseph and Mary.  No reason for this visit is assigned,
probably because it was taken for granted that every pious
Jew would take what opportunity he could to visit the Temple.
The mention of others in their company suggests the pilgrim
convoys of one of the great feasts.  The boy Jesus took the
opportunity of resorting to the doctors of the Law, both
hearing them and asking them questions.  Absorbed in this
pursuit, He got separated from the rest of the family circle,
who apparently left Jerusalem with the rest of the party
without discovering their loss.  Discovering, perhaps at the
first halting-place, that Jesus was not in the company, they
returned to Jerusalem and found Him still in the Temple.
Questioned by His Mother, Jesus made the significant reply:
'Wist ye not that I must be. . . .'  Here the Greek is ambiguous.
It might mean 'in My Father's House' (referring to the
Temple); or 'about My Father's business,' alluding to the duty
of learning as much about the religion of His people as He
could; or even 'among My Father's people.'  In the last case
it would serve to accentuate the difference between the home
circle at Nazareth and the task to which His life would later
be given, and would agree closely with later passages which
suggest that for Jesus His 'mother,' 'father,' and 'brethren' had
a wider range than these who were entrusted humanly with
His care.  Whatever the exact interpretation of the phrase, it
seems clearly to point to a wider kinship and deeper relationship than that which He possessed humanly.  The passage seems
to lift for a moment the corner of the veil of the Unique
Sonship which belonged to Him, and the curtain then falls
once more until the opening of the Public Ministry.

The Voice from Heaven at the Baptism of Jesus combines
the concepts of Sonship and Servanthood, and it appears
probable that it represents a fresh stage in the development of
our Lord's Consciousness of His own Mission.  While, no
doubt, it is true that in the second psalm the term 'Son' is used
of the Messiah in a purely honorific way, there is good reason
to believe that in this passage it may be capable of being taken

in the deeper sense which the term possesses in the light of the Filial Consciousness of our Lord. Sonship and Servanthood are here combined in a fresh and original arrangement of content. The close connexion of the Baptism and the Temptations suggests, however, that what has transpired at the Baptism has relevance to His Mission as Messiahship. The Temptations appear to establish that if the linkage of Sonship and Servanthood furnished the content of the Mission of Jesus, its form was still the traditional expectation of the Messiah. Rightly regarded, the Temptations appear as possible avenues to a Messianic Vocation which might indeed be tolerable or even attractive to others but which, Son and Servant as He knew Himself to be, Jesus was bound to reject as false trails. If it can be maintained that His consciousness of Sonship preceded His call to Messiahship, it is certainly true that this consciousness determined in no small measure the method which He took in fulfilling this Mission.

In His earthly life this Filial Consciousness remains as the background of His Ministry. But background is not foreground, and we should not therefore expect it to be extended to our view more than in the significant few intimations which we have already examined. It is—as we should expect—in His prayer-life and in statements which involve His relationship to the Father that His Unique Sonship appears.

At the Transfiguration the Voice from Heaven recurs to the combination of Sonship and Servanthood which is found at the Baptism. If the Baptism may be taken as the Inauguration of His Mission as Messiahship, the Transfiguration is not chosen at random for the second Heavenly Attestation; it opens a new phase in the Ministry in which the doctrine of the Suffering Messiah is the key feature. Jesus prepares His own for the Passion, and over this part of the Ministry and the Passion which succeeds it can be written as superscription the words of the writer to the Hebrews: 'Son though He was, yet learnt He obedience by the things which He suffered.'

This background of Sonship is left by St. Mark with the deep instinctive sense of historicity which characterizes him as an underlying fact, and is never allowed to protrude itself.

St. John, in accordance with his usual practice, makes explicit what is implicit in the other Evangelists, and, we may well believe, in the Historic Ministry itself. In view of the difference in temper, purpose, and outlook between the Synoptic Gospels and the Fourth Evangelist, the evidence of the former seems sufficient to carry the interpretation of the latter.

Finally, we must turn to the titles of the Risen Master conjoined by St. Thomas in the Fourth Gospel (*St. John* xx. 28): 'My Lord and my God.' It is clear to those who follow as a whole the development in the understanding of their Master by Christians between the opening of the Public Ministry in the Gospels to the period of the Council of Nicaea three centuries later that it is only here that the Christian thought and conscience can take its rest. The reasons why this must be so will be given in the concluding pages of this chapter. Before then, we must examine first the use of the title 'Lord' in the Gospels and the evidence in the Gospels drawn from titles and images which seem to align our Lord to God and not to man.

The title 'Lord' occurs very freely in the Gospels as a vocative, and less freely in other cases. The use of the title as a form of address does not by itself convey all that the term 'Lord' means on the lips of a professing Christian of any subsequent century. It could be just the conventional form of respectful address used normally in the Greek world. In many contexts in the Gospels it can as easily be translated 'Sir' as 'Lord.' This does not imply that in others it may not possess a warmer significance and a deeper meaning; we cannot, however, find any external criteria for determining this, and the exact shade of meaning may have in each separate instance to be deduced from the context. The meaning varies from mere outward respect to deep inner devotion and only the feel of the passage can help us to estimate the shade of meaning. An interesting feature may be traced with some probability in St. Matthew's Gospel. It is well known that this is the most ecclesiastical of the Gospels, and a tendency towards liturgy may be traced in certain passages. Thus, for example, in St. Matthew xv. 22 and xx. 30–1 occurs one of the earliest fixed parts of the Christian liturgical pattern, 'Lord, have mercy upon us.' There is no reason to believe that its use suggested the Bartimaeus story instead of the more usual belief that the liturgical cry is drawn from the Gospel story. Its introduction in a passage to which Mark has no parallel suggests the hand of Matthew the Liturgiologist. If part at least of the motive which led him to combine into one two stories of the healing of the blind may have been the desire to save space for his non-Marcan material, the advantage of being able to reproduce more exactly the current form of the liturgical cry can hardly have escaped him. A similar liturgical cry, 'Lord, save [or help] me [or us],' occurs twice in St. Matthew's Gospel. In the first instance (*St. Matt.* viii. 25) it replaces the despairing cry of the disciples recorded in Mark (*St. Mark* iv. 38): 'Master, carest Thou not that we perish?' Luke stands closer to Mark here, simply omitting the words which imply lack of thought or care in Jesus. The second instance belongs to Matthew solely—it is his account of the unsuccessful attempt made by St. Peter to cross the waves to Christ (*St. Matt.* xiv. 30), while a similar phrase with a slight alteration of the verb, 'Lord, help me,' occurs in the Matthaean narrative of the healing of the daughter of the Syrophenician woman (*St. Matt.* xv. 25). It is clear, then, that its use as a vocative must be read in the light of the disciples' estimate of Jesus rather than used as direct evidence for the content of this expectation.

The noun 'the Lord,' in any case other than the vocative as a mere form of address, is more informative. It has a varied and characteristic usage with an interesting background and history. It is sufficient to say at this stage that any one addressed as 'the Lord' was by that very act placed on the Divine side of the gap between God and creatures. In Gentile circles the term 'Lord' was used freely of the patron deities of the Mystery Religions which have been described not ineptly as 'Hellenic Nonconformity.' This description is true at least in the sense that they gave to their adherents a warm spiritual satisfaction which the official State-cult never pretended to offer. We hear, for example, of Lady Isis and Lord Serapis. One document associated with the latter which was discovered at Oxyrhynchus

in Egypt caused some comment at the time. It was an invitation sent out by a certain Chaeremon to 'supper' with the
'Lord' Serapis. Parallels to the Lord's Supper of 1 Corinthians
xi. 20 and the association at Corinth of the Supper with a social
meal immediately suggested themselves. Deities described as
'lord' were the worshipful masters and mistresses of the cult
communities associated with them. These facts suggested to
scholars at the beginning of the present century that in such
Hellenistic circles the Christian Church might have appeared
as just one such cult community. The theory to-day—on
adequate grounds which we cannot go into at this stage—is
virtually dead. One piece of evidence may, however, be
relevantly quoted here because it concerns this title 'lord.' In
1 Corinthians viii. 5–6 St. Paul shows himself fully aware of
the existence of 'Gods many and Lords many.' Over against
these he sets the claim of 'One Lord Jesus Christ.' He treats
them as rivals, not as allies, and their claims and those of
Christ as mutually exclusive. It does not therefore look very
likely that the Christian borrowed any clues towards the
interpretation of its Master from these associations. It was
indebted to these solely for the provision of battle-cries and
for the creation of rallying-points. But the really decisive
objection to this theory derives from the quotation of the
Aramaic phrase *Maranatha* (Our Lord Cometh) by St. Paul in
1 Corinthians xvi. 22. This has been called not inaptly the
Achilles heel or fatal weakness of this particular theory of
indebtedness to Greek pagan cult communities for the title
'lord.' It is less likely that an original Greek title was translated back into Aramaic and used by St. Paul in writing to a
Church with a predominantly Gentile background than that
it was part of the Christological stock-in-trade of the Church
before it came into contact with the Greek-speaking world.

But there is another and more probable theory of the origin
of the title 'lord' in the early Church. The Greek version of
the Old Testament, the Septuagint, uses the term 'Lord' to
translate the Hebrew 'Jahveh.' To safeguard against any
unintentional breach of the Third Commandment ('to keep
holy the name of Jahveh thy God') Jews had become accus-

tomed for some centuries past to write the consonants of the
name Jahveh and to add the vowels of the word *Adonai* or My
Lord, which was pronounced in place of the sacred name
itself. It was the Greek equivalent of *Adonai* (that is, *Kurios*)
which is used in the Septuagint of Jahveh and in the New Testament of Jesus. It could therefore represent the simplest possible
way of affirming that centrally and essentially, in the depths of
His Being, Jesus stood on the side of God rather than on that of
creatures. It is already noticeable that in the New Testament,
Old Testament passages referring to Jahveh are being used
without any trace of theological self-consciousness of Jesus
Himself. One example is the text from Joel ii. 32: 'Those who
call upon the Name of the Lord shall be saved,' applied to
Jesus in Acts ii. 21 and Romans x. 13. A similar passage from
Isaiah xxviii. 16 (LXX text): 'Every one that believeth on Him
shall not be put to shame,' is referred to Jesus in Romans x. 11.
The familiar Old Testament theme of the Day of the Lord is used
to describe the day of Christ in the New Testament, even to
the extent of transferring the imagery associated with the one
to the imagery belonging to the other. Such a transference is
highly significant and must be accounted one of the earliest
and best authenticated signs of the treatment of the Old Testament as a Christian book.

Such a usage would be most natural in the light of the
Resurrection of our Lord and might indeed naturally be
expected to arise in the immediate post-Resurrection period.
It might therefore appear probable that the title used in the
Gospels of the Incarnate Life of the Master might represent
a simple and pardonable anachronism. We must examine
briefly the instances in which the title is used in the Gospels
themselves. In Mark it occurs but twice, in neither case free
from difficulty. The first example occurs in v. 19 where the
Gadarene demoniac is bidden to tell the 'great things the Lord
hath done for thee.' In view of the many injunctions to
secrecy which occur in this part of the Gospel and especially
with regard to demoniacs, this command is at least curious. It
might well be better interpreted here as Jahveh rather than
Jesus. The second instance is even more difficult. St. Mark xi. 3

records that the disciples sent in search of the colt to be used at the Triumphal Entry are bidden to tell the owner: 'The Lord hath need of him.' This is followed by a phrase which can be translated in one of two ways. It can either mean 'And he [that is, the owner] will immediately send him,' or 'He [that is, presumably, Jesus] will immediately return him.' It is possible therefore that the phrase, 'The Lord hath need of him,' may mean something like 'On His Majesty's Service' or 'On the King's business.' It is difficult to be certain of the interpretation here. Matthew has only one significant instance, referred to the Risen Christ (xxviii. 6). Luke, however, uses the title of Jesus some fourteen times, mostly in the material peculiar to his Gospel. The Johannine use of the title is also interesting. The Fourth Gospeller uses the title ten times (rather less than St. Luke), thrice only before the Resurrection. It looks, therefore, as if the unambiguous use of the term in the pre-Resurrection period is rather of the nature of a Lucan speciality. That Jesus was declared to be Lord through the Resurrection fact and the Resurrection experience is plainly implied in Acts ii. 36 and Philippians ii. 5–12.

There remain for consideration a number of interesting terms and phrases which appear to confirm our belief that behind the Person of Jesus in the Gospels there exists a mysterious hinterland of Sonship in which Jesus is at one with God. The first is an arresting phrase, 'I am' (*ego eimi*), in which no attentive reader of the Gospels can miss the echo of the great phrase of Divine Self-Manifestation in the Old Testament. It occurs thrice in St. Mark's Gospel, though the translation offered in each case conceals the allusion. The first is on the occasion of the stilling of the storm where Jesus says, 'Fear not, I AM,' where the solemnity of the occasion in the light of the alarm of the disciples suggests a crashing affirmation of His control over natural forces (*St. Mark* vi. 50). A second instance is found in the answer to the adjuration of the High Priest where Jesus answers, 'I AM,' and continues with a prediction of glory of the Son of Man in His Coming (*St. Mark* xiv. 62). Here again a tremendous affirmation is more probable than the weaker meaning 'Yes.' The third passage is concerned

not with Jesus Himself but with false Christs who are to come
with the same affirmation, 'I am.' It is again more probable
that a statement of Messianic affirmation is meant than a weaker
and less apposite meaning, 'It is I.' If this interpretation is on
the right lines, it affords the appropriate Synoptic dovetail for
the sevenfold 'I am' of the Fourth Gospel and the clear echo
of the Sinai Self-Revelation of God, 'Before Abraham was, I
am,' of St. John viii. 58.

It has been suggested that traces of a so-called 'Wisdom
Christology' can be found in the Gospels, and can be attributed
with some probability to Jesus Himself. The concept of the
Wisdom of God is one which had a growing significance in
the Old Testament. The earliest sources speak of Wisdom as
deriving from God in the sense of special skills being His gifts.
For a brief period emphasis was laid upon the Wisdom of God,
that is, of Wisdom considered as an attribute of God displayed
particularly in creation, while the latest and most significant
phase of this development took place in the post-exilic period.
Here in the light of the increasing separation felt in the relation
of God and man, certain of His attributes, of which Wisdom
was the chief, as it were 'moved in' to close the gap. In the
light of the poetical character of the passages in which this
phase is preserved, it is difficult to be sure whether the relation
between God and His Wisdom can be better described
as 'personification' or 'personalization,' whether Wisdom is
merely thought of poetically as distinct from God or whether
it is really conceived as a separate personality.

Such is the background of interpretation of some of the New
Testament data. It is not in doubt that in various passages in
the Apostolic Age (such as the later Pauline letters like Colos-
sians, and the Prologue to St. John) the Divine Wisdom and
the related concept of the Word are laid under contribution
for the better understanding of Jesus. The question is whether
and, if so, in what way these terms played any part in the
Gospels. At best they can provide only an undertone.

Attention has been called first to a Q passage (*St. Matt.* xi. 19;
*St. Luke* vii. 35) which opens in both forms with the words:
'Wisdom is justified.' After this the versions divide. The

Matthaean version reads 'from [or arising from] her works.' This makes excellent sense, and reads like an ordinary proverbial saying. Even so it must not be forgotten that the saying is connected with the contrast between Jesus and John the Baptist. The justification is to be found in the actions of Jesus. The Lucan version is more interesting. This runs 'is justified of her children.' This may mean one of three things. It may mean first that Jesus is justified against the Jews who should have been His disciples; or that He is justified in and through His disciples; or, least probably, that God is justified in Jesus and His works. Opinions will differ on the directness of the link between Jesus and the Wisdom. It at least proves that Jesus found no difficulty in applying or associating with Himself a passage referring to the Wisdom of God. There is a similar passage, which is also in basis Q (*St. Matt.* xxiii. 34–6; *St. Luke* xi. 49–51), where again two possible interpretations can be maintained. Luke introduces the saying with the phrase: 'Thus saith the Wisdom of God,' whereas Matthew breaks right into the saying: 'Behold, I send unto you prophets and wise men and scribes, and some of them ye shall kill and crucify.' It is possible that we are to interpret these two passages as an exact exegetical equivalence between 'the Wisdom of God' and 'I'; but it appears altogether more probable that the words 'thus saith the Wisdom of God' are, as it were, the reference and not part of the quotation. Its source is unknown but it might be derived from a lost Wisdom work. In any case, Jesus is closely associating the action of the Wisdom with Himself, though it cannot be regarded as certain that 'I,' even if identical with the Wisdom, really refers to Jesus Himself. A final similar passage is St. Matthew xi. 28–30: 'Come unto Me, all ye that labour and are heavy laden, and I will give you rest. Take My yoke upon you, and learn of Me; for I am meek and lowly of heart: and ye shall find rest for your souls.' Here the passage is obviously based upon the invitation given by Wisdom to men to seek her 'house of instruction' (*beth ham midrash*) (*Ecclus.* vi. 24–8, li. 23 f.; *Prov.* viii. 32). Here is strong evidence that Jesus was prepared to use ideas and images associated with the Divine Wisdom and to apply them to

Himself. If the evidence cannot be overpressed to prove that Jesus habitually spoke or taught about Himself as the Divine Wisdom in person, it is not without significance that He can from time to time and with perfect naturalness use of His own Person and work language associated at earlier times with the third stage of its development.

John Wick Bowman notes a somewhat parallel passage in St. Matthew xviii. 19–20: 'Again I say unto you, that if two of you shall agree upon earth as touching any thing that they shall ask, it shall be done for them of My Father Who is in Heaven. For where two or three are gathered together in My Name, there am I in the midst of them.' There is an interesting and significant parallel in the Rabbinic writings in *M. Aboth* iii. 2 in the form of a Midrash or popular exposition of Malachi iii. 16. The passage runs: 'Rabbi Hananiah ben Teradion said: If two sit together and no words of the Law are [spoken] between them, there is the seat of the scornful. But if two sit together and words of the Law between them, the *Shekinah* [the visible sign of the presence of God] rests between them, as it is written, They that feared the Lord spake one to another; and the Lord hearkened and heard and a book of remembrance was written before Him.' There are good grounds for believing that the Rabbi in question lived before the revolt of Bar Cochba in A.D. 135. It is certainly possible that here is a traditional pattern of interpretation. For the general thought we can compare the Emmaus journey with its theme, 'Where two talk together of the Christ, He Himself draws near and makes a third.' It is, of course, most improbable that St. Luke, good Gentile as he was, had a Rabbinic passage in his mind. That the idea of the *Shekinah* might be used of our Lord is suggested by the Prologue to St. John where the connexion between 'tabernacled' and 'glory' strongly suggest the Jewish concept of the tabernacling glory called in later Jewish thinking the *Shekinah*. The echo of the passage is certainly Jewish, but whether it is Jesus or the fourth Evangelist that we are hearing here must be left undecided. Here again, however, we may notice how natural it was for concepts associated with God to be applied to Jesus Himself.

St. Paul in 2 Corinthians i. 20 speaks of Jesus as the Amen of the promises of God. In Christ God said 'Yes' to the anticipations and broken lights of the Old Testament. In the Gospels we have seen the foreshadowings of the Old Testament focused and gathered together in Him. All the various strands of Messianic and religious expectation are collected and summed up in Him as in no other. Son of David, Son of Man, Son of God, Teacher, Prophet, and Servant are all fulfilled in Him. Yet here is no mechanical fulfilment. Expectation and realization are not applied to each other like the application of one figure to another in geometry. If we speak in these terms we must be prepared to be confronted by a Christ Who goes on where these stop, and for a fulfilment which surpasses expectation.

At this point, if we were concerned solely with the evidence of the Gospels about our Lord, we might well close, for here is the evidence so far as we can trace it and so far as we have ability to interpret it. The modern reader may, however, ask somewhat impatiently what all this amounts to, and why, in plain speech, we regard the evidence as pointing to the belief in the essential divinity of Jesus Christ.

i. We can start with the character of His teaching. This struck His contemporaries as a new teaching, a teaching with authority. Whatever be the case with Rabbinic parallels, there still remains an obvious sense in which no one hearing Him would have said simply, 'Here is a Rabbi like other Rabbis.' One example of the difference may be given here. When one Rabbinic authority wished to quote an opinion from which he differed, he would put the point in the form, 'There is a teaching which says'; while his own preferred opinion would be put in the form of a gentle 'I might infer.' This is by no means the case with Jesus. He never quotes authorities or balances opinions. He goes straight to the point: 'Ye have heard that it was said by them of old time; but I say unto you.' When it is realized that among the authorities which He so sets aside in favour of His own authority was the Sacred Law, divinely instituted as it was, something of the dimensions of His claims begins to appear. This is no Rabbi contradicting another Rabbi, but One Who can fulfil or even abrogate that Law of which many were at that time beginning to assert pre-existence.

ii. There is, secondly, His sureness of touch in the things of God. Jesus never fumbles or gropes in the things of the Spirit. His stature is such that His participation in the Baptism of repentance of John the Baptist raised a genuine problem. Even the category of a prophet is left behind here. We can detect no trace of the inner tensions which characterize the message of a Hosea or a Jeremiah. Though He speaks less about His own Person than He does about the Kingdom of God, the question arises and refuses to be hushed. Who then is this who speaks with this authority? If Jesus teaches about God with such assurance, it can ultimately be only because He belongs to the Godward side rather than the creatureward side of the divide between God and creatures.

iii. John Wick Bowman calls attention to the important point that there is something unique in the way in which He demands of men that they should rise up and follow Him, that they should come unto Him. This contrasts sharply with the Prophets whose message is given as: 'Thus saith the Lord,' and even to John the Baptist who, though he possessed disciples, pointed to One Who should come. Without any sense that He is doing anything outrageous, Jesus points men to Himself: He calls them and they obey Him.

iv. It is, in fact, not too strong an inference to say that an attitude taken up towards Him is an attitude taken up towards God. To confess Him before men is to be confessed by Him before God. To deny Him before men is to be denied by Him. To receive those whom He sends is to receive Him and to receive Him is to receive Him that sent Him. The rubrics 'for My sake' and 'in My Name' cannot be attached to any merely human activity; they place Him irrevocably on the side of God in His claims before the sons of men.

v. Some of the functions which He claims in the future or exercises in the present are in effect Divine functions. He is the channel or the vehicle of Divine Judgement. He can supersede the Sabbath, God-given institution though it be; He can forgive sins, the prerogative of God alone. Like Jahveh in the Old Testament He would gather Jerusalem under His wing; like the Divine Wisdom He will bid people take His yoke upon them. Such functions carry us well beyond the level of a mere prophet; they carry us further and deeper into the Being of God.

vi. His mastery over disease and control over nature is an indication of this. We have seen that modern man is less inclined than a second-century Christian to take this as the conclusive argument which it once appeared to be. It is at least congruous or corroborative evidence. It must, however, be taken closely into connexion with the mastery of Jesus over the human soul.

vii. He is finally the agent of a Divine Act of Rescue in the Cross and Passion. If this pattern of action reveals His essential humanity, it also has its roots in His action considered as being in all essentials the Act of God Himself.

All this is focused in the Cross and vindicated in the Resurrection. It is also continued and carried over into the Life of Jesus after the Resurrection. It is a significant fact that we too, like the first disciples, can hear His call and follow Him. We too, like them, can receive the pattern prayer and learn through Him to say 'Our Father' with real force and meaning. We too, entering into the joy of our Lord, can with St. Thomas hail Him as our Lord and our God. Faithful as the Evangelists normally are to the reserve and the silences of Jesus, patiently as they trace the gradualness of understanding which attended His earthly life, they never disguise the fact that they are now living on the other side of the Resurrection and that in consequence they have a fuller understanding and a firmer grasp of Jesus than they had in the days of His flesh. It is neither dishonest nor surprising that they should have permitted this deeper insight to overflow from time to time into their narrative of the Incarnate Lord. The greater wonder is that, especially in the earlier sources, we trace so clearly the words and works of Jesus and hear even in our day the authentic accents of His voice.

# PART IV

## THE TEACHING OF JESUS CHRIST

## Chapter IX

# THE KINGDOM OF GOD

WE pass now from a consideration of our Lord's Person to a review of the principal heads of His teaching.

The Kingdom of God, judging from the number of occasions in which it occurs in the Gospels, can be considered to be the chief subject of the teaching of Jesus. It must certainly be authentic to Him because, although the term itself does indeed occur elsewhere in the New Testament, other themes take the central place.

For us the word 'Kingdom' inevitably suggests a corporate whole, a form of society in which government is exercised. It is in this context that two later interpretations of the phrase arose: the first, which goes back to the time of St. Augustine, which identified the Kingdom of God with the Church, and the other (especially favoured in the last century and the earlier decades of this), which spoke of building the Kingdom of God in the sense of establishing a better and more righteous order of society. It may well be that both these concepts are the corollaries of the Kingdom of God; it must be recognized at the outset that they are extensions of the original meaning of the phrase.

The Greek word *Basileia*, as well as the Aramaic word *Malkuth* which Jesus Himself probably used, means centrally Kingship rather than Kingdom; the state or condition of being King rather than the sphere in which that Kingdom exercised. It is the Rule of God rather than His realm. Obviously the second significance was bound to be involved in the first; it is, nevertheless, a kind of outer circle on the fringe of the central significance. Since God is not an *emigré* ruler or the head of some puppet government with a certain authority but no subjects, the central idea of rule extends itself into realm; but the latter is an extension of the primary idea of the word.

It must be said at the outset that there is no distinction of meaning between the term 'Kingdom of Heaven,' which normally though not quite universally occurs in Matthew, and 'Kingdom of God' which is found uniformly in Mark and Luke. The word 'Heaven' was for Jews at the time of our Lord (as, indeed, sometimes even to-day) a convenient periphrasis for God. A Jew vocalized 'Heaven'; he meant 'God.' This use is one of the many marks which suggests that St. Matthew's Gospel stands very close to a Jewish circle within Christianity.

Like the word 'Father,' which Jesus used to express the deepest level of His relationship to God, the phrase 'Kingdom of God' was not invented by Him; it had its counterpart in the literature of His day. The evidence is collected in Dalman's work *The Words of Jesus*, and sufficiently summarized in the early pages of C. H. Dodd's *Parables of the Kingdom*. It is apparently used in two senses: as a present reality and as a future expectation. The first sense relates to God's sovereignty over Israel mediated through the *Torah* which was given to them. Thus 'to take upon oneself the *malkuth Jahveh*' meant for the Jew of our Lord's day to accept and to fulfil an unquestioning obedience to the *Torah*, or Law, considered as the instrument of God's Fatherly Rule over His people. But it also occurs in a second sense as the something which is to be brought about in the last stages of history by Divine action whether through or apart from a Messiah. The Kingdom of God is in such passages *to eschaton*, the last thing, and this is the meaning which underlies the English words 'eschatology' and 'eschatological' which are applied to this kind of thinking.

Our first task in this chapter will be to examine the use of the word in the Gospels before proceeding to discuss the chief interpretations of the word among scholars.

It is used freely in the phrases, 'to preach the Kingdom' or 'the good news of the Kingdom.' This is stated of our Lord, of the Twelve, and of our Lord with the Twelve. A would-be disciple is bidden to 'report' or to 'proclaim' the Kingdom of God (*St. Luke* ix. 60). There is 'the word of the Kingdom' (*St. Matt.* xiii. 19), the 'Mystery' or the 'Mysteries' of the

Kingdom (*St. Mark* iv. 11, singular; *St. Matt.* xiii. 11, *St. Luke* viii. 10, plural). Verbs used in connexion with the Kingdom are 'enter' (very frequent), 'receive' (*St. Mark* x. 15 and parallels), 'give' (on the part of God) or 'take away' (*St. Luke* xii. 32; *St. Matt.* xxi. 43). It can be 'inherited' (*St. Matt.* xxv. 34). It can be described as belonging to the poor in spirit (*St. Matt.* v. 3; *St. Luke* vi. 20 Q) or to the childlike (*St. Mark* x. 14 and parallels). Renunciations even of the most radical kind may be demanded for the sake of the Kingdom (*St. Matt.* xix. 12; *St. Luke* xviii. 29). It 'has drawn near' or 'is here'; it has come by anticipation upon men or is actually among them (*St. Matt.* xii. 28; *St. Luke* xi. 20 Q). It exercises its force or is violenced (*St. Matt.* xi. 12; *St. Luke* xvi. 16). It is 'within you' or 'among you' (*St. Luke* xvii. 20–1). There can be places of prominence with ranks of least or greatest within the Kingdom. The scribe who asks about the great commandment is 'not far from the Kingdom of God' (*St. Mark* xii. 34). It must be 'sought' and 'sought first of all' (*St. Matt.* vi. 33; *St. Luke* xii. 31 Q).

When we pass to parables, we find a bewildering number of people, objects, and situations which are comparable to it. These divide roughly into three classes. We have first parables of growth. The sower sowing good seed (or is it the seed which he sows?), a grain of mustard seed which becomes a spreading plant, seed growing secretly, wheat among which are tares, are all images used for the Kingdom of God. Or it might be leaven which, small though it is, penetrates and permeates the whole lump of dough. There are parables of effort. A collector, willing to sell his whole collection to secure a master pearl or a speculator taking risks to buy a field in which he believes that there is a treasure hidden, point towards the Kingdom. There are parables which point to a consummation either of judgement or of fulfilment. Thus we hear the Parable of the Great Assize, of an absentee landowner coming to take account of his stewards or his servants, or a king returning from a far country and finding his responsible subjects either faithful or dilatory. The parables of future fulfilment usually have a feast—the Messianic Banquet of

Jewish expectation—as their theme. It is a Wedding Feast for which not all the invited guests are ready or willing to come and others have to replace them. Some who deem themselves sons of the Kingdom will not be there, and others outside the privileged and invited circle will be brought in.

Indeed, to put it more widely, there is hardly a feature in the day-to-day life of a provincial town which cannot be laid under contribution to illustrate either the Kingdom directly or, less directly, some quality required of those who take the Kingdom and its business in hand. Clearly, then, the Kingdom of God is a concept of uncommon range and power, and it would not be surprising if no single explanation of its meaning will cover all the passages with which we have to deal.

It is possible that we can best approach its meaning more nearly by considering various interpretations which have been offered in recent times to explain the term. It would be well to bear in mind that each interpretation builds upon some element which is really present in the evidence but that many seem to take one strand of the evidence and either ignore or underestimate the rest. Here as in many other spheres of New Testament study it is easier to emphasize one part of a total picture than to be sure that our conclusions are adequate to the meaning of Jesus.

1. *The Kingdom considered as a consummation lying entirely in the future.* The stimulus to an eschatological interpretation, caused by the rediscovery of many documents of the apocalyptic type which had been lost for centuries, naturally had a considerable impact upon the interpretation of the Kingdom of God in the Gospels, particularly as for some time such ideas had been tacitly ignored in the study of the Life and Teaching of Jesus. It was the merit of Johannes Weiss and Albert Schweitzer to bring them to the notice of scholars, and it was Schweitzer's book, *The Quest of the Historical Jesus*, which forced them upon the notice of English readers. It is in many ways a baffling book, in which audacious improbabilities alternate with flashes of genuine insight. The book is not made any easier by being cast in the form of a series of reviews of the work of earlier writers down to the last few pages in which

Schweitzer sets out his own theory. There is no careful and systematic review of the Gospel evidence, but merely a rapid sketch of the whole field in the light of the assumption that in every passage the Kingdom of God points to a reality which has not in any sense already come. Aside from all these difficulties is a more serious defect. In his review of earlier pictures of the Life of Jesus, Schweitzer continually warns his readers against accepting any interpretation which builds upon assumptions or links which are not actually present in the narrative or upon aspects of the Gospels treated selectively. The reader expects something generically different in Schweitzer's own exposition. We shall see as we go on that he is unfortunately doomed to disappointment.

An outline of Schweitzer's sketch might run somewhat as follows: Jesus entered fully into the expectation of a future consummation which was the idea of the Kingdom of God current in apocalyptic circles in His own day. The Kingdom of God was the coming, in-breaking day of God, which to Jesus represented the good news of the Kingdom. Jesus was not Himself in the days of His flesh the Messiah. The manner of His coming into history did not fit the expectation of a *Parousia* in the clouds of glory which was customary in this tradition. To Himself He might be Messiah-designate or -predestinate, to outsiders He might with His mighty acts of power rather resemble Elijah who was expected by later Judaism (see especially the Book of Malachi) before the coming of the Messiah. Jesus Himself saw John the Baptist in this role, but the qualifying clause, 'If ye can receive it,' in St. Matthew xi. 14, suggests that Jesus did not expect others to see in John the Baptist the coming Elijah.

Everything falls into place when once the futurist conception of the Kingdom is accepted. The data which Wrede had interpreted as forming the basis for his theory of the Messianic Secret—and which we have ventured to explain in terms of a Messianic cross-purpose between Jesus and His contemporaries —Schweitzer sees in the light of a predestinate conception of the coming Kingdom. 'Unto you it is given to know the mystery of the Kingdom of God' (*St. Mark* iv. 11 and parallels).

'He that hath ears to hear let him hear' (*St. Mark* iv. 9 and parallels; *St. Mark* iv. 23 and parallels; *St. Mark* vii. 16, where it is probably no part of the true text; *St. Matt.* xi. 15, xiii. 43; *St. Luke* xiv. 35, without parallels in any other Gospel). 'Blessed art thou, Simon bar Jona, for flesh and blood hath not revealed it unto thee, but My Father which is in Heaven' (*St. Matt.* xvi. 17, no parallels).

It seems as if Jesus expected this *Parousia*, which would reveal Him as the true Apocalyptic Messiah, within His own lifetime. The disciples, twelve in number, are chosen partly with the judgement of the Last Day in view (*St. Matt.* xix. 28; *St. Luke* xxii. 30 Q). They are sent forth with the promise that the *Parousia* would come before they had finished their preaching tour of Palestine (*St. Matt.* x. 23, no parallels). A similar saying, introduced with the same solemn formula of emphasis ('Verily, verily I say unto you'), occurs in St. Mark ix. 1, which might be the proper counterpart and control for this passage: 'Verily, verily I say unto you, there be some who stand here who shall not taste of death until they see the Kingdom of God having come with power' (*St. Mark* ix. 1; the parallels have slight but significant variations). Other facts in the Gospels fit easily enough into this framework. The tribulations or woes which are expected, and against which the Lord's Prayer offers a petition, 'lead us not into temptation' (*St. Matt.* vi. 13; *St. Luke* xi. 4 Q), are not personal temptations nor the persecutions which Jesus and His followers might expect, but the Messianic Woes. The Feast which occurs in many parables of expectation (*St. Matt.* viii. 11; cf. *St. Luke* xiii. 28–30; *St. Matt.* xxii. 1–14; cf. *St. Luke* xiv. 16–24, probably Q) is a typical apocalyptic description of the Consummation. The disciples are 'sons of the bridechamber' or 'sons of the Kingdom,' whereas those who thought themselves sons of the Kingdom are cast out. The divine predestination is taking effect (cp. the man without the wedding garment in St. Matthew xxii and the wise and foolish virgins of St. Matthew xxv. 1–13). The Feeding of the Five and Four Thousand are better represented as eschatological sacraments which partake of the nature of sealings against the

Coming Day and before the Final Feast, rather than as super-natural feedings of the hungry. The Ethics of Jesus, sharply, even impossibly, conceived must be thought of as an *Interims-ethik*—an ethical system appropriate to the short interval before the *Parousia*.

The Kingdom, promised and predestined by God, is taken by storm (*St. Matt.* xi. 12; *St. Luke* xvi. 16 Q) perhaps by the number of penitents crowding into the Kingdom or perhaps even by the violent action taken by Jesus Himself to force on its coming when it tarried. The hour of fate is at hand, but still the clock does not strike the decisive moment. Jesus therefore goes up to Jerusalem to die and by His death to force its coming. 'The wheel of fate would not turn, so Jesus flung Himself upon it and is left there hanging still.'

This is a profoundly original contribution towards the understanding of Jesus and His message, but in its original context it comes somewhat as an anti-climax. Schweitzer has spared no pains to show the subjective selectivity of many previous Lives of Jesus, but is his own interpretation really exempt from such criticism? In general he builds much upon the material special to St. Matthew. That is natural, because this Gospel is the most plainly eschatological in its emphasis of all the Gospels; but it is possible that at least in some passages Matthew has stepped-up the original sayings of Jesus. Some of his key passages are notorious *cruces* (like *St. Matt.* x. 23), and, although difficult passages cannot be treated as if they did not exist, it is asking for trouble to make them the pillars of a theory. If I might add here material which has never, so far as I am aware, been published before, Streeter once told me that he asked Schweitzer in conversation what he made of St. Luke and received the reply, 'St. Luke is an enigma.' So cavalier a treatment of one of the principal witnesses to the Life of Jesus does not increase our confidence in his conclusions.

Again, Schweitzer complains that other theories have to supply links and connexions which do not exist in the text itself. But is his own theory free from fault in this direction? It is not clear that the predestinarianism which he finds so significant in the narrative is really there. At least, as we shall see, other explanations might reasonably be given to cover the evidence. It is not clear that Jesus goes to Jerusalem simply to die, and not rather to make a final appeal for the soul of the nation which might (and actually did) end in death. And where is the evidence that Jesus is by His death seeking to force on the *Parousia* rather than to secure the salvation of the world? Certainly Schweitzer appears to have no right to draw so sharp a contrast on grounds of method between his own theories and those of his predecessors.

But the objections to Schweitzer's theory do not end with such preliminary observations.

i. His interpretation of the relation of John the Baptist to our Lord really will not bear critical examination. The resemblances between John the Baptist and Elijah seem deliberate and close. Both are men of the wilderness with the typical dress and food of near-desert dwellers. The asceticism of John is, in fact, sharply contrasted with its absence in Jesus. John's mission is connected with the Jordan fords where Elijah formerly passed from human ken. John was the preacher of repentance whose conduct before Herod Antipas recalls that of Elijah before Ahab. Jesus, on the other hand, is the bringer of good news. Jesus puzzled His contemporaries not because He was so like Elijah but because He was so unlike John the Baptist.

ii. The evidence for the predestinationist strain in the Gospels is far weaker than Schweitzer imagines. The cryptic 'He that hath ears to hear, let him hear' is better understood in terms of the law that spiritual truth requires a corresponding response on the part of man. The difficult passage on the meaning of parables need not in effect have been originally as predestinationist as it reads to us. T. W. Manson, for example, sees here an original Aramaic particle which might mean both 'in order that' and a mere connecting relative 'for, if they did, they would.' Manson's theory may not be capable of strict proof, but it does suggest that there are working alternatives to Schweitzer's extreme interpretation.

iii. The suggestion that the Ethic of Jesus is an *Interimsethik* must be reserved for further consideration in the next chapter. It is enough to note here that, as a general rule, where the eschatology of Jesus is at a maximum, His ethical teaching does not appear rich and distinctive, and that in primarily ethical contexts the eschatology falls rather in the background.

iv. In the course of his theory Schweitzer finds it necessary to transpose the Confession of Caesarea Philippi and the Transfiguration. This is no casual alteration of order. It is necessary to fit into his predestinationist theory. But, as T. W. Manson has abundantly shown, the Marcan order here is not accidental; it is crucial to Mark's conception of the unfolding of the Ministry. A view which demands at such a place a necessary transposition is weakened and not strengthened by such an assumption.

Such criticism of details in Schweitzer's theory could be multiplied to wearisome length. It is more important at this stage to underline its importance as a document of its time than to refute its claim to represent the whole truth. It did call attention to the many passages in which the idea of the Kingdom was admittedly and clearly future in significance. It resembled nothing so much as a large stone cast into the middle of a stagnant pond with ripples extending over the whole surface. The interpretation of the Gospels could never be the same again, and most advances in the interpretation of the Gospels during the generation which followed should be studied in the light of the situation which Schweitzer created. If the picture of Jesus which Liberal Lives gave before Schweitzer could never explain why Jesus ever came to be crucified, Schweitzer's own interpretation—despite his own strange, eventful history—could assign no reason why Jesus should still be followed. Neither the gentle peasant teacher of Renan nor the eschatological stormtrooper of Schweitzer is satisfactory as an account of Jesus, and for precisely the same reason that they both overestimate some of the evidence and ignore the rest.

2. *The Kingdom of God conceived as a reality partly in the present but mostly in the future.* The first step forward from

Schweitzer's theory of Futurist eschatology was taken by
Rudolf Otto in his difficult but important work *The Kingdom
of God and the Son of Man*, which might be summarized as
'anticipated eschatology.'

Otto starts from the same premises as Schweitzer that the
primary sense to be given to the Kingdom of God is the
*eschaton*—the Divine consummation which in Hebrew expectation was to break into the world process as an act from God.
His picture of Jesus is, however, better shaped and less craggy
than that of Schweitzer. For Otto, Jesus is rather the dynamic
or charismatic evangelist than the preacher of the Last Things
Who believed their coming to be somehow associated with
His own mission. Jesus and John the Baptist are more correctly
contrasted than approximated. John is the successor of the
Old Testament prophets who proclaimed a Day of the Lord
for which preparation was to be made by repentance and by
participation in an eschatological sacrament. Repentance
before a great and terrible day of the Lord and the good news
of the Kingdom are not one thing but two.

Jesus does not come once merely in order to tell us that He
is coming again in the *Parousia*. His very presence, and the
acts of power which He does, are themselves the pledge and
earnest of that which shall be more fully hereafter. Indeed,
according to Otto, there is an exact parallel between the
concepts of the Kingdom of God and of the Son of Man. He
Who came is interpreted in similar fashion to that which
He brought. Otto offers a rather specialized interpretation of
the title 'Son of Man' based upon a debatable assumption of
the unity of 1 *Enoch* and a disputed reading in the last chapter
as representing the Messiah as 'present before His power.'
This offers certain suggestive interpretations of the title as used
by Jesus, though its basis is not sufficiently strong to make it
more than a possibility worthy of some consideration. In
similar fashion he interprets the Kingdom of God in the
Gospels as neither wholly present nor fully future but as
present 'before its power' or by anticipation. In this sense it
can be described as present with Jesus, but not as yet all that it
will be hereafter. Otto offers a correction of the usual descrip-

tion of the relation of Jesus to the Kingdom. Usually we speak as though He brought the Kingdom with Him; Otto thinks that the Kingdom brings Him with it. The dynamic Kingdom brings with it the dynamic man. Here there is certainly room for two opinions. The equation of discipleship of Himself with membership of the Kingdom which the latter half of St. Mark's Gospel increasingly suggests would not altogether support this view, and the fact that Jesus can apparently speak of 'My Kingdom' as well as of 'My Father's Kingdom' would again tell against this particular part of Otto's theory.

Otto, again, unlike Schweitzer, offers a careful exegesis of particular passages. He examines first the group of passages in which the Kingdom is said to have *eggiken*—'drawn near.' This word is the perfect indicative active of a verb meaning 'to draw near,' and therefore can in his opinion be best rendered 'has drawn near' or 'is on the threshold.' An alternative rendering might however be 'has drawn near and therefore has already come.' The distinction might be given somewhat as follows. I am sitting in my study awaiting the coming of a pupil at a certain hour. I hear a heavy footfall in the hall outside my study. The atmosphere is big with his coming. He has 'drawn near' in Otto's sense. He knocks at the door and comes in. All that there is of him confronts all that there is of me! That would be *eggiken* in the second sense.

A second saying which he analyses is the Q passage (*St. Matt.* xii. 28; *St. Luke* xi. 20) in which the exorcisms performed by Jesus are offered as evidence that the Kingdom of God *ephthasen* upon you. The word in question has an interesting history. It contains within itself the element of anticipation, of coming before the time expected. It might perhaps be appropriate as a description of a master coming back to his form-room before he was expected and finding perhaps what he deserves for such an inconsiderate act. Certainly the root idea of an anticipatory coming belonged to the word, at least in earlier times. It has, however, been urged, as we shall see later, that the usage at this period no longer suggests the idea of anticipation.

The third interesting passage upon which Otto has views of his own is the saying of Jesus, 'The Kingdom of Heaven suffereth violence and the violent take it by storm' (*St. Matt*. xi. 12; cp. *St. Luke* xvi. 16 Q). Here a word of explanation of the form of the Greek is unfortunately necessary. The Greek language, in addition to the active and passive moods well known in Latin and other languages, has a third mood called the middle mood which often bears the significance of a reflexive. In the present tense it is in form indistinguishable from the passive. *Biazetai*, which is the Greek here, might therefore grammatically be either middle or passive. Schweitzer takes it as passive and as meaning that 'violence is done to the Kingdom of God,' either by Jesus Himself or by those who received His message. Otto, however, treats the word as a middle, and interprets it along the lines of 'exercises its own appropriate force.' An illustration of the meaning might be of an approaching thunderstorm which makes its presence felt to those who are sensitive to its coming before it actually bursts. The atmosphere is big with its *dunamis* long before it actually breaks. Thus in the active and dynamic ministry of Jesus the Kingdom of Heaven exerts its force and forceful men take it by storm. An objection might be made against this interpretation that the three significant words in the Greek of the saying are words not merely of power and energy, but of violence and force. A suggested answer might well appeal to the general manner of the presentation of His teaching by Jesus. He was never afraid of an emphatic word when it served to make His meaning plain. No great teacher took so much trouble to give the meaning which he intended to convey with the greatest possible vividness. Even so, however, the idea of 'robbery with violence' contained in the last word still raises a problem.

Otto can still, with Schweitzer, agree that the Kingdom is not as yet all that it will be hereafter. It is still possible to make good sense of a saying like St. Mark ix. 1: 'There be some who shall not taste of death until they see the Kingdom of God come with power.' Parables of expectation, whether of judgement or of fulfilment, still convey their proper meaning. The only difference is that, for Otto, the evidence suggests that the Kingdom is already in some sense present.

This interpretation is in many respects most attractive, and for the first time we see a standpoint which might make good sense of the two strands in the evidence, which points to a present Kingdom as well as to one that is to come. It is only fair to point out, however, that, though Otto might well be right here, his is not the only interpretation of the crucial Greek phrases upon which so much of his theory depends. This would not affect the truth of his theory as against Schweitzer, for in each case the alternative rendering makes the Kingdom not less but more present than Otto suggests. Nor can we be altogether happy about the parallel interpretation of the title 'Son of Man' which appears to me to be more vulnerable than his theory with regard to the Kingdom of God. The impression which his theory leaves is rather that he has called attention correctly to both elements in a problem which had previously been attacked upon too narrow a frontage than that he has chosen the best possible way of expressing the most probable relationship between the two realities.

3. *The Kingdom of God conceived as a fact already realized in the Life and Person of our Lord.* This theory of 'realized eschatology,' powerfully and resourcefully urged by Professor Dodd, has always appeared to me rather the polar opposite of the theory of Schweitzer. It appears to carry the elements of 'realization' of the Kingdom (described as 'anticipations' in the previous theory) to a point at which they appear to occupy the centre of the stage to the exclusion of nearly everything else. The chief work in which this theory is set out is *The Parables of the Kingdom.*

Dodd first of all admits that both the strains of present and future thinking about the Kingdom are present within the Gospels. It is hard, for example, to resist the impression that the phrase 'receive the Kingdom' ought to be interpreted in terms of the acceptance of the Kingdom of God illustrated for the Old Testament Jew in submission to the Torah. There is also the future expectation, 'Thy Kingdom come.' When, however, Dodd turns to his exposition of the Gospels, it becomes plain that it is rather with the Kingdom of God considered as a present fact that he is chiefly concerned. The Kingdom is indeed still *to eschaton*—the ultimate and decisive thing—but it is *to eschaton* which has appeared critically and decisively with Christ, not anticipatorily as in Otto, but all that there is of it. No doubt there may one day be a consummation in the sense of a completion, but that will be not so much the coming as the fulfilment of the Kingdom. This theory is powerfully and spiritually urged; we must, however, see what evidence is adduced in its support.

Dodd begins with two good and early passages (from Q), neither of which mentions the Kingdom of God but both of which emphasize the sense of achievement which marks the teaching of Jesus. The first passage (*St. Matt.* xiii. 16-17; *St. Luke* x. 23-4) contrasts the expectation of the great ones of the Old Testament with the privileges enjoyed by the disciples in the New Testament. They see what others had desired to see, for 'something greater than Solomon is here.' Dodd interprets this 'something greater' as the Kingdom of God. Again, in answer to the anxious question of the Baptist (*St. Matt.* xi. 2-11; *St. Luke* vii. 18-30), Jesus points to the events which are actually happening in His own Ministry and which had been in the past expected to take place when the Divine inbreaking into human life occurred. It would be natural to interpret these events as evidence that the Kingdom has already come. Against this background he sets the passages which Otto has already cited as evidence for a kind of anticipatory coming of the Kingdom. Thus he interprets *eggiken* as meaning not 'on the threshold' or as 'almost here' but as 'already arrived,' and in the light of the Septuagint and of the usage in modern colloquial Greek purges the last traces of anticipatory coming out of *ephthasen*. He can with obvious truth appeal to St. Luke xvii. 20-1, 'The Kingdom of God is within [or among] you,' in support of his theory, and presses the literal meaning of the participle in St. Mark

ix. 1, 'Until they see the Kingdom of God having come with power.'

At this point Professor Dodd turns to a consideration of the evidence which has often been urged in support of the idea that the Kingdom of God is something which should come in the future and tries to explain it in the light of his own theory. At the outset he lays down two principles each of which needs a short explanation.

i. It is certainly clear that some of the New Testament writers look for the future coming of the Kingdom in terms which do not suggest that they held this theory of 'realized eschatology.' This obviously raises a difficulty which Dodd tries to meet in the following manner. There is, first, no difficulty in believing that Jesus, Who was hailed as a prophet during His lifetime, predicted the coming of certain events which were to happen in the future. Among these was the final doom of His own people. It is possible that He thought that this would happen shortly after His own death although in fact anything that might be claimed as a direct fulfilment did not take place until A.D. 70, when the Roman armies brought a disastrous war to an end by the capture of Jerusalem under Titus. As the period of non-fulfilment lengthened, it was natural that the Church should set the prophetic message of Jesus in an eschatological setting on the analogy of the apocalyptic literature. For Jesus, however, what mattered was rather the principle which He was predicating than the time factor involved in its fulfilment.

ii. Dodd now turns to the parables, of which some at least (those which speak of judgement and fulfilment) do not as they stand really support his theory, while others (concerned with growth) point to a future consummation as well as to a present condition. Here he employs a technique with which Form Criticism has already made us familiar. The Form Critics have much to say about the Setting in Life or *Sitz im Leben* of the Gospel material. While, however, they frequently find the Setting in Life in the condition of the Apostolic Church, Dodd prefers with greater probability to find this in the earthly Ministry of Jesus Himself. On the other hand, he does not hesitate to alter the Setting in Life of the parables in question. While the Evangelists imply that these parables point to a consummation far in the future, Dodd inclines to the view that as originally used by Jesus they all pointed to a situation which fell entirely within the earthly life of the Master Himself. Thus he interprets parables of judgement somewhat along the lines of the Fourth Evangelist. The Judgement which Jesus has in mind in these parables is not a world judgement at the latter end of history but the crisis which the challenge for decision aroused in Galilee and Jerusalem. The parables of effort are to be seen in the same context. His service and the life to which it leads is the Pearl of Great Price and the Hid Treasure. The man who hid his talent in a napkin and buried it in the ground is the pious Jew of undoubted, if sterile, piety. Watchfulness is an attitude which was no less appropriate to the Ministry of Jesus with its call to discipleship than to the period before the Great Assize. The Marriage Feast is the Kingdom which has already been realized in the coming of Jesus, while the growth to which other parables refer reminds us of the Lord Who already in the days of His flesh had spoken to His disciples of fields which were 'white already to harvest.'

It is always regrettable to have to differ from a writer of the distinction of Professor Dodd, whose work on the New Testament has put all scholars so much in his debt; but there are reasons which prevent us from accepting the complete adequacy of his interpretation here.

i. His rendering of the crucial Greek words was challenged by J. Y. Campbell in the *Expository Times*, Volume XLVIII, pp. 91–4, and although Professor Dodd replied in the next number, it is clear that his interpretation of them is at least not the only one possible.

ii. A theory which demands the alteration of the setting of so much Gospel material can hardly be regarded as impregnable. It is true that Dodd can often see small indications in the passages in question which appear to favour his view; there is, however, often little reason, apart from the theory in the interests of which they are made, to make them probable.

They are no doubt possible; none of them can be regarded as unworthy of Jesus Himself. The fact is that the Evangelists put them in a different setting and that this setting is equally significant and possible. In such a case, where the possibilities are about equally balanced, it is surely reasonable to retain the interpretation by the Evangelists themselves, who are, after all, our earliest commentators and witnesses to the Intention of Jesus. There is little doubt that among the possible meanings of the phrase 'the Kingdom of God' in the Gospels is included the significance of 'realized eschatology' assigned to it by Dr. Dodd. There is, however, far more reason for hesitation in the attempt to reduce all the strands in the teaching of Jesus to this single one. In the light of the evidence we can still ask whether this is all that Jesus meant.

iii. Dr. Dodd does not appear to give a very plausible account of the changing focus of thinking about eschatology in the early period. The facts are as follows. On his theory, Jesus uniformly taught a 'realized eschatology.' But the earliest disciples of Jesus in the pre-literary period of Gospel tradition (on the evidence collected in Dodd's earlier work, *The Apostolic Preaching and its Development*) maintained a futurist eschatology. This is also evidenced in the earliest period of Pauline teaching, though the later Pauline letters and the Johannine Gospel mark a swing back to realized eschatology. The Fathers uniformly and from the earliest times hold, on the other hand, a futurist eschatology. On Dodd's theory there are two weaknesses in this suggested development which is curious enough in all conscience. It is first of all difficult to see why the earliest Christians, who did not number many men of original power or creative interpretation among them (apart from St. Paul who in his earlier period agreed with them), should so quickly lose the real clue to the teaching of Jesus, and offer an interpretation of His teaching in another idiom. It is worth while to reflect that the teaching so modified was that of their Master Himself. Nor at a different stage in the ladder of development is it easy to see why the insight into 'realized eschatology,' recaptured on Dodd's theory by the later New Testament writers, was not held by the earliest

Fathers. Is not the whole map of development better accounted for by the hypothesis that Jesus taught both realized and futurist eschatology, and that a selection of these elements was made by those who came afterwards according to their lights? It is really very difficult to assign any satisfactory reason why St. Paul and St. Matthew (for example) should hold a futurist eschatology and our Lord be a total stranger to this method of thinking.

iv. Some of Professor Dodd's interpretations with regard to judgement seem almost to lift Jesus out of the context of the Judaism in which He was cradled. For the Hebrew, deep theological principles were always expressed in terms of fore-sight; whereas for the Greek, the same subject-matter would be expressed in terms of insight. For a Hebrew the meaning of history was normally expressed in terms of End-History. This is, after all, the root significance of eschatology. It would, then, be wholly in character that Jesus should have expressed the principle of judgement by means of the idea of a world judgement. No doubt the interpretation which Dr. Dodd offers of judgement would be what the teaching of Jesus amounted to as seen through Greek, or even through modern, eyes. It is a legitimate interpretation of what Jesus said; it is, however, to be doubted whether it is what Jesus actually meant. Here the natural interpretation of the parables in question is much to be preferred to the ingenious alteration of their setting in life suggested by Dr. Dodd.

At this point it will be well to pause in our argument and to take stock of the conclusions which we have so far been able to reach.

i. We have agreed with Schweitzer that there are elements which suggest the idea of a future coming of the Kingdom, though denying that this is the sole clue which enables all the pieces in the jigsaw to fall easily into place.

ii. We have equally seen reason, with Dodd, to maintain that there are also passages which suggest that the Kingdom is also present with Jesus—the theory of 'realized eschatology'— though we have criticized the attempt to make all the evidence support this conclusion.

Can any attempt be made to work these two statements into some sort of consistent whole?

I think it possible that we can, especially in view of the evidence that within the literature of Judaism both conceptions were already present. There is no need to quote passages which indicate belief in a future coming of the Kingdom. The rabbis apparently also understood the phrase 'to receive the *Malkuth Jahveh*' of the present acceptance of the absolute authority of the *Torah*. That Jesus should be the heir of both traditions of thinking in view of the fact that He was, and knew Himself to be, the heir of the spiritual heritage of Judaism, raises no insuperable difficulties. To receive the Kingdom was for a follower of Him tantamount to the full acceptance of discipleship of Himself, whereas the new thing, eschatologically speaking, which He brought with Him was the conviction that the final hope was somehow centred in Himself as well. There is as little difficulty in seeing Jesus as the heir of the Apocalyptic Movement as in tracing its influence upon St. Paul or St. Matthew. The tradition of a coming Kingdom was taken over from Judaism, with the significant differences that the coming One was Jesus Himself, and that what He was to bring was in some way continuous with what He had already brought.

The same result appears to follow from another method of inquiry. If we take the three main groups of parables in question and interpret them in their Gospel setting according to their natural sense, we find that, although they point more directly to one conclusion than another, they possess, as it were, tenons which dovetail into the mortices provided by the other view. Parables of growth, no doubt, have their foreground in the presence of the Kingdom as a seed. But the picture which they give does not in fact stop there. The farmer sows seed broadcast which produces different crops. The tiny mustard seed becomes a plant with spreading shoots. Wheat and tares grow together until the harvest. The leaven works until it permeates the whole dough; parables of effort speak no less of future consummation than of present risk. Stewardship combines the notions of present responsibility and of future joy.

Nor again is the position different with the parables which are normally taken as pointing most unmistakably to the future. Parables of judgement direct our thoughts to a Future Assize, but they are linked to the present by the fact that the criterion of judgement is an attitude taken up now 'in My Name' or 'because they believe in ME.' The Judge is one Who is known here and now. Parables of fulfilment have a similar connotation. No doubt the Wedding Feast of the Messianic Age is still in the future; but the disciples are already Sons of the Bridechamber, and the Messianic Banquet is certainly anticipated in the Last Supper and possibly also in the Feeding of the Thousands as well.

How, then, are the two poles of Presence and Futurity related in the Gospels? Here we must walk less confidently, for Jesus was much more than a systematizer even of His own opinions. T. W. Manson, in his work *The Teaching of Jesus*, suggests a development of the thought of Jesus marked by the watershed of the Confession at Caesarea Philippi. This works well enough for St. Mark, but in the nature of the case is increasingly difficult to detect in the other Gospel sources. We have, for example, no warrant for believing that Q, the most probable of the other sources inferred by Streeter, had a sufficient background of incident to make such a criterion probable. In any case, T. W. Manson offers at best a genetic rather than a systematic approach. Otto, as we have seen, still gives the priority to the Futurist conception of the Kingdom and thus speaks of anticipation. If our starting point is rather nearer to that of Professor Dodd, we might prefer to use a term suggested by the parables of growth, and to speak of the Kingdom not as anticipated but rather as present, as it were, germinally or in principle. In this sense it is already here in the Ministry of Jesus; we do not, however, as yet see it in fulfilment or in consummation, but we know that, whether in principle or in completion, it is centred in Him; and that is well, for He Who is in both senses Lord of the Kingdom is also by that very token the present Master of His disciples.

It remains to examine briefly two further questions about the Kingdom in the Teaching of Jesus. We have so far discussed its character as both present and future and stressed its primary meaning as the Rule of God. We have concluded that it can be described as both present and future. It is both inward and spiritual, and outward and corporate.

Its inward and spiritual character goes almost without saying. It is clearly evidenced by St. Luke xvii. 20–1. The Greek preposition used here is not without difficulty. It might mean either 'within' or 'among,' but Dr. Dodd has given convincing reasons in favour of the former meaning. To go no further than its immediate context, it would be difficult to see on what grounds the statements 'Lo here' and 'Lo there' could be excluded if the phrase meant 'among you' or 'in your midst.' There is ample confirmation of the inwardness of the Kingdom in its close association with discipleship of Jesus Himself.

In what sense, however, can we speak of the corporate aspect of the Kingdom? Modern scholarship has vindicated the interpretation of the Kingdom as the Rule of God. Yet obviously, at least as corollary, this implies a Realm in which this Rule was to be exercised. If the Rule is so central a feature of the teaching of Jesus, it would be surprising if the Realm were to fall completely outside His purview. Fuller consideration of the place which the community takes in the teaching of Jesus will be the principal theme of our next chapter.

Just as we found that the title 'Son of Man,' though central to the self-designation of Jesus in the Gospels, fell rather out of account in Apostolic times, we shall find a similar fate befall the concept of the Kingdom of God. A solution to this obvious difficulty is suggested by Dr. Newton Flew in his book *The Christian Idea of Perfection*. He suggests with much probability that the rest of the New Testament is devoted not to a repetition of the teaching of Jesus about the Kingdom, but to a further examination of its implicates. These, in fact, stretch far more widely even than the term itself to cover every field of Christian thought and experience. It implies, first, a

Theology and a Christology. Who is the King of the Kingdom, and what in the Rule itself makes its message good and not bad news? That implies the whole weight of the Christian doctrine of God. Again, if Christ is the bringer of the Kingdom and teaches with such range and penetration about it, Who, then, is Christ? Thus we are led into the sphere of Christology. Again, Rule implies Realm and we are therefore brought face to face with the doctrine of the Church. And if those who belong to this Realm are men, who, then, are they, and by what means can they pass within it? So finally we pass to the doctrines of man and of salvation. But all these are the great cardinal themes of the theology of the Apostolic Age, which is occupied not with a mere repetition of the teaching of Jesus on the subject of the Kingdom but with the further exploration of the hinterland which lies behind it.

## BIBLIOGRAPHY

A. Schweitzer, *The Quest of the Historical Jesus.*
R. Otto, *The Kingdom of God and the Son of Man.*
C. H. Dodd, *Parables of the Kingdom.*
T. W. Manson, *The Teaching of Jesus.*
R. Newton Flew, *The Christian Idea of Perfection*, Chapter i.

## CHAPTER X

## THE BELOVED COMMUNITY

OF recent years there has been much debate on the question whether the foundation of a Church formed part of the Intention of Jesus. The belief that it did was regarded as axiomatic during the period in which the propositional infallibility of the Bible was taken for granted. Two sayings of Jesus recorded in St. Matthew's Gospel (xvi. 18 and xviii. 17) gave it express warrant, and substance was added to this rather slender store by the equation between the Church and the Kingdom which was current from the days of St. Augustine onwards. It was further believed during the same period in all parts of Christendom that from the New Testament as a whole a detailed and necessary pattern for Church Order and organization could be safely derived.

The development of modern critical method and its application to the New Testament led to a certain shaking of this assurance. It was realized that the equation 'Kingdom of God' and 'Church' was not as convincing as had previously been thought, and debate focused upon the authenticity of the two explicit sayings on the Church recorded in the First Gospel. A decided preference was enunciated for the material contained in the early sources, St. Mark and Q (so far as the latter could be inferred), while particular hesitation was often felt with regard to material contained in St. Matthew alone. The extreme eschatological school doubted whether, in view of the speedy *Parousia* which our Lord was deemed to have expected, He could have had any concern for the establishment of a community to carry on His work; while the theological Liberals, as represented by Harnack, regarded it almost as a dogma that the idea of a Church could not possibly have formed part of the teaching of Jesus.

In recent years there has been a slow though steady return

towards the older position, though as yet there appears to be no tendency for the wheel to turn anything like full-circle. While there has been no retreat from the interpretation of the Kingdom of God as the Rule rather than the Realm of God, it has been noted with increasing emphasis that the secondary notion of a Realm cannot be completely excluded from the picture. Even the extreme eschatological school has come to realize that the question of the approaching date of the *Parousia* is virtually irrelevant to the question, since a community of the saved is not unlikely whatever the date of the *Parousia* might have been deemed to be. If the difficulties over the two passages which mention the actual word 'Church' have not been completely dispelled, a number of other passages which are not critically under suspicion have been examined which give general support to the belief that in some sense the Church formed part of the teaching and therefore of the Intention of Jesus.

Before we turn to the evidence in the light of recent discussion, it is well to pause and to dispel a possible ambiguity at the outset. The question, 'Did Jesus found the Church?' is capable of a wider and a narrower range. If we mean, 'Did Jesus intend that His mission and message should be enshrined and mediated in a community living under His allegiance?' we can with great probability give the answer 'Yes.' If, however, we identify the Church as He envisaged it with any particular body of Christians living now, and take it to include the sum-total of their beliefs and practices, we are compelled to answer 'No.' The plain fact is that even at the most optimistic estimate of the sources we cannot secure Gospel warrant for everything that we as members of the Christian Church rightly value to-day. We may well come to conclude in our examination of the Ethical Teaching of Jesus in our next chapter that the teaching of Jesus here also, while basic, definitive, and fundamental, is not of this order.

If this be true, we must beware of two equal and opposite errors. The first would be to take an affirmative answer to the question whether Jesus envisaged a Church as implying automatically that this Church represented in its totality the branch of the Christian Church which we most greatly value ourselves. That would be to commit the logical fallacy of taking the part for the whole: it would also ignore the part played by Christian history in the evolution of the forms of thought, worship, and order which we rightly value to-day. But the second would be an even greater fallacy. It would run roughly as follows. It would imply that since the Church as Jesus envisaged it could not be identified with any single Christian denomination known to-day we should be entitled either to weaken our allegiance to any of these denominations, or to abandon them in the supposed interests of a pure Church or a ghost Church as founded by Jesus Himself. Such an attitude, whichever of the two forms it took, would virtually result in the abandonment of Christian history and lead to a form of 'archaism' as dangerous as it might be attractive to some minds. It does not fall to this particular study to analyse even in outline the answer to this problem, but those who wish to justify the principle of development are not left without an answer. We must not, in assessing the Intention of our Lord with respect to the Church, neglect the work of the Holy Spirit within the community which depends upon both alike.

We must first examine the evidence on which it is believed that the foundation of the Church can in the sense already given be ascribed to the Mind and Intention of our Lord.

We can begin with certain aspects of the teaching of Jesus with regard to the Kingdom. There are, first, parables of the Kingdom which imply (whether as the primary part of their teaching or as a secondary implication) that it has a corporate reference. Two Matthaean parables, the Drag-net (St. Matt. xiii. 47–50) and the Wheat and the Tares (xiii. 24–30), both depend directly upon this corporate conception of the Kingdom. Granted that there is to be in each parable a future act of judgement, in the one case discriminating between the fish and in the other case between the wheat and the tares, it is still clear that a present mixed community is being described. If it is objected that both these parables occur only in Matthew, a similar implication is to be found in two Marcan parables.

The first is the Parable of the Mustard Seed (*St. Mark* iv. 30-2; *St. Matt.* xiii. 31-2; *St. Luke* xiii. 18-19) which, while primarily concerned with the rapid growth of the immanent Kingdom, makes a strong point of its extension as a spreading shrub in the shadow of which the birds of heaven can rest. The comparison of a community with a growing plant is a familiar piece of Old Testament symbolism. The fact that St. Matthew places this parable in sequence with the Parables of the Drag-net and the Field with Tares and the Wheat shows that the First Evangelist certainly understood it in this sense. The second Marcan parable affords perhaps less obvious evidence, but its corporate direction is still plain enough. It is the Parable of the Workers in the Vineyard (*St. Mark* xii. 1-12; *St. Matt.* xxi. 33-46; *St. Luke* xx. 9-18).

Again, the phrase to 'enter the Kingdom of God' is a common one in the Gospels. Not every passage refers naturally to a present society but, whether the immediate reference is present or future, the idea of a corporate whole is clearly present. It is impossible to enter a Rule; it must be extended into a Realm before there can be any question of entering in. The passages in which the present connotation of the phrase is most clear are four in number. We can begin with St. Matthew xxi. 31: 'Verily I say unto you that tax-gatherers and harlots enter the Kingdom of God before you.' The passage is certainly unsupported Matthew, but its whole ring is authentic and is worthy of note as one of the few passages in which St. Matthew has retained the more primitive term, 'Kingdom of God,' instead of his more customary variant 'Kingdom of Heaven.' It is just possible that the passage is a prophetic present, or virtually a concealed future; but it is true to the conditions of the earthly ministry of the Master and may be taken as present. The second passage is St. Luke xvi. 16 (with its parallel in St. Matthew xi. 12): 'From that time [the days of John the Baptist] the Kingdom of God is preached and every one enters violently into it.' The contrast between Jesus and John the Baptist, between Then and Now, makes it quite clear that a present reality is in question. St. Matthew xxiii. 13 (with its parallel passage in St. Luke xi. 52) is probably a Q passage, though the original form of the saying cannot be now recovered. In the Matthaean form of the saying the scribes and Pharisees are rebuked because they shut the Kingdom of Heaven against men; that is, presumably prevent their disciples from entering the Kingdom of Heaven as offered by Jesus. Luke puts the same point even more fully in terms which suggest the Kingdom of God as a present reality: 'Woe unto you lawyers! because ye have taken away the key of knowledge; ye enter not in yourselves and ye hindered those who were entering.'

The remaining passages in which the phrase 'to enter the Kingdom of Heaven' occurs, while not being any the less corporate, all appear to refer to a future reality. Thus St. Mark x. 14–15 speaks of the little child: 'Whosoever shall not receive the Kingdom of God as a little child, he shall in no wise enter therein.' (There are close parallels both in Matthew and Luke.) No doubt the spiritual condition is a present and permanent requirement, but the main reference of the phrase which we are studying here is to the future. This is even clearer in St. Mark ix. 47: 'It is good to enter into the Kingdom of God with one eye than having two eyes to be cast into Gehenna.' (St. Matthew replaces the term 'Kingdom of God' by 'Life,' thus making clear the eschatological and future reference of the saying.) A third Matthaean passage, St. Matthew vii. 21, again clearly refers to the future: 'Not every one that saith unto Me, Lord, Lord, shall enter into the Kingdom of Heaven.' The Lucan parallel (vi. 46): 'Why do ye call Me, Lord, Lord, and omit to do what I say?' obviously extends the meaning of the passage to the present, but omits all reference to entrance into the Kingdom of Heaven.

Moreover, passages which speak of rank with regard to the Kingdom of God must clearly refer to a corporate whole in which this should be exercised, though here again it is not quite certain whether it is to a present or to a future reality to which it points. Thus, for example, the Q passage (St. Matt. xi. 11; St. Luke vii. 28) runs in the Matthaean version: 'Verily I say unto you, there has not arisen among those born of women a greater than John the Baptist, nevertheless he that is least in the Kingdom of Heaven is greater than he!' It is difficult to believe that Jesus is here thinking of the Final Consummated Kingdom of the Blessed rather than of a present corporate reality. It is probable, though not certain, that a Matthaean passage (v. 19): 'Whosoever shall loose the least of these commandments and teach men so, shall be called least in the Kingdom of Heaven, but whosoever shall do and teach them, he shall be called great in the Kingdom of Heaven,' should be similarly interpreted.

The best commentary on this passage is the Marcan saying (x. 43): 'Whosoever shall be great among you shall be your servant, and whosoever shall be first among you shall be servant of all' (with its parallels in St. Matthew xx. 26-7 and St. Luke xxii. 26, where 'least' and 'greatest' would appear to be identical with greatest and least in the Kingdom of God). It is further just worthy of notice that Jesus in His reply to the request to the two sons of Zebedee for places of pre-eminence in the coming Kingdom does not deny that such places of honour may exist, but asserts that they cannot be bespoken in advance and remain at the Father's disposal. While the disciples certainly and Jesus probably were thinking here of a future Kingdom, Jesus focuses their attention on the conditions of discipleship here on earth (St. Mark x. 35-45; St. Matt. xx. 20-8).

It is clear, then, that there exists some evidence for the social reference of the Kingdom even in the words and phrases used of it in the Gospels. It must be admitted that this significance is neither central nor dominant, but this serves only to throw into stronger relief the fact that it exists at all. While, as we should expect, Matthaean passages predominate, this strain of teaching is not confined to St. Matthew's Gospel, and while we might suspect it if it were confined to the First Gospel, in view of the ecclesiastical bias of its author, the supporting passages from other Gospels suggest rather that this represents a strain in the teaching which Matthew rather preserved because he appreciated its significance than invented to suit his particular purpose.

When we turn to wider considerations, the difficulty lies

rather in the selection rather than in the discovery of material to our purpose. It would be possible, for instance, to take aspect after aspect of the Teaching of Jesus and to show that each implies for its fullest understanding a social or corporate significance. It could be urged, for example, that the very proclamation of the Gospel implies an association in which this is done and which may even be itself constituted by this proclamation. The Ethics of Jesus are not complete without a community in which they are practised in the power of the Spirit. The reader may well be left to assess the weight of such considerations for himself since they represent rather contributory evidence converging towards a solution than the principal evidence itself. We can, however, select four pieces of evidence which point directly to the conclusion that the foundation of the Church was not foreign to the mind of Christ.

i. Our Lord uses metaphors and images drawn from the Old Testament where the corporate connotation is clearly marked. Thus in St. Luke xii. 32 there occurs a saying which sounds clearly authentic: 'Fear not, little flock, it is your Father's good pleasure to give you the Kingdom.' The comparison of the ruler to a shepherd is familiar to every reader of the Old Testament. 'Woe to the shepherds of Israel,' declaims Ezekiel (xxxiv. 2) against the rulers of Judah; while even outside Israel, in Egypt, the shepherd's crook shares with the flail or the dominion the privilege of being the insignia of the Pharaoh. It is not improbable that the expression 'little flock' is intended to recall the Faithful Remnant of the Old Testament—the nucleus in which the full purpose of God for His people was to be realized. We have already drawn attention to the corporate intention behind the Parable of the Vineyard in St. Mark xii, with its close parallels in both the other Synoptic Gospels (St. Mark xii. 1–9; St. Matt. xxi. 33–46; St. Luke xx. 9–19), where the natural Old Testament parallel is the Song of the Vineyard in Isaiah v. 1–6. Both these images of the Flock and the Vineyard are caught up and handled in his own characteristic way by the writer of the Fourth Gospel in the allegories of the Good Shepherd (St. John x. 1–18) and the

True Vine (*St. John* xv. 1-8). It is clear also that the fig tree was taken by Jesus as an image of the nation, whether expressed in undoubtedly parabolic form in St. Luke xiii. 6 or in the story of the Cursing of the Fig Tree, where it is an open question whether we are presented with a parable misunderstood as a miracle or with a symbolic action of the type of a prophetic *ôth*. While it is clear that in this passage it is the old Israel rather than the new which is in question, the comparison of the nation with a growing thing throws a clear and strong light upon the use of similar metaphors to describe the Church. The argument is not that in all cases which we have quoted Jesus is describing the Church, but that in the images which He uses the old Israel and the Church appear to be in some sense continuous with each other. Here, but not here alone, Jesus appears to start from the old Israel and to pass with complete ease of transition to the true or the new Israel which His Church constituted. The natural link between the old and the new is given by the idea of the Remnant, which even in the Old Testament proved the soul or nucleus of the whole people of God. That the Remnant or nucleus is in His mind is proved by the image of the 'little flock.' The Vineyard, the inheritance of Israel of old, is taken away from them and given to others. The True Vine is the inexpressibly close relationship of Christ and His own. The Fig Tree, on which our Lord expected to find fruit, bears nothing but leaves and is destroyed in consequence. We are still without the express description of the Church as the Israel of God which St. Paul gives us in Galatians vi. 16, nor have we the further, though perhaps slightly dubious, horticulture of the ingrafting of the new into the old which again forms part of the Pauline extension of this theme. As Jesus, like some new Moses, at once supersedes and fulfils the Law, so the Church, the new Israel, alike replaces and completes the old. Once again, as in the Old Testament pattern of Divine Action, God's Election is once more by Selection from within a wider possibility of choice.

ii. The corporate aspect of the work of Christ is also strongly suggested by the titles which were used of His Person and work. The Old Testament Messiah was a figure closely connected with the National Hope; his very title would be meaningless without the community in which he is set. The point is significant, even if it is admitted that the title is rather one used of Jesus than by Jesus. The title 'Son of Man,' even if we reject, as we are almost bound to do, the corporate interpretation given to the title in the Gospels by Professor T. W. Manson, has at least a corporate background. In Daniel, for instance, the title either means the idealized Israel seen as a whole against its supernatural setting, or the faithful nucleus of the Hebrew people standing firmly against their Hellenistic opponents. But the concept which most deeply influenced the thought of Jesus is the Servant of the Songs embedded in the work of Second Isaiah. Here again the corporate interpretation, whether of the nation as a whole or of the faithful remnant in particular, forms at least one ingredient in the author's mind.

iii. Even more cogent evidence is the selection of twelve men 'that they might be with Him and that He might send them forth' (*St. Mark* iii. 14). The number twelve is neither casual nor ill-chosen. It does not appear very likely that twelve were called merely because there were more than eleven or less than thirteen from whom Jesus could choose, or upon whom He could rely. The number is surely directly connected with the Twelve Tribes of Israel. This connexion is actually made explicit in a passage which occurs in slightly different forms in Matthew and Luke and which therefore probably has a basis in Q. In St. Matthew xix. 28 it runs: 'Verily I say unto you, that ye who have followed Me, in the regeneration when the Son of Man shall sit upon the throne of His Glory, ye also shall sit upon twelve thrones, judging the twelve tribes of Israel.' Luke merely states that 'ye shall sit upon thrones, judging the twelve tribes of Israel' (*St. Luke* xxii. 30), but the differences are purely verbal and non-significant. But it might also be urged that the twelve are not merely to act as judges of the twelve tribes at the Consummation; they have also a present function within the new Israel. They are either, in a metaphor suggested by military service, 'the right markers of the new Israel,' or in the more dignified phrase of John Wick Bowman, 'the nuclear Israel.' Long ago, in his fine study *The Christian Ecclesia*, Hort had said of the Apostles at the Last Supper, 'They sat there that evening as the representatives of the *Ecclesia* at large.'

iv. The idea of Covenant, as contained in the teaching and mission of Jesus, not only has roots which reach far back into the past, but also a corporate significance. Indeed, it might not be too much to say that it was the Sinai-Horeb Covenant which made Israel, a loose confederacy of tribes, into the people of God. The idea of Covenant is deepened in the new Covenant passage in Jeremiah xxxi. 31, while twice in the Servant Songs the Servant is described as a covenant of the people (*Isa.* xlii. 6–7 and xlix. 8–9). It would indeed be strange if Jesus, when He gave the blood of the new Covenant to His disciples, had taken no thought for the community within which that covenant obtained.

We are now in a position to turn to the vexed question of the two passages in the Gospels in which the actual term *Ecclesia* occurs. The former occurs in St. Matthew xvi. 17–19, the famous *Tu es Petrus* passage upon which probably more ink has been spilt than upon any other single passage in the New Testament. It may perhaps be rendered as follows:

17. Jesus answered and said unto him: Blessed art thou, Simon bar Jonah, for flesh and blood did not reveal it to thee, but My Father Who is in Heaven.

18. And I too say unto thee that thou art Peter and upon this Petra [*rock*] I will build My Church, and the gates of Hades shall not prevail against it.

19. I will give to thee the keys of the Kingdom of Heaven: and whatsoever thou shalt bind on earth shall be bound in heaven: and whatsoever thou shalt loose on earth shall be loosed in heaven.

The authenticity of this passage has been challenged on important grounds. Textually there seems no reason to dispute its authenticity as part of the text of the First Gospel; historically, however, doubts have been raised on three main grounds.

i. It occurs merely in the material special to St. Matthew's Gospel. This is not sufficient, as it stands, to suggest critical doubts, though it must be admitted that scholars have tended, including Burkitt and Streeter, to prefer material derived from the earlier sources of Mark and Q. Such a preference is not, however, incompatible with the belief that both in Matthew and in Luke alone are preserved material which can legitimately be claimed as authentic.

ii. It occurs in a Matthaean supplement to Mark. This is a more serious ground, since, in some cases at least, there is reason to believe that Matthew treats his supplements to Mark less as supplementary information than as Targum (explanatory paraphrases) embodied in the text.

iii. It forms one of three supplements devoted to St. Peter. The first occurs in St. Matthew xiv. 28-33, an addition to the Matthaean parallel to St. Mark vi. 45-52, of the historicity of which it is not possible to be as positive as we could wish. The third occurs in the incident of the stater in the mouth of the fish (*St. Matt.* xvii. 24-7), where it is possible to detect at least a certain amount of imaginative embroidery. The company kept by this passage does not dispel the mists of critical doubt.

It will shortly be seen that the whole tone of the passage is strongly Jewish in character. While, however, in another Gospel that might be a strong indication of authenticity, it fits in so well with the general background of Matthew as to leave open the question whether we are presented with a Targum by the Evangelist or with otherwise unrecorded words of the Master Himself.

The passage opens with the only recorded Beatitude in the Gospels addressed to an individual. St. Peter is addressed by his patronymic, a slightly formal manner of address suitable for so solemn an occasion. The saying affirms that his confession of our Lord was due to direct revelation, and continues by offering a corresponding revelation of Peter's own position within the Christian community. Much emphasis is thrown upon the name given to St. Peter. In Biblical theology the name had a more important role than it possesses in modern times. Originally the knowledge of the name gave a certain magical power over the one who bore it. Thus supernatural beings refused to give their names to men (*Gen.* xxxii. 29;

*Judges* xiii. 18). The names given by prophets like Hosea and Isaiah to their children were of the order of prophetic symbols which not only signified, but also contributed to, the woe or the weal which they denoted (*Hos.* i. 4–9; *Isa.* vii. 3, viii. 1, cp. vii. 14).

The name Peter or Cephas in Aramaic had previously been given to Simon (*St. Mark* iii. 16; *St. Matt.* x. 2; *St. Luke* vi. 14; *St. John* i. 40), though perhaps we should naturally deduce from this passage if it stood alone that our Lord was giving the name for the first time. Its relevance to Simon is not at first sight obvious. Rocks and fishes do not go naturally together. It is possible that he was so named because he was such an inveterate wobbler by nature, much as a six-footer may receive the nickname 'Tiny.' The play upon words here is even clearer in the Aramaic than in the Greek, for Cephas would cover both the name given to Peter and the stone with which it is glossed. The awkward change of gender in the Greek upon which many exegetes have raised houses of cards disappears in Aramaic.

The Rock is probably Peter himself, though a case might be made out for Peter's confession or Peter's faith. We cannot from this passage as it stands decide whether it is Peter as a private individual, or as representing the Twelve, or as the recipient of a special and unique prerogative, who is here in question. It seems impossible to take the Rock as meaning the Master Himself, since Jesus is Himself the speaker and such an interpretation would make a most awkward break in the sense. The idea is thoroughly Jewish and a very close parallel occurs in the Midrash (running commentary) on Deuteronomy. The passage runs as follows: 'When the Holy One wanted to create the world, He passed over the generations of Enoch and the Flood as unsound, but when He saw Abraham who was going to arise, He said "Lo, I have discovered a Petra upon which to build and to found the world." Therefore He called Abraham a Rock, as it is said "Look unto the Rock whence ye were hewn" ' (*Isa.* li. 1). While there is no reason to believe that either Jesus or the author of the First Gospel had this passage in mind, the parallel suggests that Peter is here designated the Forefather of the new Israel.

Upon this Rock the Church is built. While there is no agreement as to the exact Aramaic word which might have been used here, there is no lack of such words which might have been used: *qahal*, perhaps, or even *kenishta*. The shade of meaning which is conveyed here is clearly the Church Universal rather than the local congregational unit. It is further promised that the gates of Hades shall not prevail against it. Over against the House of God is set the house of Hades. If the word 'Hades' is strictly used, this means the place of the departed, and not the home of the Satanic powers which would be rendered Gehenna and is actually so rendered in other contexts by Matthew. In Babylonian thought the place of the underworld, Arallu, is represented as a walled city having seven walls and seven gates with bolts and bars. This way of depicting 'that undiscovered country from whose bourn no traveller returns' is also characteristic of Hebrew poetry (gates in *Isa.* xxxviii. 10, *Job* xxxviii. 17; bars in *Job* xvii. 16; *Ps.* ix. 13, cvii. 18). The primary meaning appears therefore to be rather the perpetuity of the Church than its victory over the mighty powers of Hell. Though it is probable that the one implies the other, a careful exegesis would beware of reading too much into the passage.

The passage continues with the grant of the 'power of the keys.' This has traditionally and popularly been understood as giving to St. Peter the role of doorkeeper in the Heavenly Kingdom, with the right to admit or to exclude to that Kingdom. It would be going too far to exclude this idea completely from the present passage, but the Old Testament background suggests a different explanation. If the thought of the future Kingdom may not be excluded altogether from the passage, it is nevertheless the present Church which appears to be more in the Evangelist's mind. The nearest Biblical parallel is Isaiah xxii. 22, where the replacement of the Grand Vizier Shebna by the more faithful Eliakim is described in the following terms: 'And the key of the house of David will I lay upon his shoulder and he shall open and none shall

shut, and he shall shut and none shall open.' There is a parallel
passage, of which the prototype must have been in Q, where
St. Matthew xxiii. 13 speaks of the scribes and Pharisees as
having shut the Kingdom of Heaven against men, and St.
Luke xi. 52 speaks of the lawyers as having taken away the
key of knowledge. Luke here mentions the key, Matthew the
Kingdom of Heaven and the shutting of its doors against men.
The possibility is therefore that here St. Peter is thought of as
the Grand Vizier rather than the doorkeeper of the Kingdom
of Heaven.

The Petrine passage follows up the grant of the power
of the keys with authority to bind and to loose: 'Whatsoever
thou shalt bind on earth shall be bound in Heaven:
and whatsoever thou shalt loose on earth shall be loosed in
Heaven.' Here the background is also unmistakably Jewish.
'Binding and loosing' is almost a Jewish technical term for
'allowing and forbidding.' Thus St. Peter, previously described as the Foundation Stone and as the Grand Vizier of the
Master in His Church, here appears as the authoritative
Christian Rabbi, the wise scribe of the Kingdom of Heaven of
another Matthaean passage. There is a verbal parallel in the
Greek historian, Diodorus Siculus (I, 27), where the goddess
Isis describes herself as follows: 'I am the Queen of the Country,
and whatsoever I bind, no man can loose'; where, however,
the idea of binding and loosing is a magical idea. But there is
certainly no hint of magic in the passage in Matthew. The
Rabbis (like Islam after them) spoke of binding and loosing
where they meant permitting and forbidding. Thus Josephus
in a passage in his Jewish Wars (I, 5, 2) speaks of the Pharisees
as binding and loosing at their pleasure in the sense of making
authoritative legal decisions both positive and negative.

It is clear, then, that in this passage we are presented with a
series of ideas and of images which have a thoroughly Jewish
flavour, and which the author, whether Jesus or St. Matthew,
associated with St. Peter. It is important, however, to note
two further points before we leave the passage. The first is
that from a passage with so poetical and metaphorical a flavour
we can hardly distil any principles of jurisdiction and order.

These are no doubt necessary for the life of the Church, but we should hardly expect to find them in this kind of passage. For these promises to be converted into principles, we should have to know whether they were made to St. Peter as typical of a certain kind of spiritual pilgrimage (wobblers made rock-like men); or as representative of the Twelve but not apart from them; or as one who is given special and unique prerogatives *de iure divino*.

These are questions which the passage does not stop to answer, and the writer may even never have envisaged them. It is, however, worth noticing that the three prerogatives given to St. Peter in the passage are all elsewhere ascribed to others. The importance of a Rock Foundation for the spiritual life is emphasized in St. Matthew vii. 24-7 and St. Luke vi. 47-9 (an obvious Q passage) without any further attempt to define where such a foundation might be found. In this passage, if Jesus is the Architect of the Church, St. Peter is the Foundation Stone. In 1 Corinthians x. 4 Jesus is Himself the Rock (cp. 1 *St. Pet.* ii. 5-8), while in Ephesians ii. 20 the place of Peter is taken by the Apostles and prophets as a whole. Again, in Revelation i. 18 and iii. 7 our Lord Himself retains the power of the keys: 'He that hath the key of David, he that openeth and no man shutteth; and that shutteth and no man openeth.' Again, the power of binding and loosing belongs, in the next passage which we shall consider (*St. Matt.* xviii. 18), to the whole Church, and is indeed so exercised in Acts xv on the first occasion of which we have any record. It does not look from the New Testament as if here were any exclusive grant of powers to St. Peter, and the diversity of interpretation which we find in the early Fathers only serves to confirm this impression.

It is possible that we may be overhearing here the struggles for pre-eminence which took place among the disciples. It is at least difficult to understand how the question of the two sons of Zebedee could have arisen (*St. Mark* x. 35-45; *St. Matt.* xx. 20-8) if this grant of powers or prerogatives had been made so shortly before to Simon Peter.

We can now pass to the second passage which mentions the

Church expressly in St. Matthew's Gospel. This occurs in
St. Matthew xviii. 15–17 in a little section which describes how
to deal with an erring brother. The whole passage runs:

> If thy brother sin, go and tell him his fault between thee and him alone.
> If he refuse to hear, take with thee one or two others, that in the mouth of
> two or three witnesses every word shall be established [*Deut*. xix. 15]. If
> he neglect them, tell it to the Church, and if he neglect the Church, let
> him be to thee as a heathen man and tax-gatherer.

There are no textual problems here of any moment. The
tone of the passage is still Jewish (St. Luke, for example, would
hardly have retained the slighting reference to 'heathen' or
'Gentile' without modification). The passage is peculiar to
Matthew, though that is not by itself a final objection. What
certainly does present some difficulty is that the dominant
interests of St. Matthew are so prominent in the passage. St.
Matthew the Churchman seems here to be speaking to the
problems of the second generation; and it is possible that the
section belongs rather to the history of Canon Law than to
the authentic sayings of Christ. It will be suggested in a later
chapter that in His ethical teaching Jesus rather gave principles
and insights than detailed applications of His ethical principles
to situations which had not yet arisen. It is possible that Jesus
was as little a Canonist as He was a Casuist. Whatever view
is adopted about the historicity of the passage, it should be
noted that the word 'Church' here must mean the local
Christian community rather than the universal body of
Christians as in the previous Matthaean passage.

It is suggested by the evidence that, though the two passages
which explicitly mention the term Church may perhaps be
suspect on critical grounds, there is even apart from them
ample evidence for the belief that the Church was part of the
Intention of Jesus. So far the Church. Can we derive anything
of significance for the Ministry of the Church from the
Gospels?

It would hardly be surprising if this were impossible
for Jesus does not normally give detailed directions to cover
situations which had not as yet arisen. Further, there are
well-attested sayings against a desire for pre-eminence. As

against the Rabbis who desired greetings in the market place and who loved to be called 'Father' and 'Rabbi' disciples of Jesus must not use such appellations (*St. Matt.* xxiii. 9). Those who follow the One Who said, 'I am among you as He that serveth,' must follow the same pattern of service and sacrifice themselves (*St. Mark* ix. 33–7; *St. Matt.* xviii. 1–5; *St. Luke* ix. 46–8; *St. Mark* x. 42–5; *St. Matt.* xx. 26–28; *St. Luke* xxii. 25–7). But these passages rather have a bearing upon the spirit in which authority is exercised than upon the question whether any authority for ministering in the Christian *Ecclesia* was left by our Lord Himself.

We turn back to the Apostles. Here we have already noted that they have special obligations and responsibilities with regard to the new Israel. The authenticity of the number is strongly confirmed by the fact that the lists of their names given in the various Gospels do not tally with each other. The fact that they were Twelve is better attested than the names of those who composed the group. Further, some of those who are included in each list do not figure prominently in the Gospel story. The attempt to fill out the blanks so left was one of the motives for writing Apocryphal Gospels whether they were heretical or not. If the heretics secured thereby the Apostolic warrant which their doctrines would otherwise lack, the claim to tell the average Church member something more about the other characters in the Gospel tradition would be a powerful recommendation for the literature which bore their names. The early Church asked questions about the less-known members of the Apostolic band for which the heretics were only too willing to supply the answer. That the number twelve had a more than casual significance is proved by the election of Matthias to take the place of the traitor Judas (*Acts* i. 15–26). It is possible, though the suggestion is mere unverifiable conjecture, that James, the Lord's kinsman, was chosen to take the place of the other James martyred so soon after the story of the Acts opens. The elaborate argument of St. Paul both in the Galatian and the Corinthian Epistles in defence of his own Apostolate not only proves that it was something to be an Apostle, but also that there existed a *numerus clausus* to the Twelve as constituted by Jesus Himself.

They are normally described as 'Twelve' or merely as 'disciples.' But the title 'Apostle' (one sent) by which they are normally described in the Acts of the Apostles is not without Gospel warrant. It occurs in the form of the verb from which the noun is derived in St. Mark iii. 14 ('that He might send them forth'). Matthew uses it without explanation or footnote as the normal way in which the Twelve were described (*St. Matt.* x. 2), while Luke adds it in a kind of footnote or bracket (*St. Luke* vi. 13). It is used both by Mark and Luke on the occasion of the return of the Twelve from their first preaching tour (*St. Mark* vi. 30; *St. Luke* ix. 10). Outside these passages it occurs only in three Lucan passages (*S. Luke* xvii. 5, xxii. 14, and xxiv. 10) in which the conjecture might be made that St. Luke is carrying back into the Gospel a usage from his second volume which would be already familiar to his readers. An exact parallel would be the use of the designation 'the Lord' also in the Lucan Gospel. No satisfactory theory can be advanced why St. Luke uses the title in these precise contexts.

It would be a tempting critical solution to take the shortest way out and to assert that, while there is good evidence for the call of the Twelve as the original foundation members of the reconstituted Israel, the title 'Apostle' is derived from the vocabulary of the Apostolic Church. Before accepting this conjecture, it would be well to consider the natural way in which St. Mark in particular introduces the term into his narrative, while restricting it to the mission on which they were actually 'apostelled.' If the idea of the apostolate was present, might not the term exist as well? But we are not left simply in the realm of conjecture. The Twelve do in fact act as the only commissioned and accredited agents of the Christ. It was natural, for example, for the father of the epileptic boy to approach them in the absence of our Lord and of the inner group for the healing of his son (*St. Mark* ix. 14–29; *St. Matt.* xvii. 14–21; *St. Luke* ix. 37–43), while the story of the strange exorcist, while it ends in a rebuke to their exclusiveness, has as its background the consciousness of authority given by our

Lord. The significance of exorcism and its bearing upon Apostolic authority must be read in the light of such passages as St. Mark vi. 7; St. Matthew x. 1; and St. Luke ix. 1.

There is also an interesting saying which appears in different forms and contexts in the Gospels. It is applied widely to any follower of Christ in St. Mark ix. 37 (cf. *St. Matt.* xviii. 5; *St. Luke* ix. 48): 'He that receiveth one such child in My Name receiveth Me, and he that receiveth Me, receiveth not Me but Him that sent Me.' But it is also used of the Twelve in particular in a form of the saying which must in origin come from Q. St. Matthew x. 40 reads: 'He that receiveth you, receiveth Me, and he that receiveth Me, receiveth not Me, but Him that sent Me'; while the Lucan form (*St. Luke* x. 16) reads: 'He that heareth you heareth Me, and he that rejecteth you rejecteth Me, and he that rejecteth Me, rejecteth Him that sent Me.' Whether their application of these words is particular or general is beside the point; their central significance is plain. The reference to Jesus as Himself the Apostle of the Father (cp. *Heb.* iii. 1) tells strongly in favour of their authenticity. If in these passages Jesus speaks of Himself as one under authority and yet possessing the authority of the Father, it would not be surprising if He had delegated a similar authority to the Twelve as commissioned by Him.

There is good warrant in later Judaism for the idea of a *shaliach*—a man sent or a personal representative authoritatively accredited. The maxim that 'a man's *shaliach* shall be as himself' occurs nine times in various contexts in the Rabbinic writings. Too much must not, however, be made of this maxim. It represents a basic axiom in legal and commercial practice. If I send a junior member of my family to the shops, the shopkeeper must be able to believe that he is my personal representative and that I will honour any implied contract of sale into which he may enter on my behalf. If he cannot reasonably expect this, it is his duty to refuse to enter into any business transactions with him. If some of the inferences drawn from this word and its usage in recent theological literature are dubious Rabbinics and conjectural theology, the significance and importance of the term itself, and the saying in the Gospels which paraphrases it, are beyond question.

The Gospels mention two other groups: one narrower and the other wider than the Twelve. The former is the inner group of three within the Apostolic band composed of Peter with James and John, the two sons of Zebedee. These three are present with their Master on a number of privileged occasions. They occur first in the Marcan, though not in other lists of the Twelve. They accompany Him to the house of Jairus (*St. Mark* v. 37; *St. Luke* viii. 51), the Mount of Transfiguration (*St. Mark* ix. 2; *St. Matt.* xvii. 1; *St. Luke* ix. 28), and the Garden of Gethsemane (*St. Mark* xiv. 33; *St. Matt.* xxvi. 37). It is probable that this represents a position of *de facto* prominence without any particular 'official significance.' We may, however, compare the three 'pillar Apostles' of Galatians ii. 9: James of Jerusalem, Cephas, and John.

Besides the three and the Twelve, St. Luke alone mentions a further group, the seventy sent out on another preaching tour (*St. Luke* x. 1–20). A variant reading gives their number as seventy-two. There is, of course, no inherent difficulty that Jesus should have extended His circle of adherents or that a further preaching tour should have taken place. It is, however, rather puzzling that no further trace of the seventy in the history of the Apostolic Church should have been left, unless we accept the rather improbable conjecture that they are somehow connected with the seven in Acts vi. 1–6. The charge to the seventy is closely paralleled to the charge to the Twelve as given in Matthew (ix. 37–8, x. 7–10), which leaves open the conjecture that Luke has transposed material from Q which belongs more naturally to the Matthaean context. It is certainly worthy of notice that seventy is the number of the nations of the world in the Hebrew text of Genesis x, while seventy-two (the variant in the Lucan passage) is the number according to the Septuagint text. It is therefore possible that St. Luke with his strongly universalist interest has here a doublet of the mission of the Twelve (which he also records) designed to throw into stronger relief the universality of the mission of the Christian Church to the world at large.

If then we can trace in the teaching of Jesus the 'little flock,' the nucleus for the new Israel, already within the circle of His historic Ministry, we can also discover the germ of the Christian Ministry within that Church. There appears to be an authoritative commission given to the Twelve, and yet at the same time a warning against the desire for personal precedence. The authority which Jesus gave must be exercised as a Ministry within, and not as a Lordship over, the Beloved Community. Here our evidence ends; for it is clear that we can expect as little particular guidance as to the detailed forms which the Christian Ministry was to take as we could for detailed instructions for the day-to-day life of the Christian society as a whole. The community is constituted; the commission for authority within it assigned. Both community and commission can be believed to be continuing; the forms which it was to take are left for the Church to determine for itself at a later date in the presence and the power of the Holy Spirit.

Finally, we must pass to the two Gospel Sacraments of Baptism and the Eucharist.

Water-washing as a symbol of ritual or moral cleansing is one of the key or master symbols of humanity in its quest for God. It is therefore hardly surprising that it should be familiar to the Jews of our Lord's day. Within Judaism it took two forms. The former is represented by the lustral washings of Pharisaic Judaism designed to promote ritual cleansing. It may be said at once that in view of our Lord's attitude towards them declared in St. Mark vii. 4, it is unlikely that they had any influence on New Testament Baptism. The second type of water-washing is of greater importance for our purpose. Among the rites which attended the reception of an adult proselyte into Judaism was the so-called *tebilah* or water-baptism. This was probably, though not certainly, quite as early as the times of John the Baptist and of our Lord. It is mentioned, for example, in one Rabbinic treatise as used for the reception of two non-Jewish soldiers into the Jewish Faith. Towards the end of the first or the beginning of the second century, it could be argued by two distinguished rabbis, Rabbi

Joshua and Rabbi Eliezer, whether it was circumcision or
baptism which was the central rite of admission into Judaism.
This would indicate at least a procedure of some standing.
Apparently a convert, if he were a man, was circumcised first
and then subsequently baptized, after which he was reckoned
in the full sense of the word a Jew. (The controversy might
perhaps be paralleled by the discussion of the relations between
Baptism and Confirmation as the two parts of the single rite
of Christian Initiation which is taking place to-day.) There
are interesting parallels to the Baptismal Discourse of the third
chapter of St. John's Gospel in the Rabbinic literature. Thus
Rabbi Yose ben Halafta compares a newly-converted proselyte to a newborn child and Rabbi Judah to a babe a day old.

The Baptism of John the Baptist seems more likely to be
related to this *tebilah* ceremony than to the ritual washings of
Pharisaic Judaism. The repentance to which it points was
associated with moral renewal rather than with ritual purity.
New features, however, appear to be two in number. The
eschatological reference, so clear in the records of John the
Baptist, had no parallel in proselyte baptism, except in so far
as the proselyte as a newly-won member of the people of God
shared in God's destiny for them upon earth. It is significant
that the Rabbinic Judaism which made much of this rite of
reception sat on the whole loosely to eschatology. A further
novelty lay in the fact that in his Baptism John treated even
Jews of good standing and impeccable heredity as though they
were proselytes. If we cannot perhaps regard John as the
precursor of St. Paul, who insists that all are not Jews who are
such outwardly, at least he insists that in the threatened
in-breaking of the Day of the Lord, spiritual repentance and
moral renewal must reinforce racial privilege.

The link between John the Baptist's Baptism and that
practised by the Christian Church is given by the Baptism
which Jesus Himself underwent at the hands of John. Its
deepest significance is probably to be connected with His
Messianic Vocation, but the Matthaean interpolation (*St. Matt.*
iii. 14–15) proves that grave difficulty was felt about it in the
Church at the time at which St. Matthew wrote. Did Jesus

come to His Baptism as a sinner with sinners or rather as a
Saviour Who willed to make Himself One with His people?
The root of the answer is certainly given in this Matthaean
passage, but a fragment from the Apocryphal Gospel of the
Hebrews[1] shows that the difficulty was still felt.

The relation of Christian Baptism to Jesus Himself is a harder
question to answer than appears at first sight. The Synoptic
Gospels afford no hint that Jesus Himself used Baptism as part
of the work of His earthly Ministry. Indeed, there is one point
which strongly suggests the contrary. The word 'baptism' is
twice used in contexts which refer figuratively to His death.
Thus St. Luke xii. 50 records: 'I have a baptism with which to
be baptized, and how am I straitened until it be accomplished?'
It is possible, though not really probable, that this anticipates
the 'baptism into the death of Christ' of which St. Paul later
speaks. In St. Mark x. 38 Jesus asks the sons of Zebedee: 'Can
ye be baptized with the baptism with which I am baptized?'
The fact that Matthew omits these words (Luke deletes the
whole incident) indicates strongly that the saying was out of
accord with the mind of the Apostolic Church, which laid
considerable store by Baptism as a Sacrament. The Fourth
Gospel does indeed contain a curious little note that Jesus
baptized in the land of Judaea (*St. John* iii. 22), and adds the
comment of the Baptist when this was reported to him: 'He
must increase and I must decrease.' But in the following
chapter (iv. 2) the writer appears to retract his earlier statement
with the qualification that 'Jesus did not baptize but His
disciples did.' It is not impossible that we may deduce from
these statements the inference that for a short time in Judaea,
before the opening of the Ministry in Galilee, Jesus and John
the Baptist may have worked along parallel lines. The discourse to Nicodemus, which contains the writer's theology of
Holy Baptism in the third chapter, is perhaps parallel to the
Eucharistic Discourse of the sixth chapter, attached to the
incident of the Feeding of the Five Thousand. In both cases
we may suspect the desire to antedate certain themes which
the writer regarded as of first-class importance for the understanding of Jesus and His work.

[1] M. R. James, *Apocryphal New Testament*, p. 6.

The arguments against the view that our Lord practised Baptism during His earthly Ministry seem to me to be overwhelmingly strong. There is the silence of the Synoptic record and the absence of any injunction to baptize in the charges to the Twelve and to the seventy. Even those Gentiles with whom He comes into contact are not required to be baptized, and we should have to take into account the absence of any appeal to the precedent of Jesus Himself in the controversy which arose over the Baptism of Cornelius. On the other side might perhaps be urged the fact that the Church used the rite of Baptism almost by instinct from the day of the Pentecost onwards.

There remains the command to baptize recorded in the First Gospel (*St. Matt.* xxviii. 19–20) as given by the Risen Lord. The textual argument against this passage carries very little weight. It depends solely upon quotations from the Fathers, which are not invariably minutely exact. The principal witness to this omission—Eusebius—also quotes the full passage in other contexts. The decisive question is whether it was actually uttered by the Risen Lord or whether it rather represents the crystallization in the form of a Dominical utterance of the experience and custom of the Apostolic Church. In favour of its authenticity is the fact that the Primitive Church, which was not primarily a creative community, from the outset took Baptism as its normal rite of initiation. It cannot be lightly assumed that this would have been the case without express Dominical warrant, which we have seen no good reason to discover in His Ministry before the Resurrection. The force of this argument is not really broken by the fact that in the Acts of the Apostles Baptism is performed in the Name of Christ rather than in that of the Holy Trinity. On the other hand, it is curious that no appeal was made to such an express authority from the Master Himself to 'baptize all nations' in the case of the Gentile Cornelius, where it could have been quoted with decisive effect. This argument from silence must, however, be taken into connexion with a widespread, though not easily explicable, silence with regard to the words of Christ in the early years of the Christian

Church. It does not in any case appear very probable that any Dominical utterance of the Risen Lord contained so full and explicit mention of the Holy Trinity. While the structure of New Testament religion is predominantly Triadic in character, it may be doubted whether so clear a formula can be found so early even on the lips of our Lord Himself. It is perhaps the best conclusion from the evidence to maintain that St. Matthew is substantially correct in asserting that the practice of Holy Baptism had Dominical warrant, but that the full Trinitarian formula has been expanded from the practice of his own day. If this conclusion were accepted, we should be presented with another example of his favourite practice of Targum-ing a narrative which was substantially historical.

There is little doubt, whatever view is held of the last problem which we have been discussing, that in the Primitive Church Christian Baptism was related more or less closely with the Baptism of Jesus Himself as an act of identification with the Christ in His Messianic Vocation through the Beloved Community which depended for its existence upon the Messiah Himself. The Pauline theology of Baptism appears to suggest that this incorporation into the Christ through the act which designated Him as Messiah was interpreted as an identification with Him as dying and rising again, thus extending the process beyond the limits of His earthly life and ministry.

We pass finally to a consideration of the Eucharist in the Gospels. If the problem with regard to Baptism was the relative scantiness of the material, we are not so placed with regard to the Eucharist. We have four explicit accounts of the Last Supper in the New Testament: one in St. Paul (1 Cor. xi. 23–5) and one in each of the Synoptic Gospels. While the Fourth Gospel gives no express account of the Last Supper, it contains a rich strain of Eucharistic teaching in its sixth chapter, and its chronology of the Passion Narrative has been held to act as a control upon the Synoptic chronology of the Last Supper. It will be necessary first of all to remind ourselves of the content of these four narratives before asking, first, what light Jewish liturgical practice throws upon what was going on

from the point of an impartial Jewish observer, and finally
seeking to discover, so far as we may, what was in the mind of
our Lord Himself in the action which was so specially characteristic of Himself.

Of the four accounts, that of St. Paul has for our purpose a
special importance. It is, of course, the earliest narrative which
we possess, antedating even that of St. Mark by some years.
But it has a further element of importance in that it is introduced incidentally almost as illustrative matter, to deal with
practical difficulties over the administration of the Eucharist
which had arisen at Corinth. The order is: bread followed by
cup. A command to repeat is attached both to the bread and
to the wine; while the words over the bread and wine respectively are as follows: 'This is My Body which is on your
behalf' (or possibly 'broken on your behalf'), and: 'This cup
is the New Covenant in My Blood.' No account is given of
the context of the action, whether it were a meal or simply an
action in itself.

St. Mark xiv. 22-4, however, makes it plain that the Last
Supper took place either during or at the end of a meal. He
agrees in the order (bread and cup) with the Pauline account,
though no command to repeat is attached to either part of the
rite. The words over the bread are simply: 'This is My Body,'
while those over the cup (which in the Marcan account follow
its reception) are: 'This is My Blood of the covenant [or 'new
covenant'] shed for many.' St. Matthew xxvi. 26-8 follows
St. Mark very closely here, merely inserting the rubrics as a
good Churchman should. He is careful to add that they should
eat as well as take the bread. (Was he familiar with a tendency
to treat the consecrated Host as a charm?) The words of
administration of the cup are transposed to before its reception
by the disciples, and to them is added the phrase 'for remission
of sins.'

The Lucan account raises more problems. It has closer
affinities with the Pauline than the Marcan tradition, as might
perhaps be expected in view of the known close connexion
between St. Paul and St. Luke. Though this conclusion has
been disputed, it is more probable that St. Luke is enriching

a fundamentally Pauline account with Marcan elements than taking the Marcan account as basic and offering an interpretation of it in a Pauline sense.

The account opens with a saying of Jesus (*St. Luke* xxii. 15–16): 'With desire I have desired to eat this Passover with you before I suffer for I tell you that I shall no more eat until it be fulfilled in the Kingdom of God.' Does this mean that our Lord is eating the Passover or not? At first sight it looks as if He is, but Burkitt pointed out that the aorist, 'I desired,' might equally well be interpreted as an 'aorist of unfulfilled desire.' We can, for example, say in English, 'I hoped to do so and so,' meaning that we wished to do so but were unavoidably prevented. The latter part of the saying seems to refer to the Messianic Banquet in the New Age. Then follows a most curious passage: 'And taking a cup, He gave thanks and said, Take this and divide it among yourselves, for I tell you that I will not drink from this time forward of the fruit of the vine until the Kingdom of God come.' The action and the appended saying are clearly related to the previous saying, and continue the thought of the Messianic Age that is to come. The problem arises how this cup, which the other Synoptists do not mention, is related to the Last Supper proper. There are three possibilities. It may represent the action to which the Last Supper is attached, a mere expansion of the Marcan phrase 'and while they were eating'; or it may be an independent anticipation of the Messianic Banquet followed without a break by the Last Supper; or (just possibly) St. Luke thought of a Last Supper involving three instead of two constituent actions. The last possibility is rendered less likely by the fact that if St. Luke thought so, his interpretation appears to have left no trace upon the later liturgical tradition of the Church. We shall see that the scribes who copied the manuscripts of the Gospel were as puzzled as we are ourselves.

St. Luke then draws nearer to the other accounts. The bread is blessed and distributed with the words: 'This is My Body which is given for you; do this in remembrance of Me.' The cup follows 'after supper' with the words: 'This cup is the new covenant in My Blood which is shed for you.' He does not, however, add the second command to repeat which occurs in the Pauline narrative.

The difficult feature in this account is the preliminary cup before St. Luke rejoins the other accounts of the Last Supper. Some manuscripts offer a version which reduces the threefold action to a twofold one by including the first cup in the Eucharistic action and omitting the second cup and the command to repeat after the bread. This 'Shorter Text' has the merit of reducing the difficulty, but reverses the order of the bread and the cup given in the other three accounts. This is not wholly without parallel. The brief allusion to the Eucharist in 1 Corinthians x. 16 seems to imply such an order, though its importance is very greatly reduced by the fact that the fuller and more careful narrative given in the following chapter adheres, as we have seen, to the Marcan order. It is also the order of the curious account given in the *Didache* (IX and X), though the content of this passage and, still more, the problems associated with the whole character and provenance of this document make it a difficult and somewhat precarious witness. We should obviously prefer the more difficult reading, but it is unfortunately uncertain which reading is really the harder. Those who maintain the originality of the Shorter Text urge in its defence that it is the less liturgical reading and therefore should be preferred. It is clearly out of accord with what the scribe would find in his local Liturgy, and is therefore unlikely to have been invented. The advocates of the 'Longer Text,' however, suggest with greater plausibility that this is the reading which explains all others, and that the real difficulty lies in the incorporation of the first cup, which does not appear to belong to the Eucharistic action at all, into the pattern of the Last Supper. Nor must we forget the possibility that a merely mechanical explanation of the shorter variant might be possible—a sleepy or inattentive scribe would be specially liable to let his eye slip down the page much as young children reading mechanically are liable to leave out a line of their reader. It is not easy to be quite sure of the ground here, but the probabilities seem to be strongly in favour of the Longer Text as the Lucan original

which later scribes, realizing the difficulty, tried to pare down
to correspond with the other accounts in the New Testament.

Our next question must be to ask what an impartial Jewish
observer would have thought was going on if he had been
present in the Upper Room. A strong case can be made out
for the belief that it was actually the Passover Feast itself. The
date given at the beginning of the Marcan narrative (*St. Mark*
xiv. 1) seems to put the matter beyond doubt. This implies
that the Thursday on which the Last Supper was eaten was
Nisan 14, on which the Paschal lambs were sacrificed in the
afternoon and the Passover proper eaten during the earlier
part of the evening. There are features in the narrative which
tell in favour of this view. The meal is taken within the city
of Jerusalem and not at Bethany where Jesus was staying.
While Passover pilgrims could be accommodated outside the
Old City, the Passover proper could only be eaten within the
confines of the city itself. Josephus tells us that houses of
Jerusalem contained in their leases the obligation on the owner
or occupier to give all possible facilities for celebrating the
Passover to parties of visiting pilgrims. Would Jesus have
risked an unnecessary journey into the Old City at a time
when the storm clouds had gathered to breaking point? Jesus
sends word to the owner of the house as if He were sure that
the request to use the Upper Room were sure to be granted.
The use of the Upper Room described as 'prepared' would
fit in well with this theory (*St. Mark* xiv. 15). The meal was
apparently taken reclining (*St. John* xiii. 23–5). Although this
ran counter to the original provision for the Passover which
enjoined the worshippers to take it standing equipped as for
a journey in memory of the haste in which the journey from
Egypt was taken, Jewish practice contemporary with our Lord
seems to have abandoned this early piece of ritual in favour of
the contemporary practice at meals. A hymn was sung before
departure (*St. Mark* xiv. 26; *St. Matt.* xxvi. 30) and this has
been taken as an allusion to the *Hallel*, the series of psalms of
praise with which the Passover meal came to an end. The
return before the end of the night, although in contradiction

to the explicit earlier procedure, had again become customary by this time.

The position is not, however, quite as clear as this evidence might suggest. A different dating is suggested by other evidence. St. Paul, who is after all our earliest witness, speaks of Christ as sacrificed for us as our Paschal Lamb (1 *Cor.* v. 7). If this allusion is taken strictly, it suggests that the death of our Lord took place at the time when the Paschal lambs were killed in the Temple Courts. This would make the Last Supper occur on Nisan 14, and leave the Crucifixion to fall on the actual day of the Passover itself. This is not, taken by itself, conclusive, for it might merely be a general comparison of our Lord to the Paschal Victim under the Old Covenant without implying any closer chronological approximations. On the other hand, it is confirmed by the chronology of the Passion in the Fourth Gospel. It is true that for reasons which are not very clear St. John omits the account of the Last Supper, though he does record the Last Discourse at a corresponding point in his narrative. He does, however, make a point of the fact that Jesus died on the Cross at the very time at which the Passover lambs were being killed in the Temple Courts in preparation for the Passover which was to follow on that evening (*St. John* xix. 31). Much, of course, depends on the general view taken of the historicity of the details given in the Fourth Gospel; contemporary scholarship is not as hesitant as its predecessors in accepting much of the material contained in the Fourth Gospel as historically accurate.

A number of points contained within the Marcan narrative itself have been taken to tell against the identification of the Last Supper with the Passover meal. Strict laws with regard to work obtained for the Passover as well as for the Sabbath. We should not expect, for example, to find Simon of Cyrene coming in from the country, presumably from the fields, on Passover morning (*St. Mark* xv. 21). Neither should we expect the disciples to be carrying two swords, which would contravene the law of burdens (*St. Luke* xxii. 35-8). The Trial itself would have been an illegality, since not only was this a particular form of work, but also (as the Fourth Gospel points out) the Jewish leaders would have risked ritual defilement in entering Pilate's judgement hall (*St. John* xviii. 28). The whole atmosphere of haste and urgency, of the religious authorities working to a rather tight time-schedule, which the Marcan Gospel strongly suggests, is better understood if Passover fell that year on the Friday than on the Thursday. The interruption of the burial rites again suggests the supervening of the Passover in which work was forbidden. The view which now begins to emerge is that the Last Supper took place and Jesus was crucified on Nisan 14, on the very threshold of the Passover which began that same evening. Passover and Sabbath must therefore have coincided that year, and the burial was intended to be completed at first light after the Passover and Sabbath came to an end.

Despite these facts a vigorous defence of the identification of the Passover and the Last Supper is offered by scholars like Dalman and Jeremias. They are rightly doubtful of the view that Simon of Cyrene was coming into the city from work. It is much more likely, especially in view of his place of origin, that he was a Passover pilgrim making his way to the city from the country. But the advocates of a Passover dating are not quite so successful with their other replies. Their premise that a legal religion has to provide itself with ways of avoiding the extreme consequences of its own legalism may be regarded as in principle sound enough. They note that the provision about carrying burdens would not in any case apply to soldiers or police. Whatever the dating, those who came to arrest Jesus were not breaking the law by carrying arms. But the disciples were not of this order. Dalman suggests that they were Galileans, and that swords might have been part of their equipment, like a highlander's dirk. This is very doubtful. They can only muster two swords between them, and the idea that fishermen normally carried swords, even in Galilee, borders on the ridiculous. The burial does not present any difficulty on any theory. Climatic conditions would need to be taken into account here, but the interruption of the burial rites does tell against a Paschal dating. The women had obviously just done the necessary minimum and their return to the tomb at first light on Easter Day suggests that they intended to do what they had had perforce to leave undone before. For the possibility of the trial, even if the Passover had already begun, Dalman urges two well-known legal principles. It was held even by the strictest rabbinical Jews that a rebellious teacher of the Law could be executed on the Sabbath Day, if necessary, on the principle that one Sabbath could be broken so that other Sabbaths might be kept. An even wider principle justified action 'if the hour demanded it.' The trial and death of Jesus could be brought under either rubric. The difficulty is, however, that it does not look as if such a rubric was really invoked. There are, on any showing, illegalities enough in the trial of Jesus; it would be surprising if the latter principle had been really invoked. It was, after all, the High Priest who was exactly the person to invoke it, and if, in fact, the Jewish authorities had all the time that they needed, why did they not take greater pains to see that the legal proprieties were better observed?

The really crucial point concerns the presence or absence of the lamb at the Last Supper. Those who deny a Paschal dating find its absence significant. From the point of view of Jesus so much might have been made of its meaning in the light of His mission that it must appear very strange that He does not mention it or build it into His sayings or actions. Those who believe it to have been present are compelled to adopt the rather weak expedient of replying that it could be taken for granted, and that Jesus preferred for His own reasons to emphasize something else done with bread and wine.

On the whole, then, while admitting the strength of the case that might be made out for the Passover theory, I prefer the view that the Last Supper was not a Passover meal in the strict sense; but that Jesus, knowing that His hour was almost come did something in place of the Passover in circumstances as similar to the Passover in place and in externals as He could. No lamb is mentioned because no lamb was present. God would, however, provide Himself a Lamb for sacrifice.

If, then, our hypothetical Jewish observer might be expected (if our reasoning is right) to deny that here in the Upper Room a Passover was going on, while no doubt recognizing certain marked Paschal features about the rite, can we form any other view of what he might have identified with the action before him? Two further views have in late years been put forward. The one suggests that the Last Supper was a Passover *Kiddush*, while a more recent suggestion inclines to the view that it represents a *Haburah*, possibly the last of a series which Jesus had held with His disciples.

The *Kiddush* theory (sponsored in this country by W. O. E. Oesterley and G. H. Box) called attention to the existence of religious meals attended by devout conversation with which it became the custom of godly Jews to approach the beginning of the Sabbath. It will be recalled that the Jewish Sabbath began at 6.0 p.m., after the day's work was over. It was therefore natural that some Jews should feel the need for some means of smoothing the transition from secular to sacred. This devout practice, called the *Kiddush* because it 'sanctified' the Sabbath by preparing the minds of those who took part in it for its coming, inevitably tended to stereotype and to liturgize. It was incorporated into the legal framework of the Jewish Faith and is still practised, although certain alterations in the procedure have in course of time taken place. It is probable that at the time of our Lord a single cup of wine was blessed and passed round the company, followed by a similar blessing and distribution of bread.

The theory is an improvement upon the Paschal theory on the following grounds:

i. While the Passover was a meal in itself, the Synoptic evidence suggests that the rite instituted by our Lord occurred either during or at the end of a meal. This would suit *Kiddush* practice.

ii. The Passover cups were four in number, and each member of the party had a separate cup, whereas the cup at the Last Supper (except in the longer Lucan account) is a single one and in all accounts is shared in common.

iii. The Paschal cups came at the beginning of the meal, but the Last Supper came later on.

iv. It is perhaps relevant to note that if the Last Supper were

a Passover we might expect an annual celebration of the
Eucharist in the Primitive Church, whereas the evidence of
Acts implies at least a weekly celebration. This would fit the
weekly *Kiddush* much better.

It is therefore suggested that the Last Supper was, from the
Jewish point of view, a Paschal *Kiddush*, and that the Last
Discourse in St. John might easily represent the sort of con-
versation appropriate to such an occasion.

There are, however, certain difficulties which have led most
scholars to abandon this theory. The first is a liturgical
difficulty. The *Kiddush* contains the order cup–bread instead
of the generally accepted order bread–cup as evidenced by
the Pauline and Marcan traditions. The only witnesses in its
support are the shorter text in Luke and the *Didache*. There is,
moreover, a chronological difficulty. The Sabbath *Kiddush*
did, in fact, fulfil the purpose for which it was originally
intended; it led straight into the Sabbath and thus could be
deemed to sanctify it directly. There is no inherent difficulty
about the extension of the principle of the *Kiddush* to the major
festivals, and there is some slight evidence for this, though it is
not outstandingly strong. The difficulty remains, however,
that a Passover *Kiddush* could not sanctify the Passover as
directly as the Sabbath *Kiddush* sanctified the Sabbath; for, at
the very moment at which such a *Kiddush* would have been
most appropriate, at least one member of each Passover party
would need to be in attendance at the Temple getting the
lamb ceremonially slain for the Passover itself. A Paschal
*Kiddush* would therefore have a rather different character from
a Sabbath *Kiddush*, perhaps partaking rather of a Preparation
Service the night before.

These difficulties led to the formulation of a theory which
in England secured the powerful support of scholars like T. W.
Manson and Dom Gregory Dix. It is urged that the origin
of the Last Supper is rather to be found in religious meals of a
more general nature partaken by groups of friends with a
looser framework than the *Kiddush* itself, called *Haburoth*. If it
be asked what is the difference between the *Kiddush* and the
*Haburah*, it may be replied that, while every *Kiddush* was a

*Haburah*, not every *Haburah* was a *Kiddush*. *Haburah* is the class-concept of which the *Kiddush* is a particular illustration. It is suggested that this throws light upon certain aspects of the Ministry of our Lord. If the Last Supper was merely the last of a series of such meals (or perhaps if we include the journey to Emmaus the last but one) we can better explain why St. John felt free to introduce his teaching on the Eucharist in a discourse appended to the Feeding of the Five Thousand. It would also explain how it came about that our Lord was made known in the breaking of bread to two disciples who were not present at the Last Supper. It is even suggested that the saying in the Fourth Gospel, 'Ye are My friends' (*St. John* xv. 14) might represent, 'Ye are My *haberim*,' although it is noticeable that a Hebrew scholar of the calibre of Franz Delitsch did not make use of the word in his translation of the New Testament into Hebrew.

But there are considerable difficulties in the way of this hypothesis, popular as it has recently become. The Rabbinic evidence for the existence of such *Haburoth* is very meagre and almost non-existent. Dom Gregory Dix appeals to the *Tractate Berakoth* (blessings), but while this tract gives abundant information about blessings, it does not afford any real evidence for the existence of such specific occasions for their use. A recent article in the *Church Quarterly Review* by Mr. R. D. Richardson has dealt trenchantly with this evidence. It might be urged, and such a contention would not be without its force, that if the *Haburah* was a loosely-framed association of devout Jews, with considerable flexibility in its organization, it would hardly be likely that the Rabbinic writings would devote any more space to it than the proposed Revision of Canon Law of the Church of England to the subject of parochial teas, and for the same reason!

A further and more serious objection is presented by the nature and definition of *Haburoth* as modern Judaism understands them. The article on *Haburoth* in the *Jewish Encyclopaedia* says nothing about fellowship meals, but speaks of *Haburoth* as associations of Jews banded together for the punctual and complete performance of the law of tithe. It is possible, of

course, for an institution to change its character in the course
of centuries, but such a change would be pretty far-reaching
and it might have been expected that at least some trace of its
original function would have been preserved. Certainly it
would be in the highest degree unlikely that One Who did not
regard the tithing of mint, anise, and cummin (*St. Matt.* xxiii.
23; *St. Luke* xi. 42) as specially meritorious would borrow
anything from such a source. Even if the theory were sus-
tained against these and similar criticisms, it would amount to
little more than the assertion by our hypothetical Jewish
observer that an informal religious meal with devout conversation was here in progress.

But did our Lord intend what He did in the Upper Room
to be repeated by the Beloved Community? Was He insti-
tuting a Sacrament? Here many scholars call attention to the
absence of any such injunction in Matthew and Mark. Paradoxically, its omission in Matthew is rather harder to account
for than its absence in Mark. The latter is always seeking to
align his readers to the actual events of the Passion itself and to
put them in the position of the earliest disciples. It is therefore
probable that he finds no reason to divert his narrative from
its primary purpose with a statement which was familiar in
practice to his readers in their weekly acts of corporate worship. If it is rather more surprising that St. Matthew the
churchman does not add this particular rubric, we must
weigh against this not only his well-known fidelity to the
Second Gospel but his tendency to shorten its narratives to
leave room for the new material which he wished his Gospel
to include. Strongly in support of this conclusion is the
presence of the command to repeat twice over in the account
given by our earliest witness, St. Paul, and its presence in the
longer and probably more authentic text of St. Luke. (Its
omission in the Shorter Text is normal as part of longer
omissions designed to bring the Lucan account nearer to the
Marcan pattern, which, of course, does not contain it.) We
may therefore conclude with some confidence that our Lord
intended what He did to be repeated in the Church of which
He founded the nucleus during His earthly Ministry.

But the principal question still remains to be answered. What, so far as we trace it with due diffidence, was our Lord's mind in the rite which He instituted in the Upper Room? If we have failed to discover any precise explanation which our impartial Jewish observer might have assigned to the action in the Upper Room, this is perhaps only what we might have expected. I have long felt that Jesus was doing something new with bread and wine at the Last Supper, as against those who merely believe that He was giving a different significance to an action which already existed. No doubt the natural action of the blessing of bread and wine appear to be associated with many activities within Judaism. That is only to be expected in a Faith which had its roots deep in the human quest for God. But the difficulty is that what Jesus does is not to be fitted exactly in any such occasion. Mr. R. D. Richardson makes precisely the same point when he warns us against under-estimating the creative originality of Jesus.

What Jesus is doing does not appear to be the Passover, though He follows as closely as the occasion permits the formal setting of the Paschal meal: 'With desire I desired to eat this Passover with you before I suffer,' but He knows clearly enough that His hour will sound before the Passover takes place. In the circumstances the Paschal lamb was inevitably absent, but Jesus knew that 'God would provide a Lamb for sacrifice' (*Gen.* xxii. 8). In a deeper sense the rite was a *Kiddush* not so much of the Passover but of the offering on the Cross which He was to make on the next day.

The framework of the action lay in the Old Testament conception of the *ôth* to which allusion has been made in earlier chapters, the kind of action which was not merely a symbol or representation, but an instrument as well, both prefiguring what was to come and bringing to pass what was therein prefigured.

The words which Jesus uses are rich in associations linking them to the past as well as anticipations of what was yet to come. They will repay a somewhat closer examination, although we cannot hope to do more than merely to touch upon some of their more obvious implications here. It will be convenient to put the various forms given in the four accounts in tabular form.

### The Bread

1 Corinthians xi. 24, This is My Body which is for you (or broken for you).

St. Mark xiv. 22; St. Matthew xxvi. 26, This is My Body.

St. Luke xxii. 19, This is My Body given for you.

### The Cup

1 Corinthians xi. 25, This cup is the New Covenant in My Blood.

St. Mark xiv. 24, This is My Blood of the [New] Covenant which is shed for many.

St. Matthew xxvi. 28 adds to the Marcan words, 'for the remission of sins.'

St. Luke xxii. 20, This cup is the New Covenant in My Blood which is shed for many.

It will be noticed that there is no exact correspondence between the words used over the bread and the cup. The words of institution used over the cup are richer in background allusion than those used over the bread. This is in part at least due to the use made of blood in the religious past of the Hebrew people. Past ages built doctrinal houses-of-cards from the use of the word 'is.' These have never been really convincing, for the good reason that we cannot tell in uncial Greek manuscripts which lack accents whether the word is meant to be a mere copulative or to be stressed. In any case, it seems probable that no equivalent occurred in the original Aramaic. In both cases the dependence of Luke upon Paul is as clear as the dependence of Matthew upon Mark, though the words used for the cup in Luke contain an obvious Marcan echo.

The fundamental thought behind both appears to be: 'This is I Myself,' or more exactly: 'This is My life made available through My death.' If it be urged that the words used over the bread would appear impossibly startling to Jewish ears, we may reply with Vincent Taylor that our criterion should not be merely what was possible for a Jew, but rather what was possible for a Jew who was beginning to believe in Jesus as He comes before us in the Gospels. We need only remind ourselves that the Jesus Who is in question here is not merely the Master of Galilee and Jerusalem but also the Crucified, Risen, and Ascended Lord Whose meaning and purpose would be further made plain by the Spirit Whom He was to give to His disciples. We cannot limit the potentiality of understanding simply to what the disciples possessed in the Upper Room with the enrichment and enlightenment which were to come to them in the immediate future.

When we pass to the words over the cup, we find fresh associations clustering round the words which Jesus used. Covenant sacrifices, in which the blood of a sacrificial victim played its part, go back to the very fabric of all primitive society. So far as Israel was concerned, the covenant was crystallized in the encounter with Jahveh at Sinai-Horeb, and this in turn linked historically with the original Passover of the Exodus. Jesus here appears as a better victim fulfilling a mightier Exodus-deliverance 'for many.' The concept of covenant was deepened and interiorized by the New Covenant of Jeremiah xxxi, a passage which our Lord also appears to have in mind. And finally, the Servant of Second Isaiah is twice represented as being himself a covenant to the nations (*Isa.* xlii. 6, xlix. 8). The vital words 'for many,' which have in their original context a universal rather than a restrictive connotation, also derive from the Servant Songs (*Isa.* liii. 11). Here Jesus sums up in word and deed a whole tradition which was of central significance to the religion of Israel.

But there is a greater significance still to be given to these words. They are not merely evocative of the past, they are proleptic of the future. The Last Supper is not merely the climax of much in earlier religious practice and thought; it is closely, even integrally, linked with the Cross and thus the covenant sacrifice is fulfilled in the Victor-Victim Who gave Himself once for all for all men on the Cross, and Who still in the Church, in the Sacrament of the Eucharist repeated according to His will, gives Himself to the Beloved Community with His own hand.

## BIBLIOGRAPHY

R. Newton Flew, *Jesus and His Church.*
K. L. Schmidt, *The Church.*
W. K. Flemington, *The New Testament Doctrine of Baptism.*
G. W. H. Lampe, *The Seal of the Spirit.*
G. Dalman, *Jesus Jeshua.*
J. Jeremias in *Journal of Theological Studies,* Volume L.
W. O. E. Oesterley, *The Jewish Background of the Christian Liturgy.*
G. H. Box in *Journal of Theological Studies,* Volume III.
Article by T. W. Manson in *Christian Worship* (edited by N. Micklem).
G. Dix, *The Shape of the Liturgy.*
Vincent Taylor, *Jesus and His Sacrifice.*
A. J. B. Higgins, *The Lord's Supper in the New Testament.*
K. H. Rengstorf, *Apostleship.*

## CHAPTER XI

# THE LOVE OF GOD AND THE SERVICE
# OF MAN

BEFORE we pass to the subject of the Ethical Teaching of Jesus, it will be necessary to define our terms, and to call attention to certain general considerations about Ethics which we shall do well to bear in mind.

Ethics is concerned with the problem of right conduct. We all know in experience what it means to be confronted with a duty, a choice of actions in which the word 'I ought,' rather than 'I want' or 'I prefer,' frames itself in our minds. Normally our choice appears to be immediate, and we do not think much about it; but even if we do not think much about it ourselves, our ethical experience certainly provides other people with much food for thought. It can be asked, for example, what 'duty' means, what types of conduct we consider good, and how we come by our belief that some things are good and others bad.

There are, for example, two different ways of understanding how we come by our belief in right and wrong. Some think that it is a matter of intuition—almost of instinct. They hold that we 'see' an action to be right or wrong. Others would say that it is a matter of reason, although they would agree with the former school that we usually think so quickly that our judgement looks more immediate and less rationally based than it actually is. The gap between these two views is perhaps not as great as at first sight appears, since, even if at the moment of choice our judgements are or appear to be immediate, we can nevertheless think about them afterwards and try to find out some way of explaining to ourselves or to others why we think them right or wrong. Clearly we must think about our actions if we are to see them in their correct proportions. I may, for example, think that in certain actions I am only being prudent and careful, whereas others may be quite sure that I am simply being mean. The attempt to face intellectually what we are really doing is called casuistry and, though it has sometimes, not without reason, got a bad name, it does represent a process which at some stage or other is really necessary.

An important distinction has sometimes been drawn between the Right and the Good. It is one of the great puzzles about Ethics that, while we can only have a duty or an obligation to perform a certain action, what we really applaud is a right action done from a good motive. Indeed, many would say that it is precisely to this good motive, for which we cannot have an obligation, that we assign the greatest importance in Ethics. I have, for example, a duty to pay my taxes; and if I attempt to evade them, the State will step in and see that I do so. But what really matters is that I should pay my taxes cheerfully and willingly; and this is precisely what the State cannot compel me to do, and what, indeed, I cannot have a duty to do. To be of the greatest moral worth right conduct must flow from a good heart.

Attempts to think clearly about ethical questions produce, in the main, two types of answer. We can produce an Ethics of Law which will tell us with the greatest possible detail what we ought to choose. Others, however, have sought to set before us an Ethic of Principle, which leaves the application in individual cases to ourselves. This requirement explains why there may be a wide divergence of views upon the question how an agreed principle should be worked out in particular circumstances. Each method of treating ethical questions has its own disadvantages. While the Ethic of Law makes it easy to decide what we are to do in individual cases, it soon dates and becomes old-fashioned. As the proverb says, 'Circumstances alter cases.' As against this, the Ethic of Principle, while clear in outline and not subject to variations in circumstance to the same extent as the Ethic of Law, inevitably leaves a wide margin of choice open upon the method of its application to particular circumstances. Clearly we cannot have it both ways!

We shall see the bearing of these points when we discuss in greater detail the Ethics of the Master. It is certain that He held that we ought to think about what we propose to do. He stressed the importance of a 'good heart' or a 'single eye'— the good motive out of which right conduct flows. We shall see that His ethic is one of Principle rather than of Law, giving us greater help on the general considerations which should determine our conduct than a detailed account of what we should do in certain given circumstances. Like His parables, His ethical teaching demands our co-operation in hard thought and full committal before we can really translate it into appropriate contemporary action. Both might be said to fall under the rubric, 'He that hath ears to hear let him hear,' with its corollary, 'Go and work it out for yourselves.'

We must not forget in this branch of His teaching the general conclusions which we reached in our treatment of Jesus as a teacher.

i. *He was a poet.* In poetry, form and content are closely related. The poet uses symbols and images rather than arguments and propositions. He paints a picture rather than expounds a theory. This does not mean that he does not care about truth. Quite the contrary. He often sets out in this way a truth that cannot be expressed—or cannot be expressed so well—in any other way. That is why ordinary people, who would find the arguments of a moral philosopher difficult to follow or even quite incomprehensible, can grasp the same truth readily if it is put in poetic form. But we cannot judge the insights which are expressed in this manner in quite the same way as we should weigh the arguments presented by an ethical philosopher. We should expect the latter to argue all sides of the question, to put in all the necessary qualifications, and to examine the principal exceptions. The poet is so anxious to make us see what he sees himself that he does not complicate his picture with careful safeguards and complex arguments. The philosopher will leave as little as possible to our imagination, but it is precisely to this that the poet will make his greatest appeal. A philosopher may construct an ingenious argument to show us the absurdity of egoism; the poet sketches the portrait of an egoist, and when we see it, we know that we do not approve.

ii. *He was an Oriental Who was not afraid to use figures of speech, especially hyperbole.* What Jesus is getting at is really clear enough, though the picture which He sets before us must be carefully followed. His ethical teaching has some points of contact, for example, with the method often used by those who have to deal with young children, putting an exaggerated picture of their own conduct before them and watching them take the point. A child much given to describing everything as 'the biggest in the world' can soon be cured of the habit if a grown-up adds this phrase to every single statement that he himself makes. Thus Jesus gives us the classical and un-forgettable picture of censoriousness in the exaggerated picture of the man with the hulk of timber sticking in his eye offering to remove a speck of fine dust in the eye of somebody else! It would be hard, for example, to believe that Jesus really meant us to 'hate' father or mother for His sake.

Yet some criticisms of the ethical teaching of Jesus entirely forget this aspect of His teaching, and fasten in a somewhat heavy-handed manner upon the words which He used with too little regard for the meaning which He intended these words to convey.

Perhaps the best commentary upon certain aspects of His ethical teaching can be found by comparing what He said with what He actually did. Thus He bade His disciples to 'give to him that asketh thee,' yet at times withdrew from the crowds Himself. It is certainly doubtful whether He healed all that presented themselves for healing (*St. Mark* vi. 5). He forbids His disciples to judge, and yet He offers the most sweeping denunciations of the Pharisees as a class. His warning against calling other people fools must be taken into connexion with the Parable of the Rich Fool. His counsel not to swear at all must be compared with His compliance with the adjuration or judicial oath used by the High Priest. This does not mean that there is a gap between the ethical theory and practice of Jesus, as there so often is with us, but rather that if we are to understand His ethical teaching aright, we must set it against the background of what we know of His life. This is not a warning against taking the ethics of Jesus seriously, but against interpreting it woodenly without any real regard for our *total* knowledge of His work and ways.

iii. *He was, humanly speaking, a Jew.* Many have noticed the parallels to His teaching which occur in the Rabbinic writings. It is, however, important not to press these parallels too hard. The point made by the great German Biblical scholar Wellhausen is well worth remembering here: 'Jewish scholars think that all that Jesus has said is to be found also in the Talmud. Yes, all and much more.' He goes on to remind us of the vast quantity of chaff that has to be worked through by such scholars before the genuine wheat is discovered. A modern Jewish scholar like C. G. Montefiore would agree with Wellhausen in his warning against exaggerating the parallels or of over-estimating their significance, but is inclined to go even further than the Christian scholar and to find in the ethical teaching of Jesus strands which have no known parallel in the Rabbinic writings. Jesus certainly had His ethical as well as His spiritual roots in Judaism, but His teaching does not bear the character of an anthology of the best thoughts of Judaism. It forms with His Ministry its own organic wholeness, and it has its supreme importance precisely for this reason. Jesus offers us new teaching not in the sense of a teaching without any known parallels in detail, but a teaching which is new because it is worked as an organic whole in fields of ethical understanding which are not identical with any of His predecessors. There is in their ethical premises a great gulf fixed between Jesus and the Jewish Rabbis. The latter offered an ethic of law. They made a brave but not wholly unsuccessful attempt to inform the practising Jew what was his duty in the detailed circumstances of daily life. The ethical teaching of Jesus seems to be sharply contrasted with this both in style and in objective. 'He taught as one having authority, and not as the scribes.'

The main problems which have been found in the ethical teaching of Jesus are the uncompromising directness of His sayings and the absoluteness of His claims. Various explanations of these phenomena have been proposed. Some have suggested that here we have an ethic of world-rejection as distinct from an ethic of world-acceptance. His ethical tone is extreme and severe because He sets at naught the world and its claims and duties in the interests of other and more spiritual realities. There may be a certain modicum of truth in the suggestion that our Lord gave the priority to the Kingdom of God over the kingdoms of this world, but in the strict sense of this hypothesis there is a fatal objection in the teaching about stewardship which would be clearly incompatible with a world-renouncing approach. Apart from such a matter of detail, this theory gets the explanation back to front. Our Lord's ethical teaching begins not with a certain attitude to the world but rather with the Kingdom of God, and passes on to a consideration of the world-order only secondarily or incidentally.

A similar way of putting the same point, which is exposed to very similar objections, is that the ethical teaching of Jesus is in principle ascetic. Again, in the technical sense, this view is clearly wrong. Jesus Himself is in clear contrast with John the Baptist in this matter, and His critics accuse Him of being a gluttonous man and a wine-bibber, a friend of publicans and sinners. It is true that He expected that the days would come when His disciples would fast, but if they did so, they should not appear unto men to fast. In such matters as are normally taken as the outward marks of asceticism, Jesus was no ascetic. Certainly there are many passages in which He expects His disciples to make thoroughgoing and even complete acts of renunciation; but these are never ends in themselves, but only means to the fullest possible participation in the cause of the Kingdom. The rich young ruler is called to sell all that he has, but Matthew seems perfectly correct in regarding this as a special vocation and not as an illustration of a universal ascetic principle. A similar renunciation is not, for examplef demanded of Zacchaeus, whose offer of fourfold restitution is apparently accepted. Thus it appears that neither of these two explanations is really adequate to account for the phenomena which they are designed to explain.

Schweitzer regards the ethical teaching of Jesus as an ethic of the interval before the coming *Parousia* (an *Interimsethik*). Since Jesus believed (according to Schweitzer) that the interval was likely to be very short, practicality in the present world-order was the last consideration which He had in His mind. All that mattered was complete obedience to the reckless standards of service for the Kingdom in the short span that remained.

Now such a theory has at least the tang of reality about it. It is at least possible to believe that Jesus might have held it. It asserts the primacy of the spiritual over the material in clear-cut fashion. But it is exposed to a number of damaging objections. It forms part of a total theory which we have seen good reason to reject in principle. Schweitzer presses the evidence beyond what is reasonable to believe. His theory emphasizes unduly what Jesus has in common with the Apocalyptic movement of His time and neglects the even more important differences. It thus tends to reduce Him to the level of His sources. Nor again is it really clear, surprising as this may appear at first sight, that the Apocalyptic movement had in general anything that was ethically distinctive to say or even any marked tendency towards rigorism. These preliminary difficulties are increased when we turn to the Gospels themselves. It is normally true to say that passages in which the ethical teaching of Jesus is rich and distinctive do not possess a marked eschatological character, and that passages which are clearly eschatological do not as a rule contain much that is ethically significant. The motive of Jesus is not

> Passing soon and little worth
> Are the things which tempt on earth,

but 'Be ye therefore perfect as your Father in Heaven is perfect.' His ethical thought appears to be coloured not by the thought of the impending end of the age, but by the character of God and the character which makes men citizens of His Kingdom.

It is no doubt true that all ethics until the Final Consummation are 'ethics of the Interval,' but it is a point which is hardly

very significant. We know for certain of one human institution which Jesus did regard as temporary—human marriage—
but this did not prevent Him from giving careful and important teaching about its conduct in that interval period.

Another explanation of this alleged severity in the ethical
teaching of Jesus is to suggest that it really applies not to
humanity as a whole but only to certain groups or categories
within it. It has been described, for example, as an ethic for
heroes; but this is to forget that those who originally received
it, the disciples, were very far from being moral heroes, as
the Gospels make fully clear. Or it has sometimes been
regarded as being valid only between members of the Kingdom. It is no doubt true that St. Paul blames some of his
flock at Corinth for going to law before Gentiles and thus
betrays a clear sense of the 'togetherness' of the Christian
community. It is, however, difficult to see how this criterion
would explain some at least of the ethical situations envisaged
by Jesus. The compulsory labour service, for example, concerning which Jesus enjoined the provision of going the extra
mile, can hardly have been confined to disciples or presided
over by a disciple. It is possible to suspect that some of these
explanations rest upon the mistaken belief that Jesus was giving
an ethic of Law rather than an ethic of Principle.

There remain two further theories which seem to fall under
the same criticism although their solutions are diametrically
opposed to each other. The first is that which in the case of
non-resistance is associated with the name of Tolstoi. It claims
that the teaching of Jesus is meant to be applied literally and
that failure to do so betokens simply lack of faith and of
courage. It has been said—not without some basis in truth—
that 'Christianity has not so much been tried and found
wanting, but found difficult and not tried.' This theory has
the merit of extreme simplicity, but it may well rest upon a
complete misunderstanding of what Jesus was intending to
teach. It is in all cases better to seek to understand what Jesus
was actually about before venturing to interpret it to the letter.
The second theory is given in an interesting book by Dr.
F. A. M. Spencer, *The Theory of Christ's Ethics*, which insists

upon precisely this last point, but strangely reaches the conclusion that the ethical theory behind the teaching of Jesus
represents a kind of 'higher selfishness.' Spencer certainly
reduces much that is most distinctive in the ethical teaching of
Jesus to a kind of ethical casuistry or case law. The command
to turn the other cheek, for example, might be the administration of the kind of psychological shock needed to break the
force of pathological ill-temper. We may well be in complete
accord with the author's insistence that we must first understand what it is that Jesus actually teaches without necessarily
accepting the belief that he has always put the ethical teachings
of Jesus against their appropriate background.

In our view we can best approach the ethical teaching of
Jesus in some such manner as the following:

i. In contrast with the general tendency of the Rabbis, Jesus
offered not an ethic of Law but an ethic of Principle. The
former would have been no ignoble aim, but we may confidently assume that if He had done so, His teaching would by
this time have passed into the limbo of half-forgotten systems.
He offered rather a series of insights or principles embodied
in vividly, though sharply drawn, ethical vignettes. This
method of ethical teaching not only allowed for, but actually
demanded efforts at individual application. When our Lord
said at the end of the Parable of the Good Samaritan, 'Go and
do thou likewise,' He did not mean, 'Wait until a precisely
identical situation turns up and then obey my instructions';
He meant that we should live in that spirit, and thus react
almost instinctively to the different situations with which we
are confronted. In this sense the parable has an unlimited
application to many different types of human society, whereas
detailed codes of duties could last for a few centuries at the
best. The spirit of the maxim, 'Give to him that asketh of
thee,' is dateless, whereas a set of detailed regulations about
almsgiving would be largely superannuated, for example, in
a Welfare State in which society as a whole assumes the
obligations originally performed by private enterprise.

ii. The root of the ethical teaching lies wholly in His
religion. In technical language His ethics are theocentric.

This is the cardinal difficulty about the brave and persistent, though necessarily abortive, attempt made during the last century in many quarters to retain the ethical teaching of Jesus while frankly jettisoning His religion. Such attempts are hardly likely to win much acceptance to-day. The ethics of Jesus rests not on the nature of man as such but upon the character of God, and the status of man as the child of God. Unless God is what Jesus taught that He was, the absolute worth of the human individual as Jesus envisaged it must go by the board as well. The dignity of man can only be securely based upon his dependence upon God. Positively this ethical conclusion is confirmed by the whole weight of the revelation of God in Christ; negatively it is confirmed by the progressive degradation of man which has occurred with gathering momentum as men have deserted the religion of Jesus in modern times. The Judaism in which Jesus was nurtured took for granted that religion and ethics stood shoulder to shoulder. Here the value of humanity was high. Greek thought, however, never discovered the integral and close relation between the two; and in consequence, while the small cultured minority were able to live a worthwhile life, the majority of mankind never attained any real status of dignity.

iii. The ethical teaching of Jesus is concerned not merely with external actions but also with the internal state of soul from which the action springs. Jesus 'interiorized' ethics by taking into full account the motive from which action springs. He insisted that in ethics we must work from within outwards, and not from without inwards. It is out of the abundance of the heart that the mouth speaketh. The good heart and the single eye are factors of supreme importance in the ethical life. It is not enough conscientiously to avoid murdering other people if angry and resentful thoughts which are the raw material of murder are allowed to flourish unchecked. The impure thought and the uncontrolled look are as guilty as open adultery. To cleanse the outside of the cup and the platter is of no avail if the inside is foul and unclean. The external whitewashing of tombs does not affect their grim and decaying contents. To the question, 'What ought I to do?'

Jesus returns an even more fundamental one, 'What sort of a person are you?'

iv. Thus the ethic of Jesus is an ethic of persons for persons. The ethical life is not composed simply of right reactions to felt obligations, nor of the mere fulfilment of my station and its duties. It is the satisfaction of claims made by persons on persons. Ethics, as Jesus understood them, involved the response of the whole man to whole men. Thus Jesus extends the range of ethics not only inwards but, as it were, outwards. Our neighbour is not merely a fellow Jew, but any man in need, solely because he is a man and is in need. To emphasize this point Jesus makes His typical good neighbour not a Jew but a Samaritan. Any conduct which is less than personal or given instead of—or with part of—the personality is condemned implicitly both by what Jesus said and what He did.

v. For, finally, the teaching of Jesus forms an organic whole. It is, as it were, a seamless robe. Its principles cohere with each other and, if taken together, form a single pattern of life based upon common insights. It is this unitary character of the life and teaching of Jesus which forms the most weighty positive argument for His ethical sinlessness. It would perhaps be better to speak rather of His ethical perfection than of His negative sinlessness. We know in ourselves the disappointing gap between belief and performance, the blindness and partiality of our ethical insight. Neither appears to characterize either the teaching or the Person of Jesus Himself.

Now if this be a correct perspective we might expect to find two corollaries true:

i. We have refused to discover in the ethical teaching of Jesus any suggestion of an ethic of Law. This is not to say that attempts to frame one in obedience to the principles of Jesus should not be made. We shall discover some traces of such an early attempt in certain passages in St. Matthew's Gospel. The science of moral theology has of recent years had a notable and welcome revival. So long as we realize that Jesus never made the attempt Himself, and that the work of casuistry needs to be revised to meet changing circumstances from age to age and that therefore we should not attempt to claim for our

efforts here a finality which belongs only to the differently
orientated ethic of the Master, such tasks are necessary and
should certainly be undertaken. At best, however, such moral
theology is derived from the Gospels and dependent upon
them, rather than contained within them. The root question
which Jesus asks of us is, 'What sort of person are you and
where are you going in life?' but this question does not rule
out of court two further questions which must of necessity be
asked, 'In the light of my answer to this, what ought I to do
in certain given circumstances?' and even the prior question,
'From the ethical point of view, what exactly am I doing in
filling up a pools coupon or beating my wife or giving short
measure or poor quality in my daily work?' If in the ethical
teaching of Jesus principles weigh more heavily than duties,
insights than obligations, these certainly need application to
situations which change from age to age. The solutions of
our fathers to the ethical problems of our grandfathers will
not serve for us their children. The principles remain; their
application is changing.

ii. It is even less likely that we shall be able to construct
either a sociology or a code of international conduct from the
teaching of Jesus in the Gospels alone. To do so would be as
surprising as if we found ourselves able to construct an un-
changingly true system of physical science from the Bible data.
Neither Jesus nor His disciples were humanly in a position even
to ask this sort of question. It is sometimes forgotten in such
discussion that Jesus was an unprivileged provincial within the
Roman Empire. He certainly rejected as a temptation the
suggestion that He should fulfil His Messiahship by political
means. No doubt had He chosen differently, such questions
would very soon have come to His notice. To a private
request to intervene in a disputed case of a private inheritance
He replied, 'Who made Me a judge or a divider among you?'
It would therefore have been surprising if He had set His hand
to the production of a sociology. Dr. Spencer thinks that this
might have formed part of the teaching which Jesus might
have given had people shown themselves ready to receive it.
He quotes the passage from the Fourth Gospel, 'I have many

things to say unto you, but ye cannot bear them now.' Conjecture on teaching which Jesus might have given but did not is notoriously profitless, but we can be at least sure that if Jesus had given such teaching as a detailed and applied system, it would have been superannuated long ago. This is far from saying, of course, that a modern disciple of Jesus should neglect sociology. After all, it is implied in the command to love our neighbour as ourselves. To try to distil a doctrine of the just wage from the Parable of the Workers in the Vineyard is not only to misconceive the point of the particular story but the significance of parables in general. Jesus never sought to reveal Himself either as a moral theologian or a sociologist; His ethical teaching lay at an earlier and a deeper level. Christian workers in these fields are indeed essential; but if their work is not superfluous, they will certainly not find that it has already been done for them by their Lord.

So far we have been chiefly concerned to set the stage for a more detailed examination of the ethical teaching of Jesus. We can draw nearer to the heart of His teaching by noticing the qualities and actions which He specially approved or disapproved.

It has been well said that no one can denounce sin with real effectiveness without showing what manner of man he is himself. Jesus is no exception here. Some years ago a lay Christian preaching in an Oxford college chapel took as his theme the things which Christ hated. His choice of a subject has about it the air of a paradox, since Jesus is usually conceived as the embodiment of Divine Love. But the motive behind the theme is clear enough. Love as Jesus understood it is no weak thing which covers a slack indifference to moral and spiritual issues. By its very nature it must take sides decisively against the things which spoil life and make it difficult for men to be what Jesus saw that they were intended to become, the sons of the Living God.

Our natural starting-point is the list of evil things which proceed from within recorded in St. Mark vii. 21-3. This rounds off a discussion on ritual purity which concludes: 'Not that which enters a man from outside but that which issues

from within defiles a man. . . . For from within, from the
heart of man, proceed evil thoughts.' Dr. Anderson Scott
interprets this phrase as 'evil confabulations,' the half-conscious
discussions of a divided mind, but it seems more probable that
it represents merely a generalizing summary of the whole
subsequent list. It is a long and unsavoury catalogue. Some
of the items cause no surprise. The mention of 'adultery' and
'fornication' warns us against a common fallacy that has little
enough warrant in the Gospels, that Jesus took the sins of the
flesh less than seriously. This is sometimes inferred from the
story of the woman taken in adultery recorded in St. John vii.
53–viii. 11, but the point there is not so much the innocence
of the woman as the guilt of the accusers. In any case, the
woman is told to 'go and sin no more.' It would be strange if
Jesus, cradled in Jewish ethics, had thought lightly of sins of
the flesh. Rather He carried His teaching deeper into the
thought-life that lies behind them, and focused greater attention upon the so-called sins of respectable people. But to say
that these were equally deadly was not to condone the less
respectable sins. If 'whining and whimpering sins' were sins,
it did not mean that 'crying sins' were whitewashed.

The condemnation of 'covetousness' or possessiveness brings
us to one of the distinctive features of the teaching of Jesus.
This is followed by 'wickedness,' which looks like another
general term but which really describes the choice of evil for
its own sake, or depravity. Perhaps we might paraphrase it as
positive aggressive evil, the desire to do hurt to others without
thought of any personal gain which might result from doing
so. The next term in the list refers to sneaking or underhand
evil, while the following word 'wantonness' implies the
excessive indulgence of any form of bodily appetite. The 'evil
eye' has nothing to do with witchcraft, but rather with lack
of generosity (cp. 'Is thine eye evil because I am good?')
'Blasphemy' should mean open speech against God, but in
this context might possibly refer to violent and unrestrained
speech against man. The next word, 'pride,' describes an
exaggerated sense of personal worth which leads to despising
others. It is exemplified in the little Parable of the Pharisee

and the Publican (*St. Luke* xviii. 9–14). The *Ethics* of Aristotle show how far such a quality would have been from being regarded as a vice in the aristocratic society of classical Greece. It is perhaps strange to find the list ending with 'folly' which we should normally regard as an intellectual rather than a moral defect. It must, however, be taken into close connexion with the Biblical view of folly, which sees it as crass moral insensibility. It is so used in the Parable of the Rich Fool (*St. Luke* xii. 13–21).

Further evidence of first-class importance is afforded by the denunciations of the Pharisees. It has long been disputed, particularly by Jewish scholars, whether the vices castigated by Jesus were typical of the Pharisees as a whole or merely of a small minority within the body. The evidence is not easy to handle even for an expert, and it is as well to remember that the Gospels form part of the evidence. It is hard to be sure of the ground here, but one point has not always been noted with sufficient clarity, that even if it is the vices of a minority which are in view, they are vices which belong to them as members of a system. They receive special attention from Jesus because they involve the corruption of religion, the very force which makes for righteousness in the lives of ordinary people. The vices of religious people are specially deadly because they flow from a perversion and a misunderstanding of their faith and its implications. If they appear at first sight to be relatively trivial, they have a devastating consequence quite out of all proportion to their apparent character. There is no greater enemy to true religion than a showy and pretentious religiosity which has run to seed and degenerated into triviality or worse. That is why hypocrisy, the leaven of the Pharisees (*St. Luke* xii. 1), has such a high place among the sins which Jesus condemns. It led to a preoccupation with long and repetitious prayers (*St. Matt.* vi. 5–8; *St. Mark* xii. 40) and the wrong attitude taken up towards fasting and almsgiving (*St. Matt.* vi. 1–4, 16–18). It is the outward shell of a piety which has long since ceased to exist inwardly, like the fig tree with its showy leaves and absence of fruit (*St. Mark* xi. 20–5), or whitewashed tombs whose neat exterior only hides inward decay (*St. Matt.*

xxiii. 27; *St. Luke* xi. 44). Its concern with externals is illustrated by its love of fringes or phylacteries (*St. Matt.* xxiii. 5),
its concern for personal precedence even on social occasions
(*St. Luke* xiv. 7–11), and its devotion to high-sounding titles
(*St. Matt.* xxiii. 8–10). These minister to a self-satisfaction
which can hardly believe that it has any sins to confess before
God (*St. Luke* xviii. 9–14). The religious mind is singularly
apt to take the will for the deed (*St. Matt.* xxi. 28–32).

But the indictment of the hypocrisy of the Pharisees is
carried even deeper than this by our Lord. The overvaluation
of secondary details is not merely a mark of anxious scrupu-
losity; it might also go hand in hand with a neglect, if only
by exclusion, of the weightier matters of the Law (*St. Matt.*
xxiii. 23–4; *St. Luke* xi. 42). The fulfilment of these secondary
obligations might even be offered as an excuse for not fulfilling obvious and primary ethical duties. This is probably
the point of the difficult *Corban* passage in St. Mark vii. 11,
which looks like a personal 'wangle' based upon the inviola-
bility of a religious oath or vow to the detriment of plain duty
to parents and to the personal advantage of those who pleaded
it. (It is only fair to note that the best mind of Judaism would
range itself solidly on the side of Jesus on this matter.) It issues
also in a perverted sense of values and a muddled order of
priorities. Contemporary religious leaders appeared to Jesus
like blind leaders of the blind (*St. Matt.* xv. 14) or like men
with bulks of timber in their eyes offering to remove the speck
of fine dust which had become lodged in the eyes of others
(*St. Matt.* vii. 3–5; *St. Luke* vi. 41–2). They have taken away
the key of knowledge and neither enter in themselves nor
permit others to enter in (*St. Matt.* xxiii. 13; *St. Luke* xi. 52).
They could even ascribe to the devil what really came from
God (*St. Mark* iii. 22–9; cf. *St. Matt.* xii. 27–32; *St. Luke* xi.
19–20). This is the really unforgivable sin, the sin against the
Holy Spirit (*St. Mark* ix. 38–41; *St. Luke* ix. 49–50).

This spirit which, either as an actuality or as a present though
scarcely realized threat, menaced contemporary Judaism,
tended to spread to the disciples themselves. They too must
be warned against the leaven of the Pharisees which is hypo-

crisy (*St. Luke* xii. 1). It is not enough to utter ecstatic address to Christ like 'Lord, Lord' and not to do what He says (*St. Matt.* vii. 21-3; *St. Luke* vi. 46, xiii. 26-7). They must not court titles of honour like Rabbi and Father (*St. Matt.* xxiii. 8-10). Our Lord Himself appears to reject the title 'Good Master,' not because it was untrue but because it was extremely bad for the man who used it half-unthinkingly (*St. Mark* x. 18). The desire for personal precedence needed to be sternly suppressed. There is a cup from which faithful disciples can drink, but within the wine is still red (*St. Mark* x. 35-45; *St. Matt.* xx. 20-8; *St. Luke* xxii. 24-7). In sharp contrast their Master is among them as one that serveth, and St. John records that on one occasion He performed the office of the junior member of a Rabbinic company (*St. John* xiii. 3-10). Narrow and exclusive intolerance among them is to be rebuked. The Boanerges or Sons of Thunder on one occasion wished to call down fire upon a Samaritan village which refused to receive their Lord (*St. Luke* ix. 51-6); they were to learn that what might be tolerable in an Elijah (2 *Kings* i) had no place in the mind of the Master. Their jealous opposition to the strange exorcist whom they found casting out demons in His Name earned the rebuke rather than the commendation of Jesus.

If Jesus found it necessary to give warnings to His own faithful friends, would-be disciples had their own special temptations to face. There is first the refusal to count the cost or to offer their service upon conditions (*St. Matt.* viii. 19-22; *St. Luke* ix. 57-60). It is not enough to wait for the death of a parent before fulfilling the duty of following Jesus. Here Jesus appears to be incomparably sterner than Elijah, who raised no objection to the natural request of Elisha to say goodbye at home (1 *Kings* xix. 19-21); it is, however, probable that the would-be disciple in the Gospels was asking for a longer delay than this. The King's business requireth urgency and the cause of the Kingdom must not tarry. Christ never undervalued family life and its claims, but steadily refused to treat it as an ultimate. This is probably the meaning of a sharply expressed saying in St. Matthew xix. 12. Possessions must be completely abandoned at least by some if Christ so

calls (*St. Mark* x. 17–31; *St. Matt.* xix. 16–30; *St. Luke* xviii.
18–30). Over against this the true disciple will take up his
cross for Christ, even daily (*St. Mark* viii. 34; *St. Matt.* xvi. 24;
*St. Luke* ix. 23), and follow the Master wherever He leads.
As Bultmann has pointed out, for Jesus 'half-decision is
abomination.' To fail here on the threshold of discipleship
would be to resemble a builder who began a work which he
could not complete and which would remain just one more
'folly,' or a king who embarked upon military operations
without providing against future contingencies (*St. Luke* xiv.
28–32).

If discipleship is rightly begun, it must be continued in a
similar spirit to the very end. Christ has no promises for the
well-intentioned but muddle-headed. Disciples must be faithful and wise stewards (*St. Matt.* xxiv. 45–51; *St. Luke* xii.
41–6), comparable to earthly stewards concerned with talents
and pounds (*St. Matt.* xxv. 14–30; *St. Luke* xix. 11–27). This
is at least part of the point of the Parables of Effort—the
widow who pestered an unjust judge to grant her request,
the man who, unable himself to fulfil the sacred laws of
hospitality to an unexpected guest, knocks up a neighbour to
his own inconvenience and to that of the family who was
sharing with him the truckle-bed in which they were all
sleeping. The speculator who realizes his whole estate to buy
a field in which he has reason to believe a treasure has been
hidden and the collector of pearls who sells his whole collection to buy the master pearl are both types of the faithful
disciple. Even a thoroughly dishonest steward may have a
lesson to teach a lazy, and therefore no less dishonest, disciple,
who keeps back part of the price. There must be a relentless
subordination of means to ends (*St. Luke* xvi. 1–8). If the
disciples should be harmless as doves, they should also be as
cunning as serpents (*St. Matt.* x. 16). They must be watchful
as men who wait for their Lord (*St. Luke* xii. 35–8). A discipleship which has gone sour is as useless as savourless salt or a
light put under a bushel measure (*St. Matt.* v. 14–15; *St. Luke*
xiv. 34–5).

In the dealings of people with each other Jesus condemns

first and foremost the inhumanity which puts stumbling-blocks in the way of others. Few passages even in the denunciations of hypocrisy are as stern as the threat to those who cause little ones to stumble. It would be better to have a millstone round the neck and to be drowned in the depths of the sea (*St. Mark* ix. 42; *St. Matt.* xviii. 6; *St. Luke* xvii. 1–2). 'Take heed that ye despise not one of these little ones' (*St. Matt.* xviii. 10). It is this moral insensibility which Jesus denounces in the scribes and Pharisees who bind heavy burdens upon others without any regard to the possibility of their fulfilment. (This seems to refer rather to the burden of religious obligation than to the direct physical carrying of heavy loads; the principle is, however, the same in either case.) The priest and Levite who passed by on the other side no doubt had pressing religious duties to perform, but they were blind to the plight of the unknown man lying in the gutter by the roadside (*St. Luke* x. 29–37). The rich man in the Parable of Dives and Lazarus is punished not so much for his wealth as for his insensitiveness to the needs of the beggar who lay at his door (*St. Luke* xvi. 19–31).

Equally significant is our Lord's condemnation of censoriousness. To judge others as we would be judged ourselves is the proper response of disciples of the Master Who came not to judge but to save (*St. Matt.* vii. 1–5; *St. Luke* vi. 37–8, 41–2). Those who discern specks in the eyes of others should beware of hulks of timber in their own eyes. The elder brother in the Parable of the Prodigal Son is the prototype of the censorious man (*St. Luke* xv. 25–32). The servant to whom much is forgiven should not exact full payment of a trivial debt to himself (*St. Matt.* xviii. 23–35).

Possessiveness is another sin which Jesus condemned in full measure. The rich fool planned his economy without any regard for the inescapable fact of human death. A man's wealth does not consist in the abundance of his possessions (*St. Luke* xii. 15), and Jesus lays down the searching principle that 'where thy treasure is, there shall thy heart be also' (*St. Matt.* vi. 21; *St. Luke* xii. 34).

It is no accident that the root of all these qualities which

Jesus condemned is egoism. *My* rights to the exclusion of others, *my* possessions, *my* judgements of others are set against *my* duties to others, *my* dependence upon God and the judgement of God under which *I* stand. Even hypocrisy has its basis in egoism. The hypocrite is more concerned for 'his' religion than for the service of God. Discipleship of Christ has nothing to do with any reserve price which we may set upon our own lives. It is literally true that he who does not 'say no' to self cannot be Christ's disciples (*St. Mark* viii. 34; *St. Matt.* xvi. 24; *St. Luke* ix. 23). 'He who willeth to lose his life, the same shall save it' is not, as some might think, a statement about death; it is a stark fact about life itself (*St. Mark* viii. 35; *St. Matt.* xvi. 25; *St. Luke* ix. 24; cp. *St. Matt.* x. 38–9; *St. Luke* xvii. 33).

But Jesus is no mere denouncer of sin; there are also qualities which He repeatedly and positively approves. He does not offer us a list of such qualities in a codified form like the Stoic four cardinal virtues or the seven virtues of later Christian thought. Such lists no doubt have their value, but it is in character with the aim and method of Jesus not to give one, any more than He normally offers a catalogue of the world's worst sins. Jesus leaves both virtues and vices to be deduced from His teaching. First of all comes humility: 'Blessed are the meek for they shall inherit the earth' (*St. Matt.* v. 5). Despite his good opinion of himself, the Pharisee in the parable is passed over in favour of the publican who would not so much as lift his eyes to heaven and prayed: 'God be merciful to me a sinner.' We should take the lowest place at feasts, and, so far from putting ourselves forward, should wait for others to say to us: 'Friend, go up higher' (*St. Luke* xiv. 7–14). When we have done all, we should say: 'We are unprofitable servants' (*St. Luke* xvii. 10). It is easy to misinterpret this teaching of Jesus on humility; it has nothing to do with the inverted pride of a Uriah Heap or a 'martyred doormat' attitude to life. The terrible meek to whom the earth belongs are those who claim great things from God because they ask nothing for themselves. Thus the meekness of Jesus was quite consistent with a terrible wrath against sin—the wrath of the Lamb. But this personal detachment can be misunderstood in a

different way. It is not the apathy of the Stoic sage, who is
unaffected by circumstances because they are beneath his
notice and cannot ruffle his Olympian calm. It is detachment
from self because it is attachment to God.

Next we should rank sincerity. This is at least part of the
meaning of the Beatitude: 'Blessed are the pure in heart: for
they shall see God' (*St. Matt.* v. 8). These are the single in
purpose, whose whole body is full of light because their eye is
single (*St. Matt.* vi. 22; *St. Luke* xi. 34).

Jesus also makes much of inner freedom of spirit. It is this
which underlies the much misrepresented exhortation: 'Take
no anxious thought for the morrow, for the morrow shall
take thought of the things of itself. Sufficient unto the day is
the evil thereof' (*St. Matt.* vi. 34). To interpret the passage as
though it meant, 'Be careless for anything except to-day,'
would not only gravely mistranslate the Greek, it would also
run clean counter to His teaching on stewardship. C. G.
Montefiore, the Liberal Jewish commentator, gives the best
interpretation of the passage: 'Not to be anxious is to have a
free heart, to be courageous and active, to accept our life
every day afresh from God, and to trust in Him. But such
composure is not only not a hindrance, but is even an in-
exhaustible source of strength for a successful struggle for
existence.' We can surely add an appropriate comment from
the Fourth Gospel: 'If the Son shall make you free, you shall
be free indeed' (*St. John* viii. 36).

A further characteristic is forgiveness. Peter, beginning to
learn the lesson of forgiveness, is told to forgive not until
seven times a day but until seventy times seven (*St. Matt.* xviii.
21-2). The Lord's Prayer contains the provision that we must
forgive others as we hope to be forgiven ourselves (*St. Matt.*
vi. 12; *St. Luke* xi. 4). If this forgiveness of others is so closely
joined to the Divine Forgiveness, it cannot arise from a shallow
indifferentism to sin. Nor does it possess the automatic and
mechanical character of the cynic's tag: 'God will forgive;
that's what He's there for.' It flows rather from overmastering
love of God extended to others in sin. If the forgiveness of
God in Christ is closely related to a Cross, we cannot imagine

that the forgiveness of man by man can be attended without
cost.

We can pass to love of neighbour. This is included in our
Lord's summary of the commandments, though it is sub-
ordinated and made dependent upon the love of God (*St. Mark*
xii. 28–34; *St. Matt.* xxii. 34–40). It must extend further than
our close neighbours, even to our enemies (*St. Matt.* v. 43–8;
*St. Luke* vi. 27–8, 32–3). Few positive principles of the ethical
teaching of Jesus have been so consistently and unintelligently
criticized as this. It does not mean that we must *like* our
enemies; that is hardly within our power. We are, however,
bidden to love, which, even if it cuts deeper, is paradoxically
less difficult. It involves seeking at all times their good rather
than their harm, and can, if necessary, be exercised from the
will alone; it is, however, made intelligible and possible only
in the light of the Love of God shed abroad in our hearts.

The quality of faithfulness is again prominent in the teaching
of Jesus. Although, when we have done all, we should say,
'We are unprofitable servants' (*St. Luke* xvii. 10), our Lord's
commendation, 'Well done, good and faithful servant,' may
one day be ours (*St. Matt.* xxv. 14–30; *St. Luke* xix. 11–27).
The Christian disciple must not imitate the servant in the
parable who took his talent, wrapped it in a napkin, and
buried it in the ground; he must give it to the exchangers so
that, when his Lord cometh, He may receive His own with
interest. The reward for responsibility well and faithfully
discharged is not an absence of responsibility but a greater and
more important sphere. Here St. Luke appears to strike a
truer note than St. Matthew's rather weak 'enter into the joy
of thy Lord.' Yet such faithfulness on our part does nothing
to establish anything in the nature of a claim upon God.

It is at first sight curious that one of the qualities most
implied in our Lord's teaching and displayed in His life—
courage—is never mentioned in the Gospels. It is certainly
implied in the demand for full committal to His service. At
first sight this absence of the word might appear to offer some
factual support for the theory of Nietzsche that the ethic of
Jesus is only for weaklings. But this is far too easy an assump-

tion. No doubt if we mean by courage a capacity for limitless self-assertion, we shall not find this quality in our Lord, and incipient advances in this direction by the disciples are firmly nipped in the bud. If, however, we mean by courage fortitude, the ability to stand alone or in a tiny minority without thought of consequences, then there are few qualities so much taken for granted in the Gospels. There is little need to dwell upon the courage, both physical and moral, shown by our Lord in the Passion—a few moments of reflection would illustrate this. For the same reason, the disciples must show this quality in their own lives: 'As is the Master, so shall the servant be.'

There remain for our consideration certain parts of the ethics of Jesus which have either caused special difficulty or which require a more detailed consideration. So far we have found it sufficient to collect and arrange our material; here we need discussion as well.

1. *Non-resistance to evil*

The evidence which bears upon this is largely (though not wholly) concentrated in the Sermon on the Mount in a section which might be headed 'On retaliation' (*St. Matt.* v. 38–42; *St. Luke* vi. 29–30). Jesus is here correcting and carrying deeper the old ethical maxim of the *lex talionis*—'an eye for an eye and a tooth for a tooth.' It is well to bear in mind that in its day this law was a merciful restriction of the practice of unlimited private revenge. Over against this Jesus sets a new principle, 'Resist not evil.' It does not greatly affect the meaning whether 'evil' is to be taken as masculine or neuter. The point is the same in either case: 'Do not resist personal insult or injury.' The example of our Lord in the Garden of Gethsemane or on the Cross forms the best commentary that we can find. As the martyred servant of God our Lord 'gave His back to the smiters and His cheek to those who plucked off the hair' (*Isa.* l. 6). The instances quoted in the Sermon on the Mount are worthy of close examination. There is first the smitten cheek. The language used suggests rather an insulting slap on the cheek than a vigorous punch on the jaw. It is intended to wound feelings rather than to inflict physical injury. The implication is that the victim is not worth wasting force upon. A sensitive oriental would find this even more deadly than a violent and open attack. The action of turning the other cheek would take a contemptuous opponent completely by surprise. The second illustration describes an action-at-law in which the rapacious litigant claims his victim's suit of clothes; he should be offered the overcoat as a free gift as well. The significance of this free surrender can be seen in the fact that the old Hebrew customary law recorded in Exodus xxii. 25–7 enacted that a creditor should return a cloak taken as pledge before nightfall for fear that his debtor should die of exposure in the chilly Palestinian nights. The third instance refers to the *corvée* or compulsory labour service presided over by some jack-booted jack-in-office who would be surprised out of his life by the offer of an extra mile of service from one from whom he had expected at best reluctant obedience. In each case it is the voluntary nature of the action which draws the sting out of an injury done to a single person who both knows what he is doing and why he is doing it.

Outside this section there are a few other passages which are brought into the discussion. The first occurs in St. Matthew x. 34: 'I am come not to send peace but a sword.' This is a sharp reminder that the Mission of Jesus is not a facile instrument of unification, but demands decision, and is therefore just as likely to divide men as to unite them. It is a warning of the tonic and challenging character of discipleship. The sword is clearly metaphorical rather than literal and, apart from the note of challenge and opposition which it contains, this saying has no direct bearing on the use of force.

There is also a curious passage in St. Luke xxii. 35–8. Here Jesus contrasts the early welcome which His disciples received with a more hostile spirit abroad on the eve of the Passion. At first they went out without scrip, wallet, and purse, and yet lacked nothing (*St. Mark* vi. 8; *St. Matt.* x. 9–10; *St. Luke* ix. 3, referred to in *St. Luke* xxii. 35). Now let them sell such things and even their precious and necessary overcoats and buy a sword. The disciples reply: 'Lord, here are two swords,' and

Jesus replies: 'It is enough.' The meaning of our Lord's reply has been disputed. It might mean: 'Two swords are enough.' But enough for what? They certainly did not prevent the arrest, and Jesus rebuked St. Peter who used his sword in the defence of his Master. Possibly it might mean 'enough to prevent an unauthorized private attack,' but there is little enough evidence that this was in the mind of Jesus. It is far better to interpret the passage as meaning: 'Enough of this, you have mistaken my meaning.'

A third saying is recorded in St. Matthew xxvi. 52, where Peter, having drawn sword in our Lord's defence, is bidden to put up his sword again into its sheath, for 'those who take the sword shall perish with the sword.' Here again the interpretation is under dispute. It can either be a particular statement to Peter or a general statement of a semi-proverbial nature of the order, 'Violent come, violent go.'

Finally, there is the scourge of small cords (a clutch of rope-ends) recorded by the Fourth Gospel though not by the Synoptists as used by our Lord at the cleansing of the Temple (*St. John* ii. 15). It would be rather prosaic to attempt to estimate its effectiveness as a weapon. This might well have been considerable, but it was surely the blazing anger of the selfless Christ rather than the weapon which He carried which really cleared the Temple Courts of its noisy, motley throng.

It is clear, then, that on this subject the evidence is scanty and not wholly easy to interpret. Its general sense at first sight points in the direction of non-resistance to evil and the refusal to use force. But before deciding too easily upon this conclusion it is well to notice two points. In the first place, the instances in which non-retaliation to injury is enjoined are either cases of injury to ourselves personally or a refusal to allow us to take up arms in the Master's defence. It is *our* cheek which is flicked, *our* suit of clothes demanded at law, the *corvée* imposed upon *us*. It is not quite so easy to determine what should be our attitude when the injury in question is to be done to others. There the severe note of the teaching about stumbling-blocks might very well be in point. To surrender

our own rights is one thing, to surrender the rights of others
is to surrender what it is not ours to give. The question asked
by the philosopher Paulsen, 'What ought the Good Samaritan
to have done if he had found the robbers engaged upon their
work?' is more relevant and less trivial than might at first sight
appear.

Further, to try to apply teaching embodied in this form and
of this character to modern international situations is to forget
the significance of the fact that Jesus never gives us either a
sociology or a code of international behaviour. In such a
matter application must involve a considerable amount of
translation before it can be regarded as adequate.

We can, however, add four caveats on the subject here:

i. The nearer that we approximate to the selfless anger of
the Christ in the Temple Courts, the more sure that we can
be that we are fulfilling our discipleship of Him. This must
be true of our approach to social, economic, and international
questions as well as in our personal relations.

ii. Our concern must be always the rights and needs of
others rather than of ourselves. The difference may perhaps
be one of degree rather than of kind, but it is nevertheless
necessary to bear it in mind.

iii. Christians should always seek to do something better
than force. They are not entitled to do nothing at all in the
presence of giant evils. If they cannot see any better solution
at a given moment than the use of force, then they must use
this in shame and penitence rather than contract out of doing
something. To contract out of situations is not to obey the
law of love. Pacifism may be one thing, passivism is quite
another.

iv. If non-resistance is accepted as the way for individuals
or for Christians as a whole, it should always be regarded as
part of a pattern of conscious discipleship, not as a move in a
diplomatic game or as a refined (and therefore a specially
devastating) method of applying force. Not all pacifist
tendencies at the present time are either motived or governed
by Christian principles.

## 2. Wealth

It has often been maintained that Jesus was opposed to the possession of wealth, and that we can trace in His teaching either an eschatological denunciation of wealth in the light of the approaching end of the age, or the zeal of a social reformer condemning wealth in the interests of some far-reaching scheme of social improvement. Neither of these views can be readily maintained. We have already discovered grounds for rejecting the idea of an *Interimsethik* as the sufficient explanation of the ethical approach of our Lord, and it appears to be unlikely that it applies any better to this particular subject than to a more general context. It would, for instance, be difficult to understand the relevance of the principle of stewardship as applied to the teaching of Jesus about wealth if this were the case. 'He that is faithful in little is faithful also in much, and he that is unjust in little is unjust also in much. If then ye are unfaithful in the mammon of unrighteousness, who shall entrust to you the true riches, and if you are not faithful in that which is another's, who shall give you what is your own?' (*St. Luke* xvi. 10–12). Such a passage is incompatible with the view that Jesus demanded the complete renunciation of riches because the end was near. Nor can we maintain that Jesus was concerned with any particular scheme for social improvement which might involve such a rejection. He treats the suggestion that He should act as a bread-giving or economic Messiah as a temptation, and even refuses to act as arbitrator in the case of a disputed inheritance (*St. Luke* xii. 14). Attempts to distil any doctrine of the just wage out of the Parable of the Workers in the Vineyard have proved uniformly unsuccessful; we shall have to examine the more probable interpretation of this parable later on.

It has sometimes been thought that St. Luke is really the villain of the piece, touching up the authentic teaching of Jesus in the direction of a commendation of poverty for its own sake. St. Luke's own interest in questions of poverty and riches is well known; it fits in well with the character of the 'dear doctor' of the early Church, full of sympathy and mercy

like his Lord. In the Acts of the Apostles it is he who records
the ill-starred effort towards a primitive communism of goods
in the Jerusalemite Church which reduced the 'poor saints'
at Jerusalem to being the objects of charity of the Gentile
Christians of the Pauline Mission. There are some traits in the
Third Gospel which have been taken to support an 'Ebionite'
interest in poverty on the part of St. Luke. In the account of
the rich young ruler, whereas St. Matthew makes it quite
clear that our Lord has in mind a special vocation, St. Luke
adds no qualification of any kind (*St. Luke* xviii. 22; *St. Matt.*
xix. 21). It should, however, be remembered that St. Mark
here agrees with St. Luke, and that the Third Gospel may
therefore be merely copying the wording of the second. In
that case, St. Matthew may merely be putting in an explanation
in the light of later questions which the other two Gospels
never thought of raising. While Matthew contains the
Beatitude, 'Blessed are the poor in spirit,' Luke merely renders
it, 'Blessed are ye poor' (*St. Matt.* v. 3; *St. Luke* vi. 20). The
force of this is rather blunted by the fact that the term 'poor'
in the Psalms is normally used in exactly the Matthaean sense;
and it is therefore not improbable that, while St. Luke may
have preserved the original form, St. Matthew may be closer
to the real meaning. It is not the financially embarrassed but
the spiritually dependent who are the intended recipients of
the blessing. There is no real warrant for setting the meaning
of the two versions in opposition to each other. Luke alone
records the two Parables of the Rich Fool and of Dives and
Lazarus (*St. Luke* xii. 13–21, xvi. 19–31), but in each case the
point is not so much the presence or absence of riches as the
moral insensibility which the possession of riches brings in its
train. As against the view that St. Luke has heightened the
teaching of Jesus in this particular direction can be set a number
of sayings and parables. He is particularly rich in teaching
about stewardship, which makes it impossible to believe that
he regarded the mere possession of wealth as vicious. Again,
he alone tells of the wealthy women who ministered to Jesus
of their substance (*St. Luke* viii. 1–3); clearly he must have
thought that here was one example of wealth rightly used.

We may well agree that St. Luke had a special interest in the teaching of Jesus about poverty and riches, and that he may also have made a special selection of material in the oral and written tradition which bore on the subject; but we cannot regard it as proven either that he selected such material as suggested that Jesus regarded the possession of riches as wrong, or that Jesus actually took such an extreme view Himself.

It is at this point that we must examine two parables of special difficulty which bear upon the subject. The first is the Parable of the Workers in the Vineyard (*St. Matt.* xx. 1–16). Here we have the picture of the owner of a vineyard who hires day labour to work in his holding for the wage which seems to have been a fair and adequate one of a *denarius* for the day. At other hours of the day he sent others to work in his vineyard, and when the end of the day came, he paid off his workers, beginning with those who had worked for the least time. Each labourer—irrespective of the number of hours that he had worked in the vineyard—received the full day's wage of a *denarius*. This led to complaints on the part of those who had borne the burden and heat of the day, either on the ground that presumably they should have received more or that those who had been engaged later should have received proportionately less. The owner of the vineyard then replied with what appears at first sight to be an appalling statement: 'Is it not lawful for me to do what I will with mine own? Is thine eye evil [are you ungenerous] because I am good [generous]?' With these words he rejects their wage claim. It is tempting to turn this parable into an allegory, to seek to press every detail rather than to look for a single point tellingly made; but here as elsewhere the tendency to overpress the parables leads to some surprising and unexpected results. It would, for example, make nonsense of some of the parables of effort to equate God with the unjust judge or even with the man in bed! It is not in this fashion that the parables of Jesus were constructed. In the parable before us the lesson which it was intended to teach was one and one only, that reward follows opportunity rather than achievement. Of those to whom much is committed, much will be expected.

If this appears inequitable to some minds, it is because they have not yet realized the unconditioned generosity of God.

The second parable which calls for special treatment is the Parable of the Unjust Steward, where Jesus appears to commend the conduct of an unmitigated rascal. A dishonest steward, knowing that he will shortly be found out, decides to make the best possible arrangements for himself after his impending dismissal. He therefore calls together some of his master's debtors and suggests that they should scale down their debts to the estate for goods supplied by altering their bills or invoices. This is done, be it noted, in their own handwriting and not in his! The implication is that he will not altogether pass out of mind when the frauds are discovered. So far all is plain—a good story with some shrewd touches. But the difficulty begins with the next words. 'The Lord commended the unjust steward because he had dealt wisely.' Who is the Lord, and why did He commend the unjust steward? 'The Lord' might either mean the master of the estate or our Lord Himself. In the first case, it might mean little more than a passing commendation of a clever rascal, but the second interpretation would be more difficult to justify. In any other Gospel except that of St. Luke the first would be the more probable, but in Luke there is a marked tendency to use the title 'Lord' of Jesus even in the days of His flesh. This just tips the balance in favour of the more difficult rendering. If, then, the Lord in the passage is really Jesus, the difficulty remains, for what possible reason could He have for commending to our notice a particularly dishonest character? No one could regard him as a moral example. But it is worth noticing that the passage speaks of the commendation not for his goodness but for his cleverness. Jesus commends his conduct to disciples as an example of the clever adaptation of means to ends. It is, in fact, a particularly striking example of our Lord's teaching about stewardship by means of a contrast between the shrewd capability of the sons of darkness in contrast with the dishonest inefficiency of the sons of light. Thus the approval which our Lord bestows on the man in the parable is limited and relative only. It is not that the sons of light should imitate his dishonesty; it is rather that despite his dishonesty a through-and-through rascal could teach disciples a lesson worth learning which would serve the good of the Kingdom. We may well remind ourselves once again that our Lord never promises any blessing to the inefficient but well-intentioned.

We can perhaps summarize our Lord's teaching about wealth somewhat as follows:

i. Jesus is perfectly clear on the question of the place of riches in the scale of goods. Material wealth is not the true riches: 'Lay not up for yourselves treasures upon the earth, where moth and rust doth corrupt, and where thieves break through and steal' (*St. Matt.* vi. 19–21; *St. Luke* xii. 33–4). Where thy treasure is, there shall thy heart be also. The principle is put even more succinctly in a saying recorded in St. Luke xii. 15: 'A man's life does not consist in the abundance of things which he possesses.' We are to make for ourselves 'purses which grow not old, a treasure unfailing in the heavens' (*St. Luke* xii. 33).

ii. The danger of wealth is that it can become a preoccupation amounting even to slavery. Here is the root teaching of the Parable of the Rich Fool (*St. Luke* xii. 13–21). To make personal security a major aim, to seek to contract out of the stress and strain of chance and mischance is to forget that it is precisely this that cannot be guaranteed. No one can find security against the stark fact of death, and any other form of security is brittle enough in all conscience. The pursuit of Mammon may become a veritable bondage (*St. Matt.* vi. 24), no less engrossing and committing than the service of God Himself. That is why covetousness, the disease of getting, occupies so prominent a place on the roll of dishonour in the teaching of the Gospels. The cares of this world and the deceitfulness of riches are two weighty reasons for the choking of the good seed of the Word of God so that it becomes unfruitful (*St. Mark* iv. 19).

iii. We are not therefore surprised to find that the possession of riches can be a barrier to discipleship. 'How hardly shall they that have riches enter into the Kingdom of Heaven!' (*St. Mark* x. 23; *St. Matt.* xix. 23; *St. Luke* xviii. 24). At least in some cases it must be completely cut away, not for ascetic reasons but because of its incompatibility with the conditions of true discipleship.

iv. Money may be rightly or wrongly used; it is in itself a thing indifferent. The Pharisee in the parable thanks God that he is not an extortioner as other men are (*St. Luke* xviii. 11). He has therefore avoided at least one of the wrongs attendant upon the possession of money. Some Pharisees devour widows' houses and for a pretence make long prayers (*St. Mark* xii. 40). The *Corban* passage in St. Mark vii. 11–12 certainly refers to some financial sharp practice linked with religion. Yet among the right uses of wealth is the financial support of Jesus and His disciples (*St. Luke* viii. 1–3). Possibly another right use of money is to make friends (*St. Luke* xvi. 9).

v. The final principle which seems to emerge from all this is that of stewardship. Jesus insists that wealth must be held as a trust from God to be held and used against a day of reckoning which God will one day make. The wise and careful steward is approved, the slack and careless steward blamed. What matters is neither the possession nor absence of wealth, but the use to which it is put.

If this summary is a fair one, we can see why Jesus never attempted to work out a detailed system of economics. The basic principles are, however, all laid down—the doctrine of stewardship, and the secondary place which money must occupy in the light of greater and nobler ends. Jesus leaves the working out of these principles to the moral theologian, and still more to the Christian economist, in the light of the changing circumstances of each new age.

## 3. *Family life*

Jesus was born into a nation and a religion which gave a high place to the claims of family life. 'Honour thy father and mother' formed part of the Ten Commandments, and St. Paul further marks it out as the first commandment accompanied by promise (*Eph.* vi. 2). In His condemnation of the *Corban* trick which had as its motive the desire to evade such responsibilities, Jesus would have had the vast majority of Jews upon

His side. The rich young ruler's question: 'What shall I do to inherit eternal life?' is first of all answered by a selection of the Ten Commandments, mainly from the second half of the Code, leading up to the command to honour father and mother (*St. Mark* x. 19; *St. Matt.* xix. 18–19; *St. Luke* xviii. 20). The Sermon on the Mount contains no attempt to re-phrase, still less to abrogate, this commandment. High standards of family life were among those which our Lord could take for granted among His own people.

Yet it appears at first sight surprising that the conduct of Jesus with respect to His own family does not appear to tally with the place which, at least by implication, the family may be deemed to hold in His teaching. A brief summary of the relationship between Jesus and His own family as it appears in the Gospels will serve to make this point clear. The exorcisms which Jesus performed in the early part of His Ministry led to the slander that Jesus was beside Himself, and that it was through Beelzebub, the prince of the demons, that He cast out demons (*St. Mark* iii. 23–30). Immediately after this incident, and possibly in connexion with it, His human family came to see Him while He was teaching (*St. Mark* iii. 31–5; *St. Matt.* xii. 46–50; *St. Luke* viii. 19–21). The message reaches Him that His mother and His brethren were outside wanting to speak with Him. He replies by asking the question: 'Who is My mother and My brethren?' which He Himself answers: 'Whosoever does the will of God, the same is My brother and sister and mother.' He thus enunciates a clear principle of detachment from His own family where the will of God is in question. There is a similar passage in St. Luke xi. 27–8, where a woman in the crowd cries out in a kind of ecstasy of devotion: 'Blessed is the womb which bare Thee and the breasts that Thou hast sucked!' Jesus immediately turns her rapture into more profitable channels: 'Yea, rather, blessed are those that hear the Word of God and keep it.' With this the witness of the Fourth Evangelist agrees. In St. John ii. 1–11 we have an account of the Marriage Feast of Cana in Galilee where the Mother of Jesus seeks His intervention on behalf of the bridal couple. Jesus answers her almost roughly, 'Lady, what have

I to do with thee? Mine hour is not yet come,' where the
Evangelist means us to understand that where the work of the
Kingdom is at stake and its times and seasons are concerned,
despite the close tie between the Mother and her Son, He must
travel alone. Here His Mother has no more say than any other
human person. The first kind word which she receives from
Him in the Gospels comes from the Cross, where, as St. John
records, Jesus commends her to the care of the Beloved
Disciple. The point is not that the life of the human family
mattered little to Jesus, but that the tasks of the Kingdom
mattered much more. Of a truth the King's business requireth
urgency.

As is the Master, so shall the servant be. The two sons of
Zebedee must leave their father in the ship with the hired
servants (*St. Mark* i. 20). Jesus will not allow the would-be
disciple to bury his father (probably, as has been suggested, to
wait until the old man dies). After the rich young ruler has
gone sadly away, the disciples ask almost despairingly: 'Who
then can be saved?' and Peter breaks in with the statement:
'Lord, we have left all and followed Thee.' Jesus comforts
them with the words: 'There is no one who has left house or
brethren or sisters or mother or children for My sake and the
Gospels who shall not receive a hundredfold now in the present
life, houses and brothers and sisters and mothers and children
and lands with persecutions; and in the world to come eternal
life.' Luke adds 'wife' to the list of those to be abandoned
(*St. Mark* x. 29-30; *St. Matt.* xix. 29; *St. Luke* xviii. 29-30).
Here it is possible that oriental hyperbole enters into the form
of the teaching of Jesus, but its main drift is clear enough. In
some quarters within Judaism the family may have become
almost what might be called a false ultimate. It is not that
Jesus ever undervalued family life, but that, however good it
was, it cannot stand of itself against the claims of the Kingdom.
The overriding importance of the phrase 'for My sake and the
Gospels' is emphasized here.

On marriage itself Jesus makes two important statements.
The question raised by the Sadducees about the after-life is in
the nature of a *reductio ad absurdum* based upon the implicit

assumption that in the after-life there will be a mere continuation of the conditions which subsist here on earth. It may even have been a stock weapon in the debate between Pharisees and Sadducees on the subject. Jesus replies that 'in Heaven there is neither marrying nor giving in marriage, for the sons of the Resurrection are as the angels of God' (*St. Mark* xii. 25; *St. Matt.* xxii. 30; *St. Luke* xx. 36). This has been taken by some as implying that marriage is an institution of the interim period. That is true, even perhaps a truism, so far as the physical side of marriage is concerned; it does not imply that the deep personal relationships which marriage involves will become as though they had never been. The other fundamental statement which Jesus makes about marriage shows that He regards it as a fundamental human institution rooted and grounded in the very nature of man as God had created him: 'From the beginning of the creation male and female created He them. For this cause a man shall leave his father and mother and cleave unto his wife and they twain shall be one flesh so that they are no more twain but one flesh' (*St. Mark* x. 6–8; *St. Matt.* xix. 4–6). This clear statement is enough to disprove any tendency to depreciate the institution of marriage in the teaching which we have previously examined.

This last statement of our Lord is the true background of His teaching on divorce. Deuteronomy xxiv. 1 permitted a woman to be divorced by her husband 'because he hath found an unseemly thing in her.' The problem of what constituted legal grounds of divorce on the basis of this passage was a matter of dispute among the Rabbis, and the modern commentators are not themselves agreed as to what the passage originally included. Many would, however, regard it as meaning by the phrase 'unseemly thing' either adultery or some form of impurity less than adultery. Matters are not helped by the problem of the relation of the passage to Leviticus xx. 10 which prescribes the death penalty for adultery. It has been urged that the death penalty for adultery was still being enforced in the time of our Lord, and that therefore the 'unseemly thing' mentioned in Deuteronomy xxiv. 1 as a ground for divorce cannot mean adultery. Evidence

in support for this conclusion has been found in the story of
the woman taken in the act of adultery in St. John viii, where it
looks as if the procedure outlined in Leviticus is in view rather
than the milder measures of Deuteronomy. It appears, however, to be most unlikely that the death penalty for adultery
could be imposed under Roman rule, and it is probable that
the provisions of Leviticus had by that time become almost a
dead letter. In that case it would be likely whether this were
the original meaning of the passage or not that adultery was at
least not left out of account in the interpretation of Deuteronomy xxiv. 1. This is made clear by the famous dispute
between the two Rabbinic schools of Hillel and Shammai at
the time of our Lord. Shammai held the stiffer view that the
'unseemly thing' referred to in the Biblical text simply meant
adultery or some form of physical impurity sufficiently serious
to cause the breach of the unity of flesh between a man and a
woman. Hillel, however, refused to restrict the grounds for
divorce to such narrow limits, and considered that it might
cover even such trivial offences as spoiling a husband's food
by bad cooking. A later Rabbi of the school of Hillel, the
Jewish martyr Aqiba, thought that it permitted divorce in
cases where a husband found a woman who pleased him
better, since that would be tantamount to finding something
unseemly in his present wife.

In the Marcan passage which deals with this question Jesus
treats the measures of Deuteronomy as a temporary measure
only designed 'for the hardness of your hearts,' and directs the
thoughts of His hearers back from divorce and its provisions to
marriage and its purposes. He appeals, in fact, from Deuteronomy to Genesis in a manner which is made even more
significant by the fact that, like all His contemporaries, He
believed that both passages were written by Moses. It constitutes an appeal from Moses on divorce to Moses on marriage.
An age like our own, which too often sees marriage in the
context of divorce, has much to learn from our Lord's insistence on seeing divorce rather in the context of marriage.

St. Matthew, in each of the contexts in which he deals with
divorce, adds a prescription for divorce on the grounds of

adultery (*St. Matt.* v. 31-2, xix. 9). The question is stated exactly as it appeared to the schools of Hillel and Shammai, and our Lord is made to approximate to the opinion of Shammai. Mark does not add any qualification of any kind to the implied prohibition of divorce. Which, then, is the more likely to be authentic, the unqualified statement of St. Mark or the careful exceptatory clause of St. Matthew? There appear to be good grounds for preferring the Marcan version. In the first place, it could be maintained that St. Mark is the earlier Gospel and that the Matthaean version is derivative and secondary. Further, the precision with which St. Matthew echoes the disputes of the Jewish schools leaves open the possibility that we are here listening to a learned Hebrew Christian rather than to our Lord Himself. Moreover, if we are right in the view that our Lord left ethical principles rather than detailed provisions for right conduct, we should not expect to find Him inserting careful qualifying clauses as St. Matthew makes Him do in this instance. If the Matthaean version is authentic, it would appear that an ethic of Principle was being turned into an ethic of Law; and there is little difficulty in tracing here St. Matthew, the good Churchman, trying to distil a readily applicable legal principle out of the teaching of the Master. The Church would in any case need to do this at one stage or another in her pilgrimage, and it would not be at all surprising to find that the Matthaean text represents the application of the ethics of Jesus by an early moral theologian.

If, then, we maintain that the Marcan text is the more authentic here, what would its implications be with regard to the teaching of Jesus about divorce? On any showing the Matthaean version is worthy of every respect, not only from its early date but also by reason of its intrinsic reasonableness. But does the Marcan text really mean that Jesus out-Shammais Shammai on the question? Not altogether, for to adopt this conclusion would be again to convert an ethic of Principle into an ethic of Law. Jesus was trying to set the question of divorce into a different and a sounder perspective rather than to modify in one direction or another the easements which the Jewish law provided for marriages which had broken down. At this stage on the application of the teaching of Jesus to broken marriages the New Testament scholar must hand over his papers to the moral theologian, with the rider that the Matthaean exception, if it cannot be held with certainty to represent the authentic words of the Master Himself, should be heard with the greatest sympathy and respect as an early witness of first-class importance.

## 4. The State

If the Gospels suggest that Jesus was a critical, though a conforming, member of the Jewish Church, it also appears that He was a loyal, though unprivileged, member of the Roman Empire. It was not until the reign of Caracalla, nearly two centuries later, that all those who lived in the territories governed by Rome received Roman citizenship. In the days of our Lord it was still a closely-guarded privilege, of which St. Paul could rightly boast and whose prerogatives he could proudly use. Jesus had no such legal safeguards against cruelty and injustice, and even if the lot of the average provincial might not be oppressive and hard, he knew that he had no possible redress against the vagaries of the administration or the utmost rigour of the law.

Jesus takes for granted the existence of the Roman rule, despite the fact that many Jews were chafing under its sway. He appears neither as a fervid patriot nor as a servile collaborationist. He accepts, but appears apart from some few sayings and incidents to ignore, the State. He refuses as a temptation the suggestion that He should claim political power or fulfil a political pattern of Messiahship. His conception of His Person and work was formed by the Suffering Servant of prophecy, the Son of Man of Apocalyptic, and the Sonship of His own interior life rather than by the Davidic Messiahship of nationalist aspiration. He associated with tax-gatherers, collaborationists with an alien power. He recognizes the existence of the hated *corvée*, compulsory labour service; and, instead of urging resistance, bids His followers go an extra mile as a token of generous goodwill which would draw the sting from the demand.

One incident, the question about the tribute money (*St. Mark* xii. 13–17; *St. Matt.* xxii. 15–22; *St. Luke* xx. 20–6), carries the matter a stage further. This was a real and burning issue of the day, even if it were used as a test question in order to trap Him. It presented Him with a real, and His opponents hoped an inescapable, dilemma. If He allowed the legality of the payment of tribute, He could be denounced as no patriot, and deprived of much well-meaning but confused popular support; if, on the other hand, He denounced the payment of tribute to Rome, He could be embroiled with the authorities as a potential rebel. Before answering the question, He asked for a *denarius*, the Roman coin with the image and super-scription of Caesar upon its obverse. This is no mere pictur-esque touch, still less an attempt to gain time for His reply. It is an integral part of His answer. His questioners are them-selves carrying about the Emperor's image and cannot there-fore pretend that the problem is external to themselves. He then states the principle: 'Render unto Caesar the things that are Caesar's and unto God the things that are God's.' This admits plainly enough a real sphere of operations which belongs to the secular power, though reserving a domain for God which Caesar may not touch. This is no mere shelving of the issue, though characteristically Jesus never attempts to define either sphere further. It is closely linked with the affirmation made at His trial before Pilate in the Fourth Gospel (*St. John* xviii. 36): 'My Kingdom is not of this world.'

As it stands, the reply to the question about the tribute money excludes two opposite errors on the relation between the two kingdoms: it rejects at once the conception of a soulless totalitarianism in which Caesar regards as part of his province the things of God, no less than the idea of a theocratic state in which God (or His Church) takes control of the things which belong to Caesar. Neither a totalitarianism (whether of the right or the left) nor a 'rule of the saints' (either in the form of a Holy Roman Empire or of Calvin's Geneva) can claim the support of this saying of our Lord. Still less, however, can we interpret the teaching of Jesus in the equally questionable sense that while God controls personal and family ethics, He must give way to Caesar in matters of State concern and inter-State relationships. This was a compromise at one time fashionable in Germany, though the half-truth that 'the Church must not meddle in politics' has frequently been heard in this country. The justification for the claim that no human relationships whatever can be exempted from the law of Christ is covered less by this particular saying than by the general conditions of the acceptance of His Lordship and the full implications of the commandment to love our neighbour as ourselves. This love and its corollaries apply no less to our neighbour as a member of a nation, whether our own or another, than as an individual or as a member of a family circle.

In summary, then, we can say of the ethic of Jesus that it is an ethic of Principle and of insight rather than an ethic of Law. It is therefore, on the one hand, dateless and capable of application to all sorts and conditions of men. On the other hand, it needs to be translated into the actual conditions of each new age. These ethical principles of our Lord depend directly upon the religion which He embodied. We cannot love our neighbour as Jesus requires of us unless we first love God in Whom we meet our neighbour and learn to treat him as ourselves. Here is not only the reason why we should do so but also the power to enable us to perform what we see to be our duty in Christ. The religion of Jesus opens vistas of ethical achievement which are only attainable to those who are attuned to God through Christ.

Jesus possessed an unerring instinct into humanity at its weakest as well as at its best: 'He knew what was in man.' He therefore sets ethics in their widest perspective and carries them to the deepest level. He does not stop short of the level of external act; He carries our ethical choices deeper into the sphere where they are really made, the inner life of man. He challenges humanity to revise its scale of values; to put first things first; to be on its guard against the dangerous intrusion of the secondary beyond its proper sphere. He offers to His disciples the transcendent gift of a free spirit, detached from secondary considerations and rising above engrossment in secondary goals. Those who have seen in His teaching little more than a 'slave morality' are singularly blind not only to the clarity of.insight which discipleship of Jesus involves, but also to the moral courage which it implies. Here is a Master Who is not afraid to demand the utmost for His highest, Who scorns cheap compromises and easy solutions, Who sees through our ethical shams and evasions to the place where we are really living, and refuses to allow us either to evade His challenge or to lower our standards.

He not only asks this of us; He has the right to do so because it is precisely in this way that He lived Himself in the conditions of His earthly pilgrimage. His ethics shine through His Ministry and culminate in the endurance of His Cross and Passion. That they are no mere gesture of defiance to an indifferent or hostile universe, but are a revelation of the very structure of a moral universe, is proved by the Resurrection which followed, and it is to this event and its implications that we must finally turn.

## BIBLIOGRAPHY

E. F. Scott, *The Ethical Teaching of Jesus*, is the best short account of the ethics of Jesus.

C. Anderson Scott, *New Testament Ethics*, has a useful section on the teaching of Jesus.

Hastings Rashdall, *Conscience and Christ*, is a more detailed study of some of the issues in New Testament ethics from the pen of a distinguished ethical philosopher.

F. A. M. Spencer, *The Theory of Christ's Ethics*, adopts a different standpoint from the one adopted here, but deserves careful, if critical, consideration.

*PART V*

THE CONCLUSION OF THE WHOLE MATTER

Chapter XII: THE RESURRECTION OF JESUS CHRIST

343

# THE RESURRECTION OF JESUS CHRIST

THIS chapter forms the natural climax of all that has gone before. It is not merely the 'happy ending' which turned the history of the Ministry of Jesus from tragedy to triumph; it is also the vindication of the high view of the Person of the Master which has been maintained here as the evidence of the Gospels as well as the historic faith of the Church. It is also the guarantee that the teaching which has been outlined above is not merely an interesting chapter in the history of human thought, but also the gateway of our approach to God and our understanding of His ways towards the sons of men.

It is natural that, if this be the case, we should be particularly careful in our examination of the New Testament evidence for such an amazing and breath-taking fact.

The evidence carries us well behind the period of the Gospels themselves. The Resurrection is, for example, the fundamental message of the speeches of the early chapters of Acts. Although it is possible that St Luke had a hand in their compilation, we can hardly believe that they represent merely a free composition of the second Christian generation. The doctrine of the Person of Christ which these speeches contains is in many respects so primitive and undeveloped in character that it seems to represent in the main good and early material. The Christian Church appears still to be a body of believers organized within Judaism, with its own beliefs and practices additional to the regular practices of Judaism. Neither in history nor in doctrine is the picture of the earliest days of Christianity given in the Acts of the Apostles really true to the period at which St. Luke was writing or of the circle which he himself represents.

These primitive Christians, as St. Luke depicts them, attended Jewish services and observances, although they had their own special place of meeting in Solomon's Porch, and broke bread together in each others' houses in observance of the Lord's Supper or Eucharist. They clearly did not anticipate that any one who was not a Jew would join their company, as their hesitation over the Samaritan converts and the Gentile Cornelius was to prove. Three beliefs appear to mark them off from their fellow Jews. First, they believed that Jesus of Nazareth, Who had died a few weeks before, was the Christ or the Messiah; secondly, they were prepared to modify previous views of Messiahship to include elements of suffering and to justify this from a highly original interpretation of the Old Testament; and, thirdly, they maintained that this same Jesus had been raised from the dead by an amazing and unique act of God. They possessed a strange power in their lives which they called the Holy Spirit, and which showed itself sometimes in ways which recalled the early Old Testament accounts of the presence of the Spirit among the prophets. Even more impressive than this was the witness of their own fearless courage; growing understanding of their Master; and readiness to take costly risks, as individuals and as a movement, which contrasted sharply with their weakness, blindness, and infirmities while He was still alive. Thus St. Peter on the day of Pentecost in Jerusalem, the city of Jesus' death and his own shame, is recorded to have spoken as follows: 'Him, being delivered up by the determinate counsel and foreknowledge of God, ye by the hand of lawless men did crucify and slay, Whom God raised up, having loosed the pangs of death because it was not possible that He should be holden by it' (*Acts* ii. 23-4). 'Him Whom ye slew, God raised up'—and that on the lips of one who had recently denied all knowledge of the man at the laugh of a servant girl and the silent hostility of a group of men round a courtyard fire. Even from the historical point of view such a complete and sudden transformation of character requires some explanation. St. Peter and his friends were not at a loss to account for it. They ascribed it to the effects of the Resurrection of their Lord from the dead. This evidence is in itself impressive alike from the simple and unsophisticated manner in which it is set out and from the primitive character of the documents which contain it. It forms, in effect, an inference from the effects of the Resurrection to the fact itself.

Our next witness is St. Paul. He had been converted on the Damascus Road by a vision which he explained as an appearance of the Risen Christ. It is doubtful whether he had ever seen Jesus in the days of His flesh. (The question depends upon a passage from one of the Epistles—2 Corinthians v. 16—of which the interpretation has been long in dispute; most scholars to-day do not, however, believe that it really implies any personal acquaintance with the historic Jesus.) But it is clear that his whole theology is centred on the Living Christ, Whom he firmly believed himself to know personally. So vital a part of his message is this assurance that he strains every idea that he can lay hold of to express not only what Christ means to him but also what place Christ holds not only with regard to the created order but also to God Himself. The background of many of his arguments is not easy for an ordinary, non-specialist reader to follow, and in a few cases we may suspect that he had not been able to think it out fully for himself, but his daring and original mind was trying every possible way of explaining the truth which had been given to him. We are therefore more impressed by the abiding adequacy of many of the results which he achieved than by his occasional failure to answer all the questions which he put to himself.

But St. Paul does even more than this. It is not often that he makes any detailed reference to the factual tradition contained in the Gospels. He is after all writing for Christians who have been taught the factual tradition about our Lord, and he does not therefore need to go over the ground again. His very infrequent appeals to the historical facts which his converts have received is therefore all the more impressive. Two instances alone are given in the Epistles. The former, concerned with the institution of the Eucharist, we have already examined in detail; the latter (1 *Cor.* xv. 3-8) concerns the post-Resurrection appearances. In neither case is the narrative introduced for its own sake, but forms part of an argument directed to a particular difficulty which had arisen in the Corinthian Church. He is not concerned in either case to leave on record a sample instruction of the kind which candidates for Holy Baptism must have received. Here in particular he is not arguing against people who denied the Resurrection of our Lord from the dead; rather he is quoting the list of appearances as an agreed starting-point for a discussion of the nature of the post-Resurrection life of Christians themselves. The material which he quotes acts as a kind of preface to the further question about which doubts had arisen. This fact should warn us to be on our guard against any inference based upon what the passage does not contain. The argument from silence is often precarious; it is especially dubious here. St. Paul is giving not the fullest possible account of the evidence for the Resurrection, but the barest minimum necessary to provide a background for his subsequent discussion.

The passage must be quoted in full for easier reference:

For I delivered unto you first of all that which I also received, how that Christ died for our sins and that He was buried, and that He has been raised from the dead on the third day according to the Scriptures, and that He appeared to Cephas, then to the Twelve, then He appeared to about five hundred brethren at once, of whom the greater part remain unto this day, but some are fallen asleep, then He appeared to James, then to all the Apostles, and last of all as to one born out of due time, He appeared to me also.

The first part closely resembles the corresponding clauses of the present Apostles' Creed. If in its present form this is a somewhat late document, in its simplest form it represents the Baptismal Creed of the West in quite early times. The passage assigns in the briefest possible form the Christian significance of the death and Resurrection of Christ and the statement that it was 'according to the Scriptures.' This must mean clearly the Old Testament Scriptures, for at the time at which this Epistle was written the total Christian literature as yet produced cannot have been more than a few epistles of St. Paul and perhaps a few documents which have since been lost. Clearly, then, questions of canonicity, of the inclusion of the New Testament writings into a Canon of Scripture, could not as yet have arisen. The passage suggests not only that the Resurrection was regarded as the fulfilment of Old Testament prophecy, but also that certain standard texts forming a kind of exegetical pattern may have been laid under contribution to explain it. While we cannot be sure that we have anything like a full list, the following passages may well have formed part of such a pattern. The mention of the third day suggests strongly that Jonah i. 17 (referred to by our Lord in St. Matt. xii. 39–41; St. Luke xi. 29–32) and Hosea vi. 1–2 were in the mind of the early Church. But the principal passages referred to in the New Testament are derived from the Psalms: Psalm xvi. 8–11 (quoted in Acts ii. 25–8; xiii. 35); Psalm cxviii. 22–4 (in Acts iv. 11 and 1 St. Pet. ii. 7); Psalm cx. 1 (in Acts ii. 34).

The Pauline passage makes no explicit reference to the empty tomb, though it is probably implied in the collocation of the Burial and the Resurrection. We should hardly have expected its mention here, since St. Paul is not arguing for the truth of the Resurrection against those who denied it, but making inferences from the Resurrection of our Lord to the state of Christians after death. They cannot expect any empty tomb, and therefore this part of the tradition would not be relevant to the argument. The appearances of the Risen Christ which he records form a longer list than is contained in our present Gospel record. He begins with one to Cephas or Peter, which is implied in St. Mark xvi. 7 and of which one is recorded in St. John xxi. He mentions appearances to the Twelve (he means, of course, the Eleven without Judas Iscariot), and to 'all the Apostles.' (This is probably a mere stylistic variant of the same group.) The former appearances may perhaps be parallel to those of St. Luke xxiv. 36–49 or St. John xx. 19–29, or even perhaps St. Matthew xxviii. 16–20, while the latter may just possibly be identical with the Ascension. We have no trace of any appearance to the 'five hundred brethren [Christians] at once,' but the further note that most are still alive to this day (though some had already died) adds greatly to the impression of historicity. It is a striking fact that, while during the lifetime of Jesus, James, called His brother, was not among His disciples, after the

Resurrection he was one of the leading members of the Jerusalem Church and is described by St. Paul as one of its veritable 'pillars' (*Gal.* ii. 9). If no appearance had been recorded by St. Paul, it would almost have been necessary to postulate one to account for the facts as we know them from the Acts of the Apostles. The final appearance recorded by St. Paul is his own Conversion Vision on the road to Damascus, to which he gives a similar status to the others, and the occurrence of which he explains as vouchsafed to him as to one born out of due time—an abortion or untimely birth.

No attempt is made in the passage to discuss either the nature of the appearances or their geographical locale, not necessarily because the Church lacked interest or information in such things, but because they did not concern St. Paul's immediate purpose. Nor can we assign any significance to the fact that the list occurs in an Epistle rather than in a Gospel. To attempt to deduce any conclusion from this would be to display a defective understanding of the flexibility of early Christian literature.

We can perhaps best sum up the evidence of St. Paul as follows. He puts us accidentally in possession of the information that at a stage prior to the compilation of the Canonical Gospels the Church was familiar with an ordered and relatively full narrative of the basic facts. So far from the Gospel tradition being an embroidery of an earlier and simpler tradition, it represents a mere selection of the material available for the purpose.

We can now turn to the Gospels themselves. It is at first sight remarkable that our Canonical Gospels are reluctant to offer any account of the Resurrection. The nearest approach is St. Matthew xxviii. 2–4, but it is reserved for the apocryphal *Gospel of Peter* to throw caution to the winds and to attempt to describe the event itself. For all four Canonical Gospels the Resurrection has already happened by the time that the women arrive on the scene; in each case it is made known by its effects.

Our earliest account in the Gospels raises problems which will demand a short critical scrutiny before we turn to examine the content of its evidence. Our English translations of the

Bible include a section (*St. Mark* xvi. 9–20) which is certainly not part of the true text. A comparison with the rest of the Gospel on the grounds of style, vocabulary, and even subject-matter suggest that it is by another hand; it does not read in the least like Mark. It is omitted by some manuscripts and replaced by interesting alternatives in others. Two fathers, Eusebius and Jerome, both learned in the text of the Scriptures and interested in questions of canonicity, declare it to be spurious. One manuscript ascribes its authorship to the presbyter Aristion from Asia Minor, and this would agree with the fact that its earliest witness is St. Irenaeus, who, although he was Bishop of Lyons in France, originally came from the same district. None of its rivals seems to possess any better claim to represent the original text of Mark. So far as almost unanimous critical opinion goes to-day, the Gospel ended at St. Mark xvi. 8.

But is it complete as it stands? Clearly those who wrote the alternative endings did not think that it was. Of late years, however, Dr. R. H. Lightfoot and Dr. J. M. Creed in this country and Wellhausen in Germany have been notable among those who believe that it was. On their view the mistake lay with the scribes who misconceived the situation and tried to complete a book which was already finished. As it stands, the book ends: 'They were afraid for.' Stylistically this seems a quite unparalleled ending. Dr. Lightfoot, however, who has made a somewhat close study of this point, came to the conclusion that, though this appears impossible English, it would be quite possible in Greek. The verb 'I fear' can be used absolutely without any necessary addition of any word or clause to express the object of fear. The conjunction 'for' can end a clause or a sentence if the previous word is a single noun, verb, or adjective. There is a fairly close parallel to the sentence from the Greek version of the Old Testament: 'Sarah laughed; she was afraid for.' Here, however, the tense of the verb is an aorist which expresses completed action and not the imperfect, as in St. Mark, which denotes strictly incomplete action.[1] Dr. Lightfoot's close analysis has shown quite clearly

---

[1] A partial parallel may be found in St. Mark x. 32, where the emphasis seems to fall upon fear as a *continuous* state of mind. After the Resurrection the state of alarm could only be *transitional*.

that in certain circumstances sentences and even paragraphs could so end. He has offered no proof that a book could peter out in so lame a fashion.

But even granted that it is possible that a book could so end, is it probable that this particular one could end in this way? It is worthy of note that the book opens with a modest flourish of trumpets: 'The beginning of the Gospel of Jesus Christ, the Son of God,' although the last four words are regarded in some quarters as textually suspect. It would be odd if a book which so opened, ended so lamely from the point of view of style. But in my opinion it is the subject-matter which tells even more heavily against such an ending. St. Mark xvi. 7 can best be interpreted as a promise to an appearance to St. Peter which we should normally expect to find fulfilled within the compass of the Gospel itself. What is even more difficult is the ending of the Gospel on a note of fear. Admittedly there is in the religion of the Incarnation, as Dr. Lightfoot reminds us, a note of godly fear, and there is no difficulty in the conjunction of fear and a manifestation of the Divine; this is a well-known and characteristic Old Testament theme. Neither of these observations, however, quite covers the ground. The alarm which such a theophany causes should properly be resolved into joy, for the Resurrection is not only part of the Gospel but, as many would say, the 'good news' itself. But there is yet another ground for hesitation before accepting Dr. Lightfoot's view on this point. The fear of which he speaks is godly fear leading to obedience. The real problem here is the unresolved conjunction of fear and disobedience. We cannot quite say that, if the Gospel ended here, it had foundered upon a rock; but it had at least received a check. Clearly, however, the impasse was in fact broken by the women plucking up courage and obeying the angelic message. Then why does not St. Mark say so?

But Dr. Lightfoot would question whether, if we argue thus, we had rightly seized the intention of the Evangelist. He would urge that we are reading the Second Gospel too much in the light of the other three, and thereby missing its purpose. It is agreed by Dr. Lightfoot that in the other Gospels the climax is found in a number of post-Resurrection appearances; in his opinion, St. Mark, on the contrary, throws his climax forward to the as yet undisclosed future of the *Parousia* or Second Coming. This conclusion is in part based upon a certain view of the geographical clues which the Gospels contain, which will be discussed in its place rather later on in this chapter. It is reinforced by an argument which can, however, best be discussed here. A German scholar of distinction, Dr. Erich Lohmeyer, framed a canon of interpretation that in St. Mark the verb 'ye shall see' pointed uniformly to an appearance which was to take place at the *Parousia*. The principal evidence to which he appealed was the passage in St. Mark xiv. 62, in which Jesus addressing the High Priest says: 'Ye shall see the Son of Man sitting on the right hand of power and coming in the clouds of heaven.' This clearly refers to the Second Coming, but what clinches this interpretation is not the form of the verb but the description of the object. In this passage in St. Mark xvi the situation is wholly different. The One Whom they will see is described as 'Jesus the crucified Nazarene.' Here, so far from there being any clear trace of the *Parousia*, it might be urged that every care is taken to avoid any such significance. The description points unmistakably back to the Passion, not forward to the *Parousia*. We could hardly imagine a less suitable description of Jesus from the point of view of the *Parousia*. It is perhaps significant that in his most recent work, *The Gospel Message of St. Mark*, Dr. Lightfoot does not appeal to this particular argument, although still maintaining his original theory.

In my judgement, therefore, it still remains probable that St. Mark xvi. 8 is not a natural ending for the Gospel. Two questions therefore remain to be answered: Why was the book never finished? and, What would it have contained if it had reached its completion?

It is difficult to be certain what the contents of the lost ending might have been. St. Matthew gives us no help here. Faithful as he so frequently is to St. Mark in passages where he used the Second Gospel as a source, it is clear that he is as lost as we are in the matter. It may, however, be conjectured (though this is no more than a conjecture) that the lost ending might have contained at least three items. We should obviously need some explanation of the means whereby the deadlock with which it now ends was broken. In the light of the special message to St. Peter it would be natural to expect a vision reinstating him to his position among the Twelve. We might also expect an appearance to the Twelve as a whole. It would not be surprising if such a vision contained a confession at last by the disciples that Jesus was the Son of God. Such confessions form a recurrent theme in St. Mark's Gospel. The title probably occurs in the statement of policy at the beginning of the Gospel. Jesus is so confessed by demoniacs. Significantly enough the title is not introduced at the Confession at Caesarea Philippi, though St. Matthew notes the omission and seeks to repair it. By a kind of Marcan irony such a confession is implied on the lips of the High Priest as if to frame the question which Judaism was later to ask of the Christian Church, while the centurion at the Cross perhaps acts as a kind of typical confessor for the Gentile world. Is it fitting that in this crescendo of confession the disciples should alone be dumb?

If this conjecture be a reasonable one, we are still left with the problem whether the conclusion was ever written, and if it were written, what happened to it. There are difficulties in both hypotheses. Perhaps the least unsatisfactory theory is that the last page of the manuscript somehow got detached and was lost, and that the author found it impossible (either through martyrdom or through a final separation from his manuscript) to repair the omission. The difficulty is not that such bibliographical accidents could not have occurred, but that they must have happened when the Gospel was represented by a single copy. Difficult as this view may be, it appears to be preferable to the theory, sponsored by authorities whom in other matters we should be glad to follow, that the Gospel ended at St. Mark xvi. 8.

What St. Mark has to tell us about the Resurrection is as follows. After the ending of Passover and Sabbath, the disciples were free to resume the task of paying the last rites to their beloved Master. At first light on the Sunday, the women, fitting agents for this purpose, made their way to the tomb bearing aromatic or sweet-smelling spices. As they went they were discussing how they were going to roll away the heavy stone from the door of the tomb. As they approached the tomb they found a young man (St. Mark evidently believes him to be an angel) who tells them that Jesus the crucified Nazarene is risen and, pointing to the empty tomb, shows them the place where Jesus had been laid. He adds a message from our Lord that they should meet Him in Galilee. This causes alarm to the women who went and said nothing to anybody because of their fear.

The women came not expecting a Resurrection, but intent upon completing the interrupted burial rites. The empty tomb is pointed out and a promise of appearances given. It is probable, but not quite certain, that St. Mark would have placed the appearances which he intended to record in Galilee rather than at Jerusalem. The Resurrection is made known by its effects, and we are left with a scene of bewilderment, terror, and disobedience.

We pass next to the post-Resurrection narratives of St. Matthew. It seems clear that we can glean nothing about the lost ending of St. Mark from his pages. Within the limits of his reproduction of the Marcan record there are nevertheless certain significant features. He describes a great earthquake and an angel who sits upon the stone. The guards, whom he introduces at an earlier part of his narrative, are struck as it were dead. This is the sole instance in which the effect of the Resurrection upon any one except a Christian disciple is recorded in the Gospels. He breaks the deadlock which St. Mark leaves as follows: the women leave the tomb with fear and joy and tell the disciples; Jesus Himself meets them and shows them His hands and His feet, and Himself repeats the message previously given through the angel. This clearly occurs in Jerusalem. The disciples obey their Lord's command, journey to Galilee, and receive a final appearance in which they are given a world-wide commission to preach the Gospel and to baptize all nations. Even here St. Matthew pauses to tie up a loose end and explains how the guards recover, make their report to the Jewish authorities at Jerusalem, and are bribed to hold their tongues.

From this summary of the contents of the Matthaean account it is clear that three motives have been at work. It might be put somewhat as follows: St. Matthew rationalizes, biblicizes, and ecclesiasticizes the story. He first tidies up the Marcan story, removing the contradiction with which it closes. His use of the story of the guards at least shows that he is conscious of the possible objection, that the disciples had stolen away the body, and safeguards against it. It is not impossible to believe that such a guard was actually placed. Neither motive nor means were lacking to the Temple authorities. The other Evangelists, however, ignore the effect of the Resurrection upon any one except the disciples themselves. The heightened background to the story may well be an attempt to bring the Resurrection into the context of the mighty acts of God performed in the Old Testament. The great saving facts of the Gospel should correspond as closely as possible to the mighty deeds done aforetime. It will be seen later that St. Luke makes a similar point in rather a different way. Finally, St. Matthew links up the fact of the Resurrection with the world-wide mission of the Christian Church in preaching the Gospel, in baptizing, and in the faith of the Holy Trinity. There may be parallels here, both in method and intention, with the Infancy Narratives in the same Gospel.

When we turn to St. Luke we find a different cycle of traditions laid under contribution. He does indeed start with the closing section of St. Mark. The women find not one young man (angel) outside the tomb, but two angels within it. Like St. Matthew, he omits any mention of a special message to St. Peter. Evidently both Evangelists treat it as a mere biographical detail, thus surely missing its rich devotional significance. The message of the angel is redrafted as follows: 'Remember how He said to you while He was in Galilee.' This was essential in view of the fact that St. Luke only records appearances in Jerusalem itself. It suggests, however, not merely ignorance of the Galilee tradition but also an implicit correction of it. Nothing is said about the disobedience of the women (perhaps disobedience was not a word in Luke's Christian vocabulary!), who immediately return and tell the disciples. In St. Luke disbelief is transferred from the women to the disciples themselves. A few manuscripts record a visit to the tomb by St. Peter and St. John which recalls, and was probably derived from, the Fourth Gospel. Then follows the magnificently told story of the journey to Emmaus, a village of uncertain location a few miles outside Jerusalem. This affords further testimony for the unbelieving disciples outside the witness of the women. Finally, St. Luke records an appearance to the eleven disciples at Jerusalem and a direct transition to the Ascension on the road to Bethany.

Here it is clear that, whatever may be the case with St. Mark, great evidential stress is laid upon the visions although the empty tomb still remains part of the tradition. Thus St. Luke xxiv. 41-3 mentions that our Lord ate a piece of broiled fish. The whole activity of the Risen Christ is focused on Jerusalem, and the slight but significant change in the angel's words taken from St. Mark's Gospel appears to exclude expressly the Galilean tradition. What was in St. Mark intended to be a geographical destination for the disciples is here converted into a mere historical detail attendant upon the prophecy.

There is a further difficulty about the Ascension in St. Luke's Gospel. Some manuscripts appear to omit the vital phrase to which reference to the Ascension is restricted in the Gospel, but a realization of the difficulty to which attention is being directed may be a sufficient explanation of this. If we read the narrative of St. Luke straight on, it would at first sight appear as if the Ascension took place at the close of Easter Day. If this be the case, then St. Luke must have decisively rejected the whole Galilee tradition. This is perhaps not wholly conclusive, for in the account given in the early verses of the Acts of the Apostles we find a mention of the forty-day period which gives the time factor necessary for a reconciliation of the two traditions. It should of course be remembered that the Acts of the Apostles is the second volume of St. Luke's treatise 'to Theophilus' and that the author might reasonably expect that his readers would read straight on. This fact is blurred by the separation of the two books by the Fourth Gospel in our Canonical Scriptures. There are obvious and good reasons for this, but it may do St. Luke something of an injustice. It is not perhaps quite certain that St. Luke did mean us to conclude that the Ascension took place on Easter Sunday. A break might be placed either at verse 41 or verse 44. He might have found that his book or roll was running out more quickly than he expected and therefore telescoped his material towards the end in order to round off the book. But in that case the apparently deliberate correction of the angel's message would be left in the air unexplained.

One way of accounting for all these facts taken together might be as follows. It is possible that at the time when he wrote his first volume he possessed only the Jerusalem tradition and altered his text of St. Mark xvi. 7 accordingly. Between the writing of his first and his second volumes he may have received or accepted the Galilean tradition with the chronological note of the forty-day period. He therefore added this tradition in a kind of appendix at the beginning of the second volume, in the confidence (not always justified, so far as the modern reader is concerned) that both volumes would be read together, and his earlier regarded simply as a kind of telescoped history. This explanation is not without certain difficulties, and is at best a conjecture; but there is a possible parallel at the beginning of the Gospel, where the Infancy Narratives seem to be a kind of appendix placed at the beginning, and St. Luke leaves the formal opening at the beginning of chapter iii unaltered and the genealogy of Jesus attached to the first mention of the Name of Jesus in the same chapter.

This represents a possible and in some ways an attractive suggestion to meet the difficulty, but it remains at best a conjecture, and the main argument of this chapter is not in the least affected by its rejection.

A comparison of the Lucan record with that of the other Synoptic Gospels contains features of great interest. The Marcan account is jerky and breathless. The crowning mercy of the Resurrection breaks upon us astonished and breathless.

St. Luke smooths away the discontinuities by revealing it as
the climax of a divine plan. If St. Matthew in some of his
details ranges it with the mighty acts of God in the Old
Testament, St. Luke makes the same point in revealing it as
the fulfilment of prophecy. All three Synoptic writers in their
different ways proclaim: 'This is the Lord's doing and it is
marvellous in our eyes.'

The Fourth Gospel is acquainted both with the Galilean
and the Jerusalemite traditions, and accepts both without any
difficulty. Some critics have inclined to see in the last chapter
of St. John's Gospel an appendix by another hand, but the
stylistic touches which link the last chapter with the remainder
of the book seem too strong to be gainsaid. If it is sometimes
forgotten that St. Matthew records appearances both in Galilee
and in Jerusalem, and that St. Luke records the time-span
necessary for their reconciliation to be possible, it is nevertheless true that St. John appears to give equal importance to both
traditions, whereas the emphasis of St. Matthew and St. Luke
respectively fall markedly upon one side or other of this
double tradition.

In chapter xx the narrative opens with a visit of Mary
Magdalene to the tomb, representing the visit of the women
as a group recorded in the Synoptic Gospels. She finds the
tomb empty, and returns to tell the disciples. Peter and John
run together to the tomb, enter in, and find the grave-clothes
undisturbed and the head-cloth lying neatly folded by itself.
(The author thus calls our attention to a feature which pre-
cludes any possibility of tomb-violation.) Mary finds two
angels inside the tomb (a Lucan touch) and is greeted by the
Risen Lord Himself Whom she mistakes for the gardener (we
are again reminded of a similar unrecognized companying with
Jesus recorded in the Lucan journey to Emmaus). There follow
two appearances to the disciples at Jerusalem, first without and
subsequently with Thomas. These are separated by a week,
in a manner which shows that the Evangelist is already familiar
with the appropriate designation of Sunday as the day of the
Resurrection. On the former occasion the gift of the Spirit is
imparted by insufflation or inbreathing. (Here St. John

anticipates the Pentecostal illapse or descent of the Spirit.) The disciples are also given the authority to forgive sins (a feature which corresponds to the universal commission given in Matthew). In the following chapter the scene changes to Galilee, where, in a scene reminiscent of his call in St. Luke v, Simon Peter is recommissioned after his denial of our Lord.

So far we have been concerned with describing the narratives given by the Four Evangelists. We must now turn to the factual side of the tradition taken as a whole. Here it must be said at the outset that it is virtually impossible to construct an exact factual harmony of the Gospels. Two attempts to do this have been made by able scholars. The first is an incomplete effort made by C. H. Turner in the *Church Quarterly Review* for 1912, while the latter, attempted by N. P. Williams, is contained in a short work entitled *The First Easter Morning*. That there should be discrepancies in detail should surprise no one who realizes how difficult it is to get complete agreement in detail from eyewitnesses even in relatively minor events in quite modern times. Here, however, we are dealing with an event which is almost too big to go into history, and can attach still less significance to divergences in detail. Those who speak of the Resurrection as a supra-historical event have at least this amount of truth on their side. That these accounts are left unreconciled in our Gospels without any attempt to produce a single stereotyped narrative gives us great confidence in the fundamental honesty of the Evangelists themselves. It can have been no small temptation which they resisted in refusing to produce an agreed statement on the point.

But there is a further reason for at least some of these discrepancies. The Evangelists are not simply offering a transcript from history, but also are combining with their narratives their interpretations of the great new fact. We have already called attention in our analysis of the contents of each Gospel to some of the differences which can best be accounted for on this theory. Here, no less than in the earlier part of the Gospel, historical fact and theological interpretation go hand in hand. Here, then, is another possible explanation of some of the discrepancies in the narratives.

It should not, however, be concluded that these discrepancies affect in any essential respect the principal elements within the tradition. Each narrative assumes that the tomb was found empty. St. Mark and St. John simply record the fact, whereas St. Matthew and St. John have their own ways of 'protecting' it, the former by his reference to the guards, the latter to the state of the grave-clothes. All the Evangelists, except the probably incomplete St. Mark, record appearances of the Risen Lord to His disciples. None of the Evangelists dares to hazard any conjecture as to what has happened to the Body of the Lord. The indications are that they regard it as being carried by the Risen Lord in a glorified and, as it were, super-substantial condition. If Luke alone records a physical act such as eating (*St. Luke* xxiv. 39), both Luke and John(*St. Luke* xxiv. 39; *St. John* xx. 27) mention the wound-prints in hands and feet.

Both the evidence of the empty tomb and of the visions appear to be necessary for the fullness of the Church's faith in the Resurrection to be possible. The evidence of the tomb, taken by itself, is 'blind.' It might convey the worst possible news: the removal of the Body by some human agency. (This is indeed apparently the first thought of Mary Magdalene according to St. John xx. 15). At best it might suggest some utterly inexplicable miracle which could not by itself give any assurance or sense of mission to the disciples. It therefore needs to be reinforced by the evidence of the visions. Yet, taken by themselves, these also would fail of complete conviction. If the empty tomb taken by itself might be described as 'blind,' the visions apart from it might be considered to be 'empty.' Apart from the evidence of the tomb, could we be sure that their content was objective? Would they be simply 'subjective'—evidence simply for a Jesus Who was alive only in the hearts of His faithful disciples? Or should we be able to go further and to proclaim them as 'objective'—'telegrams from heaven,' as Keim once described them; or 'veridical,' as Dr. E. G. Selwyn designates them in his contribution to *Essays Catholic and Critical*? It would be difficult without the empty tomb to be sure which of the two descriptions was the more appropriate. Taken together, the two irresistibly suggest an intelligible account of a single supernatural, supra-historical event evidenced in two different and complementary ways. What the one strand lacks is supplied by the other. It is true, no doubt, that St. Mark does not offer us any appearance of the Risen Lord; but we have good reasons for believing that his narrative is incomplete at this point. We have also seen that St. Paul does not expressly mention the empty tomb, though it may well be that it is implied in his narrative. Here also we have been able to assign sufficient reason from the purpose which he has in mind in the passage for his omission. That he assigns a paramount importance to the post-Resurrection appearances, and does not at least bring the empty tomb into any kind of prominence, is satisfactorily explained by the immediate context.

There still remains the difficult problem of the locale of the appearances. Did they occur in Galilee or in Jerusalem, or, as we have already implied, in both places? Some scholars, like Kirsopp Lake and P. Gardner Smith, strongly support the view that the Galilean tradition can alone be regarded as colourably authentic. It is first the more difficult tradition to explain, since it was Jerusalem and not Galilee which was the birthplace of the Christian Church. If we had to make a selection between them, we could therefore more easily explain the emergence of a Jerusalemite tradition. Further, this tradition receives the support of our earliest Gospel sources (*St. Mark* xiv. 28 and xvi. 7). Some of the supporters of this view also incline to the view that when the disciples scattered and fled after the arrest of Jesus, they immediately returned to Galilee. There was nothing to keep them in Jerusalem, and the narrative of St. John xxi and the apocryphal *Gospel of Peter*, which some regard as having in some respects a greater historical value than most of the apocryphal Gospels, suggest that they returned to their original habitat and vocations. They might well have considered that their discipleship was finished, and they would after all need once more to be assured of a living. At first sight this looks a strong case, but there are considerations which should make us hesitate to accept it. The last point is by no means as strong as it appears: it is far more likely that they went underground in Jerusalem itself, perhaps temporarily too stunned to make any further move, and were sheltered and fed by sympathizers with Jesus in the capital. Again, such a theory involves the complete abandonment of St. Luke as an historical witness, which appears far too high a price to pay for the establishment of any critical theory. The account of the journey to Emmaus, for example, seems to suggest a good and primitive tradition behind the Third Gospel. More significant still is the objection suggested by the Bishop of Durham: the theory involves a complete separation between the women and the disciples which seems most improbable. Did the women and the disciples live in two water-tight compartments? Despite the temporary check with which St. Mark appears to end, would the women have left the disciples completely in the air without telling them what had happened to them or would the disciples have lacked the courage or even the curiosity to probe the account given by the women of the strange experience at the tomb without going to investigate for themselves? Neither assumption appears to be very probable.

On the other hand, if we accept the Jerusalemite tradition by itself we shall find it difficult to explain the positive merits of the Galilean hypothesis to which attention has been called. It would, for example, be difficult to explain the invention of the Galilean tradition after Jerusalem had become the most important centre of the Primitive Church.

If, however, we are inclined to the acceptance of both traditions as factual supplements in the Gospel records, there are certain efforts at harmonization which will not, if we are wise, attract us too strongly. There is first the hypothesis of Resch, who suggested on the basis of some late narratives of pilgrimages to Palestine that there might be a place in Jerusalem itself called Galilee, and that therefore both traditions (apart, of course, from the mention of the lake in St. John xxi) could be harmonized without the disciples leaving the capital at all. But the origin of the tradition can be easily explained. The normal mediaeval pilgrim had a far more developed

religious than historical sense. Travel up-country might be
either very difficult or completely impossible owing to the
occupation of the country by the Moslem invaders. It would
not therefore be surprising if the authorities had provided a
place within Jerusalem itself where he could say 'Galilee'
prayers and offer 'Galilee' alms without incurring the risks of
a difficult journey through dangerous places. It is more surprising that any one should have imagined that such a source
should throw any light on the Gospel record than that the
authorities in the Middle Ages should have thought out such
a solution of a pressing practical difficulty.

F. C. Burkitt offered an explanation which is highly ingenious and received a favourable mention from Kirsopp Lake,
a determined supporter of the Galilean hypothesis. He takes
St. Mark xiv. 28 as his starting-point and calls attention to the
fact that the Greek word translated 'he goeth before you'
would more naturally mean 'he goeth at your head' or 'he
leadeth you.' The metaphor is that of an oriental shepherd
who leads rather than drives his flock. Burkitt suggests that
we should interpret the passage as implying not an independently made journey to Galilee to meet the Risen Lord, but
perhaps a journey started northwards according to the instructions of our Lord but turned back again to Jerusalem in
obedience to a vision received on the road northward—much
as in the later apocryphal literature Peter in flight from
martyrdom at Rome was turned backwards by a vision of the
Risen Lord on the Appian Way. It is only fair to notice the
very considerable diffidence with which Burkitt put forward
this theory: it is rather too apocryphal to be altogether
acceptable.

I have sometimes thought that a solution along the following
lines might be possible. As the message of the angel suggests,
our Lord expected the disciples to meet Him in Galilee. Is it
possible to conjecture that the Risen Master, finding their faith
unequal to following out His injunctions, met them in Jerusalem instead? This would have the merit of being true to our
own experience of Him; for He ever meets us not where He
would have us be, but where we are actually living ourselves.

It would not therefore be surprising that Jesus should act in a precisely similar way with regard to His first disciples, held captive as they were by their lack of faith in, and understanding of, Him. This is, however, at best an unverifiable conjecture and is not offered as being anything more.

Dr. Lightfoot, in his book *Locality and Doctrine in the Gospels*, takes a more thoroughgoing line in explanation of the difficulty. He suggests that we are wrong in interpreting 'Galilee' and 'Jerusalem' in a geographical sense. They are meant rather to stand for two different types of appearance: the one vocational and the other evidential. He urges that St. Paul apparently displays no interest in the locale of the appearances which he describes and the general tendency in the Gospels is to betray no greater interest in geographical details. There is, however, reason for hesitating in accepting the bulk of his arguments here. The argument from Pauline silence is most precarious in view of the specialized purpose for which he quotes his list of post-Resurrection appearances. It would probably not be much in point to assign a locality to each appearance which he records. Dr. Lightfoot's denial that the Evangelists showed any real concern for geography is a half-truth of the same order of his disclaimer in their special concern for biography. On both matters there is certainly room for more than one opinion, and if his real point lies in a warning that the Evangelists contain theological interpretation as well as factual information he will probably find few who wish to dispute the point. But the concern of the Gospels for geography need not and must not be minimized. If we do not possess a 'Bradshaw' knowledge of the movements of Jesus, the main outline of the places where He exercised His Ministry is clear enough. The distinction between Galilee and Jerusalem, so far as His earlier Ministry is concerned, is clearly enough made. The main centres of His activity are recorded, and a famous passage from Q, which speaks of mighty works done in Bethsaida and Chorazin (*St. Matt.* xi. 21; *St. Luke* x. 13), implies an even wider tradition which has disappeared.

Dr. Lightfoot is not in error in his suggestion that the Jerusalem appearances are largely evidential in character while those located in Galilee are normally vocational. (There is perhaps an exception in St. John xx. 21-2, where the gift of the Spirit and the authority to forgive sins is recorded in Jerusalem.) Such an association of theme and location is, however, just what we should expect. The closer that the evidential appearances are placed to the empty tomb, the more convincing they become, while, granted that the acceptance of the fact of the Resurrection imposed upon the first disciples (and no less upon their latter-day successors) responsibilities and vocations which would not have been theirs without it, the revelation of these vocations even in outline could scarcely be in point apart from a prior acceptance of the fact of the Resurrection. If the evidential appearances could only take place in Jerusalem, vocational appearances could be postponed until after their temporary withdrawal to Galilee. That the disciples made such a withdrawal need not cause either scepticism or surprise. They had a message from our Lord to fulfil, however belatedly, and there was nothing to keep them in Jerusalem after the initial acceptance of the fact of the Resurrection had taken place there.

The best solution of the difficulty appears to be also the simplest; namely, that the two traditions are true supplements to each other. A short stay in Jerusalem, for perhaps a week after the Resurrection, was followed by a return to Galilee and a final return to Jerusalem in time for the Feast of Pentecost. The forty-day period mentioned in the Acts could just cover such a time-table. It is perhaps slightly surprising that the only Evangelist who raises any difficulties on this hypothesis is precisely the one who records the chronological datum necessary for its acceptance, but we have already suggested a possible explanation of the best way out of this particular difficulty.

So far we have dealt with the exposition and defence of the factual tradition about the Resurrection and its immediate sequel presented by the Gospels. It is perhaps worth while to examine briefly some alternative theories which have been put forward with the object of explaining the tradition without admitting its truth. If we find good reason for rejecting such theories decisively, we shall derive at least a measure of negative corroboration for our more positive conclusions.

i. *Resuscitation.* It has sometimes been argued that Jesus never rose from the dead because He never really died on the Cross. What has come down to us as the Resurrection should rather be called the Resuscitation. It is noted on such theories that Crucifixion was normally a lingering form of death, and the fact that Jesus was taken down from the Cross after suffering there for only six hours gave rise to the suggestion that He was not really dead at all but revived in the cool of the tomb. But such a view has indeed formidable difficulties to face. There is even a more probable explanation of the one fact to which it could appeal. We must take into our reckoning not only the three hours on the Cross, but the terrible scourging which preceded it. Men had even been known to die under the scourge. Nor must we forget the long-continued strain and effort of the previous week which led up to the trial and arrest. If we follow the Fourth Evangelist here, the Roman authorities, surprised by the speedy death of our Lord, made sure by the lance thrust through the side. Even less can we explain on such a theory the new-found life which awaited the disciples. A half-dead resuscitated Master could not give the same pulsating confidence as a Living, Risen Lord. How on such an hypothesis did He continue and finish His broken physical life? It is perhaps not too much to say that, if this explanation is accepted, the difficulty is that in 'explaining' the Resurrection we have left the rest of the New Testament wholly inexplicable.

ii. *Mistake.* This is the theory virtually accepted by Kirsopp Lake. According to him the young man in St. Mark's last section was not an angel but simply some one who happened to be in the garden at the time, and who directed the women away from the wrong tomb in the half-light. On this theory St. Mark xvi. 6 would need to be reinterpreted as follows: 'He is not here (*pointing to the tomb before which the women were standing*), behold (*pointing to the right tomb*) the place where they laid Him.' The reference to the Resurrection must either be deleted altogether or taken as a purely general reference to the Resurrection of all men. But here again the difficulties appear almost insuperable. It would imply at the outset that Jesus was buried in a place in which there was more than one tomb. This supposition is not indeed excluded by Mark, though the Matthaean and Lucan accounts appear to exclude it by implication. In Mark it is simply stated that Joseph of Arimathaea placed the Body of Jesus in a tomb hewn out of the rock. Matthew speaks of 'his own fresh [or new] tomb hewn out of the rock' presumably in his own property and not in a public graveyard, while Luke speaks of a 'hewn tomb in which no man had ever yet been laid.' Of the women who went to the tomb one at least is recorded in the previous verse in St. Mark as having seen where He was laid. If they had made a mistake in the half-light, why did not the women thank the young man for his information and ask his help in moving the stone? (It will be remembered that this particular difficulty had already occurred to them.) That a simple mistake of fact should lead to panic fear does not appear very probable. The records are careful to guard against any impression that they had the possibility of a Resurrection in their minds. They had not come to greet a Risen Lord, but only to pay their last tribute to a dead Master. Nor again does the theory, even if we persevere with it in the face of such factual difficulties, offer any explanation of the spiritual change in the disciples which itself forms part of the historical evidence to be taken into account.

iii. *Hallucination.* This theory again deals roughly with the evidence of the women. It denies completely the tradition of the empty tomb, and offers a psychological explanation of the rest of the evidence. Those who hold it regard belief in the Resurrection as a singularly persistent and rather complicated form of 'wish-fulfilment.' But it is important to note that our evidence seems to guard most carefully against such a theory. The disciples do not understand the veiled hints and more open promises made by our Lord during His earthly life. The women proceed to the tomb on quite a different errand. The disciples to whom they finally report do not believe for joy. There is here no avid clutching at any straw. Something quite unexpected had happened, rather than something longed for having failed to occur. Again, these hallucinations cover a longish period, extend their sphere of operation, and finally reach one (and not one only) who had never possessed fellow-ship with the historic Jesus or even desire for the Risen Lord. It is true that (apart from the guards mentioned by St. Matthew) the circle of those who receive appearances is restricted to the circle of believers, but this was not, according to St. Paul, a small one. The possibility of hallucination is considerably lessened not only by the absence of expectation on the part of the inner circle of the eleven and of the women, but also by the difference of grouping and occasion of such appearances. It is difficult to make such a theory cover, for example, the appearances to James or to Thomas or even the journey of the disciples on the road to Emmaus.

iv. *Fraud.* This would cover the removal of the Body by the Romans, the Jews, or the disciples. We can, I think, safely rule out of court the idea that the Romans removed the Body. They had no expectation, and therefore no motive for doing so. Their grant of the Body to Joseph of Arimathaea suggests as much. All that Pilate was concerned with was the avoidance of a riot at Passover time and the removal by death of a possible trouble-maker. The Roman interest in the affair ended after the Crucifixion was over. The Jews were certainly interested in keeping the Body in the tomb. (That is the burden of the Matthaean mention of the guards.) Joseph of Arimathaea had risked much in asking for the Body of Jesus from Pilate; it is not likely that he repented so soon of having paid the last honours in his power to the Master and removed the Body to another resting place without informing the disciples of what he had done. If the disciples rested upon the Sabbath according to the Law, even though it meant breaking off the funeral rites upon which they were engaged, it is not likely that Joseph, a member of the Sanhedrin, 'an honourable counsellor,' as Mark describes him, would have broken the Jewish Law in such a way. The disciples then remain the only possible fraudulent agents. But it is clear that they were not expecting the Resurrection to occur, and were thus unlikely to take the necessary fraudulent steps to make it appear to have happened when it did not occur. If fraud had actually taken place, we should have expected tell-tale clues to this effect in the narrative before us; and if it be urged truly that the disciples compiled, and therefore controlled, the records, and might therefore have removed any such traces, we are still faced with the difficulty that a 'doctored' story is not likely to contain the minor discrepancies which were apparently left in the narrative. The 'fraudulent disciples' left their work of editing the narrative scarcely half-done. Finally, their subsequent behaviour does not harmonize well with such an hypothesis. Men who have the lie in the soul do not behave as the disciples do in the rest of the New Testament: a changed life based upon a conscious fraud is a moral impossibility. And, purely from the factual point of view, it is none too easy to dispose of a superfluous body.

It is therefore easier, even as a matter of historical fact, to accept the historical veracity of the tradition of the empty tomb and of the Resurrection as it has been the privilege of the Church to believe it from the earliest times.

We may perhaps summarize the argument which we have been trying to develop somewhat as follows. It is a truism that in any historical event of major significance, fact and interpretation are always closely associated. The Christian belief of the Resurrection is no exception to this rule. The fact of the empty tomb needed its appropriate interpretation before its significance for the disciples could be fully realized. This is the role of the appearances. The empty tomb could not tell its own story; the appearances by themselves could not convince us that there was a story to tell. The two together form a whole of evidence which it is not easy either to ignore or to gainsay. We have seen that there were two traditions about the appearances: one of which located them in Jerusalem and another which placed them in Galilee. We saw no good reason for refusing to accept the historicity of either. The former were in the main evidential in character, the latter vocational. Again, there is nothing here to cause any difficulty, since the disciples must not only be convinced of the truth of the Resurrection but also learn at least in outline the new tasks and fresh duties which belief in the Resurrection must impose upon them. The latter task is dependent upon the former, and must be subsequent to it. The disciples must first be convinced of a fact which, although too big for history, had happened in history. They must be taught, despite their opaque lack of understanding, that the empty tomb, on any showing, is good news and not bad. The gap between the women and the disciples must be bridged, here in Jerusalem, and by means of the appearances, or it cannot be bridged at all. But once faith in the Resurrection has been achieved, it cannot be enjoyed, as it were, in a corner. It involves challenges, responsibilities, and vocations which the disciples would not have undertaken without it. Thus the Galilee visions contain what the Duke of Wellington has called 'the marching orders of the Christian Church'—the commission to teach and to baptize all nations. St. John adds authority to forgive sins and the firstfruits of the Spirit as well. St. Peter receives again what the other disciples had never lost—a pastoral commission. In other words, the disciples were required to do, as a result of their faith in the Resurrection, very much what the Church in all ages has conceived to be its prime duty.

The period of the Great Forty Days was, however, temporary and provisional only: it may perhaps be described as a time of 'weaning' from the things of sense to the things of the Spirit. The very manner of our Lord's appearances suggests this. At one time Jesus appears openly, almost materially, showing His wound-prints and offering His Body to be touched; at another time He warns Mary Magdalene against trying to touch Him. He appears and disappears at will, flouting the barriers of material objects. The explanation of this apparent discrepancy in the tradition is less likely to be a conflation of two views about the nature of the post-Resurrection Body of our Lord than a real variation of His method of appearance designed to acclimatize the disciples to the new situation which the Resurrection had brought with it. They had become accustomed to the fellowship of sight and touch with our Lord in the days of His flesh; they needed time to realize that henceforward fellowship with Jesus would be through the Spirit Whom He gave and the Church which is His Body. It represents, in effect, the final stage of the training of the Twelve begun and continued in the period before the Passion. And those who still to-day are proud to call themselves learners in the school of Christ will find the same pattern of training, 'not as He could but as we could bear,' true of them as well. All through history our Lord meets His own where they are, and leads them on to where He would have them be.

The Ascension represents the last of these appearances after the Resurrection, the final leave-taking of Jesus in this guise only to resume His Fellowship with His own in the Spirit through the Church. The idea that the Ascension represents simply a levitation into the skies, tolerable only to those who believe in a three-storied universe, misses the whole significance of the fact. No doubt the disciples did in fact believe in a three-storied universe with Heaven above, the earth beneath, and a hell below. There was no reason why the disciples of Christ should be more perfectly informed about physical science than others of their contemporaries who held such a view. The real significance which they attached to the Ascension was not restricted to the symbolism in which they sought to express it. It meant the return of the Son to the glory of the Father whence He had come forth. If this is represented spatially in the New Testament, it is only because it cannot be represented in any other way than through a symbol. Not only the minds of the first disciples but those of the whole human race are in matters of this kind spatially conditioned. Let those who are guiltless of using spatial imagery in connexion with non-spatial subjects cast the first stone ! At the Ascension the disciples knew that this stage in their 'Pilgrimage of Grace' was over, and that another was subsequently to begin. The historical Jesus had returned, His Mission completed, to the Father from Whom He had come. But they were not to wait in uncertainty for long, for ten days later, at the Feast of Pentecost, when the Spirit descended upon them, they knew that the next stage of their journey had begun. We of a later age who, like them, acknowledge Jesus as Master and Lord, and seek to live under His obedience and in His fellowship, know His Presence through that same Holy Spirit and await, as they did themselves in the days of their earthly pilgrimage, the consummation of His Kingdom, when once again in visible form He shall return to judge the earth which He saved by His work and words in our midst.

## BIBLIOGRAPHY

A. M. Ramsey, *The Resurrection of Jesus Christ*, is the most satisfying single modern treatment of the subject.

N. P. Williams, *The First Easter Morning*, should be read as an ingenious attempt to construct a detailed harmony of the events of the morning of the Resurrection.

P. Gardner Smith, *The Narratives of the Resurrection*, and

Kirsopp Lake, *The Historical Evidence for the Resurrection of Jesus Christ*, are critical studies of the evidence from different points of view.

Frank Morison, *Who moved the Stone?* is a more popular exposition of the orthodox and conservative point of view, written by a layman for laymen.

# INDEX OF SCRIPTURAL REFERENCES

## I. OLD TESTAMENT

## II. APOCRYPHA

## III. NEW TESTAMENT

# GENERAL INDEX

380